Susan Deller Ross is an associate professor of law at Georgetown University Law Center.* She also serves as Director of the Law Center's Sex Discrimination Clinic and of its Women's Law and Public Policy Fellowship Program. She formerly served as a Special Counsel for Sex Discrimination Litigation in the Civil Rights Division, U.S. Department of Justice, and as Clinical Director of the ACLU Women's Rights Project. In addition to authoring *The Rights of Women* and several articles on women's legal rights, Ms. Ross is co-author of a law-school casebook entitled *Sex Discrimination and the Law: Causes and Remedies*.

Ann Barcher is an attorney with the Port Authority of New York and New Jersey.* An alumna interviewer for Harvard and an active member of the New York Women's Bar Association, she has also helped prepare handbooks on student rights and the rights of women in New York State. Ms. Barcher graduated from New York University School of Law and from Harvard University, Radcliffe College.

---

*The views expressed in this book are those of Ms. Ross and Ms. Barcher, as private individuals, and not those of any organization with which they are or have been associated.

Other Bantam books in the series
Ask your bookseller for the books you have missed

AN AMERICAN CIVIL LIBERTIES UNION HANDBOOK

THE RIGHTS OF WOMEN

THE BASIC ACLU GUIDE TO A WOMAN'S RIGHTS

REVISED EDITION

**Susan Deller Ross
and
Ann Barcher**

General Editor of this series:
Norman Dorsen, President, ACLU

BANTAM BOOKS
TORONTO · NEW YORK · LONDON · SYDNEY · AUCKLAND

THE RIGHTS OF WOMEN

*A Bantam Book / published by arrangement with
the American Civil Liberties Union*

PRINTING HISTORY

*Bantam revised edition / April 1983
2nd printing . . . April 1984*

ISBN 0-553-24630-5

Published simultaneously in the United States and Canada

*Bantam Books are published by Bantam Books, Inc. Its trademark,
consisting of the words "Bantam Books" and the portrayal of a
rooster, is Registered in U.S. Patent and Trademark Office and in
other countries. Marca Registrada. Bantam Books, Inc., 666 Fifth
Avenue, New York, New York 10103.*

PRINTED IN THE UNITED STATES OF AMERICA

O   0 9 8 7 6 5 4 3 2

Acknowledgments for the Second Edition

We would especially like to thank Diane Dodson for her careful editing and substantial original contributions to this edition. Sheila Mooney and Donna Lenhoff provided invaluable assistance for the chapter on "Employment Discrimination." We also thank Janet Benshoof, Lourdes Soto, Ann Teicher, Suzanne Lynn, and Madeline Kochen for the chapter on "A Woman's Right to Control Her Body."

Many others were generous in providing ideas, reviewing the manuscript, and offering helpful suggestions: Isabelle Pinzler, Wendy Williams, Kathy Bonk, Nancy Stanley, Diana Steele, Janice Siegel, Betsy Brinson, Ellen Leitzer, Mary Catherine Kilday, Margie Kohn, Holly Knox, and Laurie Woods. Finally, many thanks to Professor Sylvia Law and the students of the Arthur Garfield Hays Civil Liberties Program at NYU Law School who worked under her direction to update the charts on state laws: Pat Hennessey, Mitchell Bernard, Ellen Levine, Stefan Presser, Anita Cava, Sharon Blackman, Richard Betheil, Richard Zall, Elaine Fink, Karen Freedman, and Jed Ringel.

Susan Deller Ross
Ann Barcher

Acknowledgments for the First Edition

I would like especially to thank Ruth Bader Ginsburg for her thoughtful and thorough editing, and Barbara Babcock, Ann Freedman, Judy Potter, and Nancy E. Stanley for their valuable suggestions and ideas for various chapters and for comments on the manuscript. The chapter on "Names and Name Change" could not have been written without the research of several Georgetown University law students: Dayle Berke, Betty Branda, Lois Frankel, Sandy McCandless, Max Richtman, Faye Stank, and Grey Wilson. Bruce Green and Ruth Rowse did the painstaking research for Charts A and B. The following also were generous in reviewing the manuscript or offering suggestions: Alexandra Buek, Eleanor Lewis, Jeffrey Orleans, Eve Paul, Harriet Pilpel, Nancy Stearns, and David Zugschwerdt.

Susan Deller Ross

Table of Contents

Preface

This guide sets forth your rights under the present law, and offers suggestions on how they can be protected. It is one of a continuing series of handbooks published in cooperation with the American Civil Liberties Union (ACLU).

Surrounding these publications is the hope that Americans, informed of their rights, will be encouraged to exercise them. Through their exercise, rights are given life. If they are rarely used, they may be forgotten and violations may become routine.

This guide offers no assurances that your rights will be respected. The laws may change and, in some of the subjects covered in these pages, they change quite rapidly. An effort has been made to note those parts of the law where movement is taking place, but it is not always possible to predict accurately when the law *will* change.

Even if the laws remain the same, their interpretations by courts and administrative officials often vary. In a federal system such as ours, there is a built-in problem of state and federal law, not to speak of the confusion between states. In addition, there are wide variations in the ways in which particular courts and administrative officials will interpret the same law at any given moment.

If you encounter what you consider to be a specific abuse of your rights, you should seek legal assistance. There are a number of agencies that may help you, among them, ACLU affiliate offices, but bear in mind that the ACLU is a limited-purpose organization. In many communities, there are federally funded legal service offices which provide assistance to persons who cannot afford the costs of legal representation. In general, the rights that the ACLU defends are freedom of inquiry and expression; due process of law; equal protection of the laws; and privacy. The authors in this series have

discussed other rights (even though they sometimes fall outside ACLU's usual concern) in order to provide as much
guidance as possible.

These books have been planned as guides for the people
directly affected; therefore, the question and answer format.
(In some areas there are more detailed works available for
"experts.") These guides seek to raise the major issues and
inform the nonspecialist of the basic law on the subject. The
authors of these books are themselves specialists who understand the need for information at "street level."

If you encounter a specific legal problem in an area discussed in one of these handbooks, show the book to your
attorney. Of course, he or she will not be able to rely exclusively on the handbook to provide you with adequate representation. But if your attorney hasn't had a great deal of
experience in the specific area, the handbook can provide
helpful suggestions on how to proceed.

> Norman Dorsen, President
> American Civil Liberties Union

The principal purpose of this handbook, as well as
others in this series, is to inform individuals of their
legal rights. The authors from time to time suggest
what the law should be, but their personal views are
not necessarily those of the ACLU. For the ACLU's
position on the issues discussed in this handbook,
the reader should write to Librarian, ACLU, 132
West 43rd Street, New York, NY 10036.

Introduction

In the recent past, most books about women's rights accepted the fact that women did not have a great many rights. So they counseled that women have a right to support, that they must follow the husband when he moves, that they must take his name when they marry, and so on. In fact, most such books assumed that the only rights women would want to learn about would have some relationship to the fact that they were married.

This book is different: it assumes that, in reality, women work for pay, that they work for free, that they are students, that they bear children, that they practice birth control and have abortions, that they watch television, that they visit bars, that they break the law, that they would like to start a business or buy a house—that they are, in short, members of the general community with interests similar to men's and are not limited by marital status. This book also assumes that women will have problems stemming solely from the fact that they are women, and that meaningful rights are those which will help women to cope with those problems.

So this book will not tell you that you have to take your husband's name, or even your father's name, or that you must follow your husband. Instead, it will tell you how to cope with discrimination—on the job, at school, in the courtroom, in hospitals, on television, at the bank, and in the local bar. That is the true meaning of women's rights.

THE RIGHTS OF WOMEN

I

Constitutional Rights—The Concept of Equal Protection and the Equal Rights Amendment*

Throughout United States history, much of the discrimination women have faced has been caused or supported by the legal system itself. When Elizabeth Cady Stanton and Lucretia Mott called the first Women's Rights Convention at Seneca Falls, New York, in 1848, one of their major concerns was a legal system that profoundly discriminated against women. They detailed these "unjust laws" in the ringing Declaration of Sentiments adopted by the convention. The law deprived all women of the right to vote, "this first right of a citizen." And the law created a separate and unequal status for the married woman, by depriving her of all rights, thus making her "civilly dead," and by making her husband her "master." The Declaration specifically condemned, for example, the laws that gave the husband ownership of his wife's property (including the wages she earned),[1] as well as the power to deprive her of liberty and to beat her, and full guardianship of their children in case of divorce.

Of course, most of the unjust laws listed in the Declaration have disappeared from the books. It took a bitter 70-year fight, but women eventually gained the vote with the ratification in 1920 of the 19th Amendment to the Constitution. Women won other rights too, including increased control over property and wages and the right to custody of their children in divorce. But not all sex-based laws have disap-

---

*Readers who are not familiar with the legal system and legal terminology should turn to Chapter X, "The Legal System." Although this book was written for laypersons, use of legal terms is sometimes unavoidable. The explanations in Chapter X should help alleviate any confusion.

peared. Laws persisting into the 1970's mandated that a woman's right to a name was different from a man's, that a woman could be jailed when a man would not be, that a woman could not work extra hours to earn overtime pay when a man could, that a wife could not control property owned jointly with her husband because he had sole control, that a working wife could be denied fringe benefits of employment benefiting her spouse when a working husband got those fringe benefits automatically, that a girl was entitled to parental support only until she turned 18 while a boy should receive such payments until the age of 21, or that most jobs in the military could be marked "Men only." Government officials decided that high-school students who were girls must take homemaking and could not play on the tennis or football team, that a girl who ran away from home was a juvenile delinquent but the boy who did was a normal, high-spirited kid, and that a poor woman who wanted to enter a government training program had to wait until all poor men had the chance to do so.

Because of the prevalence of such laws and decisions, and because there appeared to be little chance of using the courts to get rid of them, women activists in the early 1970's sought an Equal Rights Amendment to the U.S. Constitution. The ERA was designed to do away with all such laws and practices. It proclaimed simply that:

Equality of rights under the law shall not be denied or abridged by the United States or by any State on account of sex.

The amendment was first proposed in 1923 and had long lain dormant, but it gained political momentum with the rebirth of the feminist movement and was approved by Congress in 1972. One decade later, on June 30, 1982, it was officially declared dead—having failed by a very narrow margin to gain ratification by the necessary 38 states.

Feminists mourned this important loss. But the demise of the ERA masked the larger victory of the women's movement. In the same decade in which ERA went down to defeat, sex discrimination law in this country was transformed. Under the pressure of the women's movement, the Supreme Court radically changed its interpretation of the Constitution;

sex discriminatory laws and practices once automatically approved by the Court as constitutional are now likely to be declared invalid.[2] Feminist pressure produced results in other areas as well. Congress and state legislatures rewrote old laws to eliminate sex discriminatory provisions and passed new laws to outlaw sex discrimination in such diverse areas as education, credit, and housing. And federal and state agencies began seriously enforcing laws against discrimination on the job. In short, despite the loss of the ERA, the 1970's gave us the legal structure for eradicating discrimination.

This book explains in detail how women can use the laws on the books to gain real equality—whether in the realm of the marketplace, academia, or the family. And this first chapter on "Constitutional Rights" explains how to use the Constitution to change those state and federal laws and the actions of government officials that still differentiate on the basis of sex. For while the incidence of such laws and practices has dramatically decreased, some remain, causing serious problems of sex discrimination. Although there is no ERA to attack such discrimination, there are a wide variety of other weapons to use, including the Constitution itself—now vastly changed by the Supreme Court interpretations of the 1970's. Thus there will often be many ways to attack a particular problem, but women should always consider an additional attack based on the Constitution. And sometimes this will be the only route possible.

What constitutional doctrine can be used to get rid of sex discriminatory laws and government practices?

The relevant doctrine is generally referred to as "equal protection" and is derived from the 14th Amendment to the Constitution. The key language in the amendment provides that:

No State shall . . . deny to any person within its jurisdiction the equal protection of the laws.

What does the Equal Protection Clause mean?

The Equal Protection Clause is generally used to combat discriminatory laws and practices. Historically, the principal concern has been with discrimination directed against blacks: segregated public schools, denial of voting rights, segregated public accommodations. But the concept of equal protection has also been used to protect the rights of other groups: aliens, ethnic minorities, voters, poor persons, even—of late—women.

Technically, the Equal Protection Clause prohibits discrimination because the courts have interpreted the phrase "no State shall deny any person the equal protection of the laws" to mean "no State shall deny any person the protection of equal laws." In other words, a state legislature may not treat its citizens differently. The state must pass laws that apply equally to blacks and whites, to Chicanos and Anglos, and that do not single out any one group for favored treatment over another group. If a state legislature does pass a law favoring one group, the courts will declare that law invalid because it violates the precept of equal treatment compelled by the Equal Protection Clause of the 14th Amendment.

This summary explanation of the meaning of equal protection bears qualification. In a variety of contexts, state laws do single out different classes of citizens for different treatment. Residents of a state for more than 30 days can vote; those who have resided in the state for less than 30 days cannot vote. People over 16 who have passed a state driver's test may drive; people under 16 and those who have not passed the test may not drive. Such distinctions are valid under the Equal Protection Clause. How, then, can you tell whether a law that provides different treatment for different classes of people is legal or illegal?

What tests has the Supreme Court used to determine whether a state law violates the Equal Protection Clause?

The Supreme Court uses three distinct tests. In a shorthand way, they are often referred to as the "reasonableness" test, the "strict scrutiny" or "suspect classification" test, and the "intermediate test." Each test looks at (1) the government's purpose in passing the law and (2) the relationship between the purpose and the classification (black or white, man or woman, 18 and over or under 18) used to accomplish that purpose.

1. The "Reasonableness" Test

The test the Supreme Court has used in the majority of cases is basically a test of reasonableness. Did the state have a reasonable purpose in passing the law? Is there some difference between the two classes of people that makes it reasonable to treat them differently? If the answer to both questions is yes, the law is valid.

While this approach sounds fair, it has proven virtually meaningless because of the Court's refusal to apply the test to the facts in any real sense. The Court will even make up or accept a spurious purpose for the law in order to justify differential treatment. A classic example of manipulating "state purpose" to uphold a state law as reasonable occurred in a famous sex discrimination case. In 1949 the Supreme Court said that Michigan could prohibit all women from holding bartender jobs without violating the Equal Protection Clause because the state's purpose was to prevent moral and social problems, and prohibiting women from bartending was a reasonable way to prevent those problems. Both steps in this reasoning were fallacious. The Court assumed without proof that Michigan had this purpose, and it ignored the more obvious state purpose, saying that ". . . we cannot give ear to the suggestion that the real impulse behind this legislation was an unchivalrous desire of male bartenders to try to monopolize the calling."[3] Since the real purpose of the Michigan law was undoubtedly to discriminate against women, it should have been invalidated—for the desire to treat equals unequally cannot be a reasonable purpose under the Equal Protection Clause.

The Court's second step was to assume—again without supporting facts—that women bartenders cause "moral and social problems," which men bartenders do not cause and which will be prevented if the state keeps women from holding these jobs. At first blush, this reasoning may have a certain logical appeal. Women cause problems; if you remove the women, you remove the problems. The logic falls apart when one realizes that the Court is indulging in pure fiction. How do we know there really were any problems? Even if problems existed, is it likely that women were the sole cause? The phrase "moral and social problems" was probably a euphemism for illicit sex. If this is the problem, why not exclude men from bars rather than exclude women from bartending? Better yet, why not simply demand that bar owners take measures, directed equally against both the male and female participants, to prevent illicit sex in bars and any attendant disruption? The Court's intellectual weakness in examining this law lay in its willingness to make up nonexistent "facts" to support its assumptions and in its refusal to examine alternatives. In short, when the Court "applies" the reasonableness test, it generally mentions the test as a cover for the fact that it is ducking the real issues, thus giving states free rein to discriminate.

2. The "Strict Scrutiny" or "Suspect Classification" Test

The second test used by the Supreme Court to decide whether a state law violates the Equal Protection Clause is much more stringent. It is a test that the Court has generally applied to racially discriminatory laws or to laws affecting certain fundamental rights, such as the right to vote. Consequently, experts say that use of the test is triggered by a law that sets up a "suspect classification" (e.g., treating blacks and whites differently) or by one that affects fundamental rights. The test itself is called "strict scrutiny" because the Court examines the law very closely. The questions are: (1) Does the state have a purpose of "overriding public importance" in passing the law? (2) Is the classification established by the law *necessary* to accomplishing that purpose? That is, both the law's purpose and the differences between the two classes of people affected by the law are looked at very critically.

It is extremely difficult to show that a law is valid under this test. For example, most states cannot prove that their purpose in passing a law was of "overriding public importance" rather than merely "reasonable." Similarly, it is much more difficult to prove that a particular way of categorizing people is "necessary" in order to achieve the state's purpose than that it is a reasonable way to do so. Consequently, the Supreme Court tends to find laws unconstitutional when it uses this test. For this reason, women's rights advocates have long pushed to have the Court consider sex a "suspect classification," thus requiring use of the strict test when examining laws or practices that discriminate on the basis of sex. The Court has steadfastly refused to do so, however.

An example of this approach is found in the Supreme Court's analysis of a Florida law that made sexual conduct between a black person and a white illegal, although the same conduct was not illegal if the two persons were either both black or both white. The State of Florida argued that its purpose in passing the law was to maintain sexual decency. But the Supreme Court could not find any differences between persons engaging in interracial sex and those engaging in intraracial sex that made it necessary to single out the first group for criminal punishment.[4] In other words, the classification—treating the two groups differently—was not necessary in order for the state to achieve its claimed purpose of maintaining sexual decency. Therefore, the law was invalid because it denied, without a valid reason, the protection of equal laws to persons who engaged in interracial sex.

3. The "Intermediate" Test

In 1976, the Supreme Court announced a third equal protection test which, thus far, has applied primarily to sex discrimination cases. It provides that classifications by sex are constitutional only if they (1) serve "important governmental objectives" and (2) are *substantially related* to the achievement of those objectives. When deciding whether any law which treats people differently because of their sex is constitutional, the Court now asks two questions: Does the law further an important goal of the government? Is the different treatment of men and women substantially necessary to accomplish that goal? (If the law could be written to deal with the problem along functional lines without referring to sex, the answer to the second question is probably no.) If the answer to either of these questions is no, the law is unconstitutional.

This test is referred to as the "intermediate" test because it falls between the "reasonableness" and the "strict scrutiny" tests. It is more difficult for a state to satisfy the "intermediate" test (i.e., to prove that the purpose of the law is important and that the classification is substantially necessary to achieve that purpose) than to satisfy the "reasonableness" test (i.e., to prove that the law has some reasonable purpose and that the classification is reasonably related to achieving the law's purpose). On the other hand, it is less difficult to meet the "intermediate" test than to show, as the "strict scrutiny" test requires, that the purpose of the law is one of "overriding public importance" and that the classification is necessary to achieve the state's purpose.

The Supreme Court first applied the new test in *Craig v. Boren*.[5] That case involved an Oklahoma law which prohibited the sale of 3.2 beer to young men under 21 years old, but only to young women who were under 18. The male plaintiff argued that it violated the Equal Protection Clause to treat 18 to 20-year-old men and women differently in this regard. Oklahoma attempted to justify the law to the Supreme Court as a measure to improve traffic safety—a worthy state objective. After examining Oklahoma's statistics on "driving while intoxicated," the Court concluded that the statistical differences in the behavior of young men and women were too insignificant to justify denying beer to the young men. Thus, although driving safety might be an important purpose to Oklahoma, treating men and women differently in allowing them to buy 3.2 beer was not really necessary for the state to accomplish its purpose. Other efforts—such as improved education about the dangers of drinking and driving, and better enforcement of drunk-driving laws—would have a more direct effect on traffic safety.

What relevance do these equal protection tests have to women's rights?

In the past, the Supreme Court's decision about which test to apply has almost invariably determined the outcome of the case. If it used the "reasonableness" test, the state law was valid. If it used the "strict scrutiny" test, the law was invalid. Since in the past the Court has almost always used the "reasonableness" test when examining sexually discriminatory laws, it has almost always upheld these laws—such as the Michigan bartender statute. Moreover, the Court has never declared sex a suspect classification, like race, which would automatically require "strict scrutiny." In May 1973, four of nine Justices voted to apply this stringent standard to a sexually discriminatory military benefits law.[6] But a majority has not emerged for this position, perhaps because some Justices were waiting to see whether the Equal Rights Amendment passed before applying the strict standard.

Meanwhile, the new intermediate test ensures that the Court will take a more critical look at sexually discriminatory laws than it did in the past, when it simply used the "reasonableness" test and usually found the laws valid. For example, the intermediate test was used by the Court in a 1979 decision to strike down an Alabama statute that required only husbands and never wives to pay alimony to their ex-spouses. (See discussion of this case on p. 213.) Although the "intermediate" test is an improvement over the old "reasonableness" test, it still allows the Court a great deal of flexibility in deciding cases. It is no guarantee that all sexually discriminatory laws will be struck down.[7] To achieve that result, an Equal Rights Amendment would be needed.

Does the Equal Protection Clause prohibit discrimination by private individuals or institutions?

No. Equal protection is limited by the concept of "state action." The 14th Amendment provides that "*no State* shall deny . . . equal protection. . . .*" The courts have interpreted those words to mean that only federal, state, and local governments are forbidden to discriminate. The prohibition covers a broad range of governmental activities—from passing discriminatory laws to engaging in discriminatory practices—but it is still limited to action in which the government is implicated. Thus, if a public school official decides to bar women from a physics class, even though there is no law requiring him or her to do so, this would be a prohibited *state practice*. But if a private school official made the same decision, it would not violate the Equal Protection Clause.[8]

State action sometimes reaches more activities than the above discussion indicates because courts have found "state action" present when a government involved itself with or supported the activities of a private institution. And a private institution fulfilling functions normally considered governmental may be deemed to engage in state action. Thus, if the government provides most of the funds for building a private hospital or if a private company owns a town where all of its employees live, the courts would sometimes say that both the hospital and the town are embued with "state action," even though they are nominally private institutions. The hospital and the company town will have to measure up to the standards of equal protection.

Understanding the state action concept is important for several reasons. First, where there is no state action, women will need other laws such as the Equal Credit Opportunity Act to protect them against discrimination. Second, where there is state action, women will be able to attack discriminatory practices although no law prohibits the specific practices. For instance, the women students who succeeded in integrating the originally all-male University of Virginia at Charlottesville were able to do so because it was a state school. Finally, courts have used the state action doctrine to expand the coverage of the 14th Amendment by finding state action where previously none had been found. It is possible, then, that a private institution appearing not to be subject to the amendment will become so if further expansion of the state action concept develops. Consequently, women should always consider using a constitutional attack based on equal protection.

Can sex discriminatory laws be changed despite the fact that the ERA was not ratified?

Of course. Committees can be formed in each state to work on the project of searching through all state and federal laws for those making sex distinctions, and proposing new laws to eliminate such distinctions. Ideally the members would include the key feminist lobbyists for the ERA, its legislative sponsors, law school professors, important legislators needed to pass the new laws, and feminist lawyers. Feminist groups should command a majority of these committees in order to assume the lead role in decision making about the kinds of new laws needed. The committees' work will have important policy implications, and there will be temptations to avoid difficult decisions and preserve sex distinctions. For instance, if the present law states that girls can marry at age 18 without parental consent but that boys must be 21, should that difference be resolved by lowering the age for boys to 18, raising the age for girls to 21, or perhaps selecting a middle ground of 19 for each? The answer will depend on whether people wish to encourage marriage at an early age or encourage more education or job training for everyone before marriage. Another reason feminists should play a key role on these committees is to ensure that certain laws are rewritten to protect *both* men and women, rather than eliminated entirely.

It will be more difficult to rally the necessary forces for legislative change absent the mandate of a constitutional amendment, but not impossible. In fact, some states have already undertaken similar initiatives. Thus women's groups in each state should make it a major priority to set up committees to study and revise state laws to conform to the equality principle, despite the failure to ratify the ERA. A substantial help in conducting such a project would be the book *Women's Rights and the Law—The Impact of the ERA on State Law,* by Brown, Freedman, Katz, and Price (Praeger Special Studies, 1977). This book includes a comprehensive survey of sex discriminatory state laws as well as models for reform.[9]

Is there any way women can assert their constitutional right to equal treatment without the ERA?

Definitely. Women should continue to bring lawsuits challenging unequal treatment under the Equal Protection Clause of the 14th Amendment. No lawsuit is guaranteed to win, but the chances are much better than they were ten years ago. Nor are all courts the same. Some federal and state court judges are much more likely than others to give women relief. California, for example, has adopted the "strict scrutiny" test of equal protection for laws discriminating against women, so it should be easier to win lawsuits based on equal protection clause.

Must any steps be taken before bringing a lawsuit based on the Equal Protection Clause?

No. All you need to do is to find a lawyer. There is no need to file charges with a state or federal agency first, as is true in the area of employment discrimination.

If you are having trouble locating a lawyer, try the local ACLU chapter. Other groups that provide legal assistance to women are listed in Chart D in the Appendix. Should you find a local lawyer who will help you but who is inexperienced in this field, the listed groups can offer assistance and possibly even participate in the case by writing "friend of the court" briefs to raise feminist issues.

Is it possible to assert the right to equal treatment without bringing a lawsuit?

Legal rights can be asserted in informal discussions and negotiations with officials or even in demonstrations and publicity engendering events. Merely raising a question of the legality of the actions of public officials will often have a commendable effect on those actions: public officials do not like to be accused of lawlessness. And an indication of a readiness to pursue lawsuits may convince officials that you are serious about your claim for fair treatment.

Are there any state constitutional provisions on which women can rely in fighting sexually discriminatory laws and practices?

Yes. Sixteen states[10] have amended their constitutions to prohibit sex discrimination. Women in these states may be more successful in combating discriminatory state laws and practices if they rely upon state rather than federal constitutional provisions. One reason is that many state courts employ a higher standard of review in sex discrimination cases brought under the state ERA's than the federal courts use in equal protection cases. Higher courts in many states consider sex a "suspect" classification and apply a "strict scrutiny" test. One state supreme court—in Pennsylvania—has adopted an absolute standard that eliminates sex as a factor in determining legal rights.[11] Federal courts apply a lower standard of review which makes it harder for women to win.

Are there any other federal constitutional rights that women can use?

Many other sections of the Constitution will be useful in fighting important women's issues. For example, the right to privacy is derived from several amendments and has been used to establish the right to practice birth control and abortion, and thus the right for women to control their own bodies. The Due Process Clause of the 14th Amendment may be invoked in a number of situations. But this chapter has focused on the concept of equal treatment because that problem pervades most of the issues women are now raising. It is thus essential to understand equal protection in order to recognize its application to different problems—and to apply it vigorously when necessary.

NOTES

1. Technically, the husband owned the wife's personal property outright and had the right to manage and control her real property, which included the right to use or lease it, and to keep any rents or profits from it for himself. Babcock, Freedman, Norton, and Ross, *Sex Discrimination and the Law: Causes and Remedies*, at 561 (detailing as well all aspects of a married woman's unequal status under the common law system).

2. In fact, the Supreme Court has now ruled that many of the sex discriminatory laws detailed above in the text are unconstitutional. See, e.g., *Kirchberg v. Feenstra*, 450 U.S. 455 (1981) (invalidating Louisiana statute making husband "head and master" with sole control of community property owned jointly with his wife); *Wengler v. Druggists Mutual Insurance Co.*, 446 U.S. 142 (1980) (invalidating Missouri law giving all working husbands, but only some working wives, death benefits for their surviving spouses); *Stanton v. Stanton*, 421 U.S. 7 (1975) and 429 U.S. 501 (1977) (invalidating Utah law under which parental support was paid for girls only up to the age of 18, but for boys up to the age of 21).

3. *Goesaert v. Cleary*, 335 U.S. 464, 467 (1949).

4. *McLaughlin v. Florida*, 379 U.S. 184 (1964).

5. 429 U.S. 190 (1976).

6. *Frontiero v. Richardson*, 411 U.S. 677 (1973). The Court invalidated the requirement that women in the military prove their husbands' dependency in order to get medical and housing benefits, while men received them automatically for their wives. The decision's sweeping language—women's legal status was once like that of slaves; "romantic paternalism" has "put women not on a pedestal, but in a cage"—should have added to its impact, but was never accepted by the full Court.

7. See, for example, *Rostker v. Goldberg*, 453 U.S. 57 (1981) (upholding federal law providing that men but not women must register for the draft); *Michael M. v. Superior Court of Sonoma County*, 450 U.S. 464 (1981) (upholding California statutory rape law making boys and men but not girls or women criminally liable for consensual sex with an opposite-sex partner who is under the age of 18); *Geduldig v. Aiello*, 417 U.S. 484 (1974) (upholding California law providing workers' disability benefits to all disabled men, but not to women workers disabled by childbirth).

8. The decision might, of course, violate other laws. See Chapter III, "Education," for a discussion of Title IX of the Education Amendments of 1972 Act.

   Other methods can be used to attack the discriminatory practices of private schools and institutions. The Supreme Court has ruled that the Internal Revenue Service properly interpreted federal tax law to prohibit private schools with racially discriminatory policies from receiving tax-exempt status. *Bob Jones University v. United States,*———U.S.———, 76 L. Ed. 2d 157 (May 24, 1983). If the courts deny tax benefits to private schools that discriminate against women, this would be a potent weapon, even if women could not force changes in discriminatory practices under the Equal Protection Clause because of a lack of state action.

In another case, a court ruled that the government cannot give racially discriminatory fraternal orders tax-exempt status or allow gifts to such fraternal orders and non-profit clubs to be tax-deductible: *McGlotten v. Connally,* 338 F.Supp. 448 (D. D.C. 1972). This ruling went further than the first because it was based both on an interpretation of the Internal Revenue Code and on a finding that a governmental grant of these tax benefits would constitute state action, thus bringing equal protection concepts into play. If the Supreme Court accepts this concept of state action, the Equal Protection Clause would have a new, broad scope and could be used against many private institutions.

 9. For another useful book, which identifies sex-based references in federal law and recommends changes, see U.S. Commission on Civil Rights, *Sex Bias in the U.S. Code,* Washington, D.C. (April 1977).

10. Alaska, Colorado, Connecticut, Hawaii, Illinois, Maryland, Massachusetts, Montana, New Hampshire, New Mexico, Pennsylvania, Texas, Utah, Virginia, Washington, and Wyoming. For the text of the state equal rights provisions, see *State Equal Rights Amendments* (Revised 1976). It is available from the Women's Bureau, U.S. Department of Labor, Washington, D.C. 20210.

11. Treadwell and Page, "Comment, Equal Rights Provisions: The Experience Under State Constitutions," "65 *California Law Review* 1086 (1977).

II

Employment Discrimination

Statistics on the sex segregation of workers and on the undervaluation of women's wages suggest that many companies in the United States discriminate against women workers on a daily basis. This costs women a lot of money and is illegal as well, but it frequently saves the companies money. Because of that harsh fact, few of these companies are going to stop discriminating if they can avoid doing so.

One of the goals of Title VII of the Civil Rights Act of 1964 was to overcome this pervasive employment discrimination against women. Yet 18 years after its passage, women, while representing a large and ever growing proportion of the work force, remain confined to low paying, low status jobs with little or no opportunity for advancement.

Women have begun to fight against this reality, but the attack is still sporadic. Most women do not fully understand the mechanisms used to discriminate or the legal weapons available to attack them. Laws already on the books enable women to mount a major and systematic attack on discriminatory employment patterns throughout the United States with the aim of opening up more meaningful and better-paid jobs for all women. This chapter seeks to give women the basic information necessary to change the present situation by explaining the laws that make discrimination illegal, advising how to enforce them, and suggesting some strategy for their effective utilization.

What is job discrimination?

The answer to this question may appear obvious—but it isn't. Discrimination of the most conspicuous kind is shown by the boss who openly brags that he pays female salesclerks less than male clerks or who tells his talented secretary that she'll never be promoted to a managerial position because he can't stand bossy women. But such blatant examples do not begin to tell the full story. A Senate committee has described how discrimination in employment operates:

> In 1964, employment discrimination tended to be viewed as a series of isolated and distinguishable events, for the most part due to ill-will on the part of some identifiable individual or organization. It was thought that a scheme that stressed conciliation rather than compulsory process would be most appropriate for the resolution of this essentially "human" problem, and that litigation would be necessary only on an occasional basis in the event of determined recalcitrance. This view has not been borne out by experience.
>
> Employment discrimination, as viewed today, is a far more complex and pervasive phenomenon. Experts familiar with the subject generally describe the problem in terms of "systems" and "effects" rather than simply intentional wrongs, and the literature on the subject is replete with discussions of, for example, the mechanics of seniority and lines of progression, perpetuation of the present effects of pre-act discriminatory practices through various institutional devices, and testing and validation requirements. In short, the problem is one whose resolution in many instances requires not only expert assistance, but also the technical perception that a problem exists in the first place, and that the system complained of is unlawful.[1]

Women, too, must adopt this broader perspective. In the past, they have often complained about symptoms, not root causes. The emphasis has been on the individual: a specific woman who doesn't get a particular job or promotion. Or they have stressed the importance of equal pay for equal work. But attacking these forms of discrimination will do little to change women's basic lot in the employment world. If feminists are serious about improving the situation, their major efforts must be directed toward something broader.

What major concepts define job discrimination?

Before analyzing specific employment practices that discriminate against women, three basic factors operative in sex-discrimination cases should be made clear.

First, any effort devoted exclusively toward solving the problem of an individual woman is likely to have minimal impact. By definition, discrimination is a class problem necessarily affecting large numbers of women—whether they be 50 women in a small company, 500,000 women in the AT&T system, or the millions of women workers nationwide. To illustrate, if a company refuses to promote Susie Smith because she is a woman, that company is really saying that all women in Susie's position are ineligible for the promotion. Susie should not just attack the particular decision not to promote her. She should also fight the general policy not to promote women. Unfortunately, women often fail to fight the general policy. When a woman complains about discrimination, she understandably focuses on her own job opportunities. Those in a position to help her often adopt the same focus rather than translating her complaint into its broader framework: a policy of discrimination against a class (women). This means that women who are afraid to risk their jobs by complaining or who fail to perceive the discrimination go unhelped. When another woman complains, the whole process must be repeated. Moreover, it is far more difficult to prove discrimination against a particular woman than discrimination against many women. Companies can always find specific reasons for not promoting Susie Smith—she was late to work three days in a row or she refused to sharpen her boss's pencils. When the employer must give reasons for a failure to promote all women, the excuses are harder to manufacture.

Thus, cardinal rule number one should be to look for the way any sex discrimination problem affects other women. In legal terms, this generally means litigating on behalf of classes of women—"class action" lawsuits. Even before litigation, the problem must be visualized as one encountered by a class of women. It is not enough to help the individual while leaving the job market situation unchanged for other women.

A second basic point in examining employment bias is to regard sex segregation of jobs and the wage discrimination that accompanies it as the prime target rather than simply equal pay for equal work. Equal pay has been a rallying cry for women. The first major federal legislation against sex discrimination, the Equal Pay Act, embodied this concept. According to public opinion polls, most people now believe in equal pay. But equal pay for equal work is not the real problem.

Women are paid less than men for doing the same work, of course, but most women don't do the work men do. Look at the statistics.

In 1978, women were:

- 99 percent of all secretaries;
- 99 percent of all pre-kindergarten and kindergarten teachers;
- 97 percent of all housekeepers;
- 95 percent of all telephone operators, dressmakers, and seamstresses;
- 93 percent of all keypunch operators;
- 90 percent of all bookkeepers, waitresses, and cashiers.[2]

These job categories alone accounted for almost one-quarter of all women workers. And salaries in these jobs won't be raised by equal pay laws because there are virtually no male housekeepers, telephone operators, or secretaries. If there are no men who get paid more than women for the same work, there is no way for women to claim they are getting "unequal pay" under the Equal Pay Act.

The statistics above show that some jobs are almost totally female. The converse is that women are almost totally excluded from such lucrative skilled jobs as electrician, plumber, auto mechanic, construction worker, and long-distance truck driver. They are also excluded from the upper-level white-collar jobs in administration and business management. We must learn to recognize this situation for what it is: sex segregation of the job market. Certain jobs are typed female—generally, the low-paying, repetitive jobs. Other jobs are male—they pay more and in many cases offer a chance to be creative as well. Sometimes the sex-typing of the job changes: cornhuskers are female in the Midwest, but male in the Far West. But jobs are almost always sex-typed, one way or the other; and whenever the job turns out to be female, it also turns out to be low-paying.

To summarize, the legal standard of "equal pay for equal work" requires that you have men workers to compare with women workers, that both do work that is substantially the same, and that both work in the same place. Only if all conditions are present does the employer have to increase female wages to the level of male wages. If women and men are segregated into very different, or unequal, kinds of work, a demand for equal pay will be futile. Since workers *are* segregated by sex in this country, women must switch their focus from equal pay, as it is now defined, and concentrate instead on the integration of jobs and on increasing the wage level of the "female" jobs.

Integrating jobs will open up more interesting work to women, who will then command the higher pay that goes with such work. Real integration will also help change the wage structure because as men enter traditionally female jobs the pay level of these jobs should rise. The classic example is the rise in pay and status of secondary school teachers and social workers as men entered these fields.

It is not enough, however, to hope for a better wage structure as a side effect of integration. The wage structure itself must also be attacked in order to help, right now, the women who have already been shunted into the low pay of "women's work." Traditionally female jobs do not pay less because the work is inherently worth less; they pay less because women do this work. It is the wage structure itself that is discriminatory, and women must seek court decisions that will end wage segregation by forcing employers to raise the pay scale for traditionally female jobs. (See questions and answers on pay discrimination when jobs are segregated, *infra*.) Of course, this will also have the effect of attracting more men to these jobs, thus promoting job integration. The cycle goes full circle.

A third fundamental concept is that many employment policies are illegal, even though they appear to be fair on the surface and even though the company never *intended* to discriminate. A good example of such a policy is the decision of a large company to upgrade the educational level of its labor force by hiring only college graduates. That looks like a fair policy—it seems to apply equally to everyone, female and male, black and white—and no one in the company has any intention of discriminating. But is it a fair policy? First of all, until very recently more men received college educations than did women. And the percentage of whites with college educations far exceeds the percentage of blacks. Thus the effect of the policy is to exclude a disproportionate number—relative to the population as a whole—of women and of blacks from jobs with the company. The *effect*, not the intention, of the policy is discriminatory. Furthermore, the company does not have a bona fide reason for discriminating in this way. It has never conducted a study to see whether a college education is really necessary to do these jobs. In fact, many current employees, persons hired before the new policy was established, do not have college degrees, which in itself is proof that a college degree is not necessary. These two factors—the discriminatory effect of the policy and the lack of any real business need for it—render the policy as unlawful as the practice of the boss who refuses to promote his secretary because he can't tolerate women in positions of authority. The Supreme Court has even ruled, in a case involving discrimination against blacks, that a policy of the kind just described is illegal: *Griggs v. Duke Power Company*.[3]

Lawyers often refer to this concept as the "neutral rule" doctrine, by which they mean that any employment policy appearing to be facially neutral but which in fact adversely affects employment opportunities of women or of a minority group is discriminatory. And if the employer has no provable business justification (which lawyers refer to as business necessity) for his policy, then it is illegal discrimination. This legal concept is at the very core of anti-discrimination law and has been used over and over in different situations against different employment policies. It is important that women understand the concept, apply it to their own work situations, and be prepared to fight for a non-discriminatory alternative policy.

Another example of such a policy is a company's refusal to hire unwed parents. Again, the policy appears at first blush to be even-handed. But it affects more women than men because it is easier for men to hide the fact that they are unwed parents and because women more often have the custody and care of children born out of wedlock. Since an employer would be hard pressed to show that the legitimacy of one's children affects work performance, the policy is illegal.

In conclusion, three key concepts should be kept in mind when attacking discriminatory employment practices. Always look for the way discrimination affects a large *class* of women, not just an individual. Go after sex *segregation* of jobs and undervaluation of women's wages. Don't just attack obviously discriminatory policies; carefully examine apparently neutral policies for discriminatory effects. With these basic concepts in mind, we can turn to the specifics of job discrimination.

Under what laws is it illegal to discriminate against women workers?

Four major federal laws and a myriad of state and city laws forbid such discrimination. The federal laws are Title VII of the 1964 Civil Rights Act (generally referred to as Title VII), as amended by the Pregnancy Discrimination Act of 1978; the Equal Pay Act; Executive Order 11246 (as amended by Executive Order 11375); and the Age Discrimination Act of 1967. Teachers have additional relief under Title XI of the Education Amendments of 1972[4] (see Chapter III, "Education").

What is the most important law prohibiting sex discrimination?

Title VII of the 1964 Civil Rights Act is the most far reaching law and has the greatest potential for forcing change in employment practices. In fact, the three key concepts of job discrimination—its class effects, the necessity to challenge sex segregation, and the "neutral rule doctrine"—are all concepts that developed under Title VII.

This chapter will cover each of the major federal laws, but will go into more detail on Title VII because of its importance.

A. Title VII of the 1964 Civil Rights Act

Is it ever legal to segregate jobs by sex?

Almost never. This question arises because of a particular provision in Title VII that allows a company to hire people of one sex only if the company can prove that being a person of that sex is a "bona fide occupational qualification." In legal jargon, this provision is referred to as the BFOQ, and companies use it as their chief justification for job segregation. Whenever a woman tries to get a "man's job," a company fighting her claim will contend that being a man is a BFOQ— a qualification—for that job.

Actually the BFOQ does not have much practical significance despite frequent references to it. After an initial period of uncertainty about whether Title VII protected women in a meaningful way, judges have found that a contested job could be reserved for men or reserved for women only in very rare cases. In *Dothard v. Rawlinson*,[5] for example, the Supreme Court approved an all-male BFOQ for the position of guard in Alabama's maximum security prisons. The reason: Alabama's prisons were "constitutionally intolerable" places of "rampant violence" and a "jungle atmosphere," where sex offenders were scattered throughout the inmate population. The Court reasoned that in this setting women guards would be peculiarly subject to sexual assault and thus unable to do their job of maintaining order. Whatever one thinks of this stereotypical reasoning, it does not create a dangerous precedent for women's ability to get previously all-male jobs, since few employers can meet the standard of the Alabama prisons!

A typical example of this narrow judicial approach to the BFOQ occurred when a lower federal court declared that only when a sexual characteristic itself is necessary to do the job can the employer refuse to hire people of the opposite sex. The court used the example of a wet nurse. Someone who employs wet nurses can refuse to hire men in general, without considering their individual characteristics, since having breasts is necessary to do the job. Female sex is in this rare instance a BFOQ. Similarly for the job of sperm donor, male sex is a BFOQ. The case limiting the BFOQ to these untroublesome situations is *Rosenfeld v. Southern Pacific Railroad Company*,[6] and it should be mentioned whenever a company tries to claim that being a man is a BFOQ for a job.

One other kind of job has been mentioned frequently as a suitable candidate for requiring one sex as a BFOQ. That is acting or modeling, on the ground that one sex may be necessary to make a role seem authentic or genuine. This example has never been tested, however, and if we remember Shakespeare's day, when boys were used to portray women in plays, even this example may not be accepted by the courts.

In practical terms, then, courts will not use the BFOQ provision to let companies hire women for some jobs and men for others. That is, jobs may not be segregated by sex.

When men and women are segregated into different jobs, but the jobs are worth the same to the employer, can the employer pay the women less than the men?

Despite the fact that job segregation is illegal, it persists. And while it is extremely important to integrate one-sex jobs, integration is going to take many years to accomplish. In the meantime it is also important to attack the wage structure of all-female jobs if we want to change women's low economic status in the job market. Eighteen years after passage of the Civil Rights Act, national statistics show women workers have made no progress in increasing their low salaries as compared to men—on the average, women still earn 59 cents for every dollar earned by a man. Many discrimination experts believe the reason is the systematic undervaluation, on the basis of sex, of wages in all-female jobs. Whether this is illegal is not clear, although the Supreme Court removed one important stumbling block to the goal of making it illegal in a 1981 case, *County of Washington v. Gunther*.[7]

Alberta Gunther and three other women prison guards at the Washington County jail in Oregon sued their employer under Title VII for paying them less than male prison guards. The lowest-paid man earned more than the highest-paid woman, and the plaintiffs claimed that at least part of the differential was based on sex. The county defended the suit by showing that the women guarded fewer prisoners, and therefore spent more time doing clerical tasks, than the men did. In other words, although the men's and women's jobs were roughly similar, they were not the same job. The Equal Pay Act, by its terms, would not reach a sex-based wage differential of this sort, because the statute is narrowly drawn to outlaw unequal rates of pay based on sex only where a man and woman are performing essentially the same job. The county argued that Title VII should be interpreted in the same narrow way, and that the women should therefore lose their lawsuit.

The women guards contended that wage discrimination can occur even where men and women are segregated into different jobs. In their case, for example, they claimed that the county had evaluated the work of all guard jobs, and that the evaluation showed the women should be paid approximately 95 percent of the male rate. Instead, the men received full value under the evaluation, while the women received 70 percent of the male rate. They thought the failure to pay them full value was based on their sex, and that Title VII was written more broadly than the Equal Pay Act and could be interpreted to cover the practice.

The Supreme Court agreed with the women, ruling that nothing in Title VII requires a showing that a man and a woman are performing the same job or "equal work," before the women can prove the existence of sex-based discrimination in wages. The importance of the case lies in its firm rejection of the view that Title VII is no broader than the Equal Pay Act. However, many troubling issues remain to be resolved. The Court sent Alberta Gunther and the other guards back to a lower court for a chance to prove their claim that men got full evaluation value while women got less. But the Court specifically said that even if the women proved these claims, the Court was not ready to rule on whether such facts violate Title VII. The Court also refused to say whether courts can use statistical techniques or other methods to quantify the effect of sex discrimination on wage rates.

How do you prove that women are being underpaid on the basis of sex when they are doing different work from that of men?

Although the Supreme Court's *Gunther* decision paves the way for further action on a variety of forms of wage discrimination, the difficult problem will be how to prove that particular women's jobs are worth the same as the more highly paid men's jobs, or that some portion of a wage differential is due to sex discrimination. On this problem, the Court expressed no opinion, except to allude to various methods strongly opposed by some employers.

One possible method of proof is job evaluation plans. In fact, two cases attacking sex-lowered wages have involved employers who used such plans. Job evaluation is essentially the process of analyzing jobs, and then awarding points to each job for various factors such as its skill, effort, responsibility, and working conditions. To illustrate, for the factor of responsibility, a job requiring the employee to supervise no employees might get 0 points, while supervising 1 to 5 employees would merit 5 points, and 6 to 100 employees, 10 points. Or, for the factor of physical effort, no lifting would merit 0 points, lifting 10 to 15 pounds at irregular intervals, 5 points, and lifting 15 to 50 pounds regularly, 10 points. A host of similar questions are asked for all jobs, and then the points are added for each job. At the end, the persons with the highest number of points should get the highest salaries.

In the lawsuits involving these plans, the employers chose not to adhere to the point rating after completing it. Westinghouse Corporation, in the most famous case, arbitrarily chose to give women workers a lower salary than men workers with the same points would receive. The initial decision to do this was made in 1939 and subsequent changes in the salary system preserved this basic feature. In another case, the University of Northern Iowa departed from its point scale by giving some workers a pay boost because of the theory that employers on the local market would pay more for those jobs (the university never actually tested the theory by trying to hire workers at the lower than local market price, where there was considerable unemployment). To no one's surprise, the recipients of this pay boost were all men.

Of course, job evaluation plans which show women workers getting paid less than male workers for jobs which are point-rated the same do not guarantee success in a Title VII suit. The women who sued the University of Northern Iowa on this theory lost their case. However, that was the first case testing the theory. Several years later, just before the *Gunther* decision was issued, a federal judge in Pennsylvania did rely in part on a job evaluation plan in ruling that an employer who paid men more than women violated Title VII. The case—*Taylor v. Charley Brothers Company*[8]—shows the kinds of proof that would be helpful in proving wage discrimination cases. The women working for Charley Brothers (a wholesaler supplying grocery and related items to retail food stores) offered evidence of severe, clear-cut, and intentional segregation of workers into different departments on the basis of sex, along with evidence that the lowest-paid male worker in the entire company received more than the highest-paid female worker, and that even where women had the same jobs as men did, the women received less pay. Finally, they used a job evaluation plan prepared by an expert they had hired to show that even in all-female jobs not held by any man, the women were being underpaid, and that these women's jobs were worth 90 percent of the male rate. The judge accepted all this evidence in ruling that Charley Brothers had discriminated in paying wages, not only against the women doing the same jobs as certain men, but also against the women doing jobs not held by any men. These women, he found, were underpaid "because they worked in a department populated only by women, and not because the jobs they performed were inherently worth less than the jobs performed by the men, all in violation of Title VII."

Other, less complicated, methods of proof might also be used in wage discrimination cases. Examples might include company documents explicitly stating that men should not be hired for "women's" jobs because men might demand more pay. Or jobs might be so obviously unequal in value that a court could not account for the pay disparity except by sex—e.g., a female chemist who is paid less than a male janitor. Or a company with plants at different locations might hire men for a certain position in one location at a higher salary than women doing the same job in a different location. Since the issue is a new one, the methods of proving wage discrimination will have to be further developed, but the discussion above gives an idea of the kinds of proof that could be used. In any event, caution dictates combining as many of these methods of proof as possible. Ultimately, further Supreme Court cases will undoubtedly be issued to clarify the methods of proof. A warning is in order, however. The Court could still close off certain kinds of wage discrimination cases— by ruling, for example, that job evaluation plans cannot be used to show that certain all-female jobs are being paid less than different all-male jobs on the basis of sex.

What should women do who want to attack this form of wage discrimination?

Women can take many steps besides filing charges with the Equal Employment Opportunity Commission and starting lawsuits. On the national level, if the Supreme Court ever adopts a rule that makes it impossible to show that a sex-based undervaluation of women's wages violates Title VII, they should work for an amendment to Title VII. Canada already has a law explicitly prohibiting the practice. On a state level, they can file lawsuits under state fair employment practices laws, and work for amended state laws where necessary. They can also push their unions to take action, or in the absence of unions, organize with other women to bargain with their employer. Some suggested ideas would be a push to have a job evaluation plan done, where there is none to date, and close scrutiny of existing job evaluation plans. Scrutiny is necessary to determine whether some job elements common to men's jobs (e.g., weightlifting) have been over-rated and other job elements common to women's jobs (e.g., the manual dexterity, speed, and attention to detail needed for typing) have been underrated. Close attention is also needed to see that all elements of women's jobs are given points, or that men are not given points for tasks they do not perform. These cautionary notes illustrate some of the ways job evaluation plans can be skewed against women. So while the plans can be helpful, women must be aware of their negative side and must therefore be fully involved in the job evaluation *process* to ensure that the end results accomplish something.

Are there any organizations which can provide help on this issue?

As this book goes to press, a coalition of women's and labor groups has formed to push for fair wages. Contact:

National Committee on Pay Equity
c/o NEA
1201 16th St., N.W., Room 615
Washington, D.C. 20036
   (202) 833-4324

Two other organizations which have foundation funding to work on the problem are:

Women's Legal Defense Fund
2000 P St., N.W., Suite 400
Washington, D.C. 20036
   (202) 887-0364

Women Employed
5 Wabash Ave., Suite 415
Chicago, Ill. 60603
   (312) 782-3902

May a company give "light work" to women and "heavy work" to men?

No. Companies have historically indulged in this practice; since "light" work is generally paid less than "heavy" work, it obviously discriminates against women. The practice was one of the first that women workers attacked under Title VII. One famous case involved the Colgate-Palmolive Company. Before Title VII was passed, Colgate-Palmolive completely segregated its women workers into light work and its men workers into heavy work, with the highest pay for light work less than the lowest pay for heavy work. After the new law passed, the company decided to allow men to do light work (giving them an advantage in times of layoff), but did not let women do the more highly paid heavy work. A federal court found this to be illegal and ordered that the women be paid all the money they had lost by their segregation into light work.[9]

A similar practice is to divide work into an A-B-C system—"A" (light) work being primarily of interest to women; "C" (heavy) work of interest to men; and "B" (moderate) work of interest to both. This system is also illegal because it continues to segregate jobs by sex. Title VII requires that companies analyze the individual qualifications of each worker—male and female—and assign jobs on the basis of those individual qualifications. The company can never prejudge the weightlifting ability, or any other ability, of female or male workers as a class, and then assign jobs on the basis of this prejudgment.

May a company deny jobs, promotions, or overtime work to women because of state "protective" labor laws?

No. The so-called "protective" labor laws are a series of state laws passed since the beginning of the 20th century to regulate women's—but not men's—work. It has become increasingly evident that these laws now restrict women more than they protect them. Some forbid women to hold certain jobs, such as bartender or mine worker. Others assume that a woman never wants to work long hours or at night, and consequently forbid her to do so. Still others, based on the assumption that all women are physically weak, declare that no woman may lift moderate or heavy weights or work before and after childbirth. Of course, none of these laws prohibits the unpaid housewife from working under such conditions; only the paid worker is "protected." And many of the "protections" are inapplicable to the least desirable "female" jobs—night work is seldom closed to charwomen. These facts provide a clue to the real effect of such "protective" laws. Companies use them to deny women jobs, and women workers have used Title VII to attack this practice. The most famous case involved Lorena Weeks, a worker at Southern Bell Telephone, who bid for the more lucrative switchman job. The company denied her bid, claiming she would have to lift a 31-pound fire extinguisher, which the Georgia law on weight lifting for women forbade. (The company conveniently forgot that she already had to lift a 35-pound typewriter.) After several years of litigation, Lorena won the job and $30,000 as well to compensate her for lost wages.

Other women have challenged laws forbidding overtime work (at overtime pay rates) and closing certain jobs to women, and they have all won their lawsuits even though the companies argued that the male sex was a BFOQ for the work or jobs which the women were trying to get. The federal courts have flatly rejected this claim and have ordered the companies to stop using these laws to discriminate against women workers. The courts have been joined by the federal agency that administers Title VII—the Equal Employment Opportunity Commission (known as the EEOC).

To convince employers or unions of the illegality of such laws, the best legal precedents to show them are the EEOC regulations[10] and the case of *Rosenfeld v. Southern Pacific Railroad Company*.[11]

May a company refuse to hire women because it must provide them with seats or lunch breaks under other state labor laws, if it would be expensive to provide these benefits?

No. An EEOC ruling said that not only must the company hire women in these circumstances, but it must also start giving these benefits to men.[12]

Other items provided for by state laws of this kind are ten-minute rest periods, restrooms, a minimum wage, and premium pay for overtime work. The last two provisions are generally available for men workers; in fact, the federal minimum wage and overtime pay law covers both men and women, and at a higher rate than all but one state law. But some men workers are not covered by the federal law and could benefit from the few state laws making a minimum wage or overtime pay available to women only—an obvious category is male agricultural workers. In Wisconsin, a group of such workers brought suit to extend the state female minimum wage to men.[13] California male employees sued— unsuccessfully—to get the rest periods provided for women under a California law;[14] the state legislature later provided the benefits, even though the men had lost their lawsuit.

The courts may greet favorably the attempts of men in other states to change such women-only laws, as indicated by a federal appellate case in Arkansas. A company called Potlatch Forest thought it saw a good opportunity in Title VII to stop paying women overtime, as required by the state law. It sued the state to have the law declared invalid. The court refused to do so, pointing out that Potlatch Forest could easily comply with both the state law and Title VII by paying men the premium overtime rates, too.[15] But other courts may interpret the law differently. In California, a state law requiring overtime pay only for women was declared invalid under Title VII.[16] The court refused to save the legal protections of the statute by extending the benefits to men. The Supreme Court refused to review either the Arkansas or the California case, so there is no final word on which interpretation should be adopted by other courts.

Women in states with labor laws applicable to women should keep in mind the distinction between laws that protect workers and laws that protect men's jobs from female competition. Laws that hinder women workers should be attacked; laws that benefit them should be extended to cover men as well.

Should any of the "protective" state labor laws for women be preserved?

No. First, some of these labor laws—maximum hour and weight limitations, for example—are so restrictive that they have been attacked over and over again by blue-collar women workers across the country. Both the courts and the EEOC have found the laws illegal because they are used to discriminate against women.

Second, laws that women workers are not attacking, like the overtime pay or rest period laws, can be preserved by giving the same benefits to men workers. This has already been done under Title VII, to some extent, and could also be carried out by legislation in every state that still has such laws on the books. Such laws would answer classic complaints—for example, that women need and want maximum hour laws so they can get home to their children. The best solution to this problem would be new laws providing that overtime work must be voluntary for all workers.[17] A voluntary overtime law would penalize neither the man who wanted to get home to his children nor the woman who wanted double-time pay to put her son through college.

May a company hire men and women only for separate departments in a plant?
No. This is just another form of illegal sex segregation.

Is it legal for a company to forbid transfers between departments when it once segregated those departments by sex in initial hiring but no longer does so?
No. Usually the "men's" department will have higher pay scales than the "women's" department. The no-transfer policy appears to be even-handed because it applies equally to all workers, but very few men will want to transfer to a department where the pay is less; conversely, many women will want to transfer to more highly paid work. This is a classic example of the illegal "neutral rule": more women than men will be adversely affected by the policy which, in effect, locks women into low-paying jobs.

An Indiana company was found in violation of Title VII for a similar policy. The company allowed women employees who worked in divisions being shut down to transfer only into the all-female jobs in other divisions. The company's argument that to permit these women employees to transfer into jobs held by men would result in prohibitively large training costs for the company was rejected by the court. It found that there was no true business necessity for the company to avoid the "high" cost of training; therefore the policy, which blatantly discriminated against women, was illegal.[18]

Can a company give seniority rights to men only?
No. This is just an offshoot of the problem of job segregation. In one case, only men had been assigned to "unionized" jobs, although some men were not union members; women

were all assigned to non-unionized jobs. Since only unionized jobs had seniority rights, only men had seniority rights—in this case, the right of a more senior person to avoid layoff by "bumping" a junior person out of his job (that is, taking his job). A woman who had worked 20 years for the Phillips Petroleum Company lost her job in a layoff to a man who had worked for a far shorter time with the company because she had no bumping rights. The court ordered the company to hire her back, saying that the company could not hide behind the policy of giving bumping rights only to people in union-ized jobs when those people were all of the male sex.[19]

The potential behind this theory is enormous. Unions have frequently ignored women workers in their organizing cam-paigns, but this case could eventually lead to giving women all the benefits the unions have obtained for their male workers.

Can a company force women employees to quit by assigning them to heavy jobs that they cannot manage?

No. This practice is the other side of the coin of excluding women from better-paying jobs requiring lifting. Both practices point up the need for treating women on an individual basis, since some women can lift heavy weights and some cannot. For those who cannot, a job assignment to lift weights dis-criminates just as effectively as a refusal to let women lift weights discriminates against strong women. If a company merges formerly segregated departments and fires anyone who cannot do heavy work, more women than men will lose their jobs. Similarly, during a layoff in departments that were once segregated, where women will have to bump men, the formerly men's jobs may sometimes be too heavy for some women. If the company lays off people who can't per-form the first job they're allowed to bump into, more women than men will be affected by the practice. Some companies have even been known to take one heavy job and distribute its heavy task components among several men to ensure that women will be forced out when they have to bump men from these heavy jobs.

All of these practices are illegal under the "neutral rule" doctrine since more women than men are unable to do heavy lifting. The EEOC has said that companies must use alternate ways of distributing the heavy work in order to avoid this discriminatory effect. The heavy work might be assigned to one or two strong workers (male or female) who can handle it all, rather than spreading it among all workers. The company might get machines to do the lifting. Or it might institute a bumping policy under which employees would be moved only into jobs they are capable of handling. In short, heavy work cannot be used as a device to force women off the job.

Can an employer refuse to hire employees below a certain height or weight, if the standard is applied to men and women alike?

No. This is another example of the "neutral rule" doctrine, and one which the Supreme Court has specifically declared illegal, in the case of *Dothard v. Rawlinson*.[20] In addition to an explicit ban on women guards in some prisons, the Alabama prison system had a system-wide policy—a requirement that all guards be 5'2" tall and weigh 120 pounds—which adversely affected women's employment opportunities. Over 41 percent of all women cannot meet this standard, but less than 1 percent of all men are similarly ineligible for these prison jobs. The Court ruled that the requirement discriminated against women because of this differential impact, and then rejected Alabama's defense that the height-weight standard was needed to pick strong guards. If strength is required, the Court stated, employers should test directly for strength, rather than rely on the inexact proxy of a certain height and weight. Since that decision, many other courts have invalidated height and weight rules, especially for police jobs.

May a company or employment agency place help-wanted ads in sex-segregated newspaper columns?

No. This practice is blatantly illegal.

Is it legal for newspapers to segregate help-wanted advertising columns by sex?

Strangely enough, this is sometimes legal even though it's illegal for any company to *use* the columns. Title VII applies only to labor unions, employers, and employment agencies. Only if a newspaper acts as an employment agency when it publishes want ads can a court say that the newspaper violates Title VII. Some federal judges have decided that newspapers are not employment agencies for this purpose and that they can segregate columns without violating the federal law, although another judge has disagreed.[21] In any case, if any newspapers persist in using sex-segregated columns in the 1980's, there are other ways to force change.

First, many states have laws similar to Title VII that do cover newspapers. Women have used these laws successfully to force the *New York Times* and the *Pittsburgh Press* to stop their discriminatory practices.[22] They can be so used in other localities.

The second method is a roundabout but effective way of using Title VII. Women could sue, in one lawsuit, all the companies and employment agencies that place ads in segregated columns. This class action lawsuit would pit the class of all women job applicants against the class of all companies and agencies using one paper's sex-segregated want ads. Because women would be suing a class, the judge could order everyone in that class to stop using the columns. And if no one could use the columns, the newspaper would be forced to stop the practice.

Once the want-ad columns are integrated, may an ad itself specify or suggest that only men or only women need apply for a particular position?

No. This practice is just as discriminatory—and just as common—as sex-segregated columns. Theoretically, under the BFOQ provision of Title VII, there might be some jobs for which the company could advertise in this way. But as already explained, the BFOQ provision is virtually meaningless, so as a practical matter no ad can use discriminatory language, such as "boy," "girl," "man," or "woman."

May a company or employment agency give job applicants employment tests if it gives the same tests to all applicants and grades them all in the same way?

It depends. If the proportion of women who pass the test is the same as the proportion of men who pass, the test is perfectly legal. However, if fewer women than men pass, the test may well be illegal under the "neutral rule" doctrine. In that case, a court will order the company to stop using the test unless it can prove that the test validly predicts who will perform the job better. Proving this is called validating the test and is required by the EEOC guidelines.[23] In conducting a validation study, the employer must consider alternative methods of employee selection which will help select capable employees without eliminating a disproportionate number of women. Readers interested in testing should read the EEOC guidelines and *Griggs v. Duke Power Co.*,[24] which set forth this theory.

The EEOC definition of tests is extremely broad and basically includes any formal, scored technique to assess job suitability. Women have launched few major challenges to the use of these tests because testing is usually viewed solely as a problem for minorities. However, women test less well than men in areas such as mathematics, science, weight lifting, and mechanical aptitude—areas that women have systematically been taught to ignore as unfeminine. A physical strength test has, in fact, been successfully challenged in a New York State case.[25] Studies have shown also that students will devalue an article if they think it is written by a woman.[26] thus any test involving evaluation of written essays by a grader who knows the sex of the test taker should be examined for sex bias. The same is true for evaluations of face-to-face interviews. Other studies have shown boys performing better than girls on mathematical aptitude tests.[27] Thus women need to be aware of and ready to challenge sex bias in testing.

Can a company maintain sex-segregated restrooms?
Of course.

Can a company refuse to hire women because it doesn't want to build a women's restroom?
No. Absurd as it seems, companies that have never hired women really do use the argument that they can't hire women now because it would cost too much money to install a toilet for women. So far, cost has not deterred courts from ordering a company to stop discriminating, and the EEOC doesn't give credence to this "restroom" argument, either. This should be a sufficient response to any company's questions on this subject, but it would be wise to be ready with some common-sense answers as well, since many men become emotional when discussing this topic. Point out, for example, that instead of building a whole new bathroom, an employer could construct a new wall in the middle of an existing bathroom and build separate entrances for men and for women. Or the

employer could install a Porta-Can in the corner of an unused room, or place a lock on a small bathroom so that only one person (of either sex) could use it at a time.

May a company refuse to hire or promote mothers because of their child-care responsibilities if it hires or promotes fathers?

No. This answer comes from one of the most famous cases under Title VII, *Phillips v. Martin Marietta Corporation*.[28] The company told Ms. Phillips that it wouldn't hire her to be an assembly trainee because she had pre-school-age children, even though it would hire fathers who had such young children. All the lower federal courts agreed with the company that this policy was permissible, but the Supreme Court disagreed, saying that it's illegal to have "one hiring policy for women and another for men—each having pre-school-age children." Ms. Phillips thus won a big battle and helped make it clear that Title VII means what it says: women and men must be treated equally on the job.

May a company fire women when they get married if it doesn't fire men who get married?

No. Notice that this is just a variation on the above question. Men and women in the same position must be treated in the same way, whether that position relates to children, to marriage, to age, or to anything else. Airlines that used to fire stewardesses when they married or when they turned 32 years old found to their surprise that they were breaking the law. (The airlines were also startled to find that they could not exclude men from employment as cabin attendants.)

Are different retirement ages or benefits for men and women legal?

No. There have been several court decisions requiring equal treatment[29] and the EEOC guidelines take the same position.[30] The following policies have all been declared illegal.

Companies sometimes force women to retire earlier than men, to the disadvantage of women who want to keep on working, and they sometimes give women an option to retire earlier, to the disadvantage of men who would like to leave earlier. Sometimes men will be allowed to retire at the same age as women but with a lower pension than the women are allowed. Another similar practice led to a major Supreme Court decision. The Los Angeles Department of Water and Power for a long time charged women employees more than men for equal pension benefits upon retirement. As a result, the women had lower take-home pay than the men had. The rationale for this practice: the average woman lives longer than the average man. In 1978 the Supreme Court declared that this was illegal because it prejudges and penalizes any individual woman who does not fit the average. In 1983 the Supreme Court ruled that another variation on this same theme—giving women lower monthly pension benefits than men—was equally illegal.[31] At the same time, however, the Court accepted the insurance industry argument that women should only get equal benefits for that portion of their benefits attributable to wages earned after the Supreme Court decision. This result allows insurance companies to postpone paying equal benefits until sometime well into the 21st century, when the women who first started working in 1984 retire—for only their pensions will be entirely based on post-1983 wages. Women who started work earlier—for example in the mid-1950's—will have a large portion of their benefits attributable to pre-1983 wages, and thus will receive much lower pensions than men with the same work history. Thus, the older the woman, the more discrimination the Supreme Court permitted in her pension checks. It is to be hoped that Congress will overrule this result in the process of acting on H.R. 100, a bill pending in Congress in early 1984 and designed to end all discrimination in insurance and pensions. Or perhaps the Court will retreat from this position in other cases raising the same issue.

May an employer discriminate against pregnant workers?
No. Congress amended Title VII in 1978 to make it clear that employment discrimination based on pregnancy, childbirth, and related medical conditions (e.g., abortion) is illegal sex discrimination.[32] This amendment was designed to override a famous 1976 Supreme Court decision, *General Electric Co. v. Gilbert*.[33] The Court ruled in that case that it wasn't sex discrimination to deny pregnant workers fringe benefits (pay while disabled from working) given other workers for all other disabilities. The Court's logic might be best summed up as the notion that discrimination based on *sex* occurs only when you have a group of *men* to compare to a group of

women. Since there are no pregnant men, obviously GE's denial of disability benefits to pregnant women was not sex discrimination! This logic had a terrible potential for women workers—almost any discriminatory policy could be justified on the theory that a particular woman had been, was, or could become pregnant.

The 1978 Pregnancy Discrimination Act firmly rejected this logic. Instead, the Act spelled out that pregnant women who are able to work must be treated like other able workers, and likewise that women disabled by pregnancy, childbirth, or related medical conditions must be treated like other disabled workers. The particular ramifications of this general theory are set forth more fully in answer to the next question. Anyone who wishes even more detail should read the EEOC's "38 Questions and Answers on the Pregnancy Discrimination Act."[34] A free newsletter (the *Pregnancy Rights Monitoring Project Newsletter*) detailing legal developments under the PDA is also available from: Women's Legal Defense Fund, 2000 P St., N.W., Suite 400, Washington, D.C. 20036; (202) 887–0364.

May a woman be fired or forced to take unpaid maternity leave just because she is pregnant?

No. The reason is fairly simple. Pregnancy is like other medical conditions; if the woman is physically incapable of working, just as a man with a broken leg may be incapable of working, she does not have to be kept on the job. But if she can work, the employer has no right to get rid of her, whether his motivation is Victorian paternalistic concern for her welfare or prudish embarrassment because she is pregnant. Moreover, even if she is unable to do part of her job, she may have a right to transfer to another job—if that is how the employer treats other employees who are temporarily disabled from doing part of their job.

Is a woman who is physically disabled by pregnancy, childbirth, or related conditions entitled to the same fringe benefits given to other disabled employees?

Yes. The EEOC guidelines state:

Disabilities caused or contributed to by pregnancy, childbirth, or related medical conditions, for all job-related purposes, shall be treated the same as disabilities caused or contributed to by other medical conditions, under any health or temporary disability insurance or sick leave plan available in connection with employment. Written or unwritten employment policies and practices involving matters such as the commencement and duration of leave, the availability of extensions, the accrual of seniority and other benefits and privileges, reinstatement, and payment under any health or temporary disability insurance or sick leave plan, formal or informal, shall be applied to disability due to pregnancy, childbirth, or related medical conditions on the same terms and conditions as they are applied to other disabilities. Health insurance benefits for abortion, except where the life of the mother would be endangered if the fetus were carried to term or where medical complications have arisen from an abortion, are not required to be paid by an employer; nothing herein, however, precludes an employer from providing abortion benefits or otherwise affects bargaining agreements in regard to abortion.[35]

This means that women disabled by pregnancy-related conditions are entitled to the same sick-leave pay that a man might get for his broken leg, to the same health insurance payments, to the same amount of time off. In short, disabled pregnant women must be treated just like all other sick or disabled employees in every employment policy relating to sickness or disability.

On the other hand, a pregnant woman who is *not* disabled from working is not entitled to sick benefits. The distinction is important because most people fail to realize that, depending on the job and the woman, there will be various periods of physical disability in any pregnancy. Some women will not be disabled until labor starts; others will hemorrhage and be sent to bed for several months. The EEOC guidelines apply only to "disabilities *caused or contributed to by*" pregnancy and childbirth—not to the entire period of pregnancy (unless the woman is disabled from doing her job during the entire pregnancy).

Most employers now treat pregnancy and childbirth less favorably than all other medical conditions. Many do not give pregnant women any sick-leave pay; others exempt childbirth from health insurance plans; still others require a woman to pay a large deductible for pregnancy, but not for other disabilities, under the health insurance plan. There are hundreds of other variations on the basic scheme of treating women disabled by pregnancy and childbirth differently from employees disabled by other conditions. All these variations are illegal.

In 1983 the Supreme Court decisively ruled that such differential treatment was illegal, even in the context of an employer's health insurance plan covering the dependents of employees.[35A] The Newport News Shipbuilding and Dry Dock Company provided comprehensive medical insurance to the spouses of company employees but imposed a $500 limit on pregnancy-related hospitalization costs for the wives of male workers. The Court threw out this restriction, stating it discriminated against male workers, since female workers got comprehensive spousal coverage but they did not.

Are women who have had abortions protected against employment discrimination in the same way as pregnant workers?

Generally, yes. Employers may not fire or refuse to hire women who have had abortions. Similarly, employers must give such women the same paid sick leave, temporary disability payments, or other fringe benefits that other workers receive. However, Congress wrote one exception into the law: employers are not required to pay for health insurance benefits for abortion unless the woman's life would be endangered if the pregnancy were continued until term or unless there are complications. The National Conference of Catholic Bishops successfully fought for this exception (although Congress did reject the Bishops' attempt to allow employers to *fire* women who have had abortions). Some women believe that the exception constitutes a violation of the First Amendment guarantee of church-state separation. Any woman whose employer has denied her health benefits for an abortion might consider starting a lawsuit under the First Amendment to challenge the provision.

How long a period of sick leave is a pregnant woman entitled to?

She is entitled to the same length of time as are employees on sick leave for other physical conditions.

Is a pregnant woman entitled to extensions of time if the sick-leave period is too short?

If employees can get extensions for other physical conditions, she can, too. Even if extensions are not available, the EEOC has said that she may be able to get a longer leave if she can show that more women than men lose their jobs because leave periods are too short. If that is true, the company may have to allow longer leave time for everyone.

Are workers entitled to voluntary time off under Title VII for rearing infants or for family emergencies?

This has not yet been tested in court, but Question 18A of the EEOC's "38 Questions and Answers on the Pregnancy Discrimination Act" suggests that the answer is yes. The theory is that if an employer grants employees leave without pay for non-job-related purposes, such leave must be granted for infant care too. While this theory may be somewhat tenuous, it is quite clear that if a company gives time to women for this purpose, it must also give the same time to men.

Is it legal to provide health insurance coverage only to employees who are "head of household"?

No. This practice would exclude more women than men from health benefits.

If a company can prove that it costs more to provide some kinds of insurance to women than to men, may it give women smaller benefits than men?

No, under EEOC guidelines and a Supreme Court decision,[36] Title VII forbids averaging costs by sex, just as it would forbid averaging costs by race. Averaging is a way of attributing to the individual the experience of the group even when the individual does not conform to average group behavior. Title VII says women are to be judged as individuals, and the cost for the group is therefore irrelevant. Employers and insurance companies have contested this concept, but the EEOC guidelines have prevailed.

Is it illegal for an employer to exclude all women of child-bearing age from jobs because the employer claims that if a woman became pregnant, the fetus could be injured through

the woman's exposure to some substance in the workplace?

Probably. As of 1980 no court had ruled on this issue, but women workers had filed charges with EEOC and some court suits attacking the practice. Employers have been using this exclusionary policy where workers are exposed to substances like lead or vinyl chloride. The practice sounds benign enough at first—after all, the employer is merely assuring that it is not responsible for miscarriages or for the birth of deformed children. However, these practices often turn out to be highly questionable, something like the Washington state law, still on the books in 1970, that required men but not women to be checked for venereal disease before marriage. Industry in its haste to protect fetuses has apparently forgotten that men have a role in reproduction, and therefore has neglected to study the effect on male workers' children of male exposure to toxic substances. On closer inspection, it has sometimes turned out that the wives of male workers also have increased miscarriages or children born with birth defects either because the substances affect the male reproductive cells (a mutagen) or because the man carries home a substance which in the home environment causes damage to a fetus through his wife (a teratogen). Another impact on a man might be sterility or impotency.

Besides the failure to study an impact on fetuses through male workers, employers have generally not considered less drastic alternatives than an outright ban on women in the workplace. For instance, most women of childbearing age are not on the verge of becoming pregnant at any one time; rather than tell women they are excluded from the job in question, an employer could warn the eligible population of the problem and offer transfers to other work to anyone considering becoming pregnant. This approach would trust women to protect their children themselves, rather than assume they are incompetent to make intelligent choices, given the necessary information.

Other features of these new policies have also made women activists suspicious of employer motivations. The typical policy is broad enough to apply to most of the female work force; only menopausal or sterile women are not affected. It is apparently being applied mostly to high-paying jobs that have until recently been reserved to men. Traditional and low-paid "women's jobs" are not targets even though they may be equally hazardous (e.g., kindergarten teachers who might be exposed to German measles or nurses exposed to various viruses). For all these reasons, then, discrimination experts think it is probably illegal to exclude women workers from jobs because of the toxic substance fetal deformity connection. Men too might well have a claim of discrimination—that they, in contrast to women, were required to work at jobs exposing them to substances that could injure their children, cause miscarriages by their wives, or render the men sterile or impotent. Put in this light, it becomes clear that the solution is to bring exposure to toxic substances down to safe levels, not to eliminate the worker from the work force.

Women faced with this problem should file charges of discrimination with the EEOC and go to court if necessary. The employer is likely to win such a lawsuit only if it can show through scientific evidence that the fetuses of women workers alone can be affected, and not those of male workers' wives. In scientific terms, this means that the substance in question must be a teratogen (affecting the fetus directly), and not a mutagen (which affects the egg *or* sperm prior to conception). Even if it is a teratogen, it must be one that cannot be carried home on a male worker's body or clothing, there to affect the fetus his wife is carrying. To provide such evidence, the employer must of course have actual studies involving *male* workers, not just studies of female workers. And even if an employer could meet this very difficult test, courts may still insist that the employer seek less drastic alternatives than exclusion, such as informing women of the possibility of fetal damage and offering transfers to those women workers desiring them.

May an employer require women to be sterilized in order to keep their job?

No. This is just another variant of the policy above, and is added here to show to what lengths some employers have gone. Any woman faced with this choice should see a lawyer immediately. One lawsuit involving this issue has already been filed by the Women's Rights Project of the ACLU, and interested women should contact the Project at 132 W. 43rd St., New York, N.Y. 10036; (212) 944–9800. For an in-depth treatment of the legal theory about this practice, they should read an excellent law review article by Professor Wendy

Williams, "Workplace Hazards to the Fetus: The Reconciliation of Societal, Employer and Worker Interests Under Title VII," *Georgetown University Law Review* (February 1981).

Is sexual harassment in employment illegal?

Unwanted sexual advances, employment decisions based on acceptance or rejection of sexual favors, and offensive remarks and pictures in the workplace are all-too-common features of women's employment. One survey showed that 88 percent of the working women responding had experienced sexual harassment on the job.[37] The problem is a serious one—especially to women entering non-traditional employment with mostly male co-workers—and the courts and EEOC have responded by declaring the practice illegal.

The essence of sexual harassment is that female employees, merely because they are female, receive treatment different from that received by male employees. Several federal courts have ruled that this different treatment based on sex is a form of employment discrimination forbidden by Title VII.[38] "Sexy" pictures and lewd comments also may amount to sex discrimination on the job if they create a work environment which is hostile and offensive to the woman worker.

Barnes v. Costle[39] is a leading case on sexual harassment in employment. Ms. Barnes was a payroll clerk at the Environmental Protection Agency. Her supervisor repeatedly subjected her to sexual remarks and innuendo, suggesting that if she had an affair with him, she would improve her employment status. When it became clear that her refusals were final, she was harassed and finally lost her job. As the federal appeals court in Washington, D.C., said in ruling that her employer violated Title VII: "Plaintiff became the target of her supervisor's sexual desires because she was a woman, and was asked to bow to his demands as the price for holding her job."

What is the definition of sexual harassment on the job?

One of the best definitions of sexual harassment is one proposed by the National Organization for Women and the Working Women United Institute:

Sexual harassment is any repeated or unwanted verbal or physical sexual advances, sexually explicit derogatory statements, or sexually discriminatory remarks made by someone in the workplace which is offensive or objectionable to the recipient or which causes the recipient discomfort or humiliation or which interferes with the recipient's job performance.[40]

This is a good definition because it reflects the wide range of behavior that may be involved and emphasizes that it is the effect on the recipient—the woman worker—that is important, not whether a man in the same position would be offended.

Continual unwelcome propositions are sexual harassment both because they are sexual advances the worker does not want and because they are repeated. Unwanted touching, sexual comments and innuendo, and offensive displays of "sexy" pictures or cartoons may also be sexual harassment. Rape and sexual assault might also meet the definition but would be more commonly handled by criminal prosecution, of course.

In 1980, the EEOC passed guidelines[41] which define sexual harassment by focusing more specifically on the required impact on a worker's job. Under the guidelines, in order to establish a violation of Title VII, you must show one of three things: (1) that you were forced to submit to sexual harassment in order to get or keep your job—even if this is "just understood" and not explicitly stated; (2) that submitting to or rejecting the harassment is the basis for an employment decision that affects you—you refuse sexual advances and are fired, demoted, transferred, or given less favorable working conditions; or (3) that the harassment itself is intended to or does interfere with your work or creates "an intimidating, hostile, or offensive working environment," whether or not there is any other unfavorable job action. It is very important to remember that simply being subjected to a work environment that is offensive to you is enough basis for filing charges with the EEOC if men are not subjected to the same environment.

If a woman is subjected to sexual harassment but does not lose her job, can she get some kind of monetary award for "pain and suffering"?

Federal courts cannot award damages to the victim for pain and suffering under Title VII, nor can they order punitive damages to punish the harasser. If the main problem is the objectionable environment, and the woman suffered no loss of wages as a result, the court cannot order the employer to pay even "back wages," there being none; however, the court can order the harassment to cease and order the employer to enforce rules against it. A few courts have made monetary awards under state law when the harassment was physical, was intended to cause severe emotional distress, or interfered with an employment contract. For example, a New Jersey woman was awarded $1500 under state law from each of five co-workers and supervisors who repeatedly mocked her with remarks about her virginity and marital status, posted offensive cartoons, blocked her way physically, and subjected her to other offensive actions.[42]

What if the harassment is by co-workers rather than supervisors?

Generally the employer is liable and must pay damages for anything supervisors do, even if the company does not know about it or has rules against it. If your boss fires you for refusing his advances, the company will have to pay. The employer is also responsible for sexual harassment by co-workers, customers, or clients, but only if the employer knows or should know what is going on. This would be the case if you complained to management about what was happening or if it was obvious to see.

Where can women get further information on sexual harassment in the workplace?

Further information is available from:

Women's Legal Defense Fund
2000 P St., N.W.
Washington, D.C. 20036
  (202) 887-0364

Working Women United Institute
593 Park Ave.
New York, N.Y. 10021
  (212) 838-4420

(The Institute also has a Legal Back-up Center, which can provide help in litigating cases of sexual harassment.)

Alliance Against Sexual Coercion
P.O. Box 1
Cambridge, Mass. 02139
  (617) 482-0327

Women Organized for Employment
127 Montgomery St., Room 304
San Francisco, Calif. 94104
  (415) 982-8963

AFCSME
1625 L St., N.W.
Washington, D.C. 20036

(AFCSME has information about what unions can do to help
women workers.)

**What steps should women take to protect themselves against
sexual harassment?**

This area of Title VII law is still a developing one, and
courts are often reluctant to impose liability. They may feel
that men are entitled to a few tries, that women flirt and
invite it, that men will not know what is prohibited conduct.
In this climate, in addition to filing charges with the EEOC,
it is important to take steps which might help eradicate the
conduct.

First, say no in very clear terms. If the first refusal does
not cure the problem, inform management *in writing* of the
problem, asking them to take steps to end it, and indicating
that the conduct in question violates Title VII. Keep a copy of
all correspondence to and from management, and take immediate detailed notes about conversations with anyone about
the subject. These documents and notes may be important
later on if it comes down to your word versus his, or if the
company tries to deny knowledge of the problem and thereby
avoid liability under Title VII. Finally, file charges with the
EEOC if all else fails, or as soon as you are denied a promotion, fired, or given a bad evaluation (see infra for the importance of filing charges fast with the EEOC).

**May a company recruit for jobs by encouraging its present
employees to bring in their friends as applicants?**

Not if the jobs are segregated by sex, for men will then tend to recruit male friends for the jobs they hold and women will recruit other women. The company has an obligation to correct sex segregation, so it must take affirmative steps to insure an integrated pool of applicants for every job.

What steps can a company take to insure an integrated pool of applicants?

There are no hard and fast rules as long as the remedy is adequate. Basically, the company must do what it takes to accomplish the result. This means changing advertising, recruiting methods, and educating company personnel. For example, if the company's advertising and brochures show men and women segregated by sex in different jobs, the company will have to change the materials. The Bell Telephone companies have historically maintained rigid sex segregation in all telephone company jobs, and their advertising reflected this. After the EEOC launched a major investigation into their practices, the telephone companies changed their ads, and pictures of a young woman perched high up on a telephone pole appeared in major magazines along with pictures of a young male operator. This is just one example of the kind of action that needs to be taken to achieve the ultimate goal of attracting both men and women applicants for all jobs.

The EEOC has issued guidelines[43] on affirmative action steps employers may take to overcome the effects of any past or present discriminatory employment practice. In 1979 the Supreme Court upheld EEOC's position that employers need not be found in violation of Title VII before they can implement these affirmative action programs.[44] The EEOC's guidelines set forth a three-step process for employers: self-analysis of employment patterns by the employer; determination of a reasonable basis for taking action; and reasonable action designed to solve the problem. If an employer follows the process set forth in the guidelines and the affirmative action plan is later challenged by men or whites as illegal "reverse discrimination," the EEOC will issue a written opinion on the validity of the plan which can protect the employer from liability in the "reverse discrimination" lawsuit.

Can training programs—whether for management or for blue-collar skilled craftwork—exclude women?

Under the law, no, although in practice this is done over and over again. Training programs are often a good place to start the attack on segregated jobs because management's claim of not finding qualified women applicants has no validity when it refers to a program designed to give people those qualifications.

Indeed, women would be advised to push for affirmative action especially in training programs, since the Supreme Court has explicitly approved it in this context. A company in Louisiana, in an effort to correct the absence of blacks in higher skilled jobs, started a new training program for both whites and blacks, with a guarantee that the blacks would get some of the training slots. When the company chose a black man who had less seniority than a white man for this training program, the white man sued, calling the company's action "reverse discrimination." The Supreme Court disagreed. The company's action was a reasonable way to correct the results of past discrimination against blacks which had led to the virtual absence of blacks in the higher-skilled jobs. While this case involved race discrimination, the same theory would apply to sex discrimination.

Is it illegal for a company to promote a higher percentage of male employees than female employees?

Tested under the "neutral rule" doctrine, this practice would probably fail unless the company could prove valid business reasons for the differential. In technical or professional fields where more men than women have the necessary qualifications, the practice would probably survive; but it would not in jobs or fields that require only the generalist background equally available to men and women in our society.

Can an employment agency deal with persons of one sex only?

No. This would be legal if there were any jobs for which one sex is a BFOQ, but there are practically no such jobs.

If a company requests an employment agency to send a man to fill a certain job, is it legal for the agency to comply with this request?

No. The fact that someone else urges the agency to discriminate does not give it a license to do so. The agency must consider and refer women applicants for the job as well as male applicants.[45] Other illegal agency practices include discriminating in employment counseling, accepting discriminatory job orders, and publishing discriminatory ads.[46]

May a labor union limit its membership to males or refer only the male members for most jobs?

Theoretically, the answer should be no. But the notion that blue-collar, skilled craft jobs are male jobs, and should be so forever, is so deeply engrained that even the government agencies that are supposed to eradicate sex discrimination long disregarded the obvious fact that these highly paid jobs are among the most male-monopolized jobs in our society. The government has allocated major resources to eradicating racial discrimination in this area but has allowed the even more pervasive sex discrimination to go unchallenged. Women, too, are raised to believe that only men should hold these jobs, but they must re-educate themselves and challenge the barriers. For one thing, women might more than double their incomes if they do so, an incentive particularly important for women with little formal education who are now trapped in low-paying, dead-end jobs.

Several groups of women who understood this reality decided to change it. They sued the U.S. Department of Labor to force the Department to carry out its responsibility for enforcing Executive Order 11246, which prohibits contractors who receive federal funds from discriminating against women in the skilled craft jobs that constitute the bulk of some contractors' work. Rather than fight, the Department decided to settle the lawsuit. Under the resulting court order,[47] the Department is required to issue periodic numerical goals and timetables for training and hiring women at all levels of the skilled craft trades. Each federal contractor must meet these goals or explain why it did not. The goal for 1980 was 6.9 percent. Theoretically, if a contractor did not meet that goal in each job category, it was subject to the penalties of Executive Order 11246. And if the contractor argued that it could not meet the goal because the unions were not cooperating in referring or providing women for the jobs, the union was referred to EEOC for Title VII review. But in fact, even with the court order, the Labor Department has done little to enforce these goals and timetables. Much more pressure is needed in this area.

May a labor union use its bargaining power to negotiate contracts that discriminate against women?

No, under the law, although unions do it all the time. Besides suing such labor unions, women members will undoubtedly find that an excellent remedy against this practice is to seize some power for themselves in the unions so that women do the negotiating, too.

Are there any other illegal employment practices that have not been mentioned?

Hundreds. The practices detailed here are designed to give the reader some sense of the kind and degree of discriminatory employment practices, but the list could go on and on. The best guide is simply to trust one's own judgment as to what is discriminatory. Under Title VII, discrimination can be classified under one of two headings: practices discriminatory on their face, which are judged by the standards of the BFOQ; and apparently neutral practices, discriminatory in effect, which are judged by the standards of business necessity. Each kind is almost always illegal since the courts have rarely found a company's BFOQ or business necessity claim to be genuine. So whenever a woman senses that she has been discriminated against, she should do something about it, whether or not she has the information needed to prove it and whether or not some court has already declared the practice illegal. Proving the facts and changing the law are up to those charged with responsibility for investigation and presentation of her claim. Her responsibility is to identify the practice and to demand strict adherence to, and vigorous enforcement of, antidiscrimination policy.

What federal agency administers Title VII?

The Equal Employment Opportunity Commission, often called the EEOC.

How does a women enforce her rights under Title VII?

Your first step is to contact an EEOC office, where an intake worker called an Equal Opportunity Specialist will immediately determine whether your complaint comes under Title VII. You can go to the office in person or write or phone. If you send a letter, you should outline your complaint, briefly describing what was done to you (or to a group of women) that was unfair and how men were treated differently. Once the EEOC decides that Title VII covers your complaint, you will be asked to come in for an interview with a Specialist. On the basis of this interview, the Specialist will fill out a form, called a "charge" because you are "charging" the company with discrimination. The interview lasts from two to three hours. If you are unable to come to the EEOC office, the interview can be conducted by phone. Arrangements will be made for you to call collect at the appointed time. The original copy of a charge drafted during a phone interview will be sent to you for you to make sure it is accurate and complete. The EEOC will then send your employer a copy of the charge and investigate your charge. If it believes you, the Commission will try to get the company to stop discriminating; and if that doesn't succeed, you have the right to go to court to enforce your rights.

What action does EEOC take after receiving your charge?

If you live in a state or city that has passed a law against sex discrimination in employment (see Chart A in the Appendix for the state laws), usually called a fair employment practice law (FEP law), the commission's first step will normally be to send a copy of your charge to the state or city FEP agency. The EEOC does this because Title VII requires that any person filing a charge with the EEOC must first file the charge with her local or state FEP agency. To ensure that this is done, the EEOC files your charge for you. At one time the EEOC was also required to wait up to 60 days to begin its investigation of your charge in order to give the FEP agency a chance to investigate first. At the end of this time, the EEOC would either review the state or local agency's findings (if the investigation was complete) or begin its own investigation. This procedure often resulted in duplicated efforts and complaint resolutions that took far too long.

In an attempt to improve the situation, the EEOC and most state and local agencies have entered into work-sharing agreements. Officially these agreements divide incoming charges into various categories. These divisions of responsibility are different in various parts of the country.

If the EEOC has primary responsibility for the kind of charge you have filed, it will notify the state agency of your charge and will proceed to investigate without waiting to allow the state or local agency to act first. If the state agency has primary responsibility for the kind of charge you have filed, the EEOC will allow it to investigate the charge first. The EEOC usually will take no further action until it reviews the final findings and orders of the state agency. However, if the state agency does not do anything or if it begins to investigate, but it appears that there will be a long delay before the matter is resolved, you should request the EEOC to take over responsibility as the law provides. The EEOC will also take over from the beginning if the charge is against the state agency itself or if it is necessary to get immediate or temporary court action while the charge is being investigated and processed. The practical result of many work-sharing agreements is that, regardless of category of charge, whichever agency receives the complaint first investigates it.

The EEOC will sometimes review a state agency decision, but not always. Depending on the reputations of your area EEOC and your state agency, then, you may have a preference about which one conducts the investigation of your complaint. Check with a local women's organization to find out how the work-sharing agreement between the EEOC and your state agency operates. If the office that first receives the charge investigates, ask which agency is more responsive. This information will help you decide whether to file your complaint with the EEOC or the state agency first. If you file with the state first, file also with the EEOC just to protect your rights. If you are not satisfied with the state investigation, you can and should ask EEOC to review it (otherwise, EEOC probably will not do so).

If you decide to file with the state agency, or if your charge is sent there, you should cooperate fully with the investigators. The agency's final findings and orders are considered very seriously when the EEOC reviews them, and they are almost always adopted without further investigation.

How does the EEOC investigate your charge?

Most of the charges the EEOC investigates are handled by a part of the office called the fact-finding unit, using a procedure called rapid charge processing (RCP). (Charges that are referred to other offices of the EEOC are discussed in the answer to the next question.) The goal to rapid charge processing is to bypass extended investigation and to resolve your complaint at an early fact-finding conference which you, the employer (or other discriminating party such as a union), and the Equal Opportunity Specialist assigned to your case will attend.

Upon receiving your charge, the Specialist in the fact-finding unit will decide what data and evidence should be presented at the fact-finding conference. Within ten days, he or she sends a notice of your complaint and a request for particular information on your charge to your employer (or union).

The fact-finding conference is usually scheduled for three weeks after the employer receives this notice. The Specialist will determine if it is necessary for either you or the employer to have witnesses at the conference to explain what they know of the discriminatory event. The employer almost always presents witnesses, including the person whose action you believe discriminated against you and someone from the management level to explain the policy behind the action. The Specialist may hold pre-conference interviews with any of these witnesses or with the employer, if the response to the written request for information needs clarification.

You will be asked to come to the office early on the day of the fact-finding conference so the Specialist can explain the conference format, indicate who will be attending and determine your feelings toward settlement—what action you think the employer should take to end the discrimination and to reimburse you for any loss. The conference itself is informal; it is not a trial. It will be controlled and directed by the Specialist. You and the employer will speak to each other through the Specialist. A full record of the conference will be made by an EEOC staff member. Witnesses will only be present in the room when they are called in to tell what happened or to explain a particular policy. Both you and the employer are allowed to bring an attorney to the conference. However, the attorney can only give you advice; he or she will not be permitted to speak for you or to cross-examine any witnesses.

At the conference, the Specialist first reads an opening statement explaining the conference purpose and procedure. Then any written evidence—for example, employer handbooks or personnel reports—submitted to the Specialist before the conference or brought to the conference by you or the employer will be presented. The Specialist will then read your charge, you will state your version of what happened, and the employer will respond. Witnesses may be called in to speak. Then the Specialist will summarize the points in dispute and try to resolve them, considering all the evidence which has been presented at the conference, both the written materials and the statements made by you, the employer, or any witnesses.

At any point during the conference, the Specialist, you, or the employer can ask for a recess to discuss settlement of the charge. In settlement discussions, you and the employer will take turns meeting privately with the Specialist. If settlement discussions fail, the conference will reconvene and the investigation will continue.

At the end, the Specialist will again (or for the first time) request that a settlement be considered by both parties. If a settlement is reached, the settlement agreement will be typed and signed by both parties before the conference is ended. This will close your case.

If the conference ends without a settlement, the Specialist writes a conference report and submits it, along with your case file containing your charge and the evidence submitted at the conference to another EEOC office called the continued investigation and conciliation unit (CIC or investigation unit). In the investigation unit a new Specialist will analyze your case and decide if there is enough information to submit your case for legal review. If more information is needed, the investigation unit will do further investigation, which can include an on-site visit of the place where you work, interviews with additional witnesses, and further analysis of reports and records. Once sufficient information is assembled, the EEOC will decide whether "reasonable cause exists to believe there is discrimination." The finding of "reasonable cause" means the commission believes you could win your case in court.

Where the commission finds "reasonable cause," EEOC personnel make a final effort to settle the case, technically referred to as conciliation efforts. If conciliation fails, either because you cannot accept what the company offers or because the company will not offer anything, the commission will give you a "notice of right to sue," and you may then take the company to court. You may also sue even if the commission finds "no cause," although it will then be more difficult to find a lawyer. Another, somewhat remote possibility is that the EEOC or the Justice Department (in cases involving state and local governments) will bring a lawsuit on your behalf.

Must the EEOC go through this fact-finding conference for all charges?

No. Some kinds of charges cannot be resolved by the single fact-finding hearing, and then the charge will be referred immediately to the investigation unit. They include charges in which the person discriminated against wishes to remain anonymous (or has had someone else file charges on her behalf); charges in which the parties live so far apart that it is not practical to meet for a conference; charges in which the employer admits using a discriminatory policy but claims it is required by business necessity; charges selected by the EEOC to handle as class complaints* in the early litigation identification (ELI) program; and charges filed by the EEOC itself, including system-wide charges against particular employers.

A full investigation rather than a fact-finding conference is used for different reasons in these cases. If another person or organization files a charge on your behalf because you want to remain anonymous, you will not want to resolve your charge by confronting the employer face-to-face at a conference. However, if your charge does not become a "class" charge, the employer will eventually learn your individual identity either when corrective action is discussed or a lawsuit is filed.

If you live in a different city or state from that of the employer charged with discrimination, either you or the employer may have to travel too great a distance to make a conference practical. When the employer acknowledges that the policy affecting you is discriminatory but considers it necessary for business reasons, investigation beyond a single fact-finding conference will be necessary. For example, if you charge an employer with administering an employment test that discriminates against women, little can be resolved on evidence submitted and statements made at a conference. The investigations unit will have to analyze the test, collect statistics on the test scores of men and women, and determine if the test evaluates skills necessary for the job. Only then can the EEOC decide if its discriminatory effect is legal.

If your charge describes discriminatory events or policies

---

*A class complaint means that many people are affected by the policy and the EEOC tries to help this entire class, not just the individual who first complained about it.

which affect more women than just you, your charge may be chosen for special treatment as a case on behalf of the whole class of women by the ELI program. For example, if you charge that your employer did not treat your childbirth leave in the same manner he or she treats leave for other disabilities, no doubt other women employees who took maternity leave were treated in the same way you were. In this situation, you may be asked if you are willing to have your charge expanded to a class charge to include other women affected by the same policy. If you are, your charge will not go through rapid charge processing with its single fact-finding conference. It will become a class charge and undergo a much broader investigation. The investigation will be oriented toward litigation so that if conciliation (settlement) fails, the EEOC will be in a good position to file a lawsuit against the employer.

EEOC maintains a list of six or seven discriminatory actions or policies which can trigger a special ELI investigation. This list is the same in every EEOC office. Charges against specific employers can also trigger an ELI investigation. Each EEOC office maintains a list of employers in its area whose overall employment of minorities and women is very low or whose employment of minorities and women in certain job categories is low compared to the number of women and minority employees working in other categories for the employer. Both lists change as new issues or employers are targeted by the program. When you file a charge on an issue the EEOC is especially interested in pursuing under the ELI program or when your charge is against an employer which has been targeted by the EEOC because of its poor record, you should be allowed to decide whether you want to participate in the ELI program—with its full investigation and possible help for a "class" of women—or whether you prefer the rapid charge processing which will usually take only 60 to 90 days but will apply only to your own case. An EEOC attorney or a member of the investigation unit will attend your first interview to discuss your choice with you. It takes much longer to process a charge under the ELI program because the case is being groomed for court. It will usually take at least six months to investigate the charge and decide whether there is "reasonable cause" to believe there is discrimination. (Sometimes there will be a finding that there is "no cause" to believe there has been discrimination against women employees as a group. Your charge can still be processed as an individual charge in that event.) The EEOC usually spends approximately three months trying to conciliate or settle the case. If the employer will not settle and the EEOC files suit against the employer in order to enforce the law, the litigation can last for months, even years.

Although "class" treatment takes longer, there are advantages to it. The EEOC usually looks for greater corrective action in charges under the ELI program because the action will affect more people than in an individual case. (However, the corrective action, including back pay, will have to be one which can apply to all class members. You will not be able to get a different result for yourself.) In addition, your employer may be more likely to settle the case if your charge is processed under the ELI program because of the increased likelihood that the EEOC will go to court for you if the case is not settled. (Then again, the employer may be more likely to fight it out.) The EEOC rarely goes to court on an individual charge—you have to get your own attorney to do so. Finally, your name and the names of other individuals involved remain confidential when your charge is processed under the ELI program. And the EEOC does not wait 60 days for the state agency to investigate in these cases.

If you want your charge expanded to a class charge and processed under the ELI program, you should be aware that all potential ELI charges are reviewed by EEOC management and only some are chosen for ELI processing. This is because ELI processing requires more money and personnel resources than does processing an individual charge. If your charge is not selected for this special program, there is no appeal procedure to challenge the decision and your charge will be handled in the ordinary way.

If you decide not to have your charge processed under the program, it will be handled by a fact-finding conference in the rapid charge processing program or by the investigation unit.

The last category of charges that do not go to fact-finding conferences are "systemic" charges. Systemic charges are filed by the EEOC against employers whose practice of employment discrimination is the most serious and widespread. The EEOC initiates systemic cases which will have a significant impact on the overall employment opportunities available to women. While it is similar to charges handled in the

ELI program in that a whole class of women will be affected, a systemic charge by the EEOC is not set off by an individual complaint. Systemic charges go after large employers, even whole industries, while ELI charges are usually brought against small- to medium-size employers. An individual cannot ask to have her charge processed as a systemic charge, but if your employer is being investigated under a systemic charge your individual charge may be added to that case.

How long will it take EEOC to resolve your complaint?

New charges handled through the rapid charge processing program take an average of three to six months to resolve. The process takes longer if further investigation beyond the fact-finding conference is required or if your charge is referred to the investigation unit.

Before rapid charge processing it took two to three years, on the average, to resolve a complaint. As a result, a tremendous backlog of unresolved cases developed, with new complaints waiting their turn at the bottom of the list. To alleviate this problem, the EEOC has divided the processing of new and backlogged charges. A separate unit now handles the old, backlogged charges. In most EEOC offices, the special unit for backlogged charges handles charges that were filed before January 29, 1979, but in the Chicago, Baltimore, and Dallas offices, where rapid charge processing was first initiated, these units handle charges filed before February 26, 1977. Under this separate system, the number of backlogged charges has decreased dramatically.

If the EEOC is not handling your complaint rapidly enough or to your satisfaction, is there any action you can take?

Yes. You have an automatic right to bring suit 180 days after EEOC acquires the power to act on your charge (that is, 180 days from the time you filed a charge with EEOC where there is no state FEP, or 180 days after the EEOC assumes responsibility for a charge that was handled first by a state agency). If you want faster action than the EEOC can give you, and you can find a lawyer to take your case, request the EEOC letter giving you the right to sue (the "notice of right to sue"). Although you are not technically entitled to a right-to-sue letter before the 180 days are up, the EEOC will sometimes give you such a letter upon request if the EEOC will not be able to complete processing your charge within

180 days. Don't ask for this notice until you have a lawyer, though, because she or he must start the lawsuit within 90 days of your receipt of the notice and will need time to prepare the case.

Are there any timing problems to watch out for?

Definitely, and they are extremely important. You can even lose your lawsuit if you don't comply with certain time requirements under Title VII, even though you were really discriminated against.

The first timing problem involves the date you file your charge with the commission. Title VII says you must do so within 180 days of the date you were discriminated against if there is no state or local FEP agency. If there is a state or local agency, you must file with the EEOC within 30 days after the state or local agency finishes with your case or within 300 days of the date you were discriminated against, whichever is earlier. (It is best to file with EEOC right away, even if you decide to file with your state or local agency first.)

Even if you think you have missed the time deadlines, you may still be able to comply with this requirement. Several courts have said that if the discrimination is of a continuing nature, such as a policy the company has never countermanded, then a charge is always filed within the time limits because the discrimination is still going on. You should, therefore, always tell the EEOC that the discrimination is continuing, instead of limiting your charge to a particular date. When you think about it, almost every form of discrimination can be viewed in this manner. Thus, if the company refuses to promote you on August 11, 1980, because you are a woman, you can visualize the situation in two ways. You can either say you were personally discriminated against on August 11, 1980, or you can say that the company has a continuing policy of refusing to promote women into certain jobs, which you became aware of on August 11! The second way is always better, not only because it avoids this timing problem but also because it makes the point that other women besides yourself are affected by the policy.[48]

Another reason to file your charge as soon as possible is to increase the amount of money you can win in a lawsuit. Under Title VII, you can win back wages, that is, the amount of money you would have earned if you had not been discriminated against. But you can collect back wages only for a period of time dating from two years prior to filing the charge up to the end of your lawsuit. The later you file your charge, the later the date from which the judge will compute the back pay due you. For instance, if you file on January 1, 1980, and ultimately win your lawsuit, you will collect back wages from January 1, 1978, up to the date you win the lawsuit, and the company will be ordered to increase your future wages to what you should be earning. If you wait to file until September 1, 1980, the back wages will be computed from September 1, 1978, and you will lose eight months of back wages that you are really entitled to.

The second timing problem posed by Title VII involves going to court. You have only 90 days after the day you receive your EEOC "notice of right to sue" to file the court complaint that starts the lawsuit. Never ask for the notice until you have a lawyer and make sure that your lawyer understands that the complaint must be filed within that time period, or you will lose your case. (If by some chance this happens to you, your lawyer has been extremely negligent, and you should go to another lawyer to sue the first one for malpractice.)

Who can file a charge of discrimination with the EEOC?

Anyone who believes she has been discriminated against can file the charge, or an organization can file on her behalf. Women workers who are afraid the company will find out and fire them if they file charges should ask an organization to file for them. However, the organization filing the charge must get the women's authorization, and the EEOC will check to see that it did so. If an organization files, the EEOC will ask for the workers' names and addresses, but will keep this information confidential.

While labor unions are commonly considered organizations, under Title VII they are also considered "persons." Since any injured person can file a charge, a union can file a charge on behalf of itself or on behalf of one or more of its members. Your union may therefore file a charge against your employer challenging a discriminatory action or policy that has affected you without getting your authorization or submitting your name to the EEOC.

Whom can the charges accuse of discrimination?

Four kinds of entities can be charged: an employer, a labor union, an employment agency, and, in some cases, a joint labor-management committee controlling apprenticeship or training. The employer must have at least 15 employees to be covered by Title VII, and the labor union must have at least 15 members. The only important exception to the 15-employee rule is the United States government, which is not covered by Title VII in the same way that other employers are covered. (Questions on federal employees are discussed a little later.)

Are school teachers and employees of state and local governments protected by Title VII?

Yes, as long as the school boards and governments have at least 15 employees. These two groups were added to the coverage of Title VII by amendment in 1972. Rights of employees of state and local governments and school teachers are the same as those of other employees covered by Title VII, with one difference: only the Justice Department can sue on their behalf, and not the EEOC. These employees can still bring their own lawsuits, though.

Will your employer or union find out if you file a charge?

Yes. Ten days after someone files a charge with the EEOC, it sends a notice of the charge to the employer or union, and the notice includes the name of the person filing the charge. To avoid this, women can have an organization file on their behalf, but the company will usually find out the names of the women at some stage, because the EEOC will have to discuss remedies for specific people with the company.

If your company fires you when it finds out about a charge, or if some other retaliatory action is taken against you, is there anything you can do about it?

Yes. Retaliation for filing a charge of discrimination is just as illegal as the discrimination itself. If your company retaliates, file another charge with the EEOC and sue the company for damages. If you need to get your job back or end any other retaliation immediately, request the EEOC to bring a lawsuit to accomplish this. Under the 1972 amendments to Title VII, the commission has the authority to bring lawsuits for what is called "temporary or preliminary relief"—i.e., relief for you pending final disposition of your initial charge. If the EEOC won't help you, ask your lawyer about bringing a suit to force the company to reinstate you.[49]

Will women be able to afford the court costs and attorney's fees for a Title VII lawsuit?

Title VII provides that the court may award court costs and attorney's fees to the successful party. Although courts have frequently awarded both items to successful plaintiffs, they almost never require an unsuccessful plaintiff to pay the company's fees. The awards of attorney's fees have sometimes been very large—substantial awards have ranged from $20,000 to $225,000. These facts should encourage attorneys to take your case—and to take them on the basis that if you win, they'll get their fee; if you lose, they won't. You should not accept a contingent fee basis, which means that lawyers will take their fee from a portion of *your* earnings because the statute clearly allows the court to make a separate award for the attorney, based on the value of the lawyer's work. Another approach is to make it clear that the lawyer should first attempt to get a separate award for attorney's fees; and if that does not cover the value of the work, the lawyer can then make up the difference between the award and the value on a contingent fee basis. (Careful time records should be kept by the attorney in order to support the claim for a substantial attorney's fee award.) If the attorney is adamant about a contingent fee basis, try to get another lawyer. As for court costs, you probably will have to reimburse the lawyer for these as the case progresses, even though ultimately you can expect to win them back.

How should women go about finding a Title VII lawyer?

The best source of information may be your local EEOC office, which maintains a list of Title VII lawyers. If that doesn't work, try the sources suggested under the same question in Chapter VII, "Divorce and Related Issues," and also check Chart D in the Appendix.

What can women read in order to understand more of the legal technicalities about Title VII?

It cannot be overemphasized that laywomen are capable of reading and understanding the statute and regulations, which set forth in more detail all the procedures described above. Women should also read the cases cited in the "Notes" at the end of this chapter and any pertinent law review articles. The statute (Title VII) is found in 42 U.S.C. §2000e et seq. The regulations are found in 29 C.F.R. Part 1601 (the sections dealing with procedures) and Part 1604 (the section dealing with sex discrimination). A convenient place to find all federal laws and regulations dealing with sex discrimination in employment is a book produced by the Commerce Clearing House, Inc. (CCH), *Employment Practices Guide*, Volume 1. Another publisher, the Bureau of National Affairs (BNA), has a similar book, *Fair Employment Practice Manual*. Ask a law librarian to help you locate these works and then turn to the section on federal laws.

Are federal employees covered by Title VII?

Yes, but to enforce their rights they must follow different procedures than do other employees.

What agency enforces the Title VII rights of federal employees?

EEOC was given the responsibility for enforcing the Title VII rights of federal employees under President Carter's Civil Rights Reorganization Plan of 1978. That responsibility was transferred from the Office of Personnel Management (the old Civil Service Commission) as part of the effort to consolidate Title VII enforcement within one federal agency.

Does Title VII define discrimination against federal employees differently from discrimination against other employees?

This question arises because federal employees are not covered by the same section of Title VII as are all other employees. The section that outlaws employment discrimination against federal employees was added to Title VII in 1972 and requires federal employees to follow different procedures from other employees. Given this separation of employees into two groups, it becomes important to know whether the definition of what constitutes discrimination for other employees is the same for federal employees. The answer is that courts have been using the same definition of discrimination for both groups. Therefore, for the purpose of challenging sex discrimination in federal employment, women should use the standards of what constitutes employment discrimination under Title VII that have already been set forth and should look for the same remedies.

Do federal agencies have any obligation under Title VII to develop affirmative action programs?

Yes. This is another separate requirement imposed only on the federal government. Thus the government has two duties under this law: (1) it must not discriminate; and (2) it must develop affirmative action programs to increase opportunities for minorities and women. Both duties also arise under Executive Order 11478, which has been in effect for a longer time. (See "The Executive Orders," later in this chapter, for more detail on the meaning of affirmative action.)

Each federal department or agency must draw up national and regional Equal Employment Opportunity (EEO) plans, which are reviewed annually by the EEOC. The agency must also prepare periodic progress reports on its program, again with review by the EEOC. When the EEOC finds that these affirmative action plans or the progress under them are inadequate, it has the authority to require improvement or impose corrective action. Finally, a special requirement to set up training and educational programs to encourage maximum advancement by every employee has also been imposed by Title VII.

In 1978 Congress added to these Title VII affirmative action requirements for the federal government by requiring the development of a special Federal Equal Opportunity Recruitment Program (FEORP). The purpose of this program is to eliminate underrepresentation of minorities and women in specific federal job categories. Federal guidelines issued by the Office of Personnel Management (OPM) now require every federal agency to step up recruitment of minorities and women in every job category where their underrepresentation is identified. Reports on recruitment plans must be submitted to the EEOC with the agency's annual EEO plan and the plans may be reviewed by both the Office of Personnel Management and the EEOC.

Women employees of the federal government should demand that they have a say on these EEO and recruitment plans in order to ensure that the plans become a real instrument for change.

What procedures should be followed by a federal employee to assert her Title VII right not to be discriminated against?

In rough outline, she must first consult with an Equal Employment Opportunity (EEO) counselor in her agency or department, who will try to resolve her complaint informally. If the counselor cannot do so, the employee should file a formal, written complaint of discrimination with the agency, which will be followed by an agency investigation and, if the employee so requests, a hearing. The agency then reaches a decision.

If the employee is unhappy with the result, she may appeal the employing agency's decision either to the EEOC or, in special cases, to the Merit System Protection Board (MSPB). The EEOC or the MSPB, as the case may be, can order the agency to pay lost wages and correct the discrimination, including hiring or reinstating the injured employee. If the employee is still unhappy with the results, she can start a Title VII lawsuit against the agency, either at this stage or at several earlier stages.[50]

A special note about the MSPB appeal procedure is in order. The Civil Service Reform Act of 1978 split up the old Civil Service Commission into two agencies—the MSPB and the Office of Personnel Management (OPM). The MSPB generally handles appeals from employment decisions involving claimed violations of the civil service law. If a federal employee charges that some adverse action, such as a discharge, suspension, reduction in rank or pay, or unsatisfactory performance evaluation, is *both* discriminatory and in violation of civil service laws, her case is considered a mixed case and her initial appeal must go to the MSPB rather than to the EEOC. Those cases which just involve a claim of discrimination are appealed only to the EEOC.

May an organization file a complaint of discrimination with a federal agency on behalf of an individual?

Yes, but it must be with the person's consent. In addition, EEOC regulations allow organizations and other third parties to file general complaints of class-wide discrimination, unrelated to individual complaints. This might be a potent weapon to develop.

May a woman be represented by another person during the procedures before the agency and the EEOC or MSPB?

Yes. An employee may be represented by someone else at any stage of the proceedings. The representative does not have to be a lawyer, although this probably would be useful.

Are there any time problems of which federal employees should be aware?

Yes. The original contact with the EEO counselor must be within 30 days of the discriminatory action, although the counselor may make exceptions to this rule. The employee has only 15 days after her final interview with the EEO counselor (which will follow the informal conciliation efforts) to give the employing agency a formal, written complaint. Later, if she wants to appeal the agency's final decision on her written complaint to the EEOC or MSPB, she must do so within 20 days of receipt of the agency's decision. Finally, if she chooses to go to court, rather than appeal to the EEOC or the MSPB, she has 30 days from receipt of the employing agency's final decision to do so. If she appeals first to the EEOC or MSPB and then goes to court, she likewise has 30 days from receipt of the final decision of the EEOC or MSPB to do so. The courts are apt to enforce these limits strictly by throwing women out of court who do not abide by them, so it is very important to get a lawyer and move fast when you want to sue.

Another set of time limits protects the worker's right to go to court fast. Congress wrote some safeguards into the act, so that if the employing agency or the EEOC or MSPB stalls, the employee can get action by going to court. Once she files her formal complaint with the agency, she may go directly to court if the agency does not reach its final decision within a certain time period. She may go to court after 180 days if the complaint is one of "pure discrimination" (the kind of case that is appealable to the EEOC). She may go even sooner— after 120 days—if the charge mixes discrimination and civil service violation claims (the kind of case that is appealable to the MSPB). If instead of going to court she appeals the employing agency's final decision to the EEOC or the MSPB, the EEOC has 180 days to take action and the MSPB has 120 days before she again has the right to go to court, whether they have acted or not.

Can a court award attorney's fees and court costs in a successful suit against the federal government?

Yes. Again, this is an important feature because it should encourage attorneys to take such cases.

Can each federal agency discipline agency personnel responsible for discriminatory practices?

Yes, and this remedy should be pressed, as it is likely to have a salutory effect on other agency personnel inclined to discriminate.

Is there anything women can read to better understand employment discrimination procedures for federal employees?

Yes. For a more complete description of the procedures, read the EEOC regulations, set forth at 29 C.F.R. §§1613.201–1613.401, the MSPB regulations, set forth at 5 C.F.R. §§1200–1202, and the parts of Title VII dealing with federal employees, 42 U.S.C. §2000e-16.

Do other laws besides Title VII make it illegal to discriminate against women workers?

Yes. They all cover some of the ground covered by Title VII, so the rest of the chapter will not discuss them in as much detail as Title VII. They include the Equal Pay Act, two executive orders, the Age Discrimination Act, and many state fair employment practice laws.

B. The Equal Pay Act

What does the Equal Pay Act forbid?

The name of this law suggests the answer: companies may not pay women who are doing the same work as men less than they pay those men. However, "equal pay for equal work" is not as simple as it first appears. The law is surrounded with a lot of technical distinctions. The work of the men and women must be compared to see whether it meets certain standards before there can be a decision that it is "equal work" so as to require "equal pay."

First, both the men and the women must work in the same "establishment"—that is, a distinct physical place of business or location (such as a complex of buildings). The jobs of each must require equal skill, equal effort, and equal responsibility—each factor to be examined separately. The work must be performed under similar working conditions. Finally, the work itself must be "equal"—which means that the tasks involved in a woman's job are substantially similar, even if not identical, to those in the man's job. If any one of these standards is not fulfilled, a company does not violate the Equal Pay Act when it pays women less than men—which leaves companies with a lot of loopholes.

Can an employment practice be legal under the Equal Pay Act but illegal under Title VII?

Definitely. As the previous question indicated, the Equal Pay Act covers one very narrowly defined form of wage discrimination. In contrast, Title VII covers a panoply of discriminatory practices and can be used to force change in employment patterns where the Equal Pay Act cannot. For instance, a company that assigns all its assembly line work to men and all its clerical work to women, with the men receiving a salary double that of the women, does not violate the Equal Pay Act since the jobs are in no way equal. But this practice does violate Title VII because the company has assigned jobs on the basis of sex and denied women the chance to double their incomes. The women could sue under Title VII to force the company to integrate the two jobs and to recover the income lost in the past. Integration would be a major change in employment patterns, and it would probably lead to other changes as well. The men workers in the clerical jobs might well force the wage scale up—which would also benefit the women clerical workers. Viewed in this light, Title VII offers a far greater chance for meaningful change in employment practices than the Equal Pay Act does.

May a company avoid complying with the Equal Pay Act by transferring all the men who receive higher wages into another job so that only women are left doing the first job at the lower rate?

No. Once the company establishes a higher rate for men, it must pay women that rate even after the men are transferred out. Be aware, also, that it would violate Title VII to transfer workers out of a job on the basis of sex.

May a company comply with the Equal Pay Act by lowering the wages of the more highly paid men?

No. One of the provisions in the act says that companies must always *raise* the wages of the more lowly paid sex (women) and not lower the wages of the other sex.

May a company avoid the Equal Pay Act by giving men extra weight-lifting tasks?

No, although several companies have tried to do this. When the Wheaton Glass Company was sued, it listed 17 extra tasks its male selector-packers had to perform to try to justify higher wages for men, but the court found that the work of both men and women workers was "substantially equal" and warranted equal pay.[51] The amount of back wages the women won shows the importance of this concept. The women were underpaid by only 21 cents an hour—but this added up to almost a million dollars under the final court order.

May a company avoid responsibility for unequal wages when a union threatens to strike if the company pays equal wages?

No. It is just as illegal for the union to try—by any method— to force unequal wages on the company, as it is for the company to pay them. In such a situation, both would be found guilty of violating the act.[52]

What kinds of jobs have been found to be equal under the Equal Pay Act so that companies must raise the wages of women workers?

Jobs found to be equal include: nurse's aides and orderlies in hospitals; assembly line workers in factories, where some of the men do a little heavy lifting; janitors and maids in colleges; and salesclerks in department stores, no matter what kind of merchandise they sell. Other jobs where women gained back wages were bank teller, laboratory technician, inspector, press operator, machine operator, and packer. The list could, of course, continue; so women who suspect they are being paid less than men for doing the same work should be sure to challenge the practice.

Which federal agency enforces the Equal Pay Act?

The Equal Employment Opportunity Commission administers this law. Responsibility for enforcing the law was transferred to the EEOC from the Wage and Hour Division of the Department of Labor on July 1, 1979, under President Carter's Civil Rights Reorganization Plan No. 1.

How should women enforce their rights under the Equal Pay Act?

Contact a local or area office of the EEOC. Explain that you believe you or other women are being paid less than men; give the name and address of the company and your own name and address so you can be contacted for further information. If you have a lawyer, you can bring a lawsuit against the company immediately without going to the EEOC at all.[53]

Will the EEOC keep women's names confidential on request?

Yes, in an equal pay investigation, the EEOC should go to great lengths to protect the anonymity of anyone who fears exposure. For example, if the only woman faculty member in the English department of a university files an Equal Pay Act charge and wants to remain anonymous, the EEOC will investigate a number of departments at the university, not just the English department. This way the investigation will include a number of women faculty, not just the complainant, and the complainant can remain unidentified.

If the charge includes both an Equal Pay Act and a Title VII violation, it will be more difficult to protect women's anonymity (see p. 61 for the procedure on filing an anonymous Title VII complaint).

May an organization report unequal wages to the EEOC?

Yes, and there is no requirement that the organization obtain the permission of any of the affected women.

What steps will the EEOC take to enforce your rights?

The EEOC's Equal Pay Division will send investigators to your company to find out whether there is a violation of the Equal Pay Act. It may do this even without receiving any complaints. If a violation is found, the investigator will try to collect the wages that are due to the underpaid women and will ask for a formal agreement by the company to increase the wages of women workers to the level of the men. Failing that, the EEOC will bring a lawsuit on behalf of the underpaid workers, both to obtain the past wages due and to force the company to change its future pay rates.

But remember, you can always bring your own equal pay lawsuit without even filing a complaint with the EEOC.

Will the EEOC refer your Equal Pay Act charge to a state FEP agency for initial investigation?

No. There is no requirement that the EEOC give state agencies a chance to act first under the Equal Pay Act. If your charge claims a violation of Title VII in addition to a violation of the Equal Pay Act, the state agency gives up any right it may have to investigate first on the Title VII part of the charge. This allows the EEOC to begin processing both parts of your charge immediately, and for that reason it would be good to add an Equal Pay violation whenever possible to any charge of discrimination.

How long will it take the EEOC to act on your complaint?

Because of the limited kind of charge brought under the Equal Pay Act, it will usually not take as long to process as a Title VII charge. When your charge alleges both an Equal Pay Act and a Title VII violation, a Specialist from the equal pay unit and a Specialist from the rapid charge processing (Title VII) unit are supposed to work together through the investigation, data preparation, and fact finding stages of your complaint. This joint work may slow down the whole process, however.

What companies are covered by the Equal Pay Act?

The official definition is that the company must be "engaged in commerce" or "engaged in the production of goods for commerce." This definition is not very helpful, but the courts have interpreted it broadly to reach many companies and even some public institutions like schools and hospitals. If in doubt, act as though your employer is covered until you find out differently. If your employer must comply with the federal minimum wage and overtime pay law, called the Fair Labor Standards Act, he must also obey the Equal Pay Act.

In addition, executive, administrative, and professional employees, who are exempt from the minimum wage and overtime provisions of the Fair Labor Standards Act, are included under the Equal Pay Act. If you cannot find out if you are covered, contact a local EEOC office.

Are there any timing problems under the Equal Pay Act?
Only one. You must bring the lawsuit within two years of the discrimination, or within three years if the company discriminated "willfully." Obviously, if the company is still underpaying its women workers, there is no problem. But if the company recently decided to comply with the law, you must start the lawsuit within two years from the time the company stopped discriminating.

The two-year limit also affects the amount of back pay. You can collect only for the two years prior to starting the *lawsuit;* hence, the sooner you sue, the more money you'll collect. (Compare this to Title VII, where the time you file your charge with the EEOC is the relevant date for computing back wages. Unlike that situation, filing a complaint with the EEOC under the Equal Pay Act will not increase your back wages; here the relevant date is that of starting the lawsuit, so it is important not to waste time in doing so.)

Remember also that going to the EEOC is not the same as starting a lawsuit. One woman complained to EEOC about wage discrimination immediately, but did not start her lawsuit until more than three years later. She lost her case under the Equal Pay Act because of this delay.[54] So be sure to keep track of the two- (or three-) year deadline for starting your equal pay lawsuit, even if you file a Title VII complaint with the EEOC about the same incident.

What may women win in a successful lawsuit under the Equal Pay Act?
They can win the wages they should have earned, up to two years worth ("back wages"), plus the same amount as punishment for the company, plus attorney's fees and court costs. Since Title VII does not provide for the recovery of "double" back wages, an Equal Pay Act charge should be added to every Title VII lawsuit. The provision for attorney's fees will help women locate a lawyer, just as the Title VII provision does. A court may also award back wages for three years,

doubled as punishment for the company if the lawyer can prove that the company discriminated "willfully." However, in a suit brought by a worker or workers, the judge cannot order the company to raise the salaries of the women to the legal level for the future (as he can in lawsuits brought by the EEOC).[55]

What can women read to understand better the Equal Pay Act?

The statute is found in 29 U.S.C. §206 (d). The EEOC has temporarily adopted the Labor Department's old Equal Pay Act regulations, published in 29 C.F.R. §§800.0-800.166, to the extent they are not inconsistent with recent court decisions. Both are also found in the CCH *Employment Practices Guide* and the BNA *Fair Employment Practice Manual*. The EEOC will be issuing new regulations which will interpret the relationship of the Equal Pay Act to Title VII. An article worth reading is Berger, "Equal Pay, Equal Employment Opportunity and Equal Enforcement of the Law for Women," 5 *Valparaiso Law Review* 326, 338–350 (1971), which will also refer readers to some of the more important cases. Two other articles are Blumrosen, "Wage Discrimination, Job Segregation," *The University of Michigan Journal of Law Reform* 397 (1979), and Murphy, "Female Wage Discrimination, a Study of the Equal Pay Act 1963–1970," 39 *University of Cincinnati Law Review* 615 (1970).

C. The Executive Orders

What are executive orders?

Executive orders are directives issued by the President, telling the executive branch of the government to take certain action as set forth in the order. In most respects, an executive order has the force and effect of law.

What executive order forbids employment discrimination against women workers?

Executive Order 11246, issued by President Lyndon Johnson, requires any employer that has a contract with the federal government not to discriminate. Initially, E.O. 11246 forbade race discrimination only, but the President later issued E.O. 11375, which amended the former order by adding sex discrimination to its prohibitions.

Which employers are covered by E.O. 11246 (as amended by E.O. 11375)?

The executive order applies to any company or institution that has a contract for more than $10,000 with the federal government, whether it be to sell typewriters to the government, to do scientific research, or to produce missiles. The order also applies to subcontractors of the contractor (both are referred to in this chapter as contractors) although the order is seldom enforced as to subcontractors. Finally, anyone applying for federal construction money (referred to here as "applicant") is also covered and must obtain promises of non-discrimination from the contractors who will perform the construction work for the applicant.

The executive order applies to all branches of a company that has a contract with the government, even though only one branch may have the contract. It does not apply directly to any unions involved with the company although strong pressure is exerted on the unions indirectly.

What action must the executive branch take under the executive order?

Every agency or department in the executive branch must obtain a promise from any contractor with whom it has a contract that the company will not discriminate against its workers. The agency must also demand that applicants for federal construction money agree to put the same promise in their contract with the construction company doing the actual work. Pertinent portions of the promise, generally called the Equal Employment Opportunity (EEO) clause, read as follows:

During the performance of this contract, the contractor agrees as follows:
(1) The contractor will not discriminate against any employee or applicant for employment because of race, color, religion, sex, or national origin. The contractor will take affirmative action to insure that applicants are employed, and that employees are treated during employment without regard to their race, color, religion, sex, or

national origin. Such action shall include, but not be limited to the following: Employment, upgrading, demotion, or transfer, recruitment or recruitment advertising; layoff or termination; rates of pay or other forms of compensation; and selection for training, including apprenticeship.

Unless the contractor or applicant agrees to this clause, he cannot get the contract or the federal money. For example, if Columbia University wants a federal contract to do research on guinea pigs, it will have to agree to these conditions before the government will give it the contract. And if New York City wants federal money for a construction project, it will have to put this clause in its contract with the Big Bull Construction Company, which will actually do the work.

What practices by a contractor constitute discrimination against women workers in violation of the EEO contract clause?

Discrimination under the executive order is generally measured by the same standards as discrimination under Title VII; therefore, if something is illegal under Title VII, it is almost always a violation of the contract, too. (There are some variations, but they are not very important.) Given this fact, women workers should consider and use all the legal standards of what constitutes discrimination set forth for Title VII when they want to bring charges against a contractor, including the charge of retaliation, which is illegal under both laws.

Must the contractor do anything besides refraining from discriminating?

Yes. Under the EEO clause, he must also take "affirmative action" to insure fair treatment to women workers. All contractors have this obligation if they want the federal contract, and therein lies the chief difference with Title VII. Whether or not anyone ever files a charge against a particular contractor, he will have to undertake "affirmative action" under the executive order.

Under Title VII, a company almost always has the same theoretical obligation because affirmative action is necessary to correct the effects of past discrimination and most companies have discriminated in the past. However, a company is not specifically required to take affirmative action under Title VII unless a court makes a finding of discrimination. Few companies have elected to comply with the spirit of Title VII to correct the effects of past discrimination and implement affirmative action, unless there was such a finding. In fact, the decision of one company to implement an affirmative action plan was challenged by a white man on the theory that *voluntary* affirmative action resulted in reverse discrimination and was forbidden by Title VII. The Supreme Court upheld the company's action as legal because it was within the objectives of Title VII.[56] But as a practical matter, few companies, unless covered by E.O. 11246, will voluntarily undertake affirmative action. They will gamble that women will not sue under Title VII, and thereby avoid the trouble and expense of affirmative action. Of course, if women *do* sue under Title VII, the company will have to take action and recompense the women for its failure to do so earlier, but that is a gamble many companies are willing to take.

What exactly is an affirmative action plan?

This is the formal plan the contractor (at least, those with 50 or more employees and a yearly aggregate of $50,000 or more in federal government contracts) must draw up to meet its affirmative action requirements.* Generally the contractor must analyze those jobs in which it underutilizes women, set numerical goals and a specific timetable for increasing the utilization of women, and describe in detail the methods it will use to do so, including which company personnel will be responsible for the program. Setting goals and timetables constitutes the heart of the program. An example would be an agreement by the company to increase women blue-collar workers to 10–15 percent of its work force during the first year of the contract and to 12–17 percent during the second year.

The requirements for the affirmative action plan are too elaborate to discuss in detail, and readers interested in learning more should read the applicable government regulations. They are found at 41 C.F.R. Part 60-2 and are commonly referred to as Revised Order No. 4.

---

*The Reagan administration has proposed changes in the regulations about which employers must have affirmative action plans, and what they must contain, but no changes have been finalized as this book goes to press.

If the contractor fails to meet the numerical goals it sets on the specified time schedule, will the government penalize it?

Not necessarily. All the government requires is that the contractor make an effort in good faith to meet the goals. Even if the company fails but can demonstrate that it took action in good faith, it will be home free.

What government agency enforces Executive Order 11246 (as amended by E.O. 11375)?

It is enforced by a special office in the Department of Labor, the Office of Federal Contract Compliance Programs (OFCCP).

How does OFCCP enforce the executive order?

There are two basic methods: compliance reviews and complaint procedures. In theory, the OFCCP conducts periodic reviews of contractors to see whether they discriminate or have fulfilled their duty to take "affirmative action." In addition, OFCCP regulations require reviews of certain large contractors before they are awarded a contract. In actual practice, compliance reviews (either before or after contracts are awarded) are not conducted regularly. OFCCP is so understaffed and disorganized that it is impossible for it to do its job and most companies have never been subjected to review.

OFCCP has also established a complaint procedure under which any employee of or job applicant with a contractor can accuse the contractor of discrimination by writing to OFCCP. This is the second way of turning up evidence that a contractor is violating the terms of its EEO contract clause.

How should women file complaints of discrimination with the OFCCP?

Send a letter to the Director of OFCCP, Department of Labor, 200 Constitution Avenue, N.W., Washington, D.C. 20010, or to any OFCCP regional or area office, setting forth: (1) your name, address, and phone number; (2) the name and address of the contractor; (3) a description of the discrimination (using the Title VII standards set forth in the first half of this chapter); and (4) any other pertinent information. Organizations may file on behalf of the person who is discriminated against. The regulations also require that the complaint be filed within 180 days of the discrimination unless the time limit is extended for a good reason. (Don't forget to use the concept of a continuing policy of discrimination.)

What will OFCCP do with such a complaint?

Individual complaints will be transferred to the EEOC where they will be processed under Title VII. Class and systemic complaints will be investigated by OFCCP. Women should thus file only the class and systemic complaints with OFCCP, and should make clear in the complaint that it concerns class-wide discrimination.

What penalties can OFCCP impose when it finds that a contractor discriminates against women or has not carried out its affirmative action plan?

OFCCP may hold up funds on the contract until it gets compliance (including back pay for the class of affected women), cancel a contract or part of the contract, or order the contractor debarred from future contracts with the government. All of these penalties could have an enormous impact on companies that depend on government contracts for most of their business, for if they lose government work they will often go out of business.

An alternative penalty is to refer the company's case to the Justice Department. The Justice Department can sue the company to enforce the provisions of the contract in which the contractor agreed to provide equal employment opportunity.

Will OFCCP usually impose any of these penalties?

Emphatically not. OFCCP has often been criticized severely for its failure to use the very powerful sanctions it has available. To some extent, the inaction was probably due to gross understaffing, but it has clearly been a political decision as well. Whatever the reason, OFCCP rarely imposes any of the penalties that the executive order requires. As of 1982, fewer than 30 contractors had ever been debarred.

Given the failure of OFCCP to penalize significantly contractors who discriminate, should women bother to file complaints under the executive order?

It depends on what the women hope to accomplish. If their purpose is to force the company to stop discriminating, this is not the best way to do it because there is no way they can force OFCCP to take action against a company. On the other hand, the executive order complaint is an excellent way to put some extra pressure on the company, especially when this method is used in conjunction with other laws. The courts do not have the political freedom to refuse to act on a Title VII or Equal Pay Act complaint the way OFCCP refuses to act on an executive order complaint. Courts may try to duck the issue, they may find the facts against you, but they cannot refuse to act at all; and you can always appeal to higher courts if you don't like the result. Morever, some courts have reached excellent decisions under Title VII and the Equal Pay Act, which have forced companies to take effective action to end discrimination. Given these factors, women should concentrate their main enforcement efforts on Title VII and use executive order complaints and negotiations as a backstop to the main action.

Some women have failed to understand this point and have used the executive order as their main weapon. That way was once useful in the area of university discrimination against teachers, who were not protected by Title VII until the March 1972 amendments and therefore had no other way to protest sex discrimination. But executive order complaints should not be the prime route for women protected by Title VII, which now means most women workers. Any woman covered by Title VII should use a lawsuit under that statute as her main enforcement method. It can't hurt to file complaints with OFCCP in addition to such a lawsuit, because that will maximize the pressure on the company. Even if OFCCP does nothing in the short run, action may be taken during a compliance review if OFCCP finds that women have lodged a number of complaints against a company.[57]

May women bring a lawsuit under the executive order against a federal contractor if OFCCP refuses to take action?

No. Several persons have tried this, and to date the courts have always said that there is no right to sue under the executive order.

What can women read to understand the executive order better?

Read Executive Order 11246 (as amended by E.O. 11375) and the OFCCP regulations. The first is found at 3 C.F.R.

1966–1970 Comp., p. 685; the second at 41 C.F.R. Parts 60–1, 60–2, 60–3, and 60–20. Both are also found in the CCH and BNA books. Part 60–1 of the OFCCP regulations deals with compliance reviews and complaint procedures. Part 60–2 discusses the affirmative action program and is the part generally referred to as Revised Order No. 4.

A book, *Federal Civil Rights Enforcement Effort—1977, To Eliminate Employment Discrimination—A Sequel,* is available from the U.S. Commission on Civil Rights, Publications Warehouse, 621 N. Payne St., Alexandria, Va. 22314. There is no charge for single-copy orders. The book is now somewhat out of date as it was written before President Carter's Civil Rights Reorganization Plan which transferred enforcement of the Equal Pay Act and the Age Discrimination in Employment Act to EEOC. However, the report provides good histories of the various laws, explanations of how they work, and criticisms of the laws in operation.

The Subcommittee on Employment Opportunities of the House Education and Labor Committee has published its October 1978 and July 1979 hearings on the enforcement of equal employment opportunity laws. The publication contains the testimony of agency heads and public interest groups before the subcommittee. A copy can be obtained by writing to the Subcommittee on Employment Opportunities, Committee on Education and Labor, House of Representatives, Washington, D.C. 20515.

What steps can women take besides filing complaints to protect their rights under the executive order?

One possibility is to get involved in helping the company develop its affirmative action plan. Women workers who hesitate to start a lawsuit might still make a significant impact on company policy by insisting on a voice in these plans. Women at all levels in the company should be involved—not just the professionals. Many women caught in dead-end, low-paying jobs, like that of telephone operator, clerk, salesperson, or assembly line worker, will have strong ideas about how to improve their job situation.

Another step is to ask to see the company plan in order to monitor the company's compliance with it. In general, OFCCP encourages companies to reveal these plans although the regulations do not explicitly require this. The company could be pressured about its good faith if it is unwilling to let women employees see what it promised the government it would do. OFCCP has published a *Compliance Manual*, and women should seek copies of it. Comparing the program to the requirements of the manual is another way to monitor the company's progress.

Finally, women's groups can and should start pressuring OFCCP genuinely to enforce the executive order. Pressure from women has already forced OFCCP to amend its regulations to require affirmative action plans for women workers and pushed OFCCP to conduct reviews of colleges and universities. (See note 57.) Federal agencies are vulnerable to pressure, and much more needs to be applied to this one.

D. State Antidiscrimination Laws

What are state fair employment practice laws?

Most states have passed one or more laws forbidding employment discrimination, often using language or concepts parallel or identical to the federal laws discussed in this chapter. States have their own equal pay acts, fair employment practice acts modeled on Title VII, public works laws modeled on Executive Order 11246, and public employees laws modeled on Executive Order 11478. The federal and state laws cover much the same practices, although state laws are often interpreted more conservatively. Chart A in the Appendix sets forth the type of laws each state has and several details about these laws.

E. Age Discrimination Laws

What laws forbid discrimination on the basis of age?

A federal law, the Age Discrimination in Employment Act of 1967, forbids discrimination against workers aged 40 to 70. Most federal workers are protected by the act without any upper age limit. The act is found at 29 U.S.C. §621 et seq.; the regulations, at 29 C.F.R. Part 860. Several states have passed age discrimination laws, some with different age limits; these laws are listed in Chart A in the Appendix. Both the federal and the state laws provide another avenue of redress for older women, who often face virulent discrimination, especially if they are entering the labor market for the first time. Women should be aware of the potential of these laws although this book will not discuss them in detail.

Which federal agency enforces the Age Discrimination Act?

It is enforced by the EEOC under a transfer of authority from the Wage and Hour Division of the Department of Labor on July 1, 1979. Both the EEOC and Wage and Hour Division offices will accept complaints. For more information contact the EEOC.

F. General Considerations

Why is it important to understand the differences among all these laws?

Different laws prohibit different practices and help different workers. For instance, Title VII forbids segregating jobs by sex; the Equal Pay Act does not. On the other hand, Title VII does not protect workers in companies with fewer than 15 employees, but many state fair employment laws do.

If a woman turns to the wrong law, she will not succeed in changing her situation, even though another law may offer her protection; thus it is crucial that women know the range of laws available and the details of their application. Sometimes, too, there is overlap among the various laws. When more than one prohibits the same practice, women can maximize the pressure on their employer or union by resorting to *all* the applicable laws to stop the discrimination.

What are the chief differences between each of these laws?

First, each differs drastically in the number of discriminatory practices covered. Title VII is the broadest law of all, covering almost all forms of discrimination; the Equal Pay Act goes to the opposite extreme, prohibiting only a very narrowly defined kind of wage discrimination; Executive Order 11246 (as amended by E.O. 11375) lies somewhere in between, primarily because the agency that enforces it is oriented more toward setting up affirmative action plans than toward compensating particular women for past discrimination. The number of practices prohibited by state laws generally parallel these three federal laws, but often with significant differences. For example, many state fair employment practice laws forbid newspapers to carry segregated help wanted advertising columns while Title VII reaches only the advertiser.

A second difference is found in the kinds of entities covered by each law. Title VII covers employers, unions, and employment agencies; the Equal Pay Act is limited to employers and unions; Executive Order 11246 reaches only employers; and there are wide variations among the state laws. Within each covered group, there are other differences, with Title VII reaching employers of 15 or more, the Equal Pay Act directed at producers of goods for interstate commerce, and the executive order limited to contractors with the federal government. Many state fair employment practice laws reach employers with fewer than 15 employees.

Other important differences concern the nature and extent of the relief available under each law; whether there will be a practical necessity for getting a lawyer; how vigorously an agency will enforce your rights; and the number of procedural obstacles, such as strict time limits, to bringing successful lawsuits.

As emphasized throughout this chapter, women should try to use Title VII whenever possible. It reaches the most discrimination and holds out the best hope of getting an effective remedy. But if getting a lawyer is a problem or you want to preserve total anonymity, consider using the Equal Pay Act, even though it is much narrower than Title VII. The executive order may provide an effective organizing and negotiating tool in some instances, although it provides little or no guarantee of any effective relief. State laws can be useful where a small company is not covered by any of the federal laws, to get faster action than might be available in a federal forum, or to get back pay for a longer period of time; generally, however, state agencies are too conservative to offer effective relief.

The foregoing is not a comprehensive list of the relevant factors to consider, and women will have to gain experience with all the laws in order to understand how best to use them. In summation, however, the best advice is to start with

Title VII, supplement it with action under as many other laws as possible, and turn to other laws where Title VII is not available or is tactically disadvantageous.

What concrete proof must someone have of discrimination before she can file a charge or complaint?

Absolutely none. Women often believe that they must have some conclusive evidence that their employer or union discriminates before they can walk into a federal or state agency and ask for help. They hope to discover the incriminating memorandum from the company president stating that he will never, in a thousand years, hire a woman salesman. In fact, it is the agency's job to do the investigation that uncovers evidence of discrimination, not the woman's job.

Women who have nothing stronger than their own suspicions can walk into the right agency and fill out a complaint. It might read, for instance, that Company X refuses to promote women into management positions because of their sex. That will be enough to require the agency to look into the matter.

There is a significant practical caveat to the statutory requirement that an agency investigate such a complaint. Most agencies are overworked and understaffed. The more specific information women can point to, the better the job the agency will do for the women. Therefore, they should analyze the work situation in light of all the concepts in this chapter, as well as their own gut feelings of fairness, in order to identify specific discriminatory practices and point them out to the agency in charge. For instance: Are all the secretaries women and all the managers men? What are the comparative pay scales and fringe benefits of "male" and "female" jobs? Analyze the collective-bargaining agreement—are sex distinctions built into it? Some companies and unions have so clearly conceived of particular jobs as either male or female that the contract will describe some jobs using female pronouns and other jobs using male pronouns. What does the contract say about fringe benefits? Are pregnancy leaves excluded from the sick-pay and medical insurance provisions? Are women allowed to retire earlier than men or are they forced to retire earlier? And so on. In considering these questions, women should remember that they know their own job situation better than anyone else, and their analysis of its discriminatory nature is therefore potentially better than that of anyone else, no matter how expert that other person may be.

How do lawyers and agencies prove that someone has been discriminated against on the basis of sex?

There are many different ways. One of the most important is the use of statistics. Courts have said that if statistics show a lopsided distribution of particular population groups into certain kinds of jobs, they will presume that the company or union has discriminated. Unless the company can come back with some evidence showing that this effect is absolutely necessary to the conduct of its business, the people complaining of discrimination win their lawsuit. The ramifications of this point are enormous since the statistics in almost every company show discrimination. For instance, many companies hire a lot of women, but a closer look at the statistics will reveal that women hold only 0 to 1 percent of the managerial or highly paid blue-collar jobs and 95 percent of the low-paid secretarial jobs. Those statistics prove a "prima facie" case of discrimination. Another example is a company that hires very few women overall compared to other companies; here the statistics show discrimination in the hiring process rather than in the assignment of particular jobs. Lawyers generally use statistics to show not only a disproportionate distribution of men and women, but also to find out at what point in the employment process the maldistribution takes place.

Another way to prove discrimination is through company documents, which will often set forth blatantly discriminatory practices. The pension plan booklet, when read carefully, may reveal that men and women must or may retire at different ages, solely because of their sex. The health plan will show that pregnancy is not covered or is minimally covered, although full coverage is provided for all other medical conditions. The collective bargaining agreement may use female pronouns for certain jobs, male pronouns for others— clearly indicating that the company reserves some jobs for men, others for women. The company may place help-wanted ads in segregated newspaper columns or use sex-typed language in the ad copy. All these documents can be introduced at trial to prove discrimination.

Still another way to prove discrimination is through the

testimony of various workers and officials. Co-workers may be willing to testify that the manager told them he would never hire a woman for a particular job because it's not suitable for women, or that they knew of the existence of a discriminatory job practice, or that the company's claim that women do different work from men is untrue.

What can women workers do to help their lawyer prove discrimination or to convince the EEOC or other agencies that they have been discriminated against?

The workers are the people who best know their job situation. They also have friends in the company or union who have access to important documents proving discrimination. If women will study the concepts of what constitutes job discrimination set forth in this chapter, and analyze their job situation in the light of those concepts, they can help their lawyers enormously. For, unfortunately, many lawyers and agencies do not understand all these concepts, nor do they have the time and energy to go after the necessary evidence, nor do they always care about sex discrimination. The more kinds of discrimination women workers analyze, therefore, and the more statistics, documents, and testimony or affidavits of friends and sympathizers they produce, the more likely they are to win their case. In other words, trying to end discrimination must be a joint venture between the women on the one hand and the governmental agency personnel and lawyers on the other hand.

If you win a lawsuit, what can the judge order the company to do?

First, he can order the company to pay you any wages you lost because of the discrimination. The amount of "back wages" available depends on the statute in question. (See the questions on pages 60–61 and 73 for a discussion of how the wages are computed under Title VII and the Equal Pay Act.) The judge can also award you money to cover the costs of bringing the lawsuit, the lawyer's fees, and interest for the company's use of your back wages.

Second, under Title VII the judge can order a company to change its employment practices in the future. This applies to any discrimination and is a way of forcing the company to recruit and hire more women, to transfer them to better jobs, to train them for different positions, to change the health plan, to increase their wages, and so on. (Under the Equal Pay Act, only the wages can be increased.) It is this power to change employment practices that makes Title VII such a powerful weapon.

Can women get back wages and changes in company practices through negotiations with the company?

Yes. Under both Title VII and many of the state fair employment practice laws, the company will be asked by the appropriate agency to negotiate a settlement of the case. Women should be wary of accepting settlements, though, that do not effectively provide the relief they want. This is particularly so of settlements negotiated by state agencies, which are often more responsive to business interests than to women workers, and the settlements they propose are at times so vague as to be meaningless. Since a court may later refuse to award you the relief you are entitled to because you signed such a settlement, it is important not to enter into one lightly. Thus, if you believe the proposed settlement is inadequate, reject it and keep on pursuing your legal remedies— including suing the company, if necessary.

What role can women's paralegal groups play in the field of employment discrimination law?

First, they might establish a counseling service to help women who call in with complaints of job discrimination. After studying employment discrimination law and procedures, the paralegal groups can direct these women to the proper agency or agencies and make sure that they comply with all the necessary procedural steps. More important, these groups can help women analyze the discrimination at their company, question them to find forms of discrimination that the women may have overlooked, and make sure they fill out the charge or complaint forms with all the discriminatory practices that can be identified. The woman worker who calls or walks in the door may have seized on a single form of discrimination because it is particularly onerous at that point in time; the chances are she faces a myriad of other discriminatory practices in her job, all of which should be attacked at once in order to maximize resources.

Counseling can continue even after the charge is filed with

the appropriate agency. Paralegal advisors can help women locate evidence of discrimination by telling them what to look for and can refer these women to lawyers. They can also try to convince other women workers to join in the lawsuit by alleviating fears and explaining what the lawsuit is about and the advantages of joining in.

Besides individual counseling, paralegal groups can also take on a very important educational function. Most women simply do not understand the full extent of their rights. Speeches should be made, radio and television programs developed, printed materials distributed—all with the aim of helping women understand their rights and how to assert them.

A third paralegal project would be to start organizing women workers. Women need to push their labor unions to help them with sex discrimination problems, and new unions should be formed where the workers are unorganized. A labor union lawyer, with the force of the union behind her, can accomplish broad institutional changes—often without having to bring a lawsuit. For instance, the International Union of Electrical Workers has taken action on a broad front to eliminate sex discrimination in IUE companies. The program has included educating the workers to understand sex discrimination, asking locals to fill out questionnaires to find out what the discriminatory practices are, attempts to inspire local union action, negotiating with the companies for institution-wide changes when new developments in the law occur, and bringing lawsuits on behalf of women workers when a company remains recalcitrant. Much more action of this kind is essential if women want to make real changes in the employment world.

The workers themselves can also do much by organizing other women in the process of bringing employment discrimination lawsuits. One excellent example of this technique involved Suann Hecht, who worked for CARE and wanted to challenge CARE's discriminatory practices. When she started her campaign, she was alone, and her major complaint was that CARE refused to send women overseas and paid women less than men. Instead of proceeding solely on her own behalf, she studied the CARE operation and thought of all the ways CARE discriminated against its women workers, which she listed when she filed her charges with EEOC. As

EEOC proceeded with the case, Ms. Hecht gradually enlisted the support of other women in CARE; and when she started her lawsuit, other women were ready to join her. She finally even found male employees who were willing to testify about the discriminatory effect of CARE policies. This kind of concerted effort can force an employer to make some major changes in its policies; just as important, it can heighten the consciousness of many women workers who are too frightened initially even to discuss the subject of discrimination. This is the kind of action women must take to achieve real change.

NOTES

1. S. Rep. No. 91–1137, 91st Cong., 2d Sess. 15 (1970).

2. U.S. Department of Labor. Bureau of Labor Statistics, *Employment and Earnings* 153–154 (January 1978).

3. 401 U.S. 424 (1971). See also *Dothard v. Rawlinson*, 433 U.S. 321 (1977). In that case, height and weight standards for correctional counselors in the Alabama state penitentiary system, which appeared on the surface to be neutral job requirements because they applied to both men and women, were found to exclude more women than men from the job; thus they were held to be sexually discriminatory and illegal under Title VII.

4. See Chapter III for general information on Title IX. In 1982, the Supreme Court ruled that Title IX prohibits sex-based discrimination not only against students but also against employees in federally funded education programs. *North Haven Board of Education v. Bell*, 102 S. Ct. 1912 (1982).

5. 433 U.S. 321 (1977).

6. 444 F.2d 1219 (9th Cir. 1971).

7. *County of Washington v. Gunther*, 452 U.S. 161 (1981). For other cases on the issue, see *IUE v. Westinghouse Electric Corp.*, 23 FEP Cases 588 (3rd Cir. 1980); *Christensen v. State of Iowa*, 563 F.2d 353 (8th Cir. 1977); *Lemons v. City and County of Denver*, 620 F.2d 228 (10th Cir. 1980).

8. 25 FEP Cases 602 (W.D. Pa. 1981).

9. *Bowe v. Colgate-Palmolive Co.*, 416 F.2d 711 (7th Cir. 1969).

10. 29 C.F.R. §1604.2.

11. 444 F.2d 1219 (9th Cir. 1971).

12. 29 C.F.R. §1604.2 (b)(3)–(5).

13. *Bastardo v. Warren*, 332 F. Supp. 501 (W.D. Wis. 1970).

14. *Burns v. Rohr Corporation*, 346 F.Supp. 994 (S.D. Cal. 1972).

15. *Potlatch Forests, Inc. v. Hays*, 465 F.2d 1081 (8th Cir. 1972), *cert. denied*, 409 U.S. 1108 (1973). But see *State v. Fairfield Communities Land Co.*, 538 S.W.2d 698 (Ark. 1976), *cert. denied*, 429 U.S. 1004 (1976).

16. *Homemakers, Inc. v. Division of Industrial Welfare*, 509 F.2d 20 (9th Cir. 1974), cert. denied, 423 U.S. 1063 (1976).

17. Another possibility is to provide for voluntary overtime on the basis of seniority. That is, the most senior employees—male and female— may decline overtime, while the most junior employees must accept it (if there are not enough volunteers).

18. *Chrapliwy v. Uniroyal, Inc.*, 15 FEP Cases 795 (D. Ind. 1977).

19. *Danner v. Phillips Petroleum Company*, 447 F.2d 159 (5th Cir. 1971). Of course, the *Danner* decision may not be extended to other union benefits. The only solution then is to make increased efforts to unionize women workers.

20. 433 U.S. 321 (1977).

21. *Brush v. San Francisco Newspaper Printing Co.*, 315 F.Supp. 577 (N.D. Cal. 1970); *Greenfield v. Field Enterprises, Inc.*, 4 FEP Cases 548 (N.D. Ill. 1972); *Morrow v. Mississippi Publishers Corp.*, 5 FEP Cases 287 (S.D. Miss. 1972).

22. *Pittsburgh Press Co. v. Pittsburgh Commission on Human Relations*, 413 U.S. 376 (1973). Such laws have an added clause covering anyone who "aids or abets" someone else in discriminating; at the very least, the newspaper aids and abets discriminatory companies when it gives them the sex-segregated column which enables them to discriminate. States with such laws include Alaska, Arizona, California, Colorado, Connecticut, Hawaii, Illinois, Indiana, Iowa, Kansas, Kentucky, Maine, Massachusetts, Michigan, Minnesota, Missouri, New Hampshire, New Jersey, New Mexico, New York, Ohio, Oklahoma, Oregon, Pennsylvania, Rhode Island, South Dakota, Utah, and West Virginia. See Chart A in the Appendix, FEP column, for the legal citations.

23. Uniform Guidelines on Employee Selection Procedures (1978), 43 Fed. Reg. 38290 (August 25, 1978); 29 C.F.R. Part 1607.

24. 401 U.S. 424 (1971).

25. *Berkman v. City of New York*, 536 F.Supp. 177 (E.D.N.Y. 1982); see also *Sontag v. Bronstein*, 33 N.Y.2d 197, 351 N.Y.S.2d 389, 306 N.E.2d 405 (N.Y. Ct.App. 1973).

26. See Bem and Bem, "Case Study of a Nonconscious Ideology: Training the Woman to Know Her Place," in Bem, *Beliefs, Attitudes and Human Affairs* (1970). The Bems cite a study by Goldberg, "Are Women Prejudiced Against Women?" *Transaction* (April 1968).

27. *Ibid*. The Bems cite Brown, *Social Psychology* 162 (1965).

28. 400 U.S. 542 (1971).

29. *Arizona Governing Committee v. Norris*,——U.S.——, 77 L.Ed. 2d 1236 (July 6, 1983); *Los Angeles Dept. of Water & Power v. Man-*

hart, 435 U.S. 702 (1978); *Bartmess v. Drewry's U.S.A. Inc.*, 444 F.2d 1186 (7th Cir. 1971); and *Rosen v. Public Services Electric and Gas Company*, 409 F.2d 775 (3rd Cir. 1969), followed by 5 FEP Cases 709 (3rd Cir. 1973).

30. 29 C.F.R. §1604.9 (f).

31. *Arizona Governing Committee v. Norris,*——U.S.——, 77 L.Ed. 2d 1236 (July 6,1983). See also the cases cited therein at 1246–1247, n.9.

32. P.L. 95–555, referred to as the Pregnancy Discrimination Act; its principal provision is found in Section 701 (k) of Title VII, 42 U.S.C. §2000e-(k).

33. *General Electric Co. v. Gilbert*, 429 U.S. 125 (1976).

34. They are published as an Appendix to 29 C.F.R. Part 1604. In addition, women should read the more general guidelines on pregnancy, published at 29 C.F.R. §1604.10.

35. 29 C.F.R. §1604.10(b).

35A. *Newport News Shipbuilding and Dry Dock Co. v. EEOC,*——U.S. ——, 77 L.Ed.2d 89 (June 20, 1983).

36. *Los Angeles Dept. of Water & Power v. Manhart*, 435 U.S. 702 (1978); 29 C.F.R. §1604.9(e).

37. Safran, "What Men Do to Women on the Job: A Shocking Look at Sexual Harassment," 148 *Redbook* 149 (1976).

38. *Barnes v. Costle*, 561 F.2d 983 (D.C. Cir. 1977); *Tomkins v. Public Service Electric and Gas. Co.*, 568 F.2d 1044 (3d Cir. 1977); *Garber v. Saxon Business Products, Inc.*, 552 F.2d 1032 (4th Cir. 1977). In *Miller v. Bank of America*, 20 FEP Cases 462 n.1 (9th Cir. 1979), the Ninth Circuit assumed, but did not decide, the issue.

39. 561 F.2d 983 (D.C. Cir. 1977).

40. Brief *Amici Curiae* of the National Organization for Women and Working Women United Institute in *Continental Can Co. v. Minnesota* (Minn. S.Ct. No. 4988) at 15–16.

41. 29 C.F.R. §1604.11. The Reagan administration has targeted these regulations for review, but as this book goes to press no proposed change has been published.

42. *Kyriazi v. Western Electric Co.*, 461 F.Supp. 894 (D. N.J. 1978).

43. *Affirmative Action Guidelines*, 44 Fed. Reg. 4422 (January 19, 1979) (to be codified in 29 C.F.R. Part 1608).

44. *Steelworkers v. Weber*, 443 U.S. 193 (1979).

45. Women in the Minnesota Public Interest Research Group conducted an interesting study of employment agency discrimination. MPIRG sent male and female applicants with identical qualifications to several agencies. Not too surprisingly, the men were treated much better than the women. Such a study could be used by paralegal groups to get change through publicity; it would also provide good evidence for use in lawsuits against agencies. For a copy of the "MPIRG Report: Sexual Discrimination in Employment Agencies"

(October 1972), write to: MPIRG, 1926 Nicollet Ave., Minneapolis, Minn. 55403; (612) 376–7554.

46. *Ruhe v. Philadelphia Inquirer*, 14 FEP Cases 1304 (E.D. Pa. 1975).

47. *Advocates for Women v. Marshall*, No. 76-0862 (D. D.C. Dec. 5, 1978).

48. For the limits on this concept, see *United Airlines, Inc. v. Evans*, 431 U.S. 553 (1977).

49. Note for lawyers. The Fifth Circuit has decided that an employee could maintain such an action prior to issuance of the "notice of right to sue." *Drew v. Liberty Mutual Insurance Company*, 5 FEP Cases 1077 (5th Cir. 1973). If the court did not allow such an action, it might be possible to file suit under the Declaratory Judgment statute. Although the company would not be bound to follow such a judgment, most companies would probably hesitate to violate it.

50. In August 1979 EEOC initiated a pilot program to overhaul the federal employee complaint process. Under this pilot program, the EEOC, not the agency, investigates the complaint using the fact-finding conference procedure. The goal of the program is to speed up the complaint resolution process (which currently averages 441 days), and to decrease the large backlog of complaints. While the pilot program should eventually result in the adoption of new procedures for handling federal employee discrimination complaints, nothing has been finalized as this book goes to press.

51. *Shultz v. Wheaton Glass Company*, 421 F.2d 259 (3d Cir.), *cert. denied*, 398 U.S. 905 (1970).

52. *Hodgson v. Sagner, Inc.*, 462 F.2d 180 (4th Cir. 1972).

53. The EEOC and the Department of Labor have signed an agreement that Wage and Hour Division offices of the Department of Labor will continue to take complaints under the Equal Pay Act. After taking the complaint the Wage and Hour Division office will transfer the complaint to the EEOC. This arrangement was made because there are many more Wage and Hour offices than EEOC offices around the country and because workers are familiar with filing Equal Pay Act complaints at Wage and Hour offices. Although the arrangement is to continue indefinitely, you should play it safe and file directly with the EEOC whenever possible because most Wage and Hour employees who used to handle equal pay complaints have been transferred and soon very few Wage and Hour employees will be familiar with the Equal Pay Act.

54. *Wells v. Pioneer Wear, Inc.*, 19 EPD ¶9244 (10th Cir. 1979).

55. This problem can be remedied by bringing the lawsuit under both Title VII and the Equal Pay Act because the court can order the company to raise salaries under Title VII.

56. *Steelworkers v. Weber*, 443 U.S. 193 (1979).

57. *WEAL v. Califano*, No. 74-1720 (D. D.C. Dec. 29, 1977), was an action brought by women's groups to require OFCCP and HEW to enforce Executive Order 11246 and Title IX, the law prohibiting sex discrimination in federally funded education. (See Chapter III

for more detail on Title IX.) The court ordered OFCCP and HEW (now the Department of Education) to process complaints and conduct an appropriate number of compliance reviews within specified time frames. OFCCP and the Education Department must make periodic reports to the court to ensure that they are complying with the order.

III

Education

Less than 140 years ago, Oberlin College opened its doors and made history by admitting both blacks and women to a college education for the first time in the United States. At first, women were considered too stupid to take the same course work as men—their minds couldn't assimilate "men's" fare, it was thought. The college preserved a clear aura of male dominance in other areas as well. Women were required to wash the male students' clothes, care for their rooms, and serve them at table. Nor were women permitted to talk in public. Lucy Stone, the famous feminist and an early Oberlin graduate, refused to write a commencement essay because only a male student would have been permitted to read it to the audience.[1]

Given this "beginning," it is not too surprising that academia is still afflicted with deep-seated and largely unrecognized sexism. Although male dominance continues today, women have begun to challenge it with some new, but limited, legal weapons. Feminists are using these laws imaginatively, but much more remains to be done.

Are there any clearly defined national rights against discrimination in education?

Yes and no. In the 1970's Congress finally discovered the subject of sex discrimination in this nation's schools and colleges and passed a variety of new laws designed to end sex discrimination in education. However, each of these laws suffers from some defect. The most far-reaching of them—Title IX of the Education Amendments of 1972 Act (usually referred to as Title IX)[2]—forbids sex discrimination in public and private schools receiving federal money, and thus provides important protection to women in academia. But the law presents some problems, too; as initially passed, it specifically allowed several forms of discrimination, and Congress has added to this list over the years. Then the agency enforcing the law got into the act and decided to allow even more ways to discriminate. Moreover, until 1979 it was not even clear whether women could bring lawsuits against discriminatory schools (they can), so the law did not encourage the major litigation which would have established a national definition of women's rights in the academic world, as lawsuits under the comparable employment discrimination laws have done. This major litigation should be a task for the 1980's, however.

Other laws passed by Congress are much narrower in scope than Title IX or suffer from other defects. One law—an amendment to the Public Health Service Act[3]—is addressed only to the problem of sex discrimination against students in the health professions. Another law—Title II of the 1976 Amendments to the Vocational Education Act of 1963[4]—dealt with the important problem of sex discrimination in vocational schools, but failed to provide a way to sue discriminatory schools. Congress also amended Title IV of the 1964 Civil Rights Act[5] to allow the U.S. Attorney General to sue schools and colleges for sex discriminatory policies, but the Attorney General has rarely done so. In yet another law, the Equal Educational Opportunities Act of 1974,[6] Congress acted ambiguously. In a grand preface, it declared that "all children enrolled in public schools are entitled to equal educational opportunity without regard to race, color, sex, or national origin." But the small print then inexplicably allowed various forms of sex discrimination (e.g., while the law prohibits deliberate segregation of students by *race* and employment discrimination against teachers and staff on the basis of *race*, it fails to mention deliberate segregation by *sex* or employment discrimination based on *sex*).* Despite the wide variety of new laws passed in the 1970's, then, their gaps in coverage and the relative lack of litigation under them has led to an inadequate definition of what constitutes illegal

---

*Of course, there is a wide variety of other laws prohibiting sex discrimination in employment, including academic employment. See Chapter II.

sex discrimination in academia, or worse, explicit permission to practice some forms of sex discrimination.

The picture has been slightly different in the area of constitutional doctrine. As Chapter I indicated, the Equal Protection Clause of the 14th Amendment can be used to attack discrimination carried out by state or local governments. Consequently, women could and did sue public elementary, junior high, or senior high schools, and state colleges and universities, for practicing sex discrimination in violation of the 14th Amendment. The courts' reactions to these lawsuits, however, have been mixed.

Although a wide variety of ways to attack sex discrimination problems in the academic setting now exists, women do not yet have a strong national definition of their rights. The effort for the 1980's must be to undertake comprehensive litigation efforts designed to attack in depth the major problems remaining in academia. Some important examples are the strong sex segregation in many vocational, professional, and graduate education programs, which in turn leads to and reinforces the existing sex segregation in the employment world; the virtual absence of women from top administrative and faculty positions; and the exclusion of women from many sports, or the severe underfunding and lack of support for other sports of interest to women. Another goal of the 1980's could be to seek legislation to eliminate the gaps in coverage of the laws now on the books.

A word remains to be said about the organization of the rest of this chapter. Section A discusses the rights of women to equal educational opportunity under the Equal Protection Clause and the various federal statutes, with a focus on Title IX. In reading this section, the reader should bear in mind that although the issue discussed may refer to a particular statute or to the Equal Protection Clause, it may be possible in future lawsuits to assert the same right under other statutes as well. Moreover, even a decision upholding some form of discrimination does not mean that a case with different facts might not have a different result. Thus the function of Section A should be primarily to alert readers to different kinds of discrimination that are practiced in academia. Section B describes procedures for asserting rights under the different laws, as well as the remedies (e.g., school admission, job promotion, attorneys' fees) which are available.

A. Rights to Equal Educational Opportunity under the Equal Protection Clause and Various Federal Statutes

Both public and private schools play a vital role in educating women in this country. Despite many differences between them in ideology, educational philosophy, and affiliation, public and private schools share one trait: both frequently discriminate against women. However, all laws do not apply equally to all schools, and the following distinctions must be kept in mind when considering whether a particular practice at a particular school is illegal under a particular law. The Equal Protection Clause applies to public, but not private, schools because of the requirement of "state action"; similarly, Title IV of the 1964 Civil Rights Act, as well as the Equal Educational Opportunities Act of 1974, apply only to public schools. On the other hand, Title IX applies to most educational institutions which receive federal money and, therefore, reaches the discriminatory practices of some private schools and colleges as well as public ones. The laws dealing with discrimination in schools for health professionals and in vocational education likewise apply only to institutions which receive federal money. Thus, those private institutions which receive no federal money can discriminate with impunity.

Do women have a right to attend all-male public schools?
Under the Equal Protection Clause, the answer has been: sometimes yes, sometimes no. In an important 1982 case, the Supreme Court ruled that the Mississippi University for Women could not exclude men from its School of Nursing.[7] Justice O'Connor, the first woman to sit on the Supreme Court, wrote the Court's opinion and decisively rejected the state's "educational affirmative action" rationale for its ban on men. She noted that most nurses are women, so that the all-female policy actually reinforced traditional stereotypes of nursing as a woman's field. She also pointed out that there is evidence that the exclusion of men from nursing helps to depress nurses' wages—in other words, the all-female policy may actually work to penalize women.

There have been other favorable cases as well. Women—and the ACLU—scored an important victory when they succeeded in desegregating the previously all-male University of Virginia at Charlottesville, the most "prestigious" school of the state university system.[8] High-school students knocked down the all-male barrier at highly rated Stuyvesant High School in New York City. Concerned parents forced the equally prestigious Boston Latin and Girls Latin public schools to use the same admissions standards for boys and girls, thus allowing some girls into the over 300-year-old, formerly all-male Boston Latin.[9] And a San Francisco girl won the right to attend Lowell, a top academic high school which imposed a higher admissions standard for girls than for boys in order to equalize the number of male and female students. The school's justification for this discrimination—that a balance of the sexes was essential for a good high-school education—was found insufficient.[10]

But other attempts have not been so successful. A Philadelphia girl failed to gain admission to the all-male Central High, one of the city's two academic high schools and the one with the best reputation and the most prestigious graduates. The other academic school, the all-female Girls High, was good, but, as its name indicated, not quite on a par with "Central." The appellate court ruled in favor of "separate but equal," emphasized that Central and Girls High were comparable in quality, academic standing, and prestige—and ignored the superior science facilities and reputation of Central. The Supreme Court agreed with this result, but gave no reasons.[11] Where does this leave us? It is hard to say. First, the Mississippi University decision was in one sense quite limited. It only outlawed the ban on men at the Nursing School, and did not explicitly reach the ban on men in the rest of the university. Second, since Mississippi had no all-male school, the Court did not need to decide whether "separate but equal" schools violate the Constitution. Further litigation will be needed on these issues before we know where the Supreme Court stands.

Under the Equal Educational Opportunities Act of 1974, federal courts have struck down plans by southern school districts to use sex segregation in order to avoid complete racial integration.[12] So far this law has been successfully applied only in the context of racial integration, but women may try to use it to gain admission to other sex-segregated schools. However, this did not work in the Philadelphia high-school

case. Another possible statute to use in attacking sex segregation in schools is Title IV of the Civil Rights Act of 1964.

Title IX also prohibits one-sex schools, but only graduate,
professional, and vocational schools that receive federal funding are affected. Other single-sex schools are theoretically
permitted to continue to exclude the other sex. However,
this clause did not help the Mississippi University for Women.
Thus, Title IX yields to the Equal Protection Clause when
the two are in conflict.

**Are there any differences between the successful and
unsuccessful suits under the Equal Protection Clause that
suggest strategy and tactics for future attacks on sex-segregated
school systems?**

Yes. There are important lessons to be learned from comparing the successful suits with the failures. The most important single factor in explaining the women's success in
desegregating the University of Virginia was the thorough documentation of the discrepancies in education available to men
and to women in the state. Among the shocking differences
discovered by ACLU lawyers: The men's college offered the
highest average faculty salaries in the state. The state appropriation per student at the men's college was more than
double that at each of the two women's colleges. Men had
access to sophisticated astronomy and science facilities; women
did not. Men could take degrees in astronomy, Latin-American
studies, and nine foreign languages—all unavailable to women.
The men's college offered a far greater variety of courses in
almost every department, especially in government, astronomy, economics, English, history, physics, geology, geogra-
phy, sociology, and anthropology. In short, the lawyers showed
in detail that the state reserved its highest-quality educational
facilities "For Men Only."

The lawyers topped this factual survey by extensive questioning of university officials to see whether they could offer
any cogent reasons for excluding women. Even the judge was
embarrassed by the answers the school officials gave: allowing
women to use dormitories built for men would not be feasible
because women need more diminutive furniture; the shower
heads were set at the wrong height; and so on, *ad ridiculum*.

In contrast, lawyers for the men who unsuccessfully tried
to enter all-female Winthrop College in South Carolina ap-

parently conceded that there was no difference between the quality of education available at Winthrop and that available at other public colleges in the state, which included the all-male Citadel and several integrated schools. Since the men failed to document any disparity, it is impossible to tell from the court's opinion whether Winthrop offered an identical education to that of the male school. However, the law establishing Winthrop had emphasized that the school should offer certain "courses thought to be especially helpful to female students." These included:

> . . . stenography, typewriting, telegraphy, bookkeeping, drawing . . . designing, engraving, sewing, dressmaking, millinery, art, needlework, cooking, housekeeping and such other industrial arts as may be suitable to their sex and conducive to their support and usefulness.

The men's school, the Citadel, is an engineering and military school. Thus, there were clear differences between the two schools, and, at the very least, women in South Carolina were deprived of some forms of education available only at the Citadel. Yet the men never pointed to such facts. Instead, the men sought to show that maintaining single-sex schools was inherently lacking in rational justification and thus violated the Equal Protection Clause. This is analogous to whites saying that "separate but equal" schools for whites and blacks inherently violate the Equal Protection Clause, rather than showing in detail that the schools are not, *in fact*, equal. The time may not be ripe for men—or women—to challenge segregation per se. First, they must build up the cases that will illustrate cogently just how unequal *in fact* are the opportunities for women.

What schools are prohibited from discriminating by Title IX?

Title IX covers any school—from the pre-school level through graduate education—that receives federal funds. But it does not reach religious schools if a particular religion's tenets require the sex discrimination that the school practices. (If the religion's tenet does not require sex discrimination, then the school's practices are reached.) Title IX also exempts military schools, which are defined as schools training individuals for the United States military services or for the merchant marines.[13]

What discriminatory practices does Title IX prohibit?
Discrimination is defined very broadly:

No person in the United States shall, on the basis of sex, be excluded from participation in, be denied the benefits of, or be subject to discrimination under any education program or activity receiving Federal financial assistance.

In 1975, after a three-year delay, the Department of Health, Education, and Welfare (HEW)—the agency which administered Title IX until 1980*—finally published regulations defining which discriminatory practices are forbidden.[14] Some of the regulations are comprehensive. Others are clearly compromises and could themselves be attacked as unconstitutional because they specifically permit some forms of discrimination. The most important regulations will be discussed in the questions in the rest of this chapter.

Does Title IX permit any schools to discriminate in admissions?
Yes. Title IX specifically allows several kinds of educational institutions to discriminate in admission policies. Presumably, this means schools may either exclude women completely, set up quota systems to limit their enrollment, or demand that women meet higher admissions standards than men. The schools that may so discriminate include pre-school, elementary, and secondary schools, whether public or private; private undergraduate colleges (such as Harvard, Yale, or Princeton); and public undergraduate colleges that have always been single-sex institutions.†[15] Title IX in effect licenses many of the schools that practice the most blatant forms of discrimination to continue doing so. In fact, the only institu-

---

*In 1980 the new federal Department of Education took over the responsibility for Title IX from HEW.

†Vocational schools at these levels, however, may *not* discriminate in their admissions policies.

tions prohibited from using discriminatory admissions policies are public and private vocational schools at all levels, already integrated public undergraduate colleges, and public and private graduate and professional schools. Again, insofar as Title IX permits discrimination in admissions, it could be attacked as unconstitutional. Thus, if a woman is denied admission to an all-male school protected by Title IX she should still sue the school under the Equal Protection Clause and other statutes, if possible, and in the process attack the Title IX provision as unconstitutional. In fact, this is what Joe Hogan did in his successful effort to attend the Mississippi University for Women. (See note 7.) The Supreme Court accepted his view that the Equal Protection Clause guaranteed his right to attend the school, despite the Title IX language.

Another major loophole in the law is that each school, college, or department of a university which has a separate administration is considered a different educational institution for admissions purposes.[16]

Thus, even if one school openly discriminates in admissions, the university as a whole would theoretically not be in violation of Title IX; a separate showing of discrimination would have to be established for all the other university schools to establish a university-wide violation.

Of course, once schools admit women, they must treat them in a non-discriminatory manner in all other respects.

Does Title IX permit any school organizations to discriminate?

Yes. Although most school organizations and activities are forbidden to discriminate on the basis of sex, a 1974 amendment to Title IX permitted college sororities and fraternities to limit membership to one sex and allowed such groups as the YMCA, YWCA, Girl Scouts, Boy Scouts, and Camp Fire Girls to exclude members of the opposite sex.[17] Congress amended the law once again in 1976 to exempt certain American Legion activities, such as Boys State, Boys Nation, Girls State, and Girls Nation. The 1976 amendment also permits schools to sponsor mother-daughter and father-son activities with the condition that if such activities are provided for boys, girls must be given the opportunity for "reasonably comparable" activities.[18] Although Title IX allows this and other forms of sex discrimination it does not protect these actions from constitutional attack under the Equal Protection Clause.

Does Title IX permit schools to discriminate in providing housing for students?

Yes and no. Title IX specifically allows the practice of segregating living facilities by sex. Of course this is not a clear-cut issue. Many students prefer segregated dormitories, and a prohibition would have eliminated the possibility of choice in this area. Others, however, want coed dorms and they will not be helped by Title IX, although the law does not limit the school's option to provide integrated living facilities either for all students or for students who wish accommodations of this kind.

However, the Title IX regulations do require schools which provide housing for men to provide housing for women which is comparable in quality and cost.[19] For instance, a university cannot house its male students in two-room private suites while crowding its female students into dormitory doubles. The number of housing units made available to women must be in proportion to the number of women who apply for housing. In addition, schools must take steps to ensure that off-campus housing is available to men and women on the same terms.

Do college women have the right to equal treatment in campus living rules?

Sometimes. The regulations for Title IX[20] explicitly prohibit colleges from applying different housing rules and regulations to men and women, charging them different fees, or offering them different benefits or services, such as free cleaning services for men only. On-campus residency requirements, curfews, and other parietal rules for women only are now illegal.

Cases on this subject brought under the Equal Protection Clause rather than Title IX have had mixed results. Women at one school—Southeastern Louisiana College—succeeded in forcing administrators to let them live off-campus in their own apartments, as men were already allowed to do. College officials claimed that they had to force all women under 21 to live in the dormitories to ensure collecting enough money to pay off the federal debt on the dormitories. The judge did not agree. He reasoned that the college was requiring women to shoulder more of the cost of education than it required of men. Forcing women to pay off the debt was just as arbitrary at it would be for the army to draft only blacks, he declared. Thus the school policy was irrational and in violation of the Equal Protection Clause. "All must pay, or none."[21]

But a Kentucky woman unsuccessfully challenged restrictions on hours for women under 21 at a state college (girls could have the restriction waived with parental consent, but boys did not need parental consent). She lost her case when the appellate judges ruled the state needed to protect women students on the streets at night from attack; a later curfew on weekends was allowed on the theory that many coeds have dates then and should be permitted to stay out later.[22] Today, she would probably win such a case if she brought it under Title IX.

Both cases suggest interesting attitudes about women students which must be attacked. The college regulations often imply that girls are more immature than boys and need to be closely supervised. Alternately, they suggest that girls are more vulnerable to danger and must be "protected" by restrictions on their *own* freedom. Always lurking in the background is the fear young women will indulge in sex and a desire to limit their opportunities to do so. College officials who are willing to make rules on the basis of such paternalistic motives and such stereotyped assumptions about girls may be just as prone to denigrate women in their educational policies. A persistent intention to prevent women from assuming responsibility for their own lives is at stake in these policies—not some issue of unfair financial costs. Lawyers handling such lawsuits, and judges, must begin to confront these attitudes and the degrading impact they have on women.

May schools give out scholarships restricted to men or discriminate in the award of financial aid in other ways?

The Title IX regulations forbid sex discrimination in financial assistance.[23] Schools may not give male and female students different types or amounts of financial aid nor may they use different eligibility requirements for males and females. For instance, a school may not give scholarships to all men with a 3.0 average but only to women who have a 3.5 average, nor may it award larger scholarships to men than to women with the same financial need.

However, once again the regulations do not forbid certain forms of discrimination. A school may administer sex-restricted scholarships and fellowships established by will or trust or by foreign governments (e.g., the Rhodes Scholarships which were once restricted to men), with the proviso that the overall effect must not be to discriminate against women—whatever that means. Women who are otherwise eligible for financial aid must not be denied aid because of a shortage of unrestricted funds. Thus, the school cannot make scholarships available to men with less need or lower academic qualifications simply because there are more endowed scholarships available for men.

If a woman who is married to a non-resident attends a state university in her home state, can she be forced to pay non-resident tuition rates because of her husband's out-of-state residence?

Not if she can show she is in fact a resident of that state.

State universities often charge non-residents higher tuition rates than residents pay. In determining residency, some universities apply the common law rule that a married woman's residence follows that of her husband instead of the modern view that each may establish his or her own residence. As a result, married women students sometimes discover they are classified as non-residents for tuition purposes although they may have lived in the state since birth. (Of course, non-resident women benefit from such rules when they become eligible for lower in-state tuition by marrying a state resident. Either way, such rules discriminate on the basis of sex and marital status.) This practice can be attacked on several grounds.

Married women at state universities in Pennsylvania who had been charged out-of-state tuition because their husbands were non-residents sued the universities and demanded a return of the excess tuition they had paid. Rejecting the universities' argument that administrative convenience and the preservation of fiscal integrity required the residency rule, the judge decided that the rule violated the Equal Protection Clause. He ordered the universities to stop presuming that in-state married women had the same residence as their out-of-state husbands and to refund excess charges to any woman who could prove she was entitled to the lower in-state rate.[24]

Another avenue of relief may be available under state law. At least one state—California—has passed a law providing that for tuition purposes a married woman may establish her own residence without regard to that of her husband.[25] In addition, the Title IX regulations specifically forbid sex discrimination in applying residency rules to determine eligibility for in-state tuition or fees.[26] Thus a state could not apply the common law rule that a wife's domicile is that of her husband.

Do girls have the right to take the same courses as boys and to refuse to take girls-only courses?

Yes. With a few exceptions, the Title IX regulations forbid excluding a girl (or boy) from a class or activity because of sex, or offering separate courses to girls and boys. This applies to courses in health, physical education, industrial arts, business, vocational and technical subjects, home economics, and music as well as traditionally integrated courses. Schools may group students in physical education according to physical ability and may separate girls and boys for participation in wrestling, boxing, rugby, ice hockey, football, basketball, and other contact sports. Sex education classes may also be held in separate sessions for girls and boys. Choruses which are selected on the basis of vocal range are permitted to be one, or predominantly one, sex.[27]

A few girls have succeeded in challenging discriminatory course assignments—such as metalworking for boys and home economics for girls—under the Equal Protection Clause.[28] Under this theory, girls could not be forced to take a course that is required for girls but not for boys. The threat of a lawsuit may motivate a recalcitrant board of education to eliminate illegal course segregation.[29]

May school counselors steer girls into courses "suitable" for females or advise them to prepare only for jobs which women have traditionally held?

No. This common practice violates Title IX regulations. Counselors may not indirectly preserve male-only courses, like woodworking, by channeling girls into more "feminine" fields, or discourage girls from taking "masculine" subjects like physics or calculus.[30] However, such discrimination is often insidious and difficult to eradicate because counselors are unaware of their own biases or honestly believe they are merely being realistic about the job opportunities for women. Schools which find that a disproportionate number of boys or girls are enrolled in a particular course or program of study are required to investigate the situation in the school's counseling and testing program, but it is doubtful this self-monitoring will be very effective.

Many of the standardized vocational interest tests employed by counselors to assist people in making the "right" career choice have a built-in sex bias. Tests often use different questionnaires for males and females or evaluate boys' and girls' answers according to different standards so that a boy and a girl giving the same answers would get different career advice. They may rate a boy's aptitude for jobs traditionally held by men and a girl's for jobs traditionally held by women, rather than rating both boys and girls for all jobs. Such discriminatory tests and counseling materials are now forbidden by Title IX regulations. Parents' and women's groups should investigate the tests used in their community schools to make sure these discriminatory tests are not still being used.

May schools use textbooks which show women only in traditionally female jobs or contain other sexual stereotypes?
Yes, under the Title IX regulations.

Although gender-biased textbooks tend to socialize girls into subservient "female" roles and to reinforce the stereotypes of women as passive, dependent, emotional creatures, the regulations issued under Title IX specifically exempt textbooks and other curricular materials from coverage under the law.[31] The reason is a possible conflict with the First Amendment to the Constitution, which protects freedom of speech and press from government interference.[32]

However, there may be other avenues of legal help. For example, California has passed legislation requiring schools to use instructional materials which portray the contributions of women in all fields and forbidding the use of materials which treat women as inferior.[33] Many women's groups are working to develop unbiased textbooks, educational materials, and courses, and to eliminate sex-role stereotyping in schools.[34]

In response to their efforts, other states may have adopted laws or official directives to replace, forbid, or supplement discriminatory textbooks and other materials.

May a school exclude pregnant students or unwed mothers?

No. Title IX regulations forbid schools to exclude pregnant students or students who have had a child or an abortion.[35] Pregnant students may ask to attend special schools or educational programs, but their requests must be truly voluntary. Schools cannot pressure pregnant students into withdrawing from regular courses or refuse to allow them to return after their babies are born. A pregnant student must also be allowed to take a leave of absence for as long as her physician thinks necessary and later resume school attendance, even though the school does not usually permit leaves of absence. If the school maintains a separate, voluntary program for pregnant girls, it must be comparable in quality to that offered to other students.

A few states—e.g., Michigan[36]—also have laws which guarantee the right of pregnant students to stay in or to return to public schools. However, federal constitutional challenges to the practice of expelling or suspending pregnant students have had uneven results. One court ordered a school to readmit an unwed mother, but said the school could still exclude her if it showed she was so lacking in moral character that she would "taint the education of other students." The judge also implied that the school could exclude a pregnant girl; only after having the baby would she be entitled to return.[37] But in another case, the judge ordered school officials to permit an unwed, pregnant girl to continue regular attendance without restriction.[38] In Georgia, a ninth-grade girl who had had a baby was forced to attend night school instead of returning to regular daytime classes. The judge ruled that this policy was permissible, theorizing that students who become parents are more precocious than other students and might disrupt school discipline.[39]

May students who are pregnant, married, or parents be excluded from extracurricular activities?

This practice is forbidden by Title IX regulations.[40] In addition, a number of courts have ruled that married students or parents cannot be barred from extracurricular activities in an effort to discourage early marriage or to curb discussions of sex. A Texas judge decided that a 16-year-old girl who had been married, divorced, and had given her child up for adoption, could not be excluded from such extracurricular activities as chess, choir, drama, and the National Honor Society. He emphasized that she was an exceptionally good student and that success in these activities would enhance her chances to get into college or win a scholarship.[41] In another case, a school was ordered to allow a married high-school senior to participate in extracurricular activities and other school functions. The judge decided that the school regulation, whose sole purpose was to punish perfectly legal marriages, infringed upon the girl's fundamental right to marry.[42] Several married male high-school students have also won the right to play on varsity or interscholastic athletic teams.[43]

Do women have an equal right to participate in school athletic programs?

In the 1970s the struggle of women to win equal athletic opportunities produced numerous lawsuits and a great deal of controversy. Most of the girls who have sued their schools under the Equal Protection Clause to challenge their exclusion from all-male teams have succeeded—at least in "non-contact" sports. Girls in Minnesota, Nebraska, Colorado, Tennessee, and Kansas established their right to join all-male golf, tennis, cross-country track, cross-country skiing, soccer, and baseball teams.[44] In one case, a physically qualified girl even won the right to play football.[45]

On the other hand, girls in Illinois[46] fared less well, and in Tennessee an attempt to strike down restrictive playing rules failed. A female guard who wanted her team to play "boys' " rules persuaded a lower-level judge that the special girls' basketball rules (e.g., split court, guards prohibited from shooting) denied her equal protection and handicapped her in competing for a college athletic scholarship. Although Tennessee was one of only five states which imposed separate rules, the appellate court disagreed, in a decision based more on stereotype than reason:

When the classification, as here, related to athletic activity, it must be apparent that its basis is the distinct differences in physical characteristics and capabilities between the sexes and that the differences are reflected in the sport of basketball by how the game itself is played. It takes little imagination to realize that were play and competition not separated by sex, the great bulk of the females would quickly be eliminated from participation and denied any meaningful opportunity for athletic involvement. Since there are such differences in physical characteristics and capabilities, we see no reason why the rules governing play cannot be tailored to accommodate them without running afoul of the Equal Protection Clause.[47]

The successful suits have generally been brought under the Equal Protection Clause by individuals suing only on their own behalf (not on behalf of an entire "class" of girls) and have involved "non-contact" sports. The absence of a girls' team seems to be a critical factor in the decisions. Several courts have explicitly expressed reservations about integrated teams in "contact" sports. However, in two lawsuits under state equal rights amendments, courts have struck down restrictions on girls' participation in contact sports. In Pennsylvania, a judge found unconstitutional a by-law of an interscholastic athletic association that prohibited high-school girls from practicing or competing with boys in football, basketball, wrestling, soccer, baseball, and several other sports. He ruled that girls must be permitted to play on boys' teams, even where there was a separate girls' team.[48] In Washington, two high-school girls who had qualified for the boys' football team won the right to play with their teammates when state judges ruled that the athletic association regulation which barred their participation violated the state equal rights amendment.[49]

The regulations issued under Title IX provide some, but not enough, protection against discrimination in athletics.[50] Although in theory schools may not bar any student from playing in interscholastic or intramural athletics because of his or her sex, in practice the regulations permit schools to sponsor separate teams for girls and boys when team selection is based on "competitive skill" or the activity is a "contact" sport.* Most teams are covered by one or the other of these

---

*The regulations define "contact" sports as boxing, wrestling, football, rugby, ice hockey, basketball, and other sports involving bodily contact.

exceptions. If the school has only one team, girls must be allowed to try out for it, unless it involves a "contact" sport. The regulations also mandate "equal athletic opportunities" for both sexes but do not require equal amounts of money to be spent on girls and boys. These regulations are a particularly strong candidate for a lawsuit attacking them as unconstitutional, especially by girls who have the skills to make an all-male team. However, the regulations can be used to improve inadequate female sports programs in many instances.

Should women try to win more than the right to participate on "male" athletic teams?

Yes. Women must make some difficult strategy decisions in seeking to establish equal rights to participate in athletic programs. Should they ask for equal funding for separate male and female sports, integrated sports programs, or a combination of the two? The latter is probably the most desirable. Integrated sports would provide the opportunity for the most athletically talented girls to compete with athletically talented boys. By also asking the schools to fund sports diverse enough to attract most girls, and by insisting that the average per student expenditure be equal for boys and girls, women would also provide opportunities for those girls who are not interested in, or lack the muscular development for, some of the traditionally male sports. More adequate funding of different sports than are currently emphasized would also help those boys with a similar lack of interest in or muscular development for sports like football. Eventually the schools might find themselves providing meaningful athletic programs for all students, sorting the students into sports roughly by interest and skill rather than by sex.

What laws protect women from discrimination in vocational education?

Discrimination in vocational education has helped to concentrate women in domestic, clerical, and other low-paying, low-status, dead-end positions, while men monopolize the more lucrative skilled-craft jobs in trade and industry. A major factor in perpetuating this pattern is the virtual exclusion of women from many occupational training programs. For example, in 1972, 37,277 men but only 34 women were being trained as plumbers.[51]

To alter this situation, Congress amended the Vocational Education Act in 1976 to require states to take affirmative steps to end sex discrimination in vocational education.[52] To qualify for federal money, states must collect data on the enrollment of women in training programs, reduce sex-role stereotyping and sex bias in job-training programs, and assist schools in making vocational education opportunities available to women. The law also provides grants to states for job training for homemakers who are seeking paid employment and for women in traditionally female jobs who want employment in "male" fields.

States which do not comply with the law risk the termination of federal funds. The law does not specifically authorize women to bring private lawsuits to enforce its provisions, but it is possible that such a lawsuit might be allowed.

In addition, Title IX forbids sex discrimination in all school policies—whether admissions, course assignments, or financial aid—in those vocational schools which receive federal money—and most do. Thus it should be possible to challenge all-male or all-female vocational schools under Title IX, as well as otherwise integrated schools with single-sex vocational programs. In some cases, the Equal Educational Opportunities Act of 1974, Title IV of the 1964 Civil Rights Act, and the Equal Protection Clause also could be used to challenge the assignment of students to vocational schools or programs on the basis of sex.[53]

What educational problems should women seek to address under the Equal Protection Clause or the various federal statutes?

The Citizens' Advisory Council on the Status of Women outlined many problems needing attention in the area of education. In any local community, the council would look for:

. . . the degree of sex discrimination . . . with respect to (1) schools restricted to one sex; (2) courses of study in coeducational schools restricted to one sex; (3) the per-capita expenditure of funds by sex for physical education courses and other extracurricular activities; (4) sex stereotyping in textbooks, library books, and other curriculum aids; (5) school activities, such as hall patrols, safety squads, room chores, etc.; and (6) promotion of teachers.[54]

Many of these practices continue at the college level and above. In addition, guidance counselors offer sex-stereotyped advice about jobs and careers to students, and consequently many vocational, professional, or graduate programs are effectively sex-segregated, despite the absence of official bars to the entry of one sex. Some schools have restrictive quotas on the admission of women and unequal scholarship aid. Many of these practices are prohibited by the regulations for Title IX. However, HEW enforcement has been ineffective so far and it is not yet clear whether the new Department of Education will do a better job. Women should challenge these practices in lawsuits brought under the Equal Protection Clause or the federal statutes barring sex discrimination in education. Success is likely on restrictive admissions quotas and unequal scholarship aid in public schools and colleges. The outcome of litigation in other problem areas is uncertain. Women should push for legislation forbidding all the discriminatory practices discussed here, particularly those that are less likely to be ruled illegal in lawsuits under the Equal Protection Clause or current statutes.

Should any national planning be undertaken before attempting to establish these rights?

Yes. Feminists—and particularly feminist lawyers—should definitely plan strategy for nationwide legal action to abolish discrimination in education. The lack of coordinated planning to date may already have led to some bad losses, which will make it more difficult to win in the future.

Planning should define the kinds of discrimination to attack initially, the priorities thereafter, and the theoretical Equal Protection development needed. The cases adjudicated so far, and past experience in eradicating racial discrimination in education, suggest that women ought to start with—and carefully document—the most blatant forms of discrimination: outright exclusion of women from certain courses; exclusion of women from schools; admitted restrictive quota systems; and denial of access to all athletic programs. Later they can move on to issues that will seem less obviously discriminatory to hostile judges: de facto quota systems on admissions; segregated athletic programs; and sex-role-biased job and career counseling programs leading to de facto sex segregation in schools and training programs. Tactically, it is better to break down the segregation bars by focusing on factual comparisons of facilities for men and women which will demonstrate that the state allocates much less money for women.[55] After that job is done, the time may be ripe to ask judges to declare all segregation inherently illegal. Similarly, it seems wise to start the attack with public schools and colleges since current law is so solidly against finding state action at private schools.[56]

Do students in the health professions have any additional rights against discrimination by their schools?

Yes. Under an amendment to the Public Health Service Act, two sections—§§799A and 855 (formerly §845)[57]—specifically prohibit schools and training programs in the health professions from discriminating against students on the basis of their sex. The prohibition applies only to schools and programs receiving financial assistance under Titles VII and VIII of the Public Health Service Act, but the vast majority of these schools do receive such assistance. The prohibition also applies to hospitals insofar as they operate medical schools, training programs, or even internships. Those affected may now protest and seek legal redress if a hospital refuses to hire women interns, if a medical school limits its enrollment of women or refuses to admit people over 30 (which affects women more than men), or if a nursing school refuses to admit men.

In 1975 HEW finally issued regulations[58] to interpret these sections of the Public Health Services Act. The regulations, which are independent of those under Title IX, afford stronger protection against discrimination in admissions, but omit athletic programs and provide less protection against discriminatory employment practices. Otherwise they parallel the Title IX regulations in the areas of student housing, student financial aid, equal benefits and services to men and women students, and the treatment of pregnant and married students.

Are teachers, other school employees, and students protected against employment discrimination by the sex discrimination provisions of the Public Health Service Act and Title IX of the Education Amendments of 1972 Act?

Yes. In 1982, the Supreme Court ended a long legal controversy on this issue. It ruled that Title IX protects employees in federally funded education programs from discrimination on the basis of sex in their employment.[59] Thus, Title IX helps teachers, administrators and other school employees, as well as students. There has never been any real doubt over whether the PHSA covers employment discrimination; it does. But this law protects only those teachers and employees who work directly with students.

Are there any other laws that protect teachers against sex discriminatory employment practices?

Yes. Both Title VII of the 1964 Civil Rights Act and the Equal Pay Act have been amended to protect teachers against sex discrimination. Both laws are discussed in Chapter II, "Employment Discrimination."

Until these amendments were passed, college teachers had only one very ineffective remedy against sex discrimination: Executive Order 11246, as amended by E.O. 11375. (See Chapter II for a discussion of its weaknesses.) Now all teachers may sue in federal court under the Equal Pay Act and Title VII to recover lost wages and to force the school to change discriminatory policies. The executive order may still be used to apply additional pressure, but teachers will no longer have to rely on federal agencies that do not wish to enforce the order.

Public school teachers already had the right to sue in federal court under the Equal Protection Clause. They too will gain from the amendments, since courts have been much stricter about eliminating sex discrimination under Title VII than they have been under the Equal Protection Clause.

Should teachers use all laws available to combat discriminatory practices?

Yes, since this maximizes the pressure on school officials. Teachers now have a wide range of remedies: court action under Titles IV and VII of the 1964 Civil Rights Act, the Equal Pay Act, Title IX, and the Equal Protection Clause (if they are public school employees); and differing forms of agency action under Executive Order 11246 (contract cutoff), Title IX (grant, loan, and contract cutoff), and the Public Health Service Act.

Do any state laws prohibit sex discrimination in education?

Yes. Many states now have laws forbidding at least some forms of discrimination, some of them modeled on Title IX (e.g., Washington, California, and Michigan). Other state statutes prohibit types of discrimination not covered by federal law. In addition, women in the several states which have adopted state equal rights amendments[60] may challenge discriminatory practices in public facilities or those facilities with state involvement as violations of the state constitution.

A few other states have laws prohibiting educational discrimination on the basis of race, religion, or national origin, but not sex. (See Chart B in the Appendix for a list of and citations for all such laws.) It is difficult to know how effective these state laws are. Some, administered by state civil rights agencies, provide for a complaint procedure and full enforcement powers. Others merely forbid some forms of discrimination and provide no apparent enforcement mechanism. Even where there is a comprehensive program on paper, personnel in state agencies and courts can undermine the effectiveness of the program, as can a lack of funding.

Women who have encountered discrimination should check whether their states have laws prohibiting sex discrimination and whether these laws are adequately enforced. Because the Department of Education has been so slow in handling complaints, since HEW enforcement responsibility passed to it in 1980, women should file a complaint with the appropriate state agency as well as with the U.S. Department of Education's regional office. In some cases the state agency may be able to get quicker results. Filing complaints in both places will also maximize pressure on schools to correct their discriminatory practices.

In states without laws on this subject, women should work for the inclusion of provisions in existing civil rights laws forbidding sex discrimination in education or for passage of comprehensive laws prohibiting all forms of educational discrimination. If the problem is the lack of enforcement of an existing law, women should lobby for adequate funding for the agency charged with enforcing the law and for the hiring and training of capable, dedicated staff and appointment of a director with a strong history of working against sex discrimination as well as other forms of illegal discrimination.

B. Procedures to Follow in Seeking Remedies

A right which exists only in theory does no one any good. For example, a school principal may be acting illegally when he prevents a woman from enrolling in a course just because she is a woman, but until he has been forced to stop, the woman merely has a theoretical right not to be discriminated against. She has not yet gotten the results she needs. Occasionally a woman can change the situation by telling the principal (or other authority) that she has a right to do certain things and by referring the official to the appropriate law or appropriate enforcement agency; if he then changes his actions, she has gotten her result. All too often, however, a lawsuit or some other legal action will be required to enforce her right.

The rights guaranteed by the Equal Protection Clause and the various federal statutes are generally enforced in different ways. If a woman sues under the Equal Protection Clause or Title IX, she can ask for an end to the discrimination, but if the Department of Education (formerly HEW) rather than the individual woman takes action under Title IX, the remedy might include a cutoff of federal funds to the offending school, although in almost all cases the Department of Education will seek to end the discrimination through conciliation. Also, administrative action in the form of a threatened cutoff of funds often comes too late (if at all) to help the individual victim of discrimination. The remedies available to women under the various laws and the procedures for obtaining them will be discussed in detail in this part of the chapter.

1. The Equal Protection Clause

How can a woman challenge a discriminatory practice under the Equal Protection Clause?

A woman can enforce rights under the Equal Protection Clause by bringing a lawsuit against the discriminating school or official. Of course, she will need a lawyer, preferably one experienced in the area of women's rights. (The groups listed in Chart D in the Appendix can assist in locating a lawyer.)

Usually the women will sue for an "injunction"—a court

order telling someone to do something or ordering them to stop doing something. For instance, a judge can order a school to admit a woman or to stop enforcing a rule which applies only to girls. Occasionally a woman will want money damages or some other award. An equal protection claim also may be combined in a single lawsuit with a challenge to the discriminatory practice under a state equal rights amendment (if one exists in that state) or with a claim under one of the federal or state laws discussed here.

Cases which have already established that certain discriminatory practices are illegal under the Equal Protection Clause were discussed in Section A. Women should now move on to attack additional forms of discrimination under this constitutional provision. (Remember, however, that the Equal Protection Clause prohibits discrimination only by public schools and colleges.)

2. The Equal Educational Opportunities Act

How may women enforce rights under the Equal Educational Opportunities Act?

This statute is enforced in two ways: A woman may bring a lawsuit in a federal district court to enforce her rights or the U.S. Attorney General may begin one on her behalf. The Attorney General is also authorized to intervene in lawsuits begun by private individuals.[61]

3. Title IV of the 1964 Civil Rights Act

How can women enforce rights under Title IV?[62]

This law only permits the U.S. Attorney General to sue a discriminatory school or college. Thus a woman's role is limited to requesting the Attorney General to bring such a lawsuit when she has been discriminated against or is aware of a discriminatory practice.

What kinds of discriminatory practices can be attacked in such a lawsuit?

To date, the Attorney General has used Title IV principally to desegregate public schools. In the course of such lawsuits,

Justice Department lawyers have also attacked other forms of discrimination—both against students and teachers—but these moves have always been incidental to the main issue of desegregation. This seems to indicate that Title IV can be used against all the forms of sex discrimination mentioned in this chapter, but that the Justice Department may not be inclined to do so unless women raise these issues in the context of segregated schools. Women should still request the Justice Department to fight other forms of educational discrimination in integrated schools, if for no other reason than to help educate Justice Department lawyers on other sex discrimination issues. Title IV applies both to lower schools and to colleges, so complaints about college-level discrimination should also be sent to the department.

How should women request the Attorney General to bring such lawsuits?
Send a letter to:

> Attorney General
> U.S. Department of Justice
> Washington, D.C. 20530
>   Attention: General Litigation Section,
>   Civil Rights Division

At the elementary- and secondary-school level, the letter should be sent by the parents of affected children. At the college level, women students can raise the complaint.

Describe the school system and the discriminatory practices, and give as many facts as possible. It also helps to identify other women who share the same problem. The Justice Department will be more interested if it is a widespread problem because the Attorney General must certify that the lawsuit will further desegregation efforts. Although it is impossible to know whether the Justice Department will follow through, it is probably worthwhile to make the effort—certainly so for women who cannot find or afford their own lawyers. Even for those who have access to counsel, requests for Attorney General intervention may serve as a means of publicizing the discrimination and awakening government officials to its existence and effects.

4. Title IX

How are discriminatory schools punished under Title IX?
Any federal agency that awards money—whether as grants, loans, or contracts—to a school can cancel that assistance if it finds that the school discriminates. The agency may also refuse to award such assistance in the future, or refer the case to the Justice Department for a lawsuit against the school. Although many federal agencies administer grant programs to educational institutions, the Department of Education (formerly HEW) is the main grantor and as such is the chief enforcement agency.

The threat of a cutoff of federal money is a powerful weapon, since many schools depend on this money for a major portion of their budget. Of course, the Department of Education must be willing to make this threat and to carry through in the event of noncompliance if the law is to be effective. It remains to be seen whether the agency will be willing to do so. HEW, the enforcement agency until 1980, was not.

Are there any other ways to enforce rights under Title IX?
Yes. In 1979 the Supreme Court explicitly ruled that women may bring their own suits in federal court under Title IX against discriminatory schools.[63] In addition, the Justice Department (through the Attorney General) can bring such lawsuits.

How should women enforce their rights under Title IX?
If they want a Department of Education investigation which threatens the school with a possible cutoff of federal funds, they should send a letter detailing their charges of discrimination, and the name and address of the school involved, to the nearest regional office of the Department of Education, or to:

Assistant Secretary for Civil Rights
Office of Civil Rights
Department of Education
Washington, D.C. 20202

Include as many facts as possible about the school's practices, and use the advice on how to file complaints from the chapter on employment discrimination (see Chapter II). For example, give statistical evidence of discrimination (e.g., percentages of men and women enrolled in different programs); do not limit your charges to those you are sure you can prove—add those you think may be true (it is the responsibility of the Department of Education to investigate and prove or disprove your charges); and mention anything that you believe is discriminatory, whether or not legal authority already supports you. Only by raising new issues will new law be made. If you know which federal program gives money to the school, you should also add its name. The Department of Education will find out which agency gives grants to your school if you don't know; and the department will also send your letter to the proper federal agency if it is not in charge of the grant program (or programs) at your school.

Once the Department of Education receives your charge, it must investigate and possibly hold a hearing to find out whether the school discriminates. Women complainants may participate in these hearings only as witnesses or as "friends of the court"; they may not present their side of the matter by having an attorney call witnesses or present evidence. Only Department of Education lawyers do these things unless a special arrangement is made. However, if a woman is unhappy with the results, she can ask a United States court of appeals to review the Department of Education action. Sometimes women's organizations may also be allowed to participate as "friends of the court," which means they can offer their opinion as to what the result should be but they cannot present evidence or control the course of the hearing unless they are invited to do so.

If a woman wants to bring her own lawsuit in federal court attacking discriminatory education practices forbidden by Title IX, she can do so. She need only find a lawyer to bring suit for her; there is no requirement that the women file anything with the Department of Education before suing.

Has Title IX been adequately enforced by the responsible federal agency?

Emphatically not. HEW was the enforcement agency until 1980. It took HEW nearly three years just to write regulations to implement the law. A study[64] of HEW's record in handling Title IX violations in elementary and secondary schools turned up some shocking statistics. Between 1972 and 1976 HEW managed to resolve only one out of five complaints filed with the agency, a total of 179 cases. The average delay on cases which it did resolve was 14 months, but some women had to wait two or three years. Many complaints were dismissed after a cursory investigation or none at all. HEW also piled up a large backlog of unprocessed complaints. In this same four-year period HEW conducted "compliance reviews" (investigations not begun by formal complaints) on a mere 12 of the nation's 16,000 school districts.

The study concluded that understaffing did not account for this sluggish enforcement effort. Between 1973 and 1976 HEW received an average of only six complaints per year for each investigator assigned to handle sex discrimination in the public schools—hardly an overwhelming workload. Indecision about what Title IX meant, bureaucratic inefficiency, political pressures, and a low priority for sex discrimination cases contributed to the neglect of Title IX enforcement. HEW bureaucrats (mostly male) did not view sex discrimination as a pressing problem.

Feminist groups, outraged by this neglect, sued HEW to compel it to enforce the law. The result was that in 1977 HEW agreed to a court order[65] that laid down timetables and procedures for eliminating its complaint backlog and for processing new cases.

What did the court order tell HEW to do?

The court order required HEW to eliminate its backlog of complaints by the end of 1979 and process a certain number of new complaints each year. The court order also established procedures and timetables which bind the Department of Education in handling new complaints under Title IX after 1980. When the department receives a letter of complaint, it must notify the woman within 15 days whether her complaint contains all the information it needs to begin an investigation. If the complaint is incomplete, the department must tell her what additional information is required and give her 120 days to supply it. If the information is not received within this period, the department may close the investigation.

If the complaint is complete, within 15 days the department must inform the woman and the school when it intends to start the investigation, what procedures it will follow, and whether a department investigator will go to the school to collect information and to conduct interviews. In any investigation the department must at least interview the woman who complained, school officials, and any witnesses who know about the discrimination. If the department makes a preliminary finding that the school did not discriminate, it must notify the woman and let her reply to any evidence which the school presented to the department.

When the department finishes its investigation, it must send a "letter of findings" containing its conclusions to the woman and the school. If the department decides that the school did discriminate, it must try—through negotiation—to persuade the school to comply voluntarily with the law. The woman has the right to be kept informed of the progress of the negotiations. If the negotiations fail, the department has another 30 days to bring formal administrative action against the school on the cutoff of funds.

Finally, even if no complaints have been filed, each year the department must conduct a number of "compliance reviews" of schools, including vocational schools in the South, to find out whether they are obeying the law. Although the court order has some loopholes, the procedures look good on paper. It remains to be seen whether the Department of Education will improve upon HEW's poor record.

How can a woman assist (or pressure) the Department of Education while it is handling her complaint?

Nothing is guaranteed to work, but the following steps may help mobilize the bureaucracy.

In the initial letter to the department, provide as much information as possible, especially such useful items as the names, addresses, and phone numbers of people who should be interviewed. If several people have suffered from the same discrimination (e.g., five other girls were excluded from the same shop class), all of them should join in the complaint. This guarantees that if one of the girls moves or graduates before the department takes action, there will be someone else who can assist it in correcting the discriminatory practice.

Answer any letters received from the department officials quickly. If they do not get a reply within a reasonable time, they will conclude that you are no longer interested in pursuing your complaint and will close the investigation.

Call the department regional office and find out the name and phone number of the investigator assigned to the complaint. Maintain friendly contact with this person. The department still has a great deal of discretion over which cases it handles and how thoroughly it investigates them. A complainant who is cooperative and remains interested in resolving her case may receive more attention.

If nothing seems to be happening on a complaint, call the department to find out what action is being taken or planned. Contact the Congressperson for your district and tell him or her about the discrimination and the lack of action on it. A letter from a Congressperson to the Department's regional office may work wonders.

Does Title IX provide adequate protection against sex discrimination in educational opportunities?

Definitely not. In fact, some women might see the law as a sellout by Congress, particularly since Title IX was considered several weeks after the overwhelming congressional approval of the Equal Rights Amendment. Male presidents (or their representatives) of the big-name, high-prestige schools, descended on Congress to plead for the right to discriminate against women students. Harvard, for example, wanted to bring its 4 to 1 male-female quota system slowly "down" to 3.5 to 1.[66] Women's colleges, too, sought to preserve their present admissions practices. The schools won that "right"—which explains why the law does not touch the admissions policies of so many kinds of schools. With time, schools have won further opportunities to discriminate without violating Title IX—for instance, the right to exclude women from all-male contact sports teams or to force students to attend sex-segregated events like Boys State and Girls State (when the real world they are preparing to enter has at least nominally integrated legislatures). It still does not forbid sex discrimination across the board.

The enforcement mechanism provided in Title IX is also weak. Experience to date demonstrates that women cannot rely with any confidence on federal agencies to enforce their rights.

Should women who want to challenge discriminatory practices in public schools use both the Equal Protection Clause and Title IX of the Education Amendments of 1972 Act?

Yes; because each provides a different remedy, both together would maximize the pressure on school officials. Women should remember, though, that Title IX allows many public schools to follow various discriminatory admission policies. In these instances, the Equal Protection Clause provides the only remedy. (Women students at private schools, of course, can use only Title IX and not the Equal Protection Clause because of the lack of "state action.")

5. The Public Health Service Act

How are the antidiscrimination provisions of the Public Health Service Act enforced?

The Department of Health and Human Services (formerly HEW) must cancel any federal financial assistance—whether in the form of a grant, a loan guarantee, or a subsidy on interest payments—received under Titles VII or VIII of the Public Health Service Act by a school or program that discriminates. Theoretically, cancellation can occur in three ways. If the school fails to give HHS a written assurance that it will not discriminate, HHS must cut off or refuse to award the funds. HHS also conducts routine reviews to check for discrimination. Finally, someone can file a complaint with HHS, charging a program with discrimination. HHS would then conduct a hearing and cancel any financial assistance if it finds discrimination. Although women will not be allowed to participate in these hearings except as witnesses or "friends of the court," they will be able to ask a federal court to review HHS action.

To file a complaint, send a letter detailing the charges to the nearest Health and Human Services regional office, or to:

Director, Office of Civil Rights
Department of Health and Human Services
330 Independence Avenue, S.W.
Washington, D.C. 20201

Although there has been no court ruling on the point, it may also be possible to sue the discriminatory schools in federal court, under the same theory used to allow private lawsuits under Title IX.

Are there any differences between the sex discrimination provisions of the Public Health Service Act and those of Title IX?

Yes. The Public Health Service Act does not contain the numerous exceptions that Title IX does. Thus, women in the health professions who are not helped by Title IX—such as applicants to private undergraduate schools—may still be able to get relief under the Public Health Service Act.

Should women who can challenge sex discrimination under both laws do so?

Yes. This may help maximize the pressure on the school, even though the remedy under both laws is of the same nature—a cutoff of federal funds.

6. New Legislation

What can women do to close the gaps in Title IX?

Let your congressional representatives know that you want strong provisions against discrimination, and that Title IX needs to be strengthened. When women were lobbying for the Equal Rights Amendment, they were told repeatedly by male lobbyists that they would have to compromise if they wanted to get anything through Congress. The women remained firm and got the amendment they wanted; they realized that to settle for less was to negate completely the principle they were striving to establish. Legislators are used to giving up easily and to the process of compromise—but if women organize the same strong lobby for a solid bill against discrimination, they can succeed.

What provisions would a strengthened Title IX contain?

First, it would not exempt any school or admission policy from coverage. Even religious schools would be forbidden to discriminate, since the law would cover only schools receiving federal funds. If a religious school wants to discriminate, it should not be allowed to do so with federal money, particularly since part of that money comes from female taxpayers. The same holds true for military schools. Many military schools teach valuable employment skills and offer other benefits that cannot be acquired anywhere else. For example, commercial airlines hire almost all their pilots from those trained by the Air Force. The prestige private schools likewise deserve no special break. Supposedly they provide some of the best education in this nation, and it is outrageous that Congress is willing to continue funding, with federal money received from female taxpayers, schools that blatantly limit women's enrollment.[67] Similarly, women's colleges receiving federal funds should be required to open admissions to men. The price paid for maintaining all-female institutions is the maintenance of all-male institutions, and that price is too high to tolerate. All the other special exemptions for admissions policies should be eliminated. Finally, all the other specific discriminatory policies allowed under Title IX or the regulations should be eliminated.

7. Paralegal Action

What can women's paralegal groups do in the education area?

As in other fields, they can teach women their rights, help them file complaints or find lawyers, and lobby for new and better laws. In addition, Title IX offers a unique organizing opportunity since it protects all the women in a particular school or campus from sex discrimination, whether the women are students, research assistants, teachers, secretaries, or maids. All these women can coalesce to study campus discrimination as it affects them all and then together file charges with the Department of Education. This concerted action will produce a much stronger attack on discriminatory practices, and it should also help women in very different circumstances understand some of the factors that unite them. An excellent source of technical information about and assistance in action to eradicate sex discrimination on college campuses is:

The Project on the Status and Education of Women
Association of American Colleges
1818 R St., N.W.
Washington, D.C. 20009
(202) 387-1300

Write for the project's newsletter, *On Campus with Women*.
Other groups which work on education discrimination issues include:

PEER (Project on Equal Education Rights)
1029 Vermont Ave., N.W., Suite 800
Washington, D.C. 20005
(202) 332-7337

WEAL (Women's Equity Action League)
805 15th St., N.W., Suite 822
Washington, D.C. 20005
(202) 638-1961

A third group, the National Women's Law Center, provides legal advice and representation to women and girls
experiencing sex discrimination in educational programs and
for groups working to strengthen federal policies for sex equity in education. They also have excellent legal training
materials on sex discrimination in education. Their address is:

National Women's Law Center
1751 N St., N.W.
Washington, D.C. 20036
(202) 872-0670

NOTES

1. E. Flexner, *Century of Struggle* (1970), pp. 29–30 and n. 13.
2. 20 U.S.C. §1681 *et seq*.
3. 42 U.S.C. §§295h-9, 298b-2.
4. 20 U.S.C. §2301 *et seq*.
5. 42 U.S.C. §2000c-6.
6. 20 U.S.C. §1701 *et seq*.
7. *Mississippi University for Women v. Hogan*, 102 S.Ct. 3331 (1982).

8. *Kirstein v. Rector and Visitors of University of Virginia*, 309 F.Supp. 184 (E.D. Va. 1970).

9. *Bray v. Lee*, 337 F.Supp. 934 (D. Mass. 1972). A few boys are also now attending the former Girls Latin School.

10. *Berkelman v. San Francisco Unified School District*, 501 F.2d 1264 (9th Cir. 1974).

11. The Supreme Court affirmed the decision without an opinion. *Vorchheimer v. School District of Philadelphia*, 532 F.2d 880 (3d Cir. 1976), aff'd by an equally divided court, 430 U.S. 703 (1977). However, a state court later reached the opposite result and required Central to admit girls. *Newberg v. Board of Public Education*, No. J822 (Ct. of Common Pleas, Phil. County, Sept. 28, 1983).

12. *U.S. v. Hinds County School Board*, 560 F.2d 619 (5th Cir. 1977); *Haymon v. Jefferson Parish School Board*, C.A. No. 77–396 (E.D. La. Oct. 21, 1977).

13. Women were admitted to the military academies by amendment to the Defense Appropriation Authorization Act of 1976. 10 U.S.C. §4342 note (Supp. V. 1975). Women must meet the same academic and other standards required of men for appointment, admission, training, graduation, and commissioning (with slight modifications for physiological differences). However, the number of women admitted has been severely restricted "consistent with the needs of the services." (See Chapter IX for discussion of sex discrimination in the military.)

14. 45 C.F.R. Part 86.

15. When this book was first published, the number of single-sex public undergraduate colleges was fairly small. It included the following all-female schools: Texas Women's University; Mississippi University for Women; Longwood College (Va.); Radford College (Va); Douglass College (N.J.); and Winthrop College (S.C.). The list of all-male public undergraduate schools was larger: Maine Maritime Academy; Massachusetts Maritime Academy; New Mexico Military Institute; State University of New York Maritime College; The Citadel Military College (S.C.); Virginia Military Institute; Air Force Institute of Technology; U.S. Air Force Academy; U.S. Coast Guard Academy; U.S. Merchant Marine Academy; U.S. Naval Academy; U.S. Naval Postgraduate School; California Maritime Academy. These male schools were exempt from Title IX coverage in two ways: they were military schools; and they had always been single-sex, public undergraduate colleges. By 1980, all the colleges but Mississippi University for Women were integrated, and that school lost an Equal Protection challenge in the federal courts in 1982, at least at its Nursing School. See text at n. 7, and n. 7, *supra*. However, the integration was token in the extreme at most schools. For example, the Virginia Military Institute had 1317 men enrolled and 11 women; the Maine Maritime Academy, 636 men and 7 women.

16. 20 U.S.C. §1681(c); 34 C.F.R. §106.15.

17. 20 U.S.C. §1681(a)(6) (Supp. V, 1975).

18. 20 U.S.C.A. §1681(a)(7) and (8) (Supp. 1977).

19. 34 C.F.R. §106.32.

20. 34 C.F.R. §106.32.

21. *Mollere v. Southeastern Louisiana College*, 304 F.Supp. 826 (E.D. La. 1969).

22. *Robinson v. Board of Regents*, 475 F.2d 707 (6th Cir. 1973), *cert. denied*, 416 U.S. 982 (1973).

23. 34 C.F.R. §106.37.

24. *Samuel v. University of Pittsburgh*, 375 F.Supp. 1119 (W.D. Pa. 1974). On appeal the court ruled that the women were entitled to restitution and that requiring each student to sue individually to recover her money imposed an undue burden. 538 F.2d 991 (3d Cir. 1976). The Supreme Court has never ruled on this issue, but has ruled favorably in an analogous case. *Vlandis v. Kline*, 412 U.S. 441 (1973).

25. Calif. Educ. Code §22847 (West Supp. 1974). Other states may have similar laws. No comprehensive survey of state law has been made on this topic.

26. 34 C.F.R. §106.31 (b) (6).

27. 34 C.F.R. §106.34.

28. *Sanchez v. Brown*, C.A. No. 69-C-1615 (E.D. N.Y. 1971).

29. State statutes in New York and Massachusetts prohibit the exclusion of either sex from courses. See Chart B in the Appendix. In addition, the Pennsylvania Commissioner of Education has issued a broad directive against discrimination in education that includes a prohibition against excluding either sex from courses. Other states may have similar rulings.

30. 34 C.F.R. §106.36.

31. 34 C.F.R. §106.42.

32. The Women's Educational Equity Act of 1974 authorizes grants to public agencies and private non-profit organizations to develop, evaluate, and distribute non-discriminatory curricula, textbooks, and counseling tests in order to promote equality in education. 20 U.S.C. §1866(d) (Supp. V, 1975).

33. Calif. Educ. Code §§9240, 9243 (West Supp. 1973).

34. See "Sex Discrimination: The Textbook Case," 62 *Calif. L. Rev.* 1312 (1974), for a discussion of the effects of textbook stereotypes and the efforts to eliminate biased books in California, Pennsylvania, and Kalamazoo, Michigan.

35. 34 C.F.R. §106.40.

36. Mich. Stat. Ann. §15.41301 (Supp. 1977).

37. *Perry v. Granada*, 300 F.Supp. 748 (N.D. Miss. 1969). Another case from the same district is *Shull v. Columbus Municipal School District*, 338 F.Supp. 1376 (N.D. Miss. 1972).

38. *Ordway v. Hargraves,* 323 F.Supp. 1155 (D. Mass, 1971).

39. *Houston v. Prosser,* 361 F.Supp. 295 (N.D. Ga. 1973).

40. 34 C.F.R. §106.40.

41. *Romans v. Crenshaw,* 354 F.Supp. 868 (S.D. Texas 1972).

42. *Holt v. Shelton,* 341 F.Supp. 821 (M.D. Tenn. 1972).

43. *Davis v. Meek,* 344 F.Supp. 298 (N.D. Ohio 1972); *Moran v. School District #7, Yellowstone County,* 350 F.Supp. 1180 (D. Mont. 1972); *Hollon v. Mathis Independent School District,* 358 F.Supp. 1269 (S.D. Texas 1973).

44. *Brenden v. Independent School District,* 477 F.2d 1292 (8th Cir. 1973); *Bednar v. Nebraska School Athletics Association,* 531 F.2d 922 (8th Cir. 1976); *Reed v. Nebraska School Activities Association,* 341 F.Supp 258 (D. Neb. 1972); *Hoover v. Meiklejohn,* 430 F. Supp. 164 (D. Colo. 1977); *Carnes v. Tennessee Secondary School Athletic Association,* 415 F.Supp. 569 (E.D. Tenn. 1976); *Gilpin v. Kansas State High School Activities Association, Inc.* 377 F.2d 1233 (D. Kan. 1973).

45. *Clinton v. Nagy,* 411 F.Supp. 1396 (N.D. Ill. 1976).

46. *Buchas v. Illinois High School Association,* 351 F.Supp. 69 (N.D. Ill. 1972).

47. *Cape v. Tennessee Secondary School Athletic Association,* 563 F.2d 793 (6th Cir. 1977), reversing 424 F.Supp 732 (E.D. Tenn. 1976).

48. *Commonwealth, Packel v. Pennsylvania Interscholastic Athletic Association,* 334 A.2d 839 (Cmwlth Ct. 1975).

49. *Darrin v. Gould,* 540 P.2d 882 (Wash. 1975).

50. 34 C.F.R. §106.41. These regulations are expanded on in a subsequent policy interpretation, set forth in 44 F.R. 71413-23 (Dec. 11, 1979).

51. Shelton & Berndt, "Sex Discrimination in Vocational Education: Title IX and Other Remedies," 62 *Calif. L. Rev.* 1121 (1974).

52. Title II of the 1976 Amendments to the Vocational Education Act of 1963, 20 U.S.C.A. §§2301 *et seq.* (Supp. 1977). For details, see *Achieving Sex Equality in Vocational Education: A Citizen's Guide to the 1976 Vocational Education Amendments,* available from Lawyers' Committee for Civil Rights Under Law, Federal Education Project, 733 15th St., N.W., Washington, D.C. 20005.

53. "How to Erase Sex Discrimination in Vocational Education," available from the Women's Rights Project, ACLU, 22 E. 40th St., New York, N.Y. 10016, suggests ways to combat sex bias in vocational education programs. Readers interested in sex discrimination in vocational education should also read the Title IX guidelines on this subject, found at 34 C.F.R. Part 106, Appendix A, with text at 34 C.F.R. Part 100, Appendix B.

54. *Women in 1971* (1972), pp. 19–20.

55. The Citizens' Advisory Council on the Status of Women has published a pamphlet, *Need for Studies of Sex Discrimination in Public Schools.* It is available free from the council (U.S. Department of

Labor, Room 1336, Washington, D.C. 20210). The Appendix lists several surveys of sex discrimination in public schools, which might be useful to women planning lawsuits.

56. Refer to the discussion of "state action" in Chapter I.

57. 42 U.S.C. §§295h-9, 298b-2 (Supp. V, 1975).

58. 45 C.F.R. Part 83.

59. *North Haven Board of Education v. Bell,* 102 S.Ct. 1912 (1982).

60. Alaska, Colorado, Connecticut, Hawaii, Illinois, Maryland, Massachusetts, Montana, New Hampshire, New Mexico, Pennsylvania, Texas, Utah, Virginia, Washington, and Wyoming.

61. 20 U.S.C.A. §§1706, 1709 (Supp. 1977).

62. 42 U.S.C. §2000c-6 (Supp. V, 1975).

63. *Cannon v. University of Chicago,* 441 U.S. 677 (1979).

64. "Stalled at the Start: Government Action on Sex Bias in the Schools," an excellent, comprehensive report of Title IX enforcement problems, is available for $1 from PEER (Project on Equal Education Rights), Suite 800, 1029 Vermont Avenue, N.W., Washington, D.C. 20005.

65. *Adams v. Califano,* C.A. No. 3095-70 (D. D.C. 1977).

66. Subsequently Harvard adopted a "sex-blind" admissions policy (applicants are considered without regard to sex) with the result that its male-female ratio is now approximately 1.5 to 1.

67. Women could even contend that this practice is unconstitutional. In effect, Title IX specifically allows the federal government to give money to schools that openly discriminate. Some women might want to sue the appropriate federal agencies to prevent them from doing so and to knock out these provisions of Title IX. One could argue that the due process guarantee of the Fifth Amendment (which makes equal protection concepts applicable to the federal government) forbids government funding of discriminatory programs, especially at *public* schools, which may already be operating in violation of the Equal Protection clause.

Another method is to attack the tax-exempt status of discriminatory private schools and the tax deductibility of gifts to these institutions. Blacks succeeded with these tactics, and there is no doubt that favorable rulings would have a powerful impact on such schools. See the discussion of *Green v. Connally* and *McGlotten v. Connally* at note 8, Chapter I.

IV

Mass Media—Radio and Television

"The Women's Rights Movement has declared war on radio and television," a leading feminist attorney once wrote. She explained why, in terms familiar to the many women who have been outraged by the media's treatment of women: "Television is one of the largest purveyors of prejudice and contempt toward women in this country. In program after program, it presents women as flighty, frivolous, simple-minded persons, childishly in need of masculine guidance. . . . [T]elevision characterizes women as incompetent, dependent and over-emotional, [and] . . . stereotypes their social roles."[1]

Women today can take positive action against this image; they need not simply avoid the problem by flicking off the television or radio. The law governing radio and television provides several avenues of attack that can be used to force these media to change their ways.

To understand this law, some background on local stations and federal regulation of them is in order. The television and radio industries are made up of local stations and national networks. Although the networks distribute most of the nationwide programming, they share advertising revenues with local stations, which do the actual broadcasting. It is these local stations that are regulated by the Federal Communications Commission (FCC).

Congress created this regulatory agency in the 1930's because of the problem of competing broadcasters who jammed up the airwaves so badly that no one could hear anything. To avoid this situation, the FCC was given the authority to grant particular stations a short-term monopoly to use a defined portion of the airwaves. Since only one station could use that wavelength at a time, the jamming was eliminated. The stations did not acquire ownership of the airwaves—which belonged to the public—but were given a *license* to broadcast for three years. (In 1981 Congress extended the license period to five years for television stations and seven years, for radio stations.) The license is granted on condition that the station operate "in the public interest, convenience, and necessity," and it must be renewed every five or seven years, as the case may be, for the station to continue to operate.

From this one seemingly simple condition of operation in the public interest, the FCC has defined many rights belonging to the general public. If a station does not act in certain ways, it is considered not to be acting in the "public interest, convenience, and necessity," and hence will lose its license. The public has the right to demand that each station act in these ways. What then are these rights of the public?

May a radio or TV station discriminate against its women employees or applicants?

No. Most stations are already forbidden to discriminate by the laws discussed in Chapter II: Title VII, the Equal Pay Act, Executive Order 11246, as amended by E.O. 11375, as well as by some state laws. Public broadcasters are also covered under the strict equal employment provisions of the Public Telecommunications Financing Act of 1978.[2] Finally, the FCC also has its own regulations that cover much of the same ground.[3] Some people might ask why these regulations should be used in addition to the other laws. The answer is that if women can make a strong showing that a station discriminates, it can be one step in challenging a station's license—and without a license, the station is out of business. The chances of revoking a station's license are in fact small, but the mere threat is a potent weapon and can lead to improvements in station policy.

What do the FCC regulations on employment discrimination require?

The FCC regulations require stations not to discriminate in employment and to adopt affirmative action plans to end discrimination.[4] Stations must file such plans with the commission when they apply for renewal of their license.* During this renewal period, licensees must also provide turnover rate information and pending employment discrimination complaints. Stations with more than 50 employees must also provide job title information. All of these materials are powerful tools that can be used to prove discrimination. The stations must also compile annual statistics for the FCC on the breakdown by sex and minority group of employees in every job category. Both the affirmative action plan and the statistics must be kept on file for the public to see at the local station. If you want to find out how the station is doing, ask for FCC Forms 395 and 396 A[5] (and write to the FCC if the station refuses to show them to you). Women employees or feminist advocacy groups can back up their claims of discrimination with this information.

However, unlike the EEOC, the FCC is not concerned so much with providing a remedy for any one individual who has been discriminated against as with assuring that a station complies with its equal employment opportunity rules overall. For example, if the station is generally in line with FCC rules, the commission will take no action if one woman is fired because of her sex. Moreover, the FCC does not require the percentage of women on the station's staff to reflect the percentage of women in the area's work force, as it should, but is satisfied if the staff level reaches 50 percent of the work-force level. The commission also accepts a station's affirmative action plan if it is "adequate" and if the statistics on the station's female employment fall within a "zone of reasonableness."[6] The FCC has, however, tightened this zone over time and will probably continue to do so.

If women employees and applicants at a station suspect job discrimination, what should they do?

File a complaint with the FCC. In addition, file with the EEOC and a state or local agency which handles job discrimination. (See Chapter II, "Employment Discrimination.") The FCC complaint should be addressed to:

---

*A pending FCC proposal—not finalized as this book went to press—would delete this provision. Thus the FCC would not examine the plan automatically, but only upon special request.

Chief, EEO Branch
Broadcast Bureau
Federal Communications Commission
1919 M. St., N.W.
Washington, D.C. 20554

Send a copy to the station if you want to, but this is not required.

There is no set form to follow, but the following items are good to include: the name (call numbers) of the station; all the ways in which you believe the station discriminates (see Chapter II, "Employment Discrimination"); an analysis of the station's affirmative action program and statistics showing how inadequate its measures are; a request for an investigation; and a demand for correction of the station's job bias.

Whenever possible, the FCC refers individual complaints of discrimination to the appropriate federal, state, or local agency.[7] Even though the FCC does not take action itself, you will be building a record that the station is not operating "in the public interest, convenience, and necessity." This could theoretically lead to the loss of its license. Although no station has ever been denied a license because it employed too few women or because its women employees were concentrated in low-level positions, many licenses have been granted for only a short term and in other cases stations have been forced to go to a hearing because of employment complaints. Thus women should continue to press the FCC to enforce an effective equal employment policy. The existence of employment discrimination complaints may also add to other pressures on and complaints about the station at license renewal time.

Do women a have right to have TV and radio stations broadcast news about the feminist movement fairly?

Yes. The FCC has often told stations that they have a duty to the public to broadcast fairly under the "fairness doctrine." By this, the commission means that a station must cover controversial and important public issues, and, in doing so, it must present both sides of an issue—not just the side in which it believes. Notice that there are two steps in reaching this result: first, the issue must be controversial and of "public importance"; second, the station must present both sides. In the past, the FCC has forced stations to broadcast both sides of many issues, including civil rights, pollution, and cigarette smoking.

However, generally the FCC will not challenge a station's news judgment unless there is evidence of a deliberate distortion of the news or a consistent bad-faith failure to report news events of public importance. Thus the FCC will not challenge a station that thinks the women's movement is not "newsworthy" enough to cover at all—unless it skips enough "news events of public importance." The reluctance of the FCC to review a station's editorial news judgment has been commended by one federal appellate court because of First Amendment values.[8]

Individuals should, however, write letters to their local stations to complain about or praise their programming. Each such letter must be kept in the station's public file.* At many stations the receipt of one consumer letter often inspires a memo to the producer, and ten letters may cause a meeting. Policymakers know that for every letter of concern, thousands of viewers feel the same way but do not take the time to write.

Could the fairness doctrine be used to force coverage of both sides of feminist issues in shows other than news programs?

In theory, yes. The list of possible women's rights issues takes in a wide range of concerns—from the right to abortion to the drafting of women.

Feminists should particularly demand that TV and radio stations treat the issue of a woman's role in the modern world more fairly. This issue is a dominant concern of a feminist movement that seeks to broaden the roles women can play. Television's record on this issue is not good. One major government study found that only 30 percent of the characters in television drama were women, who were shown primarily in sex-stereotyped traditional roles and occupations.[9] In addition, there had been no significant increase in the percentage of women and minorities holding top TV jobs between 1975 and 1977. Thus the white men in charge of the broadcasting media have allowed women to be portrayed in sharply limited roles.

No one knows the psychic harm done to adult women by the one-dimensional model presented so continuously on TV. Growing children, too, must suffer from its impact. Both boys

---

*An October 1981 FCC proposal—not yet finalized as this book went to press—would delete this requirement.

and girls are taught to conform to the stiff, stereotyped sex-role lines male society has mandated.

But the inaccurate portrayal and underrepresentation of women on television not only form and reinforce stereotyped attitudes; they also result in the denial of jobs to women who act, direct, write, and manage. Thus an equally serious concern is the lost energy and talent which might otherwise be used to bring the best possible television and radio to the public.

Can women request that stations present women in more diverse roles even though the stations say they merely reflect the reality of society?

Yes. To give a concrete example: if less than 5 percent of the nation's judges are women, must the stations ever show women judges or talk about the positive reasons for giving women judicial appointments? The answer would be yes. The issue meets the "fairness doctrine" standard of being controversial and of public importance (feminists have challenged the virtually all-male appointments to the bench to the point where candidates for the presidency even raise it as a campaign issue). And TV has to date presented only one side of the issue—that judges are, and by implication should be, male. According to the fairness doctrine, TV has an obligation to show all sides of an issue. Thus a station might air an interview discussing the issue with a feminist, do a documentary on women judges now on the bench, or portray judges as women in some dramatic program.

How should women raise the fairness issue?

There are several procedures to follow. The first and easiest step is to write to the broadcasting station, protesting a particularly offensive and one-sided view of some feminist issue. Identify the program and explain that the fairness standard has been violated (keep in mind, however, that the fairness doctrine applies only to "overall programming"); state what the issue is, why you believe it is a controversial issue of public importance, and that the opposite side has not been presented; request that the other viewpoint be presented. If the station fails to take satisfactory action, you can take the next step—filing a formal, legal complaint with the FCC. To do this, send a copy of your correspondence with the station to the FCC along with a separate letter of complaint. Your complaint should include everything that was included in the original letter to the station, plus the name of the station and the date and time of the broadcast.

If you know in advance that a biased program will be shown, file a complaint with the FCC before the broadcast and let the station know that you are prepared to sue. Often this will result in air time for the opposing viewpoint.

If the FCC is unresponsive to your complaint, you can review the fairness issue in a legal proceeding to deny the station its license renewal. This last step is the most time-consuming and costly, and it will require the help of a lawyer. It will also produce the best results. (For a description of proceedings to deny license renewal, see *infra*.) Groups and individuals without time, resources, or inclination to undertake this major effort can still make a valuable contribution by letter writing and lodging complaints with the FCC. Even these tactics will help build a record of women's protest nationwide—which in time may convince the FCC that fairness on women's issues is important, as well as force it occasionally to take steps against stations that consistently violate the standard.

If a TV or radio station attacks particular women or a feminist group by name, do the women have any right to reply?

Yes, under another FCC rule called the "personal attack doctrine." The right to reply arises when someone attacks the "honesty, character, integrity, or like personal qualities" of a person or group during the broadcast of views on a "controversial issue of public importance." Whenever this occurs, the station is required to send the person or group attacked a notice of the date, time, and name of the broadcast; a transcription or summary of the attack; and an offer of equal reply time. Two exceptions to the personal attack rule allow news programs (except for editorials) and candidates for public office to attack others without a right to reply. With these exceptions, this right should be fairly easy to enforce because the Supreme Court has accepted it.[10]

If the station fails to send notice of the attack and an offer of reply time, what should women do to enforce their right to reply?

Write to the station. Identify the broadcast and ask for a transcript and the right to reply. If this is unsuccessful, send a copy of the correspondence to the FCC, Complaints and Compliance Division, and ask for help.

Do stations have a duty to plan programs to meet the needs of women viewers?

The answer appears to be yes. The FCC's "community ascertainment" doctrine requires stations to ascertain the needs of all segments of the community and to plan programs to meet those needs. In television, but not radio, as part of the ascertainment process, stations are required to consult with leaders of community groups, including organizations of or for women, on a continuing basis.[11]

The FCC has defined 14 types of programming that TV stations should broadcast: opportunity for local expression; development and use of local talent; programs for children; religious programs; educational programs; public affairs programs; editorialization by licensees; political broadcasts; agricultural programs; news programs; weather and market reports; sports programs; service to minority groups; and entertainment programs. Women could demand programming to reflect women's needs in each of these areas. For instance, a station may insist that it broadcasts sports events sufficiently to meet the needs of the public. But the events almost never depict women athletes, so girls and women who are more interested in female sports, or who need female athletes as role models, find the sports programs inadequate. Similar reasoning applies to the other programming areas. Programs for "local expression" are likely to exclude any expression by women of their interests or limit such expression to women who conform to traditional expectations about the female role. Programs for children will often overemphasize the male child (just as children's books feature little boys more than little girls). With some imagination and thought, one could set forth other needs of women not met by current or planned programs in each of the 14 areas of required programming.

In sum, women need programming that responds to them

as full human beings, participating at every level of society, as well as programming that looks at issues from a feminist perspective.

What effect would deregulation of television and radio have on these doctrines?

Efforts are currently being made to dismantle much of the FCC's regulatory power—which is the basis for the little leverage women have over radio and television programming. In 1979 several bills were introduced in Congress to revise the Communications Act of 1934, which created the FCC and gave it regulatory authority. Each of these bills would have deregulated TV, radio, and other communications media. Several versions of the proposed legislation would have discarded the "public interest" standard, "community ascertainment," and the Fairness Doctrine (except for personal attack rules); thus these bills would have eliminated the requirements that stations operate "in the public interest, convenience, and necessity;" that they cover controversial and important public issues and in doing so present both sides of such issues; and that stations determine community needs, including women's needs, in planning programming. Although Congress had not yet acted on most of these bills as of early 1982, it did extend the three-year radio and TV license terms to five and seven years, respectively. Moreover, the deregulation movement is still strong; interested women should communicate to Congress their concern about the effect of deregulation on the role of women in the mass media.

In 1981 the FCC took action on its own to reduce the regulation of the radio industry.[12] Although this action did not remove the "public interest" standard, which is part of the Communications Act, it did eliminate the specific guidelines spelling out the steps that radio stations needed to undertake to find out community programming needs and the requirement that radio stations carry news and public affairs programming. Under the FCC action, marketplace forces determine all programming—if news does not "make money," it would not have to be broadcast. This approach is unlikely to guarantee adequate treatment of feminist issues. Women should write Congress to object, since a measure was pending there to codify the FCC approach, as of early 1982.

If all else fails, how can women force stations to be responsive to women's equal employment and programming concerns?

The only way this right can be enforced is through a lengthy legal battle over the station's right to a renewal of its broadcasting license. The legal document which starts this battle, and which raises the right to be consulted and to have responsive programming, is called a Petition to Deny License Renewal. The Petition to Deny is just what its name implies: your group will be asking the FCC to deny the station's request that its license be renewed at the end of the five- or seven-year license period; in other words, you will be asking to have the station put out of business.

Will you need a lawyer to file a Petition to Deny?

Yes, since the legal proceedings involved in filing it are fairly complicated. The proceedings are much like a lawsuit, except that they take place before the FCC instead of a court.

Must a Petition to Deny be filed within any time limit?

Yes. The station must file its application for renewal at least four months before the license expires. All licenses in one state expire on the same date. Write any of the organizations at the end of this chapter for the expiration date in your state, if you are interested in pursuing this option. After the station applies for renewal, you must file your petition at least 30 days prior to the license expiration date.

Can the attack on a station's license renewal be used to raise other issues besides the right to be consulted on women's needs and to have programming to meet those needs?

Yes. In fact, the Petition to Deny License Renewal provides the ideal opportunity to raise all of the issues already mentioned: sex discrimination in employment; unfair coverage of feminist issues; a failure to consult with women and to program to meet all of women's needs.

If women have already raised these issues in letters to the station and complaints to the FCC, their case against license renewal will be even stronger. In fact, women who plan to file a Petition to Deny in the future should coordinate a campaign of letters and complaints for the interim period in order to strengthen the final effort.

Is the FCC apt to deny license renewal to a station?

Statistically the chances are somewhat slim although the commission has done so in a few extreme instances. But the basic point is not always the loss of the license. The station does not want to be tied up in expensive legal maneuvering for years in order to have its license renewed. Thus, any group challenging license renewal will have significant leverage and can use this power to negotiate with and gain concessions from the station on all issues of women's rights.

What role can women's groups play in a Petition to Deny License Renewal?

Although women's groups should not file a Petition to Deny without the aid of a lawyer, they have a vital role in the proceedings. Women must decide which station to challenge and must monitor its programs for documentation of fairness violations and inadequate programming. This is a mammoth task, but it is essential to the success of the petition that an exhaustive feminist analysis be undertaken of all station programs for a certain period of time. The success of the monitoring will, in large part, determine your success in attacking the fairness and programming issues.

Are there any other times besides license renewal periods when women have leverage over broadcast stations?

Yes. Whenever a station transfers owners or merges with another company, it must obtain the FCC's approval. Generally millions of dollars are involved in such a transfer of license and the new owners are anxious to complete this process as quickly and easily as possible. Broadcasters tend to be extremely cooperative with feminist and other community groups during the negotiations for this transfer process, in part because if a community group objects or files a petition against the transfer, the sale of the station falls into a regulatory delay at the FCC and the sale usually is suspended.

Could women apply to the FCC to take away a license for themselves?

Yes, although this action would require substantial financial backing (hundreds of thousands of dollars for radio and millions for television) and detailed planning. One precedent exists, a case in which a minority group successfully pursued this route. An interested women's group would simply compete for the license when the existing station applied for its license renewal. A lawyer's help would be required.

Although competition for licenses will be difficult for women to undertake in the short run, in the long run it may be the only real answer to the degrading fare most stations presently feature. Minority groups have discovered that economic development is ultimately the way to make sure that your views prevail. Women must learn the same lesson.

Are there any unused channels that women might apply for?

There are not very many in major cities, but small towns and rural areas frequently have unused channels, both commercial and non-commercial. It would be easier to obtain unused channels than to compete for channels already in use and often owned by the powerful major networks. In addition, the FCC has recently approved the licensing of low-power TV stations. These offer opportunities for new television stations to be built, especially in small, rural communities. If you are interested in this option, write to the FCC for the booklet *How to Apply for a Broadcast License*.

Is there any way for feminists to influence the FCC on the policy decisions it makes?

Any group or individual has the right to ask the commission to make a rule—or broad policy statement—that will set standards for the broadcasters to follow. The legal document that commences this proceeding is called, appropriately enough, a Petition for Rulemaking. The National Organization for Women has already used this procedure to great effect. When the FCC first issued regulations requiring stations to cease discriminating in employment, stations were required to take two important steps. First, they were to draw up "affirmative action" plans showing how they intended to hire and promote more minorities and women. Second, they were to file these plans with the commission. There was, however, one important difference in the second step as far as women were concerned. The station did not have to send its plan for hiring women to the commission—only its plan for hiring minorities. Naturally this made a mockery of the whole procedure as it related to women.

NOW decided not to take this exclusion sitting down and filed a Petition for Rulemaking, which proposed that the women's plan be treated the same as the minority plan—that is, that it be filed, too. Other groups, including the ACLU, supported this position. After some deliberation, the FCC finally granted NOW's petition and changed its rule. The moral of this story is that sometimes it is not difficult to get an agency to take action—partly because the agencies are so unaccustomed to citizen action. This was a relatively simple legal proceeding and did not cost much money to initiate, but it laid the groundwork for effective action: every time a station files for a renewal of its license, the FCC is now supposed to examine the station's employment program for women (although in early 1982 the FCC was re-examining this requirement). However, in other rulemaking cases, petitions have been filed and action delayed for years.

Individuals and groups should, however, be encouraged to write to the FCC on policy issues. Or, while in Washington D.C., make an appointment to meet with FCC commissioners or staff.

What groups are concerned with broadcasting issues?

The National Organization for Women, which has long been involved in media issues, has a Media Reform Project. The project focuses on equal employment opportunities, public affairs and informational programming on women's issues, and female ownership of stations. For more information, contact:

> Media Reform Project
> NOW Legal Defense and Education Fund
> 425 13th St., N.W.
> Washington, D.C. 20004
> (202) 785–0345

The Media Access Project is a public interest law firm which specializes in petitions to deny license renewals and Fairness Doctrine complaints. It also represents citizen groups in rulemaking before the FCC and has opposed deregulation of radio. For legal assistance, contact:

Media Access Project
1609 Connecticut Ave., N.W.
Washington, D.C. 20009
   (202) 232–4300

Two other important public interest groups, concerned with equal and civil rights in broadcast licensing and deregulation, are:

Office of Communications
United Church of Christ
105 Madison Ave.
New York, N.Y. 10016
   (212) 683–5656

Citizens Communications Center
1424 16th St., N.W.
Washington, D.C. 20036
   (202) 483–0170

In addition, the FCC has opened an office to help consumers wade through its government bureaucracy. For help in any area of the broadcasting or cable industries, contact:

Office of Public Affairs
Consumer Assistance Office
Federal Communications Commission
1919 M. St., N.W.
Washington, D.C. 20554
   (202) 632–7000

NOTES

1. Nancy E. Stanley, "Federal Communications Law and Women's Rights: Women in the Wasteland Fight Back," 23 *Hastings Law Journal* 15, 16 (1971).
2. 47 U.S.C. §§309, 398.
3. 47 C.F.R. Part 73.
4. Chapter II, "Employment Discrimination," contains details on the definition of an affirmative action program.

5. Form 395 is the one containing the statistics. Form 396A is the affirmative action plan, which is filed with a station's application for license renewal or for a transfer.

6. "Nondiscrimination in the Employment Policies and Practices of Broadcast Licensees," 60 F.C.C. 2d 226, 228 (1976); *National Organization for Women, New York City Chapter v. FCC*, 555 F.2d 1002 (D.C. Cir. 1977).

7. "Nondiscrimination in the Employment Policies and Practices of Broadcast Licensees," 60 F.C.C. 2d 226, 244, 247 (1976).

8. *National Organization for Women, New York City Chapter v. FCC*, 555 F.2d 1002, 1010 (D.C. Cir. 1977).

9. A recent report by the U.S. Commission on Civil Rights documents the underrepresentation of women in television dramas and their portrayal only in traditional, stereotyped roles and occupations. U.S. Commission on Civil Rights, *Window Dressing on the Set: An Update* (Washington, D.C., 1979).

10. *Red Lion Broadcasting Company v. FCC*, 395 U.S. 367 (1969).

11. "Ascertainment of Community Problems by Broadcast Applicants, First Report and Order," 57 F.C.C. 2d 418 (1976), Appendix B, pp. 441–442.

12. *FCC: Inquiry and Proposed Rulemaking: Deregulation of Radio*, 44 *Federal Register* 57636 (Oct. 5, 1979); the final approval is set forth at 84 FCC 2d 968 (1981).

V

Crimes and Juvenile Delinquency

When a woman law student asked her male law professor for leads on studying women convicted of committing crimes, his reaction was: "Women criminals? There aren't any!" He was wrong, of course. Many women and girls are convicted of committing crimes and juvenile offenses. And the laws defining these crimes and offenses, as well as the men who enforce the laws, are often biased against women. To correct these biases, we must analyze the laws, the sentences given women, and the treatment of women once they are convicted.

Criminal law itself cannot be discussed in terms of "women's rights." Convicted women by and large have not yet won the right to equal treatment in the criminal and juvenile justice system. As the professor's remark indicated, this is because convicted women have been largely ignored—by the law schools, the courts, the lawyers, and the public. The first step toward fair treatment is understanding their condition.

A. Sentencing

Is a law allowing women to be given longer sentences than men for the same crime constitutional?

No. One right convicted women do have is the right to equal sentences. Laws providing for unequal sentences have been attacked in Connecticut, Pennsylvania, and New Jersey. Courts have struck down these laws on the ground that they violated the 14th Amendment guarantee of equal protection,[1] or a state equal rights amendment.[2] In Connecticut and Pennsylvania, the courts released women who had already served sentences longer than the maximum a man could serve.

Differential sentencing laws offer a valuable lesson of the danger to women of laws that purport to accord them "favored" treatment. Most laws defining a particular crime also prescribe the maximum sentence for that crime. However, in the Connecticut and Pennsylvania cases, the women concerned were each sentenced under a law applicable to women only—one providing for what is termed indeterminate sentencing. This law provides, for example, that if a *woman* is convicted of any crime having a maximum sentence of less than three years, she must be given an indeterminate sentence of a full three years. Notice that if the crime is punishable by less than three years—say one and one half years—the maximum time she may have to serve is greater than the maximum time she would get without indeterminate sentencing. Since the indeterminate sentencing law applies only to a woman, her sentence is potentially longer than the time any *man* could serve for the same violation.

It was originally thought that indeterminate sentencing was a progressive measure, beneficial to women. People believed that it placed more emphasis on a prisoner's behavior and that a woman, if she were a model prisoner, could get out on parole after a brief period. This procedure contrasted with the usual practice of setting both a *minimum* sentence, which a prisoner must serve before getting out, and a *maximum*. In practice, however, the parole boards that determined when a prisoner could leave for good behavior were more prone to let people stay the *maximum* time than to let them out earlier; hence, most women in states with indeterminate sentencing for women only ended up serving longer sentences than men.

Many states have indeterminate sentencing laws for prisoners of both sexes and in these states, whatever other problems may exist with this form of sentence, sex discrimination is not an issue. However, wherever there is a special, "good" law for women, they end up in a worse position than men.[3] The moral is clear: never work for laws that apply only to women; support laws that apply equally to men and women in order to prevent later abuse of women under the guise of "beneficial" single-sex laws.

How many states have laws that permit longer sentences for women?

No one has yet made a careful study to find the answer. Experts believe, however, that a close study of the laws and their operation would reveal a high incidence of different sentencing laws and practices for men and women. Such laws are not always readily ascertainable, but a study should be undertaken with an eye to ending this practice.[4]

Do any states give men longer sentences than women?

Yes, and one court has upheld this practice. A man who escaped from a Maine prison farm was sentenced to from 6 to 12 years, although the maximum penalty for a woman convicted of escaping from a woman's reformatory in Maine is 11 months. The Maine court upheld the difference, using stereotypical views of men and women to find that different treatment was reasonable, and the Supreme Court refused to review the case.[5]

In addition, one study suggests that courts may treat adult male criminals more harshly than adult female criminals.[6] In grand larceny and felonious assault cases during 1962, there were statistically significant differences between the treatment of men and women: a smaller percentage of men were released on bail; had their cases dismissed or were acquitted; or received suspended sentences or probation when convicted. The study has limited value, however, since there was no attempt to control for the severity of the crime. It is possible that women received less harsh treatment because they in fact stole property of less value or committed less violent assaults than did men on the average. Certainly this would accord with the social conditioning most women receive.

The study raises enough questions to merit further studies, scientifically controlled for the severity of the crime, to find out whether the enforcement of criminal laws is even-handed for men and women. If the studies showed unequal enforcement, they would reveal serious equal protection issues that should be included in the defense of male defendants affected by such enforcement patterns.

B. Juvenile Delinquency

Do girl juvenile delinquents ever get longer sentences than boys?

Yes. This happens in two ways. National statistics show that girls serve longer sentences on the average than do boys, even though girls are sentenced for less serious matters.[7] This situation does not seem to arise from any laws but rather from the informal practices of courts and correction authorities, who apparently are more shocked by girls who misbehave than by boys; thus they see to it that girls serve longer sentences as a more severe punishment.

In addition, all juveniles are likely to serve longer sentences when there is no adult willing to take them home, and girls' families are often so incensed by their sexual activity that they refuse to let them return home. Authorities then ought to, but do not, neutralize the effects of the families' prejudices by releasing the girls anyway.

Many states, moreover, have passed juvenile delinquency laws that make girls liable under them at a later age than boys.[8] For example, a juvenile delinquency law forbidding running away from home may apply to girls up to 18 years old, but to boys only up to 16 years. Here a 17- or 18-year-old girl is subject to punishment for conduct that is not punished at all in a boy of that age. Sometimes the discrimination under these laws runs in the opposite direction, as when the juvenile delinquency law covers behavior that would be criminal if done by an adult. In this instance, a juvenile will receive more favorable treatment under the juvenile delinquency law than under the adult criminal law; hence, the 16-to-18 age differential works in favor of the girl. But where the juvenile delinquency offense is something like running away from home, there is no criminal penalty for adults and the age differential thus favors boys.

Do longer sentences for female juvenile delinquents also violate the Equal Protection Clause?[9]

One of the courts that struck down longer sentences for adult women later faced the same question for minors. Connecticut law allowed girls under 21 to be sentenced for three years, but boys under 21 (convicted for the same offense) for only two years. The judge said this was illegal and ordered the release of Ada Sumrell, who had already served *more* than two years—the maximum for a boy—for "breach of the peace."[10] In another case, a court struck down a New York juvenile delinquency statute that punished girls for being "persons in need of supervision" until age 18, but boys only until 16. The "PINS" law did not prohibit any crimes and thus discriminated against girls.[11] Similarly, although a state court upheld an Oklahoma juvenile delinquency law that operated to discriminate against boys, saying that the law was based on the "demonstrated facts of life," a federal court later found the law unconstitutional.[12]

No one has yet challenged the practices of those judges and social workers who give longer sentences to girls than to boys—not because a statute requires them to, but because of their biases. This is a widespread problem, and lawyers should begin challenging the practice. They will have to develop evidence to document the charge that girls get longer sentences than boys, which may involve looking into the statistical pattern of the sentencing decisions of selected judges and comparing girls' to boys' sentences, over a period of time, for particular offenses. This would be a good project for women's organizations to undertake under the direction of a feminist lawyer.

May girls be convicted under juvenile delinquency laws for acts for which boys are not punished?

Yes, in many jurisdictions. Sometimes it is blatantly written into the law. For instance, Connecticut makes it a crime to be an unmarried girl between 16 and 21 who is in "manifest danger of falling into habits of vice." No boy can be convicted of this.[13]

Far more often the practice is simply a result of the attitudes of social workers and judges. If girls run away from home, disobey their parents, have a child without marrying, or are promiscuous, they are branded as juvenile delinquents. Boys engaged in the same conduct are seldom even referred to juvenile court.

A major attack on these unjust practices should be launched. This means educating girls to demand that their lawyers raise the defense that boys are not punished for these acts, and it

means educating lawyers to raise that defense. It also means
working for new laws sharply defining which acts constitute
juvenile delinquency and stipulating that the same standards
must be applied to boys and to girls. Finally, it means watch-
ing to see that new standards are in fact enforced equally
against girls and boys.

This campaign should not be too difficult in the long run. If
judges are shocked when they learn girls receive longer sentences than boys for the very same offense, they will be even
more shocked when they learn girls are punished for some
things boys are not punished for at all.

C. Prison Conditions

**May a convicted woman be sent to a more restrictive institu-
tion than a man guilty of the same crime?**

Probably not. One court has dealt with this practice and
found it unconstitutional.[14] A woman sent to a state penitentiary wanted to go to the county jail, where men were sent
for less serious crimes like hers. She did not want to be sent
to the penitentiary where "confirmed, hardened criminals
convicted of more serious crimes" were sent. She eventually
won the right to the county jail sentence. Ironically, this
particular problem arises out of the fact that there are so few
women criminals; consequently, there are very few criminal
institutions for women, and a whole range of women—from
those awaiting trial to those who are hardened criminals—
tend to be thrown together in one setting.

**Must women prisoners be given facilities, training, and
education equal to those given men?**

Yes. In 1979, women inmates in Michigan won an important lawsuit challenging a host of conditions at the all-female
prison as sex discrimination in violation of the Constitution.[15]
The judge's opinion detailed myriad deficiencies in the Huron
Valley Women's Facility. For example, the vocational training offered women prepared them in only five broad areas—
office occupations, food service, graphic arts, building
maintenance (really, custodial techniques), and general shop.
Men had access to 20 different vocational programs, including
automobile servicing, heating and air conditioning, machine

shop, and drafting. Even where both men and women received training in the same broad area, the men's training was superior; where women were taught home-cooking skills, the men learned commercial cooking skills. Men were offered apprenticeships in many trades (millwright, machinist, machine repair, tool maker, tool-and-die maker, industrial maintenance electrician, draftsman, and tool-and-die designer); women were offered none. Men were given jobs in prison industry, with its higher wages and bonuses; women were given none.

A multitude of similar problems led the judge to find:

> . . . the rehabilitation opportunities afforded [women prisoners] are substantially inferior to those available to the State's male prisoners in terms of both the quality and variety of programming offered. By providing them with fewer and poorer educational and vocational programs, as well as less adequate facilities and equipment, and by denying them access to supplemental programs like work pass and incentive good time, the State has unnecessarily deprived women inmates of valuable rehabilitative experience.

As a result, the judge ordered Michigan to take comprehensive action, including upgrading the women's post-secondary education program to make it comparable to the men's; undertaking an extensive vocational counseling and testing program to inform women of the job possibilities and wage scales in traditionally male fields; starting new vocational programs in areas in which the women expressed an interest; giving women apprenticeship training and prison industry programs, as well as work-pass and correctional camp work; and installing a legal education program for women.

In the wake of this decision, women in other state prisons have started similar lawsuits. For further information, contact the lawyer who handled the Michigan case:

Center for Urban Law
1500 David Scott Building
Detroit, Mich. 48226
  (313) 962–9015

These cases are particularly important to bring because the training and education now offered women prisoners are clearly designed to funnel them into the lowest-paying jobs of our society: waitress, household worker, beautician, housewife—the classic "female" jobs. While the training at men's prisons is far from adequate, it at least offers somewhat better options.

Training is not the only area in which women's institutions are deficient. On the surface, women's prisons are gentler and less violent places than men's prisons. It does not follow that they are better equipped or better staffed. Indeed, the conditions in women's prisons are usually ignored. Women often lack libraries (especially law libraries) and sports and recreation facilities. Nor do women receive adequate medical and psychiatric care or individual counseling. In all these areas, lawyers should seek to bring to women prisoners the same facilities and opportunities men have. On the other hand, if women's prisons have more physical comforts and less rigid social control than men's prisons, the effort ought to be to bring the men up to par.

It is important to remember that the training facilities and care available in men's prisons are often in a deplorable state. We are not talking about unequal protection of the laws in the classic sense that men always get good treatment and women bad treatment. The major reason that women should focus on the treatment of *women* prisoners is not only that they receive unequal treatment. It is also that no one else is interested in women prisoners, and their situation is usually at least as bad as, if not worse than, the situation of male prisoners.

Other conditions in prisons have improved because of recent litigation. Women prisoners have won the right to wear slacks, to have contact visits, to get regular outdoor exercise, to have better work release opportunities, and to have improved access to legal research facilities. Others have been granted the right to outside medical specialists and psychiatric care, methadone maintenance programs, annual physical examinations, and prenatal care for pregnant inmates.[16]

(The effort to achieve better treatment for women prisoners should not blind us to a central fact. Most women now in prison are confined for sex-related offenses, such as prostitution, and should not be in prison at all—if they were men, they would not be there for such offenses. So although prison reform efforts must be made, the major thrust should be to get these women out of prison. This coincides with the broader current movement to decriminalize many activities and to eliminate prisons for non-violent criminals.)

What can women's groups do about unequal treatment in prisons?

One of the most severe problems faced by women prisoners is isolation. No one is interested in them; no one offers to help; no one communicates. An immediate way to alleviate this condition is simply to establish contact.

In Washington, D.C., Ann Cuningham started a Visitors' Services Center at the suggestion of chaplains working in D.C. jails. People working for the center make regular visits to the prisons, help arrange transportation and baby-sitting so that families can visit the prisoners, bring reading materials and make telephone calls for the prisoners, and help provide community contact when the prisoner comes out of jail. Even more important, the center helps straighten out courtroom mixups. The center provides an invaluable service in itself, and people working there will also learn in more detail about the basic problems and needs of women's institutions. Those interested in starting such a project should contact:

Visitors' Services Center for D.C. Jails
261 17th St., S.E.
Washington, D.C. 20003
  (202) 544–2131

It may even be possible to get federal funding for such a project, as the Visitors' Services Center did. The Law Enforcement Assistance Administration, a federally funded granting agency, along with private foundations and church groups, funded this project.

A second project would be to study and compare the conditions in jails, prisons, and other institutions to see how men and women, and girls and boys, are treated. This could be done under the direction of feminist lawyers and could lead to a campaign for legislative change. Where the differences between men's and women's treatment are blatant, the study might lead to a lawsuit. Feminists should be careful, though, to avoid the old pitfall of establishing different standards for men and women. Such standards can be the basis for later mistreatment of women, even unintentional mistreatment. Examples include recent concern about the sex life of male criminals and about the relationship of female criminals to their children. There has been discussion of ways to allow the men—but not the women—some heterosexual relations while in jail. This is fine, but women have sexual needs, too, and they should be equally protected. Similarly, some attention has focused on practices that deprive women prisoners of their children; no attention is paid to men, presumably on the ground that they are not interested. If methods can be established to allow a woman to keep her children, and even to see them while she is still institutionalized, the same effort should be made for men. Otherwise we are back setting up societal pressures that force women to care for children and teach men that they should not.

A closely related problem is that of pregnancy. Here, obviously, women have unique problems: the availability of abortions for those who do not want to give birth; the quality of health care for those who do. The indications are that practices in institutions will have to be corrected on both scores.

A third project feminists might undertake is to teach women prisoners and juvenile delinquents their legal rights. The absence of the "jailhouse lawyer" among women prisoners is conspicuous, and it is a problem that might easily be rectified. Students in a course on "Women and the Law" might assist in such efforts. Women students at Rutgers University Law School in New Jersey have engaged in a project of this kind, under the direction of women lawyers. They have taught women prisoners in the Correctional Facility for Women at Clinton, New Jersey; the course covers the rights of criminal defendants and prisoners and also focuses on such issues as indeterminate sentencing and the treatment of women in women's prisons. The students report that the women prisoners are enthusiastic about the course. Similar projects are under way in Philadelphia (led by Villanova students) and New York (Carol Shapiro supervises work at the women's prison in Bedford, New York).

For further information, contact the supervisor of the Rutgers seminar:

Prof. Nadine Taub
Rutgers University Law School
15 Washington St.
Newark, N.J. 17102
    (201) 648–5637

Is it legal to maintain separate prisons for women and men?
At the moment, it seems reasonably clear that no court would ever find separate prisons illegal because they violate the Equal Protection Clause. Under state equal rights provisions, however, separate prisons might be illegal except for a separation of sleeping and bathing facilities, in the interest of privacy.

D. Prostitution and Other Sex Offenses

Do men and women have the same legal right to engage in sexual activity?
Emphatically not—and the denial of women's rights in this area is particularly severe, since a woman is often sent to prison or centers for juvenile delinquents if she attempts to assert her rights. This, after all, is the meaning of laws that make prostitution and solicitation a crime and that brand as juvenile delinquents young girls who are promiscuous or who become pregnant out of wedlock. Although it seems obvious that the central focus of all these laws is to punish *sexual activity*, that focus has been obscured by the technical definition of prostitution. Thus many women have not sensed as clearly as they should the essential injustice of sending the female prostitute to prison but allowing the male customer to go free.

Of course, it is not just the laws that mandate this result. Unequal enforcement, which results from the fact that most officials who administer the criminal system are male, also has its effects. Male district attorneys do not prosecute men for "patronizing a prostitute" (often a crime, though defined as less serious than prostitution) or for "aiding and abetting" (always a crime) a woman to commit prostitution. Nor are judges likely to find men guilty under such statutes. In fact, one of the few times this was ever attempted, the public uproar was immediate and powerful. In the summer of 1970, the Washington, D.C., police instituted an aggressive program of arresting male suburban customers—but the male outcry brought the program to a halt in four weeks. Even then the purpose of the campaign was revealing. The police basically wanted to protect men against "dangerous" ghetto prostitutes and get the men to go to other, "safer" spots. There was not the slightest hint that the campaign was intended to equalize enforcement of the laws.

In response to the argument that these laws and attitudes show a sexist bias against women, some people reply that male homosexuals are also actively prosecuted for solicitation. If males are prosecuted, it is thought, the law must not be biased. This response is inadequate, however, because the only males punished are those considered "deviant" by the male establishment. In fact, neither women nor "deviant" men should be punished for solicitation that leads to sex between consenting adults—just as "normal" men are never punished for such activity.[17]

Is there any way to establish an equal right to sexual activity?

Yes, but the solutions are long-term ones. First, push for legislative repeal of the laws that make women's participation in sex illegal, that is, all prostitution, solicitation, and juvenile delinquency laws used to punish females, but not males, for sexual activity.

Second, litigation strategy warrants attention. Lawyers for women prosecuted under these laws could try to establish that the laws violate the Equal Protection Clause. It will be a difficult issue to win, so firm is the conviction that the act of receiving money, rather than giving money for sex makes a difference. Two courts have in fact ruled that the practice of arresting the prostitute, but not her male customer, violates the Equal Protection Clause,[18] but others have condoned this discrimination.[19]

Lawyers could also argue that the laws are invalid because they violate the constitutional rights to privacy, to freedom of expression, and to freedom of association, and they are unconstitutionally vague and overbroad. These arguments, however, have also been rejected by two courts,[20] though they may still be tested elsewhere.

It may be easier to win the right to sexual activity for

juvenile girls than for adult women, since most of the laws girls are sentenced under theoretically apply equally to boys. If the lawyers can prove that more girls than boys are punished under these laws, then it will be clear that the law is being enforced unequally, which should be a violation of the Equal Protection Clause.

A third strategy for establishing an equal right to sexual activity for both girls and women might be to push for enforcement of aiding and abetting and "patronizing a prostitute" laws against men. A really firm campaign to do this—instead of challenging enforcement of the laws directed against women—would probably upset men so much that they might even join in the effort to get rid of the laws altogether.

If the laws against prostitution and solicitation were repealed or struck down, would any problems remain?

Perhaps. People who talk about legalizing prostitution often want to set up special centers for prostitutes and certify them medically safe for the customer. In other words, there is still a strong urge, among those who oppose the laws, to impose restrictive conditions on women prostitutes but not on men customers. In fact, it is rarely the women professionals who spread VD. Here, as elsewhere, the guiding principle should be to seek equal treatment. If a woman must have periodic health examinations to protect the men from VD, then the male customers should also be screened for VD in order to protect the women. If the male customer is exempted, then so too should be the woman professional.

E. The Crime of Rape

Does the law protect women against rape?

Theoretically, yes; in reality, very little. The reasons stem from a complex of mutually contradictory male ideologies about women, which have been enshrined in the law of rape. Ideology number one is that women are vindictive and/or psychopathic creatures who frequently turn in an innocent sex partner to the police as a rapist out of spite or revenge. A prominent legal authority on rules of evidence asserts, for instance:

Modern psychiatrists have amply studied the behavior of errant young girls and women coming before the courts in all sorts of cases. Their psychic complexes are multifarious, distorted partly by inherent defects, partly by diseased derangements or abnormal instincts, partly by bad social environment, partly by temporary physiological or emotional conditions. One form taken by these complexes is that of contriving false charges of sexual offences by men. [21]

Ideology number two is that most women want to be raped, and ask for it by wearing sexually suggestive clothing and by walking around in strange places instead of staying home. This helps account for the popularity of the suggestion, frequently advanced when a rash of rapes occurs, that a curfew ought to be imposed—but on the female victims rather than the male aggressors!

Ideology number three is that only a "pure" woman can be raped; if she has ever indulged in sex before, particularly with the accused rapist, she could not possibly have been raped. If she doesn't drink or smoke, this will strongly support her story.

Ideology number four is that women are chaste, delicate creatures, belonging to particular men, and that rape is thus a particularly heinous crime since it involves a violation of both the woman's unique purity and the man's property rights. In Bangladesh, for instance, husbands refused en masse, out of a sense of outraged male ownership, to remain with wives who had been raped by the invading Pakistanis.

These ideologies form the basis for several legal doctrines that have the net effect of making it extraordinarily difficult in many states to convict a man of rape, but that subject the woman victim to humiliating treatment by the police and the courts. All kinds of special evidence rules, unique to the crime of rape, are set up in order to protect the accused male against woman's vindictive spirit. These rules reflect two basic assumptions about women and rape: that "the woman will usually lie," and that "the woman really consented, so it wasn't rape."

"The Woman Will Usually Lie"

The most important manifestation of this assumption comes with the requirement that various aspects of the crime—unlike any other crime—be corroborated by evidence other than the victim's testimony, since it is presumed that the woman victim will lie. The word of the victim is not enough, as it is in other crimes. Thus in many states, to convict a man the prosecutor must prove through evidence independent of the woman's testimony that she was penetrated, that force was used, and/or that the man accused was the actual person who did it. In some cases, these things are difficult, if not impossible, to prove. Many women's first step after being raped will be to douche themselves, thus destroying the sperm which is the proof of penetration. In addition, many rapists are ejaculatory impotents and do not deposit sperm in the woman's vagina even when there is penetration. Proof of penetration, in these cases, is never possible. Proving force is even more difficult. A woman victim can point to her bruises to show that force was used, but many men, including judges, believe that women enjoy a little violence as part of normal sex—and thus refuse to consider bruises as evidence of sex without consent. Finally, corroborating the identity of the assailant is a third difficult problem. This rule practically requires that a third-party eyewitness be present at the rape—and that, of course, is quite rare. Such strict standards of corroboration make a conviction for the crime of rape almost impossible. The statistics for New York City show the depth of the problem: in 1971, of 1085 arrests for rape, the state secured only 18 convictions.

The belief that the woman will lie leads to other legal doctrines besides corroboration. A woman's failure to go to the police promptly can be used to attack her credibility on the witness stand. So deep is this distrust of women that in some states the court can allow the defendant's lawyer to have the *victim* subjected to psychiatric examination and present the results to the jury. Victims of other crimes are not normally subjected to such treatment.

"She Really Consented, So It Wasn't Rape"

The second element of protection for the accused male lies in inferences the law permits in determining whether the woman was a willing partner. A woman's prior lack of virginity or her reputation for unchastity can be used by the accused rapist's lawyer as evidence to cast doubt on her claim that she did not consent. Her prior consent to intercourse with the accused male also can be used in the same way to disprove a rape. In practical effect, this can amount to licensing any man who has once slept with a woman to rape her in the future with impunity. And finally, some states require that the woman must have resisted before the state will say she did not consent to the act. This is absurd in a day when most women are told by the police themselves—and have ample reason to believe—that it is best not to resist, in order to save one's life.

In conclusion, it must be said that some of these defenses have probably been created because the penalties for rape are often unreasonably high. Rape has been equated with murder in terms of the sentences imposed; understandably, this harshness contributes to an extreme reluctance to find a man guilty.

What is the practical effect of these evidence rules for the rape victim?

The rules discussed above are not mere abstract injustices. Because these rules exist, both the police and lawyers will often ask the woman probing and humiliating questions about her past sex life, whether she ever slept with the accused, what kind of clothes she was wearing, what she was doing in that part of town anyway, and on and on. If the woman decides to go to court to testify against the rapist, much of this questioning will take place on the witness stand, often with much publicity. The best tactic the accused man's lawyer can use is to throw doubt on the woman's every word. He will do everything he can to make her appear promiscuous or vindictive or hostile toward men, or perhaps even sexually disturbed. What would a nice girl be doing at that time of day, in that part of town, with that clothing on? This will be the implication behind every question. And while it is theoretically the duty of the prosecuting lawyer to object to those questions, most of the prosecuting lawyers are men, who may secretly believe in the implications behind the questions and therefore not object to improper questioning. The net result will be that the rapist goes free, the woman suffers unnecessary humiliation, and other women learn the lesson: don't bother to report a rape or attempted assault to the police, because neither the police nor the courts will help you.

What can be done to make the laws more effective in protecting women against rape?

All special rules applied solely in rape trials must be done away with. This means doing away with the assumption that women will lie: there should be no special corroboration requirements, no inferences drawn from the fact that a woman didn't go to the police right away, and no suggestion that the victim be psychoanalyzed.[22] Reform also requires a realistic notion of consent: there should be no requirement that a woman resist, and no inference drawn because she has slept with other men or even, in the past, with the rapist himself.

The requirement that a woman be penetrated should also be abolished. Whether or not a man merely touches his genitals to an unwilling woman or penetrates her makes no difference in terms of the intended humiliation and invasion of her privacy that lie at the core of the crime of rape. And the requirement of penetration leads to degrading and meaningless searches for sperm—meaningless if the man is an ejaculatory impotent or if the victim douches before she goes to the police.

By itself, abolishing these rules will do much to eliminate the unjust treatment a woman can receive when she is raped. Today, the woman victim still is often subjected to intense humiliation from the salacious inquiries the police sometimes indulge in to the outrageous cross-examination the woman is often subjected to when she testifies about the crime in court. If the special evidence rules were abolished, these humilating questions would no longer be relevant and therefore could no longer be asked.

Since this chapter was first written in 1973, almost half of the states and the federal government have reformed their rape evidence laws.[23] The usual reform is to restrict the use of evidence concerning the rape victim's past sexual behavior or reputation for chastity. The new laws provide that such evidence must be presented first to the judge, sitting alone without a jury, who then decides whether it is relevant and may be admitted at trial.[24] Eight states have also repealed their special corroboration requirements for rape cases[25] so that a rape victim's testimony alone is legally sufficient to make out a case. The real impact of these reforms is difficult to assess, but they should improve the treatment of rape victims at trial, and they should be sought in the remaining states.

How do women go about changing these rules in states where no reforms have occured?

The first effort should take place in actual trials, where lawyers can ask the court to change judge-made rules. Feminist groups should contact prosecutors to try to convince them to raise these issues. Women victims should try to retain their own lawyers to represent them while they are testifying, and these lawyers should also challenge special rules applied solely to rape. If change cannot be achieved through the courts, a drive should be launched in the state legislatures to abolish special rules for rape.

Women should also seek new laws setting lower penalties for rape, penalties parallel to those imposed for aggravated assault, for instance. Although it sounds anomalous to urge lower sentences, actually this should help to assure more convictions. Experts are convinced that one reason the special evidence rules have been created, and so few convictions obtained, is the legitimate reluctance to give a man a life sentence for the act of rape. If the penalties are lowered to a more realistic level, the emotional climate in favor of the accused will be reduced. A step in the right direction occurred when the Supreme Court ruled that the death penalty for rape is a cruel and unusual punishment forbidden by the Eighth Amendment[26] and can no longer be imposed for this crime.

Can a man be convicted of raping his wife?

Not in most states.

Current laws give women virtually no protection against rapes by their husbands (although a husband can be prosecuted for assisting a third person to rape his wife). Most states exclude rapes within marriage from the coverage of rape laws, even where husband and wife are separated. The rationale for this exclusion is the common-law view that by marrying, the wife has consented to all future sexual contacts with her husband, including violent ones.

In the past few years, several states—e.g., Oregon, New Jersey, Iowa, and Delaware—have rewritten their rape laws to protect wives from being sexually assaulted by their husbands. Indeed, in a much publicized case, an Oregon man was prosecuted under one of these revised laws for beating and raping his wife although the jury acquitted him. (The couple was reconciled but later divorced.) And in 1979 a Massachusetts man was convicted of raping his estranged wife in the first conviction of its kind in that state.

Women in other states should press for legislation to outlaw spousal rape. In doing so, they must consider two questions:
(1) Should rape by a spouse be prosecuted like any other rape or should it be treated as a lesser offense? (Perhaps it should be covered by domestic relations law rather than by criminal law.)
(2) Should the penalty for spousal rape be lower than for other forms of rape? (This might increase the probability that juries would convict.) Although spousal rape laws will not eliminate marital violence, their passage will at least serve notice that society no longer condones sexual assaults by husbands on their wives.

Can any practical measures be adopted to help the rape victim?

There are several practical steps women can take to avoid some of the humiliating treatment they now receive from the time they first report the crime to the police to the time they testify in court. Until these measures are undertaken, women will remain victims—victims of the police, the lawyers, and the judges.

First, when you report the crime, take a strong friend along—possibly one who is a lawyer or law student. You want someone who is cool, calm, sure of herself, and will stand up for your rights at a time when you may be least able to do so. The role of the friend will be to help you assert your rights and to protect you against salacious questioning (such as forcing you to repeat all the details of the rape over and over to inordinately curious male police officers).

Second, refuse to answer questions about your past sex life. This is no one's business, and it is irrelevant to whether or not you have been raped. Even if the police insist that your sexual experience is relevant because of the special evidence rules, reply that you will be challenging those rules and will not answer. Go to the inquiring officers' superiors, if necessary.

Third, take a friend with you when the police send you to a doctor or hospital. The friend will help you object to improper treatment. One of the most frequent complaints rape victims make concerns the rude, abrupt, and hostile medical examinations they are given by police doctors. Such doctors often refuse to treat the victim but merely examine her to make sure that she has been raped. You should also go to your own doctor for treatment afterward, including getting an anti-pregnancy pill.

An important service that women's groups could perform in this area would be to meet with the police medical authorities to explain the problems with present procedures and attitudes in order to get considerate treatment for rape victims. Another service would be to set up a panel of doctors (and especially women doctors) who would be willing to give post-rape treatment in cases where police medical treatment is inadequate and women do not have family doctors they can go to immediately. The women's groups could publicize a phone number for rape victims; women who called would be given the name of a doctor who would see them. A number of trained women could also be on hand to accompany any victim when she made her report to the police; their services could be offered at the same time the woman calls in for a doctor's name. Women's groups would thus develop relationships with sympathetic doctors and gain firsthand knowledge of the kinds of abuse most prevalent at police stations. Experience in developing a service of the kind suggested could provide ammunition for later organizational efforts to make the police change their practices.

Fourth, discuss with the prosecutor the evidence he will be using at the trial and the kinds of questions you will be asked, both by him and by the lawyer for the accused rapist. If the questions are humiliating or unnecessary, explain to him why and request that the questions not be asked or that he object to such questions by the defendant's lawyer. Go over his head, if necessary.

Fifth, try to get your own lawyer for the actual trial. You want someone who will object if improper questions, based on the special evidence rules, are asked of you by the defendant's lawyer. Of course, you will have to answer if the court orders you to do so—that is, if your lawyer has been unsuccessful in getting the court to rule that the particular questions are unnecessary.

Theoretically the prosecutor should raise objections, but he often will not, and the result can be humiliating if you don't have a lawyer whose special role is to protect your interests. Your lawyer, in fact, should explain to the judge that he or she is there to protect your reputation. Your lawyer should also discuss with you in advance the kinds of evidence that will be used at the trial so that you understand what will happen once you are in the courtroom.

Sixth, women's groups should meet with the police and prosecuting attorneys to explain what women find objectionable about present procedures, and they should seek institutional change in these procedures.

Seventh, use the employment discrimination laws to get more women into the police forces, the district attorney's office, and on the bench. A major part of the problem is that the rape victim faces an essentially all-male system from the moment she reports the crime to the day of the trial. Men in our society frequently believe that all women have secret fantasies of being raped; there is seldom a discussion of male fantasies of raping women. Men with such beliefs or fantasies cannot help but be biased against the woman rape victim.

Change in this area will not be accomplished easily. Women will be dealing with very conservative forces. Policemen, lawyers, and judges are accustomed to handling rape cases in one way. They will not welcome reports from women that they themselves are mistreating rape victims, and that reforms are necessary to correct that mistreatment. Nevertheless, if women organize, they should be able to effect change in this area as in others.

What can women's paralegal groups do in this area?
They can run a rape crisis center to help women who have been raped. Such centers can start rape hotlines and can

provide counseling (or referrals) for rape victims; advocates to help victims in their contacts with police, hospitals, and courts; companionship; general information; speakers' bureaus; classes in self-defense; and public relations information for the media. The first such center, established in January 1972, has a pamphlet entitled *How to Start a Rape Crisis Center*, available for $4 to $5. Write:

> D.C. Rape Crisis Center
> P.O. Box 21005
> Washington, D.C. 20009
>   (202) 232–0203

For other centers, see Chart D (3) in the Appendix.

NOTES

1. *Robinson v. York*, 281 F.Supp. 8 (D. Conn. 1968); *Commonwealth v. Daniel*, 430 Pa. 642, 243 A.2d 400 (1968); *State v. Chambers*, 13 Cr.L. 2330 (N.J. Sup.Ct. June 26, 1973).
2. *Commonwealth v. Butler*, 458 Pa. 289, 328 A.2d 851 (1974).
3. For a parallel situation, see the discussion of state labor laws that regulate women's employment in Chapter II, "Employment Discrimination."
4. Another important lesson to draw from indeterminate sentencing is that, at this stage in society's development, it does not help women—or anyone—to do away with the strict standards that lawyers refer to as "procedural due process." Indeterminate sentencing has been part of a broad social reform movement, which thought that giving discretion to parole boards and social workers would be beneficial to both women and children. We have come to see the disastrous consequences this approach has for children, and concerned people are working to reinstate strict standards for the treatment of juvenile offenses. The consequences are equally disastrous for adults, and we must also work to reverse the unbridled discretion given parole boards over convicted women—and men—under indeterminate-sentencing laws.
5. *Wark v. State*, 266 A.2d 62 (1970), *cert. denied*, 400 U.S. 952 (1970).
6. Nagel and Weitzman, "Women as Litigants," 23 *Hastings Law Journal* 171 (1971).
7. W. Lunden, *Statistics on Delinquents and Delinquency* (1964), pp. 258, 259; U.S. Children's Bureau, *Statistics on Public Institutions*

for Delinquent Children—1964 (1964), p. 1; President's Commission on Law Enforcement, *The Challenge of Crime in a Free Society* (1967), p. 56; all cited in S. Gold, "Equal Protection for Juvenile Girls in Need of Supervision," 17 *N.Y. Law Forum* 570, 582-584 (1971). Of course, individual judges may favor girls over boys rather than vice versa. On a nationwide basis, however, girls are serving longer sentences than boys, on the average, even though the majority of girls are confined for running away from home, sexual activity, or having a child without being married; while the majority of boys are confined for serious offenses, such as larceny and breaking and entering.

8. Since 1970 six states—Illinois, New York, Texas, Oklahoma, Kentucky and New Mexico—have eliminated disparities in jurisdictional age. See Brown *et al.*, *Women's Rights and the Law* (New York: Praeger, 1977), p. 96.

9. See generally S. Gold, n. 7, *supra*.

10. *Sumrell v. York*, 288 F.Supp. 955 (D. Conn. 1968).

11. *A. v. City of New York*, 31 N.Y.2d 83, 335 N.Y.S.2d 33 (1972).

12. *Lamb v. State*, 475 P.2d 829, 830 (Okla. 1970); *Lamb v. Brown*, 456 F.2d 18 (10th Cir. 1972).

13. On the other hand, in Massachusetts it is a crime to cause the conception of an out-of-wedlock child although this law is probably never enforced.

14. *Commonwealth v. Stauffer*, 214 Pa.Super. 113, 251 A.2d 718 (1969).

15. *Glover v. Johnson*, 478 F.Supp. 1075 (E.D. Mich. 1979). See also *Canterino v. Wilson*, 546 F. Supp. 174 (W.D. Ky. 1982), thoroughly documenting numerous sex-based disparities in Kentucky's treatment of women prisoners.

16. *Forts v. Malcolm*, 426 F.Supp. 464 (S.D. N.Y. 1977); *Kershaw v. Davis*, Civil Action No. 77-329 (M.D. Pa. 1978); *Bounds v. Smith*, 430 U.S. 817 (1977); *Garnes v. Taylor*, Civil Action No. 159-72 (D. D.C. 1976) (Memorandum and Order); *Cooper v. Morin*, No. 1411/74 (Monroe County, N.Y., Sup.Ct. 1976); *Jackson v. Hendrick*, No. 2437 (Pa.Ct. of Common Pleas 1975); *O'Bryan v. City of Saginaw*, 446 F.Supp. 436 (E.D. Mich. 1978).

17. Some people contend that solicitation by either men or women constitutes an offensive invasion of privacy. However, punishing such conduct runs into difficult issues of freedom of speech and association under the First Amendment. Even if there were no First Amendment problems with punishing solicitation, a serious equal protection problem would remain. Those people who fear invasion of privacy and would like to punish solicitation seldom discuss seriously the need to punish the "normal" male solicitation, which thousands of women encounter every day on the street. It seems obvious that elementary equal protection theory cannot sanction punishing the female and the "deviant" male for actions undertaken by "normal" males without the remotest fear of punishment.

18. *Riemer v. Jensen*, 17 Crim. L. Rep. 2042 (Calif. 1975); *In re P.* 92 Misc.2d 62, 400 N.Y.S.2d 445 (1977).

19. *U.S. v. Wilson*, 342 A.2d 27 (D.C. Ct.App. 1974); *People v. Superior Court of Alameda County*, 19 Cal.3d 338, 138 Cal. Rptr. 66, 562 P.2d 1315 (1977).

20. *U.S. v. Moses*, 339 A.2d 46 (D.C. Ct.App. 1975); *Morgan v. City of Detroit*, 389 F.Supp. 922 (E.D. Mich. 1975).

21. Wigmore, 3A *Evidence* §924a at 736 (1970).

22. It is of course true that there may be rape cases where women complainants do not tell the truth, just as there are robbery cases where complainants do not tell the truth. However, the credibility of the witness in rape cases can be tested in the same way as in other cases. There is no need for a special presumption that rape victims will lie. In one particularly shocking case, where the court reversed a rape conviction even though the victim had identified both the man's ring and his car, a dissenting judge pointed out: "Our system of jurisprudence relies on a jury to distinguish truth from falsehood, after hearing evidence and giving due weight to the requirement that one must be considered innocent until proven guilty beyond a reasonable doubt. Since these safeguards suffice for murder, robbery or burglary cases, there is no cogent reason why they should fail when the crime charged is a sex offense." *People v. Linzey*, 31 N.Y.2d 99, 335 N.Y.S.2d 45, 52 (1972).

23. Brown *et al.*, *Women's Rights and the Law* (New York: Praeger, 1977), p. 58. See this book for more detailed information on the kinds of reform which have taken place in rape evidence law.

24. Cal. Evid. Code §782 (West 1966), *as added by* Stats. 1974, ch. 569, §1; Colo. Rev. Stat. Ann. §18-3-407 (1973), *as repealed and re-enacted by* L. 1975, at 630, §1; Fla. Stat. Ann. §794.022 (1965), *as amended by* L. 1974, ch. 74-121; Hawaii Rev. Stat. §37-707 (1968), *as amended by* L. 1974, ch. 83; Ind. Ann. Stat. Ann. §§35-1-32.5.1 *et seq.* (Burns 1975), *as added by* Acts 1975, ch. 322; Iowa Code Ann. §782 (1950), *as added by* Acts 1974, ch. 1271; Mich. Comp. Laws Ann. §750.520j (1968), *as amended by* Acts 1974, No. 266; Mont. Rev. Codes Ann. §94-5-503 (Supp. 1975), *as amended by* L. 1975, ch. 2, 1201; Neb. Rev. Stat. §28-408.05 (1975), *as amended by* L. 1975, L.B. 23, §9; Nev. Rev. Stat. §§48.2, 50.4 (1968), *as amended by* Acts 1975, at 600; N.M. Stat. Ann. §40A-9-26 (1953), *as amended by* L. 1975, ch. 109, §7; N.Y. Crim. Proc. Code §60-42 (McKinney 1965), *as added by* L. 1975, ch. 230, §1; N.D. Cent. Code §§12.1-20-14, -15 (1976), *as added by* L. 1975, ch. 118; Ore. Rev. Stat., §163.475 (1975), *as amended by* L. 1975, ch. 743, §2; Pa. Stat. Ann., tit. 18, §3104 (1973), *as amended by* Acts 1976, No. 53, §1; S.D. Comp. Laws Ann. §22-45-1 (1969), *as added by* L. 1975, ch. 169, §3; Tenn. Code Ann. §40-2445 (1975), *as added by* L. 1975, ch. 44, §1; Tex. Penal Code §21.13 (1974), *as added by* Acts 1975, ch. 203, §3; Wash. Rev. Code §9.79 (1961),

as amended by L. 1975 (1st Ex. Sess.), ch. 14. See also Rule 412, *Federal Rules of Evidence*.

25. Conn. Gen. Stat. Ann. §53a-68 (1975), *as repealed by* Acts 1969, No. 828, §69, No. 74-131; Fla. Stat. Ann. §794.022 (1965), *as added by* L. 1974, ch. 74-121; Iowa Code Ann. §782.4 (1950), *as repealed and re-enacted by* Acts 1974, ch. 1271, §1; Mich. Comp. Laws §750.520 (h) (1968), *as amended by* L. 1975, ch. 109, §6; N. M. Stat. Ann. §40A-9-25 (1953), *as amended by* L. 1975, (ch. 109, §6;) N.Y. Penal Law §130.16 (McKinney 1975), *as added by* L. 1974, ch. 14, §1 (under this enactment corroboration no longer is required unless incapacity to consent is at issue); Pa. Stat. Ann. tit. 18, §3106 (1973), *as amended by* Acts 1976, No. 53, §2; Wash. Rev. Code, ch. 9, §79 (1963), *as amended by* L. 1975 (1st Ex. Sess.), ch. 14, §2.

26. *Coker v. Georgia*, 433 U.S. 584 (1977).

VI

A Woman's Right To Control Her Body*

The past decade has brought enormous changes in the rights of women in the areas of birth control, abortion, and sterilization. By two landmark decisions in 1973—*Roe v. Wade*[1] and *Doe v. Bolton*[2]—the Supreme Court declared the right of women, with their physicians, to choose whether or not to bear children to be part of the fundamental right of privacy, thereby invalidating the restrictive abortion laws of most states. Feminists hailed these decisions as a major victory in the fight to win reproductive freedom for all women. In their initial euphoria many believed that all that was needed was to implement these decisions and to clarify issues the Supreme Court left unresolved.

Subsequent to these decisions various "right-to-life" groups supported by religious groups opposed to abortion launched a major campaign to reverse the 1973 decisions and to deny to all women the right to choose abortion. The central goal of the "right-to-life" movement is to make all abortion illegal by amending the United States Constitution.

Although public opinion polls show that a majority of Americans favor abortion in a great variety of circumstances, the "right-to-life" movement has scored some notable successes, particularly in the elimination of Medicaid funds for abortions for poor women. Furthermore, since 1973, many state legislatures and some cities have passed new laws hampering access to abortion. A "human life" amendment to the Constitution, which would criminalize all abortion, has the support

---

*Janet Benshoof, Lourdes Soto, Ann Teicher, Suzanne Lynn, and Madeline Kochen are the co-authors of this chapter.

174

of President Reagan, the backing of the Republican national platform, and the momentum gathered by the outcome of the 1980 elections, which the "right-to-life" groups claim represented victories for them, although the fact is that abortion does not seem to have played a crucial role in these elections. Other "right-to-life" methods for outlawing all abortion include a movement to call a constitutional convention to pass a "human life" amendment, a human life federalism amendment to the Constitution (sponsored by Senator Orrin Hatch of Utah), and the Human Life Bill (sponsored by Senator Jesse Helms of North Carolina). Despite vigorous lobbying and litigation by pro-choice groups, the right to abortion is in jeopardy.

This chapter will discuss the rights of women under current law and will suggest steps which must be taken to preserve access to abortion.

What are the full implications of the Supreme Court's 1973 abortion decisions?

In *Roe v. Wade*,[3] the Court set the basic structure for future state laws. States may not prohibit or interfere with a woman's right, with her physician, to choose abortion during the first trimester of pregnancy. From then until viability (about the 24th to 28th week of pregnancy), the state can establish medical regulations governing abortion only if they are designed to protect maternal health. After viability, the state can prohibit abortions except where they are necessary to protect the life or health of the woman.

The Court's rationale for this structure turns on the competing interests of the woman on the one hand and the state's interest in protecting the woman and the fetus on the other. The woman has a constitutional right to privacy; the state has an interest in protecting the health of the woman and potential human life. However, the court found, until the end of the first trimester the mortality rate for childbirth is higher than it is for abortion; thus the state's interest in preserving a woman's health is not strong enough to justify regulations that interfere with the woman's choice, except that choice of abortion must be made with the concurrence of a doctor. After the first trimester, when abortion becomes more dangerous, the state's interest in protecting a woman's health may be asserted by regulations to that end. Viability means that the fetus is potentially able to survive outside the mother's womb; after that point, i.e., after approximately 24 weeks of pregnancy, the state's interest in potential life can take precedence over the mother's right to privacy and abortions can be prohibited except when necessary to preserve her life or health.

In the second decision, *Doe v. Bolton*,[4] the Court struck down several procedural regulations in a Georgia abortion statute. States may not require that abortions be performed in a hospital that is specially accredited (in Georgia's case, by the Joint Commission on Accreditation); and during the first trimester the state cannot even require that abortions be performed in hospitals. (In 1983 this ruling was extended to the second trimester. See discussion in later question and answer.) Further, the state cannot require that the abortion patient be a state resident, or that more than one doctor concur in the abortion decision.

Does Medicaid pay for abortions for poor women?

Not in most states. As of March 1982, only nine states and the District of Columbia were voluntarily paying for most Medicaid abortions.[5] In five other states, court orders are in effect requiring the states to pay for all medically necessary abortions.[6] In all other states the only Medicaid abortions available are those necessary because the woman's life is endangered,[7] and, in some states, also for victims of rape and incest.[8]

Congressional action and a 1980 Supreme Court decision[9] have eliminated Medicaid funding for most abortions. Since 1976, Congress has attached amendments, popularly known as the Hyde Amendments, to the yearly appropriations bills[10] for the U.S. Departments of Labor and HEW (HEW is now the Department of Health and Human Services). These amendments restrict federal Medicaid funding of abortion. The amendment for 1982 permits federal Medicaid funds to be used for abortions only when the woman's life is endangered.[11]

In June 1980 the Supreme Court issued a decision in *Harris v. McRae*,[12] a nationwide class action challenging the Hyde Amendments. The Court ruled that the federal Constitution does not require Medicaid to pay for medically necessary abortions, even though the Medicaid program pays for all other medically necessary procedures. The Court found that abortion restrictions in the funding context are different

from other abortion regulations and that it is legitimate for a
state to choose to promote fetal life by funding only childbirth
and not abortion—even when a woman's health is sacrificed.
By allowing a state to accomplish, by a withdrawal of funds,
what it could not otherwise do, the decision radically under-
mines the protection which the Court will accord the poor.
Under the Supreme Court's decision, not only may Congress
withhold funds for medically necessary abortions, but states
are not required under the federal Constitution to fund such
abortions. It seemed clear from the decision that the Social
Security Act at least required states to fund Medicaid abortions which are eligible for federal matching funds;[13] subsequent to the *McRae* decision, however, Congress passed an
additional anti-abortion amendment to the yearly appropriations bill, called the Bauman Amendment.[14] This amendment changes the states' obligations by permitting them to
choose to eliminate all Medicaid abortions. This amendment
has not yet been challenged in court.

The decision in *McRae* made it clear, however, that Congress and the states are free to fund Medicaid abortions if
they so choose, and therefore the fight for Medicaid-funded
abortions has been thrown back to the federal and state
legislatures. In addition, challenges to restrictive state Medicaid laws continue to be feasible based on state constitutional
and common law grounds. Such challenges have been successful or are currently underway in California, Connecticut,
Massachusetts, New Jersey, and Pennsylvania.[15]

As state policies on the public funding of abortion are still
in flux, and since a new version of the Hyde Amendment is
passed every year, women should check with the local American Civil Liberties Union affiliate, local abortion providers, or
local family planning clinics for the current policy in their
state.

Does a married woman need her husband's consent before she can have an abortion?

No. In 1976, the Supreme Court struck down a Missouri
statute which required the husband's prior written consent
for any abortion unless the abortion was necessary to save the
woman's life.[16] The Court ruled that just as the state may not
prohibit abortions prior to viability, the state may not dele-
gate a veto power over the woman's decision to her spouse.

The Court recognized the interest of the father in the fetus and the importance of the marital relationship in our society. Despite the fact that ideally the husband and wife should concur in the abortion decision, the Court ruled that the state does not have the constitutional authority "to give the spouse unilaterally the ability to prohibit the wife from terminating her pregnancy."[17] The right to decide on abortion is part of the woman's privacy right. The decision ultimately rests upon her and her physician because it is she "who physically bears the child and who is more directly and immediately affected by the pregnancy."[18]

There are additional problems with spousal consent requirements. For example, the husband is not always the father of the child. Also, the interests of unmarried fathers are not equally protected by a spousal consent requirement.

Some states have included, as part of comprehensive regulatory schemes designed to discourage women from seeking abortion, provisions which require that before an abortion may be performed the husband must be notified. Although the Supreme Court has not directly decided this issue, it would appear from their decision regarding spousal consent that a requirement for notifying the spouse is also unconstitutional. Several spousal notification requirements have already been struck down in federal courts.[19]

If a doctor should notify a husband without a woman's permission, this would be an invasion of privacy and she may be able to sue him on a variety of technical legal grounds.[20] It is possible that lack of spousal consent over abortions could be raised as a ground of "irreconcilable conflict" in a no-fault divorce proceeding, although it is unclear whether it would be considered a proper ground.

What kind of "informed consent" can a state require of a woman before she can obtain an abortion?

Obtaining the informed consent of a patient before he or she undergoes any medical procedure is an accepted doctrine which is designed to allow patients to participate with greater knowledge in the medical decision-making process. As opposed to being passive recipients of prescribed treatment, patients should be informed about the benefits and risks of alternative procedures so that they may evaluate and react to the medical decision in which they participate.

In the abortion area this doctrine has been distorted by some state statutes; "informed consent" requirements have been used by some states to discourage abortion. Since there are certain types of "informed consent" requirements which interfere with the woman's right to decide about abortion free from government intrusion during the first trimester of pregnancy, not all of these "informed consent" requirements for abortion are permissible.

In 1976 the Supreme Court stated that since the abortion decision is "an important, and often a stressful one," some sort of special informed consent requirement for abortion would be legal.[21] The guidelines laid down by the Court then were that a permissible requirement would call for "the giving of information to the patient as to just what would be done and as to its consequences," but that to require any more would not be allowed.[22]

After the 1976 decision, a model anti-abortion statute drafted by "right-to-life" lawyers was introduced in state and local legislatures throughout the country under the guise of an "informed consent" statute. These "informed consent" laws were not designed to ensure that a woman receive the information necessary to make a knowledgeable decision about whether to terminate her pregnancy. Rather, they required that the physician provide the woman with a variety of questionable and disturbing information, such as a statement that the fetus is a human being from the moment of conception, a detailed description of the appearance and characteristics of the fetus, and a list of medical risks (many of which have not been proved). They also imposed a waiting period, usually of 24 or 48 hours, between the time the woman gives consent and the performance of the abortion. These requirements were clearly intended to discourage women from choosing abortion and to burden that choice. Variations of this type of statute were adopted in a number of states and some localities, including Akron, Ohio (all of them are generally referred to as "Akron ordinances or statutes," since they first came to public attention in the Akron case), Louisiana, Missouri, Rhode Island, Maine, Nebraska, North Dakota, South Dakota, Illinois, Massachusetts, Kentucky, Nevada, and Tennessee.

Finally, on June 15, 1983—one decade after the Court's landmark decisions in *Roe v. Wade* and *Doe v. Bolton*— the Court issued another landmark decision, finding such "informed consent" laws to be unconstitutional. The case, *Akron v. Akron Center for Reproductive Health*,[23] struck down all of the pertinent Akron ordinance provisions, after first strongly reaffirming the Court's commitment to *Roe v. Wade*. Writing for the Court, Justice Powell reasoned that most of Akron's "informed consent" provisions were not designed "to inform the women's consent,"[24] but instead represented an attempt to pressure her into foregoing the abortion. Further, many of the provisions were "speculative" or "dubious," and interfered with the attending physician's discretion.[25] Consequently, the Court rejected all of the following items on Akron's "litany of information" to be recited by the doctor to the pregnant woman: the statement that " 'the unborn child is a human life from the moment of conception' "; "the detailed description of 'the anatomical and physiological characteristics of the particular unborn child,' " including such speculation as fetal sensitivity to pain; and the long list of the "risks" of abortion, designed in reality as a " 'parade of horribles' . . . to suggest that abortion is a particularly dangerous procedure."[26]

The Court also threw out Akron's requirements for other, more neutral information. With respect to this information, the Akron law was unconstitutional only because the city insisted that the physician give the information. Future laws, the Court ruled, could at most require the physician to verify that the woman received adequate counseling from people with "reasonable minimum qualifications" for counseling.[27] Information that counselors can be required to give includes a discussion of the risks of the pregnancy and the abortion procedure, the postoperative medical instructions needed for the patient's safe recovery, the fact of pregnancy and "the gestational age of the fetus," "the availability of information on birth control and adoption, . . . and the availability of assistance during pregnancy and after childbirth. . . ."[28] While the Court indicated that it will allow states and localities to require this information, Justice Powell cautioned that it can only be required in "general terms," and that the "precise nature and amount of this disclosure" must be left to the physician's discretion.[29]

Finally, the court also quickly disposed of Akron's 24-hour waiting period, characterizing the rule as "arbitrary and inflexible."[30] It too was unconstitutional, because it did nothing to further the safety of the procedure and interfered with the physician's discretion.

Does a minor have the right to obtain an abortion without her parents' consent?

Yes, in some circumstances. In 1976 the Supreme Court recognized that a mature unmarried minor has the right to decide, in consultation with a physician and without her parents' consent, to terminate her pregnancy.[31] In a 1979 decision holding a Massachusetts parental consent law unconstitutional, the Court ruled that a mature minor has the right to make the abortion decision without parental involvement.[32]

However, until 1983, the Supreme Court was divided on the question of how far a state may go in regulating minors, and it was unclear whether states could require consent in some instances. In two of the three major 1983 abortion decisions, the Supreme Court finally confronted this issue. The Court ruled that such parental consent statues are constitutional if (1) mature minors have a right to make their own decisions about abortion; (2) mature and immature minors, as a matter of constitutional law, have the opportunity, through an alternative judicial or administrative procedure, to obtain an abortion without parental consent *or* consultation; and (3) with respect to immature minors, the sole test is their own best interests.[33] Thus, minor girls will be able in some instances to get abortions without parental consent, if they can convince a court either that they are sufficiently mature to make their own decision or that, while not that mature, an abortion would nevertheless be in their own best interest. Of course, if the courts (including both the original and the appeal court) do not agree with either contention and the girl cannot convince her parents, she will be forced to continue the pregnancy.

It should be noted that the court option must be a real option. The Supreme Court rejected Akron's parental consent provision because the Akron law did not expressly authorize any court to act on a minor's request to have an abortion or set forth the standards governing the decision. In contrast, the Court upheld a Missouri law that did both things.[34]

It seems obvious that requiring young women who are already frightened, confused, and unable to secure the involvement and support of their parents, to navigate through an intimidating and awesome court process would be so burdensome that many would be discouraged from trying.[35] There is no general requirement that free legal assistance to these women be provided. Courts are not usually set up to handle applications expeditiously. Adolescents already account for the largest percentage of second-trimester abortion,[36] and further delay caused by procedural red tape could seriously increase the health risks.[37] Justice Powell attempted to deal with this issue, too, by ruling that the judicial proceeding must " 'be completed with anonymity and sufficient expedition to provide an effective opportunity for an abortion to be obtained.' "[38]

It is important and desirable for parents to be involved in their daughters' decisions, and doctors and counselors customarily encourage such involvement. Organizations which oppose mandatory third-party involvement or parental notification all recognize and encourage parental involvement in the abortion decision. For more information, women should read E. Paul and H. Pilpel, "Teenagers and Pregnancy: The Law in 1979," *Family Planning Perspectives*, Vol. 11, No. 5 (Sept./Oct. 1979); The Alan Guttmacher Institute, *Family Planning and Abortion: An Analysis of Laws and Policies in the United States* (Washington, D.C.: U.S. Government Printing Office, 1979); and P. Donovan, "Your Parents or the Judge: Massachusetts' New Abortion Consent Law," *Family Planning Perspectives*, Vol. 13, No. 5 (Sept./Oct. 1981).

Can the law require that a minor's parents be notified of her decision to have an abortion?

Yes, in some limited instances. In 1981 the Supreme Court ruled that a parental notification (*not* consent) law is valid if the minor lives with and is dependent on her parents, is not emancipated, and does not claim that she is mature enough to make the decision or that notifying her parents would not be in her best interest because of the nature of her relationship with them.[39] However, notification laws would probably still be unconstitutional if they require notification for minors who don't fall within these narrow categories.[40] For the same reasons that many adolescents may not be able to seek their parents' consent, they also cannot risk their being notified.[41] Notification statutes, therefore, also unduly burden the constitutional right to seek an abortion.

Statutes requiring parental notification have been enjoined from going into effect in several states.[42] As of the fall of 1982, six states had functioning parental notification statutes—Indiana, Idaho, Minnesota, Maryland, Montana, and Utah.[43] The

Maryland statute permits an exception where the doctor believes that notification might result in physical or psychological abuse to the young woman.

May states require that all second-trimester abortions be performed in hospitals?

No. In 1983, in a trio of abortion decisions, the Court ruled that states could not require that all second-trimester abortions be performed in hospitals, although it is constitutional to require that they be performed in licensed clinics.[44] This was an important advance, for as of late 1982, 21 states had laws limiting second-trimester abortions to hospitals,[45] although several lower courts had declared this type of statute unconstitutional.[46]

In *Roe v. Wade*, the Supreme Court laid down guidelines which allowed states to regulate abortions taking place after the first trimester, on the theory that such regulations would be necessary to protect maternal health; not allowing such health regulation was restricted to the first trimester because in 1973 abortion was safer than childbirth only during that trimester.[47] In 1983, however, the Court concluded that advances in abortion techniques had altered the situation. There is now undisputed medical research establishing that abortion performed by the dilatation and evacuation (D&E) technique up to the 18th week of pregnancy is at least twice as safe as childbirth.[48] Post-first-trimester abortions may now be performed safely in clinics[49]—and requiring that they be done in hospitals does not add to the safety of the procedure but does add to its cost.[50]

Despite the fact that most second-trimester "in-hospital" requirements are unrelated to women's health concerns, such laws were enacted throughout the country in order to hinder access to abortion. Such requirements greatly reduced access to abortion, especially in light of the limited availability of hospitals which provide abortion services. In Louisiana, for example, there are 127 public and private hospitals; not one allows abortions to take place on its premises. This is true of five other states; that is, no hospital in these states allows abortions on its premises.[51] The increased delay and cost of being required to travel to a hospital in another state that does permit abortions is not only burdensome to the abortion right but increases the health risks to women seeking abortions. Moreover, the cutoff of Medicaid funds for abortion exacerbates the problem, so that the costs of traveling and having an abortion performed in a hospital may be prohibitive.

May a state require the presence of a second doctor at a post-viability abortion?

Yes. The Court ruled on this issue in the context of the Missouri law, which prohibited all post-viability abortions except those necessary to preserve the life or health of the woman. Missouri also required the presence of a second doctor at such post-viability abortions; their charge would be to take control of the medical care of the child if one should be born alive as a result of the procedure. Justice Powell noted that such abortions will frequently be emergency operations, as they are permitted only to preserve the woman's life or health, and that the attention of the woman's doctor will thus be focused on her, while the viable fetus could be in grave danger from premature birth. In these circumstances, given the state's interest in preserving the life of a viable fetus, the second physician requirement was found to be constitutional.[52]

What other efforts are being made to make it harder for women to obtain abortions?

States and municipalities have passed a variety of laws to hinder access to abortion. Many of these attempts to stop abortion take the form of laws regulating abortion facilities. In some states, laws require that abortion clinics have blood supplies, knee- or foot-controlled sinks, wide hallways, and elevators, and that they pay licensing fees. These regulations, which are unrelated to maternal health matters, can make it prohibitively expensive to operate a clinic. Several of these ordinances have been struck down as attempts to regulate first-trimester abortions in violation of the constitutional standards of *Roe v. Wade*.[53]

Another approach has been to use licensing and zoning laws to exclude clinics. Challenges to this type of regulation have met with both success and failure.[54]

Some states enact reporting and record-keeping requirements which not only threaten the privacy of the patients by failing to provide adequate protection for the confidentiality of the specified information, but are also unduly burdensome on the clinics. They may require, for example, that a great deal of detailed and unnecessary information be reported to the state, or that the records be kept for many years. Some of these laws have been stricken as unconstitutional.[55] However, in one of the 1983 abortion decisions, the Supreme Court upheld a related requirement that a pathologist examine the fetal tissue and file a copy of the report with the state health department and the abortion facility or hospital. Justice Powell viewed the added cost of approximately $20 as too minor to "significantly burden a pregnant woman's abortion decision."[56]

Louisiana had a law requiring a special type of disposal (cremation) for the tissue remains following an abortion. The law, which was clearly designed to deter abortion, would have increased the cost and inconvenience of the procedure. It was challenged in court, and subsequently amended by the legislature.[57] In the *Akron* case, the Supreme Court invalidated a smiliar provision. *Akron* required disposal of the remains in a "humane and sanitary manner," with criminal penalties attaching to a failure to do so. The Court agreed that this language suggested "some sort of 'decent burial' of an embryo at the earliest stages of formation" and that it failed to give doctors fair notice of the forbidden conduct.[58]

Some state laws have been designed to restrict access to abortion by regulating or prohibiting the advertisement or even discussion of abortion services. These laws not only interfere with the abortion right, but also violate the Free Speech and Press Clause of the First Amendment to the Constitution. They are clearly unconstitutional, as several courts have decided.[59]

When abortion opponents fail to get their state and local governments to join their efforts, they often resort to private harassment of clinics and their patients. Their tactics consist of sit-ins, trespass on clinic property, harassment of patients, and firebombings. Clinics in several cities have been burned. A Cleveland clinic was firebombed while a woman was in the operating room. In northern Virginia, an abortion clinic was forced to obtain a federal court injunction to stop trespassing in the clinic and harassment of patients.[60]

Congress has also passed legislation to restrict access to abortion, primarily in the form of amendments to annual appropriations bills. In addition to the Hyde Amendments, which have eliminated virtually all abortions for Medicaid recipients since 1977 (see discussion, *supra*), funding for abortion has been restricted for military personnel and for Peace Corps workers and their dependents.[61] Since 1974 the Legal Services Corporation has been prohibited from bringing suits to obtain non-therapeutic abortion services for their indigent clients,[62] and in 1978, after it issued a comprehensive report on childbearing in the United States, the United States Civil Rights Commission was prohibited from even studying the subject of abortion.[63]

The Pregnancy Discrimination Act, passed in 1978, requires private employers to provide the same fringe benefits for pregnancy-related disabilities that they do for all other disabilities, but allows them to exclude coverage for abortion from medical insurance policies unless the woman's life is endangered or she suffers medical complications as a result of abortion.[64] For a full explanation of benefits under the Pregnancy Discrimination Act, see Chapter II.

Massachusetts, Illinois, Kentucky, and North Dakota have eliminated almost all abortion benefits for their public employees. Kentucky and North Dakota have also prohibited private health insurance plans in the state from covering abortion except by option and at additional premiums.[65]

Must public hospitals provide abortion services?

According to the present state of the law, the answer may differ depending on whether the abortion is medically necessary. In 1977, the Supreme Court upheld the right of a public hospital to refuse to perform *non-therapeutic* abortions.[65A] The Court ruled that the refusal to provide such services does not create an obstacle to the right to choose abortion and that the federal Constitution does not forbid a state or city from "expressing a preference for normal childbirth."[65B]

The Supreme Court has not yet decided whether the federal Constitution allows public hospitals to refuse to perform even *medically necessary* abortions. However, in its 1980 *Harris v. McRae* decision, the Court ruled that the government may refuse to provide Medicaid funding for medically necessary abortions.[65C] It would be an easy step to extend that decision by allowing public hospitals to refuse to provide most therapeutic abortions. However, a federal court has refused to draw that line and struck down a Minnesota law prohibiting public hospitals from performing any abortions except those necessary to save the life of the mother.[66]

Although the situation may not be very promising in terms of the U.S. Constitution, public and/or private hospitals may be required to provide non-therapeutic and/or therapeutic abortions under state constitutional, statutory, or common law grounds. In New Jersey three private hospitals prohibited the use of their facilities for first-trimester non-therapeutic abortions. That policy was overturned by the New Jersey Supreme Court based on state common law.[67] The court decided that in serving the public, the hospitals constituted quasi-public institutions, so that under New Jersey common law their policies must be rationally related to the public good. The Court concluded that there was no rational relationship between the public good and a prohibition on non-therapeutic abortion, and declared the policy invalid.

This issue is particularly troubling because of the large number of public hospitals which refuse to perform elective abortions. During 1977, for instance, only about 24 percent of all public hospitals provided abortion services and in ten states no public hospitals provided such services.[68] In Louisiana, there are 127 public and private hospitals; not one allows abortion. This is true of five other states. In eight of every ten U.S. counties, no physician, clinic, or hospital provides abortions.[69] The situation is especially burdensome for poor women, who cannot afford to have abortions in private facilities or to travel to distant hospitals. For the poor, therefore, a state policy of "preferring normal childbirth" can mean forced maternity, self-abortion, and even abortion by "back-street" abortionists.

Is there a constitutional right to obtain and use contraceptives?

Yes. In 1965, the Supreme Court declared that the constitutional right of privacy includes the right to make personal decisions relating to contraception free from unjustified government interference.[70] In 1972 the Supreme Court made clear that this was not only a "marital right to privacy," but a right of privacy extending to unmarried persons.[71] The right to use contraceptives applies to unmarried as well as married people.[72] This ruling was expanded by the Court in *Carey v. Population Services* in 1977, when it ruled that access to contraceptives is also guaranteed by the Constitution, since such access is essential for exercising the right to choose and use contraceptives.[73] Just as the state may not limit the use of contraceptives, it also may not restrict the sale or distribution of contraceptives in the absence of a compelling reason for the restriction.[74]

From the *Carey* opinion it appears that state laws which limit access to contraceptives can only be justified if they promote the state's interest in protecting people's health and in controlling the quality of contraceptives which are sold without a prescription. Just as with other drugs or devices, the federal government decides whether or not certain contraceptives may be dispensed by prescription only.[75] The *Carey* case involved a law which limited the category of those who may sell non-prescription contraceptives. Similar laws which limited the distribution of contraceptives to those dealing primarily with health or welfare (such as pharmacists and physicians) have also been struck down by lower federal courts.[76]

Do minors have a right to obtain contraceptives without their parents' consent?

Yes. The right to obtain contraceptives, like the right to abortion, is included in an individual's constitutional right to make private decisions about childbearing. In 1977 the Supreme Court ruled that this right extends to minors of all ages insofar as "non-hazardous," i.e. non-prescription, contraceptives are concerned. The Court struck down a New York law which prohibited the sale of non-prescription contraceptives (such as condoms, foams, and spermicidal jellies) to anyone under the age of 16, as interfering with the privacy rights of minors.[77]

Although the Supreme Court has never ruled directly on whether it would be constitutional to require parents' consent, its decisions regarding a minor's right to obtain an abortion without parental consent and to have access to non-prescription contraceptives indicate that an absolute requirement of parental consent or notification for prescription contraceptives would be unconstitutional. Lower-court decisions have recognized a minor's right to consent to contraception without parental involvement.[78] As with abortion, every effort should be made to persuade teenagers to consult their parents about contraceptives, but they should not be forced to do so.

One federal appeals court has ruled against a group of

parents who asserted that they had a constitutional right to be notified of their children's requests for contraception. The court found that no such right existed, and the minor's right of privacy was upheld.[79]

Furthermore, federal laws which mandate that family-planning services be made available under the Social Security Act and Public Health Services Act to eligible recipients as part of aid to needy families specifically require that such services be made available to sexually active teenagers who voluntarily request such services, and prohibit discrimination on the basis of marital status or age.[80] Federal courts in Utah and West Virginia have upheld the right of minors to have access to these federally funded family planning services without parental consent or notification, and have ruled that denial of services to minors who do not have parental consent violates the federal laws which created these programs.[81] (Where a federal law conflicts with a state law, the federal law applies under the so-called Supremacy Clause of the U.S. Constitution.)

One obstacle which has prevented some adolescents from receiving the family-planning services provided by the Medicaid program is that they must produce their parents' Medicaid card in order to prove eligibility. A lawsuit was recently filed in New York State in order to compel the federal government to provide adolescents with their own Medicaid cards so that they can apply for and receive the family-planning services to which they are entitled without their parents' knowledge.[82]

Many state laws provide that minors may have access to birth control without parental consent and no state statute actually prohibits a doctor or institution from providing or prescribing birth control for minors. Yet where there is no statute expressly giving adolescents the right to obtain contraceptives, doctors are often reluctant to provide these services for fear of being sued by the minor's parents, despite the fact that there is no reported case of a doctor ever being successfully sued for providing sex-related health care to a minor. Of course, a private doctor or facility which does not receive government funds is free to refuse to give contraceptives to a minor without parental consent.

Are poor women entitled to publicly funded family-planning services?

Yes. The Social Security Act requires that states participating in the federal Medicaid or Aid for Families with Dependent Children (AFDC) programs[83] offer and provide family-planning services to all eligible individuals, both married and single, who are in those programs and who voluntarily request such services.[84] This includes providing contraceptives to sexually active minors.[85] States must provide counseling and medical contraceptive services, including diagnoses, treatment, supplies, and follow-up, and individuals must be assured of their choice of the contraceptive method as well as of the particular provider.[86] In addition, federal law requires that all state Medicaid programs cover family-planning services and supplies.[87]

Other federally funded family-planning programs offer either free or low-cost family-planning services without regard to whether the recipient is actually covered by AFDC or Medicaid.[88] To find out the location of these clinics and whether or not a person is eligible, calls should be made to a local Planned Parenthood or family-planning service or to the state social services or Medicaid agencies.

Do women have a right to be sterilized?

Yes. The right to choose to be sterilized is part of the constitutional right of privacy in matters related to childbearing,[89] and voluntary sterilization is legal in all 50 states. The fact that sterilization is the second most frequently used and fastest-growing method of contraception among married couples over 30 in the country[90] indicates that earlier problems of denial of access to sterilization have declined significantly.

Formerly, the medical profession imposed its own age parity formulas on women seeking sterilization. Only if a woman's age multiplied by the number of her children reached a certain figure (e.g., $20 \times 5 = 100$!) did she qualify for voluntary sterilization. The American College of Obstetricians and Gynecologists dropped this requirement in the early 1970's and it is no longer generally applied.

State laws requiring spousal consent for sterilization are almost surely unconstitutional for the same reasons that such laws are impermissible for abortion.[91] Some private doctors and hospitals still refuse to perform sterilizations on men and women without their spouse's consent for fear of malpractice suits by the non-consenting spouse. It is unlikely, however, that a court would allow such a suit against a doctor or hospital.[92]

Although some courts have upheld the right of sectarian hospitals to refuse to perform sterilizations on religious and moral grounds,[93] courts have held that public hospitals must offer this service to those who desire it.[94] As with abortion, spousal disagreement over sterilization could possibly be raised as a ground of "irreconcilable conflict" in a no-fault divorce proceeding although it is unclear whether this would be upheld as a ground for granting the divorce.

May women be sterilized without their informed consent?

Absolutely not. Yet women have been and continue to be sterilized, either without their knowledge, without their consent, without knowing that the operation is permanent, or under such coercive circumstances that their formal acknowledgment of consent is meaningless. Sterilization abuse primarily affects poor and minority women and the retarded.

The federal government funds 90 percent of the cost of sterilization under its Medicaid and family-planning programs. The Department of Health, Education, and Welfare (now the Department of Health and Human Services), which is responsible for these programs, was under a court order requiring it to issue regulations establishing requirements of informed consent for all federally funded sterilizations.[95] The court order resulted from a suit brought on behalf of two 12- and 14-year-old black girls in Alabama who were sterilized under a federal program without their parents' knowledge and consent. The Court found that 100,000 to 150,000 persons had been sterilized annually under these federal programs, many of them minors and incompetents.[96]

The final HEW (now HHS) voluntary sterilization regulations, issued in November 1978,[97] are similar to a law which regulates all sterilizations in the public and private sector in New York City. The New York City law was fought for by women's and community groups attempting to curb sterilization abuse. The HHS regulations, which apply to both men and women, prohibit sterilization of anyone under 21, and require a 30-day waiting period after written consent is given, and counseling in the person's own language about the irreversibility of the procedure and its risks, benefits, and alternatives. Consent cannot be obtained while a woman is in labor, is having an abortion, or is under the influence of drugs or alcohol. The regulations also prohibit the use of federal funds for sterilizations of the mentally incompetent and institutionalized. The regulations provide that federal funds may not be used for hysterectomies done solely for the purpose of sterilization.

In addition, under the regulations a person cannot be asked to consent to sterilization as a condition for obtaining or continuing to receive welfare or other government benefits. Officials who coerce women into being sterilized by threatening to deprive them of such benefits may be fined or imprisoned.[98]

If fully implemented, the regulations might curb the most blatant forms of abuse. However, studies have shown that they are not uniformly followed and that some hospitals disregard them altogether.[99] Doctors in a Maryland hospital recently admitted that they often flouted the regulations by not accepting federal funds and simply allowing the hospital to assume the costs.[100] The government's enforcement power is limited to withholding federal reimbursement.

Sterilization abuse can only be altered where there is community action to pressure local hospitals to follow the HHS regulations even in connection with sterilizations not paid for by federal funds. Any person who thinks he or she is a victim of abuse should contact the ACLU or a local attorney, or complain to the state Medicaid office; if a woman, victim should get in touch with a local women's group or the National Women's Health Network.

Women who wish to obtain more information about sterilization abuse can read *Women Under Attack*, CARASA, 386 Park Ave. S., New York, N.Y. 10016; *Sterilization: Resource Guide 9*, National Women's Health Network, 224 9th St., S.E., Washington, D.C. 20003. These publications also contain further sources.

Can the right to an have abortion be eliminated by constitutional amendment?

Yes. This is precisely what "right-to-life" groups are attempting to do.[101] There are two ways to amend our Constitution: one is for Congress, by a vote of two-thirds of both houses, to propose such an amendment; the second way is for 34 states to call for a constitutional convention. In either case, the amendment must be ratified by three-quarters (at the present time, 38) of the states.

Until the last presidential election, congressional enactment of a "Human Life" Amendment (HLA) did not seem likely. Now that Congress has become more conservative, with a Republican majority in the Senate, HLA poses a greater threat.

One version of the Human Life Amendment now under consideration before Congress provides:

Section 1. With respect to the right to life, the word person as used in this article and in the Fifth and Fourteenth Articles of the Amendments to the Constitution of the United States applies to all human beings irrespective of age, health, function or condition of dependency, including their unborn offspring at every stage of their biological development.

Section 2. No unborn person shall be deprived of life by any person; provided, however, that nothing in this article shall prohibit a law permitting only those medical procedures required to prevent the death of the mother.

Section 3. The Congress and the several states have power to enforce this article by appropriate legislation.

The implications of this amendment are frightening. Not only is it intended to outlaw all abortions, but it might prohibit the use of IUD's and probably even some forms of the birth control pill because they might be considered abortifacient rather than contraceptive. Women who aborted could conceivably be charged with murder, and women who miscarry or who are thought to act improperly during their pregnancies might be subject to charges of manslaughter or prenatal "child abuse."[102]

In addition to congressional passage of a Human Life Amendment, "right-to-lifers" have been pushing the second method of amending the Constitution, namely a constitutional convention, popularly referred to as "Con Con." This route of amending the Constitution has never been used, and if used could pose a serious threat to the entire Constitution. Nineteen states had passed Con Con resolutions calling for a constitutional convention on the subject of abortion as of December 1980. This is only 15 short of the 34-state total needed to compel Congress to call a convention.[103] Con Con remains a threat because (1) there is no time limit on the call; (2) defeat does not prevent reintroduction of a resolution; and (3) the National Right-to-Life Committee, in June 1978, for the first time expressed approval of this amendment process.

The legal issues presented by a constitutional convention are manifold, but the political impact is clear. If opponents of reproductive choice should even approach success in calling a constitutional convention on the subject of abortion, Congress would probably initiate its own HLA in order to avoid the chaos of a constitutional convention.

The convention issue is a matter of concern to everyone. It is not clear whether it could be limited to one purpose because there are no procedures set up for a convention and because once a convention was called, all constitutional rights could be in jeopardy.

Readers should alert their representatives and the members of the judiciary committees of both houses of Congress that they oppose the Human Life Amendment and the abortion Con Con. In states where Con Con resolutions are pending, people should contact their legislators to voice their opposition.

Nor are these the only methods for changing the Constitution which are being proposed. Senator Hatch has proposed a "Federalism" amendment which would allow both individual states and the Congress to set their own policy on abortion, with the most restrictive law governing. Senator Helms has proposed a "Human Life Bill," which in effect attempts to amend the Constitution by a simple majority vote in Congress. These too should be opposed.

Where can women get information about obtaining abortions?

Most states now have referral groups, and there are helpful national organizations as well.

The National Abortion Federation (NAF) has established a toll-free hotline to help women choose an abortion clinic. It also provides legal and medical information about abortion procedures. The hotline number in the United States (outside New York State) is (800) 223–0618; in New York State, the number is (212) 688–8516 (outside New York City, call collect). NAF also publishes a booklet entitled *Guidelines on How to Choose an Abortion*, which can be obtained by either calling or writing NAF, at 110 E. 59th St., New York, N.Y. 10022.

The Abortion Assistance Association, 149 Lewis Rd., Havertown, Pa. 19083, (800) 523–5101, helps women east of the Rocky Mountains to find abortion clinics. For quick help, contact the Family Planning Information Service, 380 2nd Ave., New York, N.Y. 10010; (212) 677–3040. The service is operated by Planned Parenthood of New York City on behalf of the New York City Interagency Council of Family Planning. It gives complete information on abortion referral for New York City, as well as on family planning.

A useful source which contains essays describing various abortion techniques and procedures, a bibliography of resources, a listing of the key groups in each state which are working on abortion, and a directory of women-controlled health centers around the country, is published by the National Women's Health Network (NWHN), entitled *Health Resource Guide: Abortion* (1980, $4 to $5), and can be obtained by writing to NWHN at 224 7th St., S.E., Washington, D.C. 20003. Another useful source for women faced with an unwanted pregnancy is entitled *The Abortion Guide: A Handbook for Women and Men* written by Carole Dornblaser and Uta Handy.

What must people do to preserve their right to reproductive freedom?

Every woman and man who values the right to reproductive choice must now participate in whatever way they can in the struggle to preserve that right. Congress and the state legislatures need to know that the majority of people in this country oppose the various "Human Life" Amendments, the cutoff of Medicaid funding for abortions, and all the other restrictive laws that have been, and continue to be, enacted to limit access to abortion. The anti-abortion forces have gained as much ground as they have because of their diligence in making themselves visible in the legislative and electoral arenas. Now the pro-choice forces must do the same by mobilizing the silent majority to lobby their state legislators and members of Congress, and to work to defeat anti-choice legislators and to support those who are pro-choice. Constant visibility and pressure is the key to maintaining the right to abortion and other reproductive rights and to defeating the "Human Life" Amendments.

Organized efforts are always more effective than individual ones. There are several national organizations, with local and state chapters, as well as many local women's groups, that are already working on this issue. In addition to lobbying, these organizations work at the grass-roots level to alert women to the imminent threat to their right to free choice about childbearing, and to enlist their support. People should seek out these groups, and where they do not exist, form new ones. In order to gather grass-roots support, all concerned people must talk to their friends and acquaintances in their workplaces, schools, and communities, and in the other organizations to which they belong. To turn the climate of public opinion requires getting thousands of people to sign petitions, write letters, make phone calls, come out to demonstrations, and pressure their elected representatives. It is clear that if women are to have a right most basic to individual liberty—control over their own reproduction—they will have to fight during the 1980's to preserve it.

The following national organizations have state and local affiliates and chapters which are working for reproductive freedom and which regularly put out newsletters and other publications: ACLU, 132 W. 43rd St., New York, N.Y. 10036; Planned Parenthood Federation of America, 810 7th Ave., New York, N.Y. 10019 (and the 187 local Planned Parenthoods); National Organization for Women, Inc. (NOW), 425 13th St., N.W., Suite 1048, Washington, D.C. 20004; National Abortion Rights Action League (NARAL), 1424 K Street, N.W., Washington, D.C. 20005; National Women's Health Network, 224 7th St., S.E., Washington, D.C. 20003; Reproductive Rights National Network (R2N2), 41 Union Sq. W., New York, N.Y. 10003; Religious Coalition for Abortion Rights (RCAR), 100 Maryland Ave., N.E., Washington, D.C. 20002; Catholics for a Free Choice, 2008 17th St., N.W., Washington, D.C. 20009.

NOTES

1. 410 U.S. 113 (1973).
2. 410 U.S. 179 (1973).
3. 410 U.S. 113 (1973).
4. 410 U.S. 179 (1973).
5. Alaska, Colorado, Hawaii, Maryland, Michigan, New York, North Carolina, Oregon, and Washington.
6. California, Connecticut, Massachusetts, New Jersey, and Pennsylvania. See, e.g., *Committee to Defend Reproductive Rights v. Meyers*, 29 Cal.3d 252, 625 P.2d 779 (1981).

7. Illinois, Indiana, Kentucky, Nebraska, North Dakota, Rhode Island, South Dakota, and Wyoming.

8. Alabama, Arkansas, Delaware, Florida, Idaho, Iowa, Kansas, Maine, Minnesota, Mississippi, Missouri, Montana, Nevada, New Hampshire, New Mexico, Oklahoma, Ohio, South Carolina, Tennessee, Texas, Utah, Vermont, and Wisconsin. Iowa also allows payment in those cases where the fetus is "physically deformed, mentally deficient or afflicted with a congenital illness."

9. *Harris v. McRae,* 448 U.S. 297 (1980).

10. Pub. L. No. 94-439, §209, 90 Stat. 1434 (1976); Pub. L. No. 95-205, §101, 91 Stat. 1460 (1977); Pub. L. No. 95-480, §210, 92 Stat. 1586; Pub. L. No. 96-123, §109, 93 Stat. 926; H.J. Res. 610 (F.Y. 1981).

11. H.J. Res. 610 (F.Y. 1981) also permitted funding for limited instances of rape and incest.

12. *Harris v. McRae,* 448 U.S. 297 (1980).

13. *Harris v. McRae, supra; Beal v. Doe,* 432 U.S. 438, 446 n.ll; see also *Planned Parenthood of Ohio v. Rhodes,* C-2-79-687 (S.D. Ohio Sept. 26, 1980).

14. H.J. Res. 610 (F.Y. 1981).

15. *Committee to Defend Reproductive Rights v. Meyers, supra,* n.6; *Right to Choose v. Byrne,* 165 N.J.Super. 443, 398 A.2d 587 (N.J. Super.Ct. 1979), 169 N.J.Super. 543 (Chan. Div. 1979); *Moe v. Sec'y of Administration and Finance,* 417 N.E.2d 387 (Mass. Supreme Jud.Ct. 1981).

16. *Planned Parenthood of Central Missouri v. Danforth,* 428 U.S. 52 (1976).

17. *Id.* at 70.

18. *Id.* at 71.

19. *Charles v. Carey,* No. 79 C 4541 (N.D. Ill. Nov. 16, 1979) (order granting preliminary injunction), *aff'd in part, rev'd in part,* 622 F.2d 772 (7th Cir. 1980) (interlocutory appeal). But see *Scheinberg v. Smith,* 659 F.2d 476 (5th Cir. 1981).

20. See T. Hayden and J. Novik, *Your Rights to Privacy* (New York: Avon, 1980), pp. 80-83.

21. *Planned Parenthood of Central Missouri v. Danforth, supra.*

22. *Id.* at 67 n.8.

23. *Akron v. Akron Center for Reproductive Health,*———U.S.———, 76 L.Ed. 2d 687 (June 15, 1983).

24. *Id.* at 712.

25. *Id.*

26. *Id.* at 712 and n.34.

27. *Id.* at 715.

28. *Id.* at 713 and n.37.

29. *Id.* at 713–714.

30. *Id.* at 716

31. *Planned Parenthood of Central Missouri v. Danforth, supra.*

32. *Bellotti v. Baird*, 443 U.S. 622, 61 L.Ed.2d 797 (1979).

33. *Akron v. Akron Center for Reproductive Health*,———U.S.———, 76 L.Ed.2d 687, 709 (June 15, 1983); *Planned Parenthood Association v. Ashcroft*,———U.S.———, 76 L.Ed.2d 733, 745 (June 15, 1983) (opinion of Justice Powell, joined only by Chief Justice Burger).

34. *Akron, supra*, 76 L.Ed.2d. at 709–710; *Planned Parenthood Association, supra*, 76 L.Ed.2d. at 745–747, 754.

35. A. Hofmann, "A Rational Policy Toward Consent and Confidentiality in Adolescent Health Care," *Journal of Adolescent Health* 1:9–17, 1980.

36. Centers for Disease Control, U.S. Dep't. of Health and Human Services, Abortion Surveillance, Annual Summary 1978 (1979).

37. W. Cates *et al.; The Effect of Delay and Method Choice on the Risk of Abortion Morbidity*, reprinted by U.S. Dep't of HEW, Public Health Service, from *Family Planning Perspectives* 9:266 (1977).

38. *Planned Parenthood Association, supra*, 76 L.Ed. 2d. At 745, n.16.

39. *H.L. v. Matheson*, 450 U.S. 398 (1981).

40. The rationale of *Bellotti v. Baird*, 443 U.S. 622 (1979), would apply to such a situation.

41. A. Torres, "Does Your Mother Know . . . ?" *Family Planning Perspectives*, Vol. 10, No. 5, Sept./Oct. 1978; A. Torres, "Telling Parents: Clinic Policies and Adolescents' Use of Family Planning and Abortion Services," *Family Planning Perspectives*, Vol. 12, No. 6, Nov./Dec. 1980.

42. *Glick v. Bryan*, No. CV-R-81-150 (BRT) (D. Nev. Jul. 7, 1981) (preliminary injunction issued); *Planned Parenthood Assoc. of Kansas City, Missouri v. Ashcroft*, 655 F.2d 848 (8th Cir. 1981) Supreme Court decision did not address this issue); *Women's Medical Center Inc. v. Roberts*, 512 F.Supp. 316 (D.R.I. 1981), *Women's Community Health Center, Inc. v. Cohen*, 477 F.Supp. 542 (D. Me. 1979); *Wynn v. Carey*, 582 F.2d 1375 (7th Cir. 1978) (interlocutory appeal), *reaff'd*, 599 F.2d 193 (1979); *Charles v. Carey*, No. 79 C 4541 (N.D. Ill. Nov. 16, 1979), *aff'd in part, rev'd in part*, 627 F.2d 772 (7th Cir. 1980); *Women's Service, P.C. v. Thone*, 483 F.Supp. 1022 (D. Neb. 1979), *aff'd*, 636 F.2d 206 (8th Cir. 1980), *vacated and remanded*, 452 U.S. 911 (1981); *Epp v. Thone*, Civ. No. 81-L-167 (D. Neb. May 30, 1981) (order granting temporary restraining order); *Leigh v. Olson*, 497 F.Supp. 1340 (D. N.D. 1980) (North Dakota subsequently enacted a parental/judicial consent statute which has not been challenged).

43. N.D. Ann. Code Art. 43, §135E (1977); Mont. Rev. Codes, §94-5-616; Utah Code Ann. §76-7-304(2); Minn. Stat. §144.343.

44. *Akron v. Akron Center for Reproductive Health*,———U.S.———, 76 L.Ed.2d. 687, 704–708 (June 15, 1983); *Planned Parenthood Association v. Ashcroft*,———U.S.———, 76 L.Ed.2d. 733, 739 (June 15, 1983); *Simopoulos v. Virginia*,———U.S.———, 76 L.Ed. 2d. 755, 760–765 (June 15, 1983).

45. Connecticut, Georgia, Hawaii, Idaho, Illinois, Indiana, Kentucky, Louisiana, Massachusetts, Michigan, Missouri, Montana, New Jersey, Nevada, New York, North Dakota, Oklahoma, Tennessee, Utah, Virginia, and Wisconsin.

46. *Gary-Northwest Indian Women's Services, Inc. v. Orr*, 496 F.Supp. 894 (D. Ind. 1980), *aff'd mem.*, 451 U.S.934, (1981); *Planned Parenthood Assoc. of Kansas City, Missouri v. Ashcroft*, 483 F.Supp. 679 (W.D. Mo. 1980), *aff'd in part, rev'd in part, and remanded*, 655 F.2d 848 (8th Cir. 1981); 664 F.2d 687 (8th Cir. 1981) (supplemental opinion); *cert granted*, 102 S. Ct. 2267 (May 24, 1982) *Margaret S. v. Edwards*, 488 F.Supp. 181 (E.D. La. 1980); *Margaret S. v. Treen*, No. 78-2765 (E.D. La. Nov. 27, 1981) (summary judgment); *Wolfe v. Stumbo*, C80-0285-L(A) (W.D. Ky. Dec. 3, 1980); *Charles v. Carey, supra; Glick v. Bryan*, No. CV-R-81-150 (BRT) (D. Nev. Jul. 7, 1981) (preliminary injunction); *Livingston v. N.J. Board of Med. Examiners*, 168 N.J.Super. 259 (App. Div. 1979), *cert. denied*, 82 N.J. 291 (1979).

47. *Roe v. Wade*, 410 U.S. 113 (1973).

48. Forrest, E. Sullivan, and C. Tietze, "Abortion in the United States, 1977-78," *Family Planning Perspectives* 11:329-341, 1979.

49. See, e.g., M.S. Burnhill, "Vaginal Second-Trimester Abortion," in J.J. Sciarra *et al.* (eds.), *Risks, Benefits, and Controversies in Fertility Control* (Hagerstown, Md.: Harper & Row, 1978), pp. 331-347.

50. The American Public Health Association, upon whose original 1970 opinion the Court in *Roe v. Wade* relied, 410 U.S. at 145, has changed its position from supporting an in-hospital requirement. Present policy states that "current data show that abortions occurring in the second-trimester can be safely performed by the Dilatation and Evacuation (D&E) procedure. . . . Requirements that all abortions after twelve weeks of gestation be performed in hospitals increase the expense and inconvenience to the woman without contributing to the safety of the procedure." "APHA Recommended Program Guide for Abortion Services (Revised 1979)" *American Journal of Public Health*, Vol. 70, No. 6, June 1980 at 652, 654.

51. S. Seims, "Abortion Availability in the United States," *Family Planning Perspectives*, 2:88, 1980.

52. *Planned Parenthood Association v. Ashcroft*,———U.S.———, 76 L.Ed.2d. 733, 739–742, 747, 754 (June 15, 1983).

53. 410 U.S. 113 (1973). See *Margaret S. v. Edwards*, 488 F.Supp. 181 (E.D. La. 1980); *Aware Woman Clinic*, No. 77-361-O-1-Civ-1 (M.D. Fla. Apr. 21, 1978); *Florida Women's Medical Clinic v. Smith*, 481 F.Supp. 137 (S.D. Fla. 1979); *Mahoning Women's Center v. Hunter*, 444 F.Supp. 12 (N.D. Ohio 1977); *aff'd*, 610 F.2d 456 (6th Cir. 1979), *vacated and remanded*, 447 U.S. 918 (1980); *Friendship Medical Center Ltd. v. Chicago Board of Health*, 505 F.2d 1141 (7th Cir. 1974); *Mobile Women's Medical Clinic v. Board*

of Commissioners, 426 F.Supp. 33 (S.D. Ala. 1977). But see *Westchester Women's Health Org., Inc. v. Whalen,* 475 F,Supp. 734 (S.D. N.Y. 1979) (order denying preliminary injunction); *Birth Control Center, Inc. v. Milliken,* 508 F.Supp. 1366 (E.D. Mich. 1981).

54. Among the cases which have found in favor of clinics are: *Deerfield Medical Center v. City of Deerfield Beach,* No. 81-5215 (5th Cir. Nov. 13, 1981) (interlocutory appeal); *Planned Parenthood of Minnesota, Inc. v. Citizens for Community Action,* 558 F.2d 861 (8th Cir. 1977); *Margaret S. v. Edwards,* 488 F.Supp. 181 (E.D. La. 1980); *Relsco, Inc. v. Cert. of Need and Licensure Bd.,* 234857 [Jefferson (Ky.) Cir.Ct. 9th Div., filed Sept. 23, 1977]. Cases upholding such regulations include *Bossier City Med. Suite v. City of Bossier,* 483 F.Supp. 633 (W.D. La. 1980); *West Side Women's Services, Inc. v. City of Cleveland,* 450 F.Supp. 796 (N.D. Ohio 1978), *aff'd and remanded,* 582 F.2d 1281 (6th Cir. 1978), *cert. denied,* 439 U.S. 983 (1978).

55. See *Margaret S. v. Edwards, supra; Mahoning Women's Center, supra; Women's Services v. Thone,* 483 F.Supp. 1022 (D. Neb. 1979).

56. *Planned Parenthood Association v. Ashcroft,*——U.S.——, 76 L.Ed.2d. 733, 742–744, 747, 754 (June 15, 1983).

57. La. R.S. §40:1299.35.14 (1980 Amend.) was challenged by the ACLU in *Margaret S. v. Edwards,* II C-78-2765 (E.D. La. Nov. 24, 1980) (order granting temporary restraining order).

58 *Akron v. Akron Center for Reproductive Health,*——U.S.——, 76 L.Ed.2d. 687, 716–717 (June 15, 1983).

59. *Valley Family Planning v. The State of North Dakota,* 475 F.Supp. 238 (D. N.D. 1979), *aff'd,* 661 F.2d 99 (1981); *Leigh v. Olson,* 497 F.Supp. 1340 (D. N.D. 1979); *Planned Parenthood of Central and Northern Arizona v. Arizona,* (D. Ariz. 537 F.Supp. 90, 1982) (summary judgment); *Planned Parenthood Association-Chicago Area v. Kempiners,* 531 F.Supp. 320 (N.D. Ill. 1981) (order granting summary judgment).

60. *Northern Virginia Women's Medical Center v. Horan,* 617 F.2d 1045 (4th Cir. 1980).

61. Pub. L. 95-457, §863, 92 Stat. 1254 (1978). Pub. L. 96-123, 93 Stat. 926 (1979) (Dep't of Defense restrictions). Pub. L. 96-123 §109, 75 Stat. 612 restricts use of funds under foreign assistance programs for abortion and covers funds appropriated to carry out provisions of the Peace Corps Act, as amended (22 U.S.C. §2504(e)).

62. Legal Services Corporation Act of 1974, §1007 (b) (8) Pub. L. 95-355, 42 U.S.C.A. §2996f (b) (8).

63. Civil Rights Commission Act of 1978, Pub. L. 95-444 §3, 92 Stat. 1067, 42 U.S.C.A. §1975c (f) (Supp. 1978).

64. Civil Rights Act of 1964, §701 (as amended) Pub. L. 95-555 §1, 92 Stat. 2076; Pub. L. 95-598., Title III, §330, 92 Stat. 2679, 42 U.S.C.A. §2000e (k) (Supp. 1978).

65. *Family Planning/Population Reporter*, Vol. 8, No. 3, June 1979, pp. 27-28.

65A. *Poelker v. Doe*, 432 U.S. 519 (1977).

65B. *Id.* at 523.

65C. *Harris v. McRae*, 448 U.S. 297 (1980).

66. *Nyberg v. The City of Virginia*, 5-73 Civ. 72 (D. Minn. Nov. 10, 1980), *aff'd*, 667 F.2d 754 (8th Cir. 1981) *appeal pending*, 50 U.S.L.W. 3803 (May 24, 1982) (No. 81-1782).

67. *Doe v. Bridgeton Hospital Assoc., Inc.*, 71 N.J. 478, 366 A.2d 641 (N.J. Sup.Ct. 1976), *cert. denied*, 433 U.S. 914 (1977).

68. J.D. Forrest, E. Sullivan, and C. Tietze, "Abortion in the United States, 1977-78," *Family Planning Perspectives*, 11:329, 1979.

69. S. Seims, "Abortion Availability in the United States," *Family Planning Perspectives*, 2:88, 1980.

70. *Griswold v. Connecticut*, 381 U.S. 479 (1965).

71. *Eisenstadt v. Baird*, 405 U.S. 438, 453-54 (1972).

72. *Id.* at 553.

73. *Carey v. Population Services International*, 431 U.S. 678, 688 (1977).

74. *Id.*

75. 21 U.S.C. §353 *et seq*.

76. *Tice Sales Company v. The State of Minnesota*, No. 4-80-4897 (D. Minn. Oct. 22, 1980); *Postscript Enterprises, Inc. v. Whaley*, 499 F.Supp. 646 (D. Mo. 1980), *rev'd*, 658 F.2d 1249 (8th Cir. 1981).

77. *Carey v. Population Services International*, 431 U.S. 678 (1977).

78. *Doe v. Irwin*, 615 F.2d 1162 (6th Cir. 1980), *cert. denied*, 449 U.S. 829 (Oct. 6, 1980); *Doe v. Pickett*, 480 F.Supp. 121 (S.D. W.Va. 1979); *T. H. v. Jones*, 425 F.Supp. 873 (D. Utah 1975) (3 Judge court), *aff'd in part*, 425 U.S. 986 (1976).

79. *Doe v. Irwin, supra*. However, in February 1982 the Department of Health and Human Services issued proposed regulations requiring that parents of unemancipated minors be notified of their attempts to get birth control at federally funded family-planning programs. 47 F.R.———(Feb. 22, 1982).

80. Social Security Act, 402 (a) (15) (A), 42 U.S.C. §602 (a) 15 (A), 45 C.F.R. §220.21 (AFDC); Social Security Act §1905 (a) (4) (C), 42 U.S.C. §1396d (a)(4)(C) (Medicaid); 42 C.F.R. §59.5 (2) (1978) (Public Health Services).

81. *T. H. v. Jones, supra; Doe v. Pickett, supra*.

82. *Doe v. Blum*, 80 Civ. 0177 (S.D. N.Y. filed Jan. 3, 1980).

83. All 50 states participate in one or both of these programs.

84. Social Security Act §402 (a) (15) (A), 42 U.S.C. §602 (a) (15) (A); Social Security Act §1905 (a) (4) (c), 42 U.S.C. §1396d (a) (4) (c).

85. *Id.*

86. 45 C.F.R. §220.21.

87. Social Security Act §1905 (a) (4) (c), 42 U.S.C. §1396d (a) (4) (c).

88. Title V provides that "not less than six percent of the amount

appropriated [each year, under Title V] shall be available for family planning services." SSA, Title V, §502; 42 U.S.C. §702 (1970). Neither the statute nor the regulations identify eligibility requirements for family planning services. Determination of eligibility under each project "will be made by the project director or a member of the project staff designated by him." 42 C.F.R. §51a.130 (c) (11) (1976). Among the criteria for approval of a state's program of projects by HHS is the establishment of income standards "which are to be applied flexibly." 42 C.F.R. §51a.130 (b) (5) (1976).

Title X, the Public Health Service Act, authorizes a program of grants and contracts to be administered by HHS, which may be made to public agencies and non-profit private organizations to "assist in the establishment . . . of voluntary family planning projects which shall offer a broad range of acceptable and effective family planning methods . . ." PSHA, Title X, §1001 (a); 42 U.S.C. §300 (a) (1970). The law does not establish eligibility requirements for the receipt of services and information, although it does require that the Secretary of HHS, in making grants, shall "take into account the number of patients to be served, the extent to which family planning services are needed locally, the relative need of the applicant, and its capacity to make rapid and effective use of such assistance." PSHA, Title X, §1001 (b) (1970); 42 C.F.R. §59.6 (1976); cf. 42 C.F.R. §59.5 (1976).

89. *Roe v. Wade*, 410 U.S. 113 (1973).

90. K. Ford, "Contraceptive Use in the United States," *Family Planning Perspectives*, Vol. 10, No. 5, Sept./Oct. 1978.

91. *Planned Parenthood v. Danforth*, 428 U.S. 52 (1976). Only Virginia and New Mexico still have laws requiring spousal consent for sterilizations.

92. *Murray v.Vandervander*, 552 P.2d 302 (Okla. Ct.App. 1972) (court refused to allow suit by husband against doctor and hospital for sterilization performed on his wife without his consent). See also *Ponter v. Ponter*, 342 A.2d 574 (N.J. Sup.Ct. Chanc. 1974).

93. Health Programs Extension Act of 1973, Pub. L. 93-45, Title IV, §401 (b), 87 Stat. 95 ("Conscience Clause"). Cases regarding sectarian hospitals' right to refuse treatment include *Taylor v. St. Vincent's Hospital*, 523 F.2d 75 (9th Cir. 1975), *cert. denied*, 424 U.S. 948 (1976); see also *Chrisman v. Sisters of St. Joseph of Peace*, 506 F.2d 308 (9th Cir. 1974); *Watkins v. Mercy Medical Center*, 364 F.Supp. 799 (D. Idaho 1973).

94. *McCabe v. Nassau County Medical Center*, 453 F.2d 698 (2d Cir. 1971); *Hathaway v. Worcester City Hospital*, 475 F.2d 701 (1st Cir. 1973), *application for stay of mandate denied*, 411 U.S. 929 (1973).

95. *Relf v. Weinberger*, 372 F.Supp. 1196 (D. D.C. 1974), *remanded for modification, sub nom. Relf v. Matthews*, 403 F.Supp. 1235 (D. D.C.1975).

96. *Relf v. Weinberger*, *supra* at 1199.

97. 45 C.F.R. §205.35 (1979).

98. 42 U.S.C. §300a-5, §300a-8 (Supp. 1976).

99. R. McGarrah, *Sterilization Without Consent: Teaching Hospital Violations of HEW Regulations,* Health Research Group (Jan. 1975); T. Bogue and D.W. Sigelman, *Sterilization Report Number 3: Continuing Violations of Federal Sterilization Guidelines By Teaching Hospitals in 1979,* Public Citizen Health Research Group (April 1979).

100. H. Kurtz, "Sterilization Widespread in Maryland: Hospitals Ignoring Federal Restrictions," *Washington Star,* June 22, 1980.

101. The 1980 Republican party platform included a call for an amendment to the Constitution to give fetuses—from the moment of conception—all legal rights to which live human beings are entitled.

102. See, e.g., *In the Matter Concerning Baby X,* No. 46543, (Mich. Ct. App. Apr. 23, 1980).

103. So far, the following states have enacted anti-abortion Con Con resolutions: Alabama, Arkansas, Delaware, Idaho, Indiana, Kentucky, Louisiana, Massachusetts, Mississippi, Missouri, Nebraska, Nevada, New Jersey, Oklahoma, Pennsylvania, Rhode Island, South Dakota, Tennessee, and Utah.

VII

Divorce and Related Issues*

For many women, the most difficult legal problem they ever face is getting a divorce. Emotional and legal problems mingle, exacerbating each other. The husband may threaten to harm the wife or take the children away; he may remove all the money from the joint savings account. The wife may feel lonely and scared, yet find that this is the time when she is most under pressure to cope, to find a lawyer, to protect herself. Many feminist lawyers report getting phone calls from women who have acute marital problems and are on the verge of hysteria; they often believe there is nothing they can do to protect themselves. This is not true. Women who are about to be divorced can get help and they can protect themselves.

This chapter is not designed to enable women to get their own divorces or to learn the legal grounds for divorce. Rather, it is designed to show women the kinds of issues they should be concerned with in the divorce situation, and to convince them that they can and should protect their own interests. It also explores similar issues for unmarried couples and some steps that can be taken to combat domestic violence.

A. Divorce, Property Division, Alimony, and Child Support

Do most people have to go through a long, drawn-out courtroom battle in order to get a divorce?

No. In only a small fraction of all divorces do the parties engage in courtroom dramatics. In those few cases, each side

---

*G. Diane Dodson is the principal author of Sections B-E of this chapter; she also contributed to Section A.

presents evidence, and the judge makes the final decision on whether to grant a divorce, who gets custody of the children, the amount of alimony and child support that should be awarded, and who is entitled to the property acquired during the marriage. In most cases, however, the parties negotiate their own decisions about these details, and the judge merely gives formal approval. The parties make only a pro forma courtroom appearance to finalize the breakup.

Does a woman need her own lawyer for divorce proceedings even when she and her husband have a friendly agreement to negotiate the details?

Yes. No matter how amicable your relationship with your husband is, once you agree to a divorce you have interests separate from his and you should be represented separately. *This is vital.*

Should a woman retain a lawyer to whom she is referred by her husband's lawyer?

Definitely not. This will be a tempting course to follow for any woman who has had little or no exposure to lawyers before, has no idea of how to get one, and feels bewildered and scared by the whole process. Avoid the temptation. The person your husband's lawyer recommends may be a fine attorney, but, if he is brought into the case in this way, he may be more sympathetic toward your husband's interests than he should be. This may happen for several reasons. The lawyer you are referred to may need the business and may find that the other lawyer ceases to refer business if he or she represents your interests too firmly; therefore, this lawyer may make certain compromises in advocating your side, perhaps even at a subconscious level. Or the lawyers may simply be good friends, and your lawyer may find himself or herself swayed too much by the arguments of a good friend. It is even possible that there is a formal kickback arrangement between the two lawyers, whereby your lawyer pays some of his or her own fee to the original lawyer for the favor of sending the business. This is grossly unethical, of course, but it does sometimes occur.

The fact that these things can happen does not mean that in any particular case they will happen. However, there is no reason to tempt fate by accepting a referral arrangement that can lead to problems. Most husbands and wives have at least some conflicting interests. Each party considering a divorce should get a lawyer who will represent those interests fully, without any possibility of a conflict in loyalties.

How should a woman go about finding a divorce lawyer?

There are a number of ways. Probably one of the best is to ask other friends or acquaintances who have obtained divorces whether they were satisfied with their lawyers' services. If they were, this may be a good recommendation. If you are poor, you should check with the Legal Aid Society or a legal services program; they usually do divorce work and should be listed in the telephone directory. Check with them even if you are not sure whether you would qualify for free help; they might be able to refer you to a lawyer even if they can't provide free services.

Another way to find information is to contact a women's paralegal group. Such groups often counsel women who are getting divorces, and this includes helping you find a lawyer. The best way to locate such a group is to look in the telephone book for a women's center, a local chapter of NOW (the National Organization for Women), or WEAL (the Women's Equity Action League). You could also ask someone in the feminist movement to refer you to any of the existing groups in your community. (Groups that are already formed are listed in Chart D in the Appendix.)

A more traditional way to find a lawyer is through the local bar association. Such groups usually maintain a lawyer referral service, which will give out a list of names to anyone who needs a lawyer. Use this service only as a last resort—and with caution. The bar association does not guarantee that the lawyers are competent or sympathetic to women clients; it simply gives the names of all lawyers who ask to be placed on the list. You should, therefore, shop around before you finally choose the lawyer you wish to retain. Arrange a short interview before making your decision so that you can find out whether you like the lawyer and his or her manner of dealing with your questions. There is usually no fee for such a preliminary interview, but check ahead of time to make sure.

Are there any books that it would be helpful to read before seeing a lawyer?

Yes. Reading a book on divorce written for non-lawyers will help give you a clearer idea of what is going on and what to expect during the legal process. Two books that are fairly good, despite some sexist overtones, are *Making the Best of It: A Common-Sense Guide to Negotiating a Divorce,* by Newton Frohlich (New York: Harper & Row, 1971); and *The Divorced Mother: A Guide to Readjustment,* by Carol Mindey (New York: McGraw-Hill, 1969). The Frohlich book emphasizes the process of negotiating divorce settlements and explains what each side should bargain for (although the woman's side is often not thought out adequately). The Mindey book offers advice on problems such as jobs, loneliness, and finances. An excellent book is *Women in Transition,* available from its authors, Women in Transition (see Chart D (3) in the Appendix). Other recommended books are *Creative Divorce,* by Mel Krantzler (New York: Signet, 1974); *Divorce: What a Woman Needs to Know,* by Barbara Hirsch (Chicago: Henry Regnery, 1973); and *Dissolution: No Fault Divorce, Marriage and the Future of Women,* by Riane Eisler (New York: McGraw-Hill, 1977).

How much does a divorce cost?

When you pay for a divorce, you are paying mainly for the lawyer's time. Divorce fees tend to be standardized with different fees charged in different parts of the country. Shop around to find out the range of fees usually charged in your area. This will help you choose a lawyer who will not overcharge. Generally a divorce that is uncontested—that is, one your husband agrees to, and in which you can negotiate all the details before going to court—costs less than a contested divorce. A fairly standard range is $300 to $750 for a simple, uncontested divorce; this fee covers simple negotiations, drafting of a simple settlement, and standard courtroom procedures. For a contested divorce or for an uncontested one requiring further negotiations over children or over real estate or other property, the lawyer may charge an hourly fee of $40 to $75 (or $120 for a high-priced lawyer). Some court costs will also be charged, perhaps in the range of $25, although in some states standard court costs are as high as $100 or as low as $5. There may be further costs for publication of newspaper notices (up to $100) or for paying a process server to serve court papers on your husband.

You should also realize that most lawyers will charge you something every time you call them up, usually in 15-minute increments. So remember this: if you need to keep costs down, but are tempted to call the lawyer for emotional support, call your friends instead. They won't charge you, and they'll probably do a better job of comforting you anyway.

Who pays the attorney's fees for the wife's lawyer?

It depends on your situation. If you qualify for Legal Aid or a legal services program, there is no charge. If you have your own income, you'll pay for your attorney although if your income is less than your husband's, you may bargain for some reimbursement from him. If you have no independent income, your husband may be ordered by the court to pay your attorney. In some states, your lawyer can collect a part of this fee when he or she arranges for temporary alimony and child support. However, in many places, court-awarded fees are far lower than those generally charged by divorce lawyers. Many lawyers will refuse to rely on payment of fees by your husband and will look to you to pay some or all of the fee in advance and to be ultimately responsible for any part of the fee not paid by your husband. One advantage of this arrangement is that it leaves the lawyer mentally free to bargain vigorously for all you are entitled to without fear that his or her fee will be strongly opposed by your husband as a result. Unless you qualify for free legal services, you probably should assume you will have to pay at least a portion of the fee yourself, in advance, and make arrangements to borrow or save funds for this purpose.

Is it necessary to have a written fee agreement with your lawyer?

It is not absolutely necessary, but it is advisable. The agreement should specify the amount paid as an initial retainer, what services it covers, whether it is refundable and under what circumstances. The agreement should also spell out the basis for further charges—i.e., will there be an hourly charge in *addition* to the initial payment or *out of* the initial payment? Will a higher fee be charged if the divorce becomes contested? When and how will further payments be required? Who is responsible for payments, your husband or you? What extra services or costs will you be charged for? These may include court costs, photocopying, transcripts, and the like. Be sure to ask for a monthly itemized bill.

If you are unhappy with your lawyer and don't believe that he or she is representing you fairly, what can you do?

You can fire the lawyer. Many women do not realize that the relationship between a lawyer and a client is that of employer and employee. You are the employer and you have a perfect right to fire your employee at any time.

Firing your lawyer may present tricky financial problems, though. First, if the lawyer required a retainer ahead of time, he or she may try to keep it, whether or not any work has been done. The lawyer is entitled to payment only for work actually done, however, and must refund unearned portions unless the written fee agreement specifies that the retainer is not refundable. Ask for an itemized bill, setting forth hours worked and the nature of work done in that time. If the charges seem unjustified, ask for the refund. Your next lawyer may be able to help you collect it if the first lawyer proves recalcitrant.

Second, some lawyers will try to keep any original papers you have given them for the divorce, under what is called a lawyer's lien, unless you pay them the agreed-upon fee. Since you need the papers to get the divorce, the lawyer has you over a barrel until you pay the fee. Your new lawyer can also help negotiate this matter, but the best thing is to avoid the situation altogether by giving lawyers only copies of original documents. In that way, you always have the papers you need, and papers can never be withheld as a way to force you to pay an unearned fee. If your lawyer does need the originals for the courtroom proceedings, you can hand them over at that stage.

A less drastic method than firing your attorney may be to tell him or her clearly and calmly what you are unhappy about, and see whether this produces any changes.

If you believe your lawyer has acted unethically, or has failed to represent you fully, report this to any feminist group that you know of and to the bar association. The more feedback women's groups get on divorce lawyers, the more they can do something about the present situation in which many women have voiced very strong complaints about the way they are being treated by lawyers.

How can you tell if your lawyer is representing you adequately?

There are no hard-and-fast rules, but there are a few things to look out for. The lawyer should send you itemized bills for his or her services, detailed by the hour (unless you agreed to a flat fee for the entire case), and should explain any item you do not understand. You should get copies of all papers and letters prepared for your case. The lawyer should be willing to explain what is happening in terms that make sense to you. The lawyer should insist on fair property and custody arrangements on your behalf (there will be some discussion of these concepts later in the chapter), and you should feel totally confident that he or she will go to bat for you. From a feminist perspective, the lawyer should be able to perceive you as a person with individual strengths and weaknesses, and with your own unique needs, desires, and family situation, not as a stereotyped woman whose needs he or she automatically "understands" without asking any questions. For instance, a lawyer might assume that you want custody of the children; or not check to see whether you need alimony to cover expenses for additional training or education, because he or she thinks you would be satisfied to work at a low-paid job or not to work at all. Finally, your lawyer should have time to talk with you. Feel suspicious if he or she doesn't return your calls or asks you to repeat the same things over and over. If it seems your lawyer has no time, it is better to find one who does have time to devote to your case. You should use the occasion of your divorce to prepare for your future and you need a lawyer who will help you do this.

Does the husband have the right to kick his wife out of the house?

No, generally not before a divorce hearing, especially if she wants the marriage to continue. If the husband wants to end the marriage and the wife does not agree to leave the home, he will have to move out. If the husband tries to force her to leave, she can probably obtain a court order, with a lawyer's help, allowing her to stay. If the wife wants the marriage to end and the husband does not, she may have to leave the home. She should talk to a lawyer at once if this situation arises. However, regardless of who leaves, at the time of divorce the court may award the family home to either the husband or wife or order that the house be sold and the proceeds split, depending on state marital property law.

Is it all right to sleep with your husband once you have decided to get a divorce?

Never. First, in many states, sleeping with your husband may prevent you from getting the divorce at all. If you are claiming your husband's adultery as grounds for divorce, sleeping with him after the adultery occurred is legally construed as forgiving him for his actions. Thus you lose your right to divorce him.

Second, even if the divorce is uncontested (so that you don't need to prove adultery or any other grounds for divorce in court), the fact that you do have strong "fault" grounds for divorce can put you in a strong bargaining position in negotiations over the details of the divorce. You may, for example, get a better settlement on issues like child custody and alimony simply because your husband's lawyer knows you would win in court on the question of the divorce itself. Your husband may have even been advised to sleep with you for just this reason: to destroy your legal grounds for divorce and thereby weaken your position in the negotiations.

Last, so-called no-fault grounds for divorce are often based on no "cohabitation" for a certain period of time, such as 60 days or one year. In many of these states, sleeping with your husband even once will be considered "cohabiting" for legal purposes and you will have to start counting the time period all over again.

Should you ask for alimony?

Probably, if you are in the situation of most wives. Many women have begun to feel guilty about asking for alimony—perhaps in response to those men who are clamoring that alimony is "anti-women's-liberation" and oppresses men. The fact that these same men have not taken up any other banner of women's liberation provides a definite clue to their real motives. They want to get out of their marriages with as much money as possible, while absolving themselves of responsibility for the financial situation of their wives.

Marriage still places all but a few women at a tremendous financial disadvantage. Most women do not get enough training or education before marriage to maximize their wage-earning capacity; they are told that their husbands will take care of them and that they need not plan for a career. Then society encourages women to bear and rear children. This further decreases a woman's wage-earning capacity, for even when she has somehow managed to acquire education or training, she loses work experience and her own self-confidence during the years of child rearing. Many women work to put their husbands through medical school or other kinds of extended education without ever receiving comparable training themselves or even a repayment of the money. Nor are women paid for their years of work in the home even though this work has real economic value. Thus they have no way to acquire property unless the husband "gives" it to them. Finally, society also encourages most women to take custody of the children upon divorce—again without compensation. Put all these factors together, and it is clear that alimony is one way of compensating women for those financial disabilities aggravated, or caused, by marriage: unequal educational opportunities; unequal employment opportunities; and an unequal division of family responsibilities, with no compensation for the spouse who works in the home.

A husband may argue, of course, that society and not he is responsible for any discrimination his wife faces in education or employment. This may be true. The husband, however, benefits from the *system's discrimination in his favor*, and there is no valid reason to allow him to carry away the fruits of an unfair bias. Moreover, the husband is often responsible for any unequal division of housekeeping responsibilities and lack of pay for the "housekeeper." After all, husbands acquiesce in the societal demand that their wives stay home; and it is a rare man indeed who would even consider staying home himself with the children so the wife could advance her career. If the husband would help rear the children, he and his wife could come much closer to equalizing their wage-earning capacities. Unfortunately most men don't see it this way. When married, they expect their wives to assume most of the responsibility for rearing the children. When divorced, many of them expect their wives to take custody of the children, again without conceding that their wives ought to be compensated for the extra work the men are avoiding.

Thus, women should not be cowed into believing that to ask for alimony is to be unliberated, or that their husbands provide alimony out of the largess of their noble hearts. Women have earned alimony and will continue to earn it— they should receive it as well. It's a different story, of course, for women who have been married only briefly and have suffered no change in earning capacity, or for those few women who do have equal wage-earning capacity whose husbands have shared equally in the responsibilities of home life and whose husbands will continue to carry an equal burden with the children after the divorce. But until other women achieve that status, they deserve alimony.

May a woman ever be forced to pay alimony?

Yes, in some instances. The Supreme Court ruled in 1979 that an Alabama law which required husbands to support their ex-wives, but did not require wives to support their ex-husbands, violated the Equal Protection Clause.[1] As a result, Alabama and other states must now rewrite their alimony laws in sex-neutral terms.

Under these new laws, whichever spouse has the greater income or wage-earning capacity may be ordered to pay alimony if the other spouse is in financial need. Ideally, the need for the parent with custody of the children to spend time caring for them will be taken into account. Because men generally have greater income and wage-earning opportunities than their wives (as a result of low pay for women) and because few husbands have custody of the children, few wives will be required to pay alimony. But in those cases where the husband is unemployed, chronically ill, or otherwise unable to support himself adequately, it is not unfair to ask a financially able wife to help support him.

What kinds of expenses does alimony cover?

Alimony covers household and personal expenses, work-related costs, training and educational expenses, and recreation for the spouse.

Is alimony always permanent or does it just give a woman* help for a year or two to get on her feet or to receive further education?

Historically, alimony has been "permanent," at least until the husband died or the wife remarried. (Of course, it was always possible to agree in a separation agreement to payments over a shorter time.) Recently, however, in what has been a mixed blessing for women, a number of states have passed laws allowing courts to award "rehabilitative alimony" or "short-term alimony." In theory, these are available to aid a woman who may not require long-term assistance but who does need help in establishing herself in a job or in furthering her education. In practice, many feminist lawyers believe that unsympathetic judges have begun to award short-term "rehabilitative" alimony instead of permanent alimony in situations in which there is little hope the wife will ever be able to support herself adequately.

Is a woman entitled to child support payments?

Of course, if she has custody of the children. Again, women should not hesitate to ask that the husband contribute his fair share. Recent studies have shown that women usually contribute a greater share of child support costs than do their husbands.

What should be included in child support?

The standard items are fairly obvious: food, clothing, shelter, education, medicine, medical insurance. It is also important to negotiate for extra support amounts when there are high medical expenses not covered by insurance. These often include bills for eyeglasses, dentistry, and psychiatry. Extras such as summer camp and music lessons should be included. If it is financially feasible, one should also negotiate for the costs of a college education and even the cost of graduate school (although the latter is hard to get). The separation agreement should also spell out who pays for travel and long-distance calls to the out-of-town parent who does not have custody.

---

*Throughout the following discussion of alimony and child support, usage of the terms "man," "woman," "husband," and "wife" reflects traditional roles and the most frequently encountered situations. The reader should keep in mind that in theory, if not often in practice, either spouse may be awarded alimony or child support depending on financial need.

Can child support be increased to keep up with inflation?

Your separation agreement should provide for both an automatic cost-of-living adjustment and increased payments as your children grow older and have higher expenses. (Electric guitars and stereos are far more expensive than teddy bears and overalls.) If your agreement does not cover this or if the payments are based on a court order, it is possible to return to court to ask for higher payments to keep up with inflation or increased expenses. Judges in a few states have even included automatic cost-of-living increases in court orders, contingent only on the ex-husband's income increasing by the amount of the cost-of-living increase.

Will it help the lawyer increase the amount of alimony and child support if a woman documents her past budget needs and the family assets?

Yes, in fact it can't be done without your help. You must itemize all expenses that you will need covered and document them with past bills wherever possible. The lawyer must have this information in order to make a convincing case of your need for alimony and child support. Standard budget items would include rent or mortgage payments; repair bills; utility and phone bills; household supplies; furniture replacements; transportation (including car and public transportation); insurance premiums (for health and life insurance); psychiatric, medical, and dental care expenses; food; clothing; children's tuition; recreation, including vacations; such work-related expenses as lunches, extra clothes, day care, and cleaning and laundry services; education and training costs; and taxes.

You should make special arrangements for the life insurance on your husband to ensure that there will be a viable policy to cover alimony and child support if your husband should die. One arrangement is for your husband to give you the incidents of ownership on the policy, so that he cannot use the policy as security for a loan or change the named beneficiaries. Another approach is to request alimony money to make the premium payments yourself; this ensures that your husband will not let the policy lapse.

Work and education-related expenses should also be emphasized because they are the kinds of expenses most lawyers tend to overlook for a woman. Both are important for your own well-being, too, because being busy will make it easier to adjust to the change and because the vast majority of women will never receive enough alimony to live on comfortably. Most men simply do not make enough money to support two families, and few men keep the payments up anyway.[2] It is best to face these facts from the start. Thus you will have a real need to improve your education or training. Additional training will increase your wage-earning capacity and your ability to provide the kind of living you would like on your own. Having the training also reduces the pressure to remarry for economic reasons and allows you the time to find someone you really care about if you do want to remarry. Don't think, though, that education eliminates the need for alimony. Always plan for the worst. A B.A. is no guarantee of a good job to a 45-year-old woman who has been out of the labor market for a long time.

In addition to preparing a solid budget, you will need to list the family assets. You should get the original or copies of all legal documents showing property of any kind owned by either or both of you and tax returns showing your husband's income. You should do these things as soon as there is any indication of trouble in the marriage because some husbands hide these documents or change real estate, stocks, bonds, cash, and other property owned in your joint names to their names alone.

What other legal documents will your lawyer need?

He or she will need your marriage certificate and documentation of any former marriages and divorces.

Is there any reason to collect budget, property, and income information quickly?

Yes. First, as mentioned above, your husband may be acting to hide the information in order to reduce his payments; you should get copies before he does so. In fact, it wouldn't hurt if women began collecting duplicate copies of such information as a matter of course in case their husbands ever do walk out on them without much advance warning. This information would also be useful in case of sudden death and just to make you more independent.

Second, you will need this information for the temporary alimony payments your lawyer will arrange for the interval before the divorce takes place. It is extremely important to have accurate information for this round because what you get as temporary alimony will set the tone for how much you receive as permanent alimony. If you are unsure of the exact amount for any particular item and have no documentation, it is best to err on the generous side, since the judge will almost always cut back on the figures.

Is there a difference between alimony and property?

Alimony and property are separate concepts; both should be fully negotiated and settled in a separation agreement or court order. Property includes all physical and financial possessions which have been acquired in the family up to the time of divorce: cash, house, furnishings, jewels, car, boat, land, stocks, bonds, businesses or business interests, and so on. Pension rights and the value of a professional education are included in some states. At the time of divorce, property is divided between the husband and wife by separation agreement or property settlement agreement or by court order. The principles used and the resulting divisions vary widely from state to state. There may be a 50–50 split or one spouse may get all the property. However, the division of property is a onetime event and the arrangements are settled at the close of the divorce case—even if some property is still to be transferred or some payments are still to be made under the plan. It is not possible to come in two years later and ask that the question of property division be reopened (unless, of course, there has been fraud or coercion or a misrepresentation of assets). The basic rule in most states is that jointly owned property may be evenly divided by the husband and wife without either paying federal income tax on the transferred property. Tax problems do sometimes arise when the property which is transferred has increased in value since it was purchased, and the tax aspects of the property division should be fully explored with your lawyer.

Alimony, on the other hand, consists of periodic support payments to the husband or wife after the marriage has ended. There is an obligation under an agreement or court order to make support payments of a certain amount on a periodic basis (weekly, monthly, annually), until the spouse receiving alimony remarries, or the husband or the wife dies. Because it is uncertain when these events may happen, the total amount of alimony that will be received is unknown. It is possible for the wife to return to court later to ask for increased alimony if circumstances change or for the husband to ask for decreased payments if his income decreases. Alimony payments are taxable to the one who receives them and are deducted from the income of the one who makes them.

What right does a woman have to property acquired during the marriage?

In the eight community property states,[3] the husband and wife each own an undivided one-half interest in all of the community property. This includes almost all property either the husband or the wife acquired during the marriage, except inheritances or gifts—which remain separate property. Community property is almost always simply divided in two equal shares at the time of the divorce. (In some of the states, "equitable" principles are sometimes applied to vary this rule—for example, by awarding the family home to a mother with custody of the children.) However, some of these states do not provide for alimony at all. Therefore, all the woman gets at the time of the divorce is one-half of the property and no future support payments for herself. (She may get child support.) This is particularly unfair in situations in which there is little property at the time of the divorce, but the husband earns a good salary (for example, if he is a doctor just out of medical school).

In the 42 "common-law" states, property has traditionally been divided quite differently. The predominant principle has been that the property belongs to the one whose name it is in or the one who paid for it. The wife could not get a share of property the husband bought with his own money and put in his own name—which many men do. When the property was put in joint names, courts would assume it should be divided equally even if the husband supplied most of the money. However, courts tended to rule that the husband made the wife a *gift* of her joint interest in the home or other property (not that she earned it with homemaking and child rearing), and that this gift was contingent "on her faithful performance of her marriage vows." Therefore, if she was found to be at fault in the marriage—because of adultery, desertion, or abandoning the home—she would lose all interest in jointly owned property, except to the extent she had contributed her own money. Thus an adulterous wife who worked in the home might receive nothing at all, while an equally adulterous husband who paid money for the property would receive everything.

To deal with this inequitable situation, many of the common-law states recently have passed "equitable distribution" laws. Under these laws, divorce courts may divide all of the "marital property" between husband and wife at the time of divorce. As with community property, this "marital property" generally includes all the property acquired during the marriage except inheritances and gifts. Unlike community property laws, these laws do not require a 50–50 division of the assets (and of course, it is generally the wife who gets less than 50 percent and the husband who gets more). Instead, the laws provide a list of factors the divorce court should weigh in deciding on a fair division of property. These often include length of marriage; age, health, and earning ability of husband and wife; contribution of each to homemaking and care of the children, and, in money or work, to acquiring the property; and who will have custody of the children. Because these laws specify a whole list of factors, marital "fault," such as adultery, desertion, or cruelty, is often eliminated or diminished in importance in dividing the marital property.

Does a woman have a right to a share of her former husband's pension and other work benefits?

In some states, yes. Community property states and some common law states which provide for "equitable distribution"[4] of marital property classify pensions and retirement benefits as co-owned marital property which is subject to division between husband and wife at the time of divorce regardless of who earned them. Of course, the wife owns an interest only in the part of the benefits earned while she and her husband were married.

Other states consider pensions the separate property of the one who earned them rather than a part of the "marital property" and therefore refuse to give wives a share of their husband pensions at the time of divorce. This is very unfair. Often the husband's pension is the largest or second-largest asset the couple has (after the family home) and the wife truly is denied a fair share of property acquired during the marriage when she does not get a share of the pension. Women's groups would do well to lobby with their state legislatures to make sure pension and retirement benefits are considered co-owned marital property which should be divided on divorce. But even when the wife does not get an ownership interest in the pension, her lawyer may still be able to start legal proceedings (attachment, garnishment) to receive part of it if her husband fails to make his alimony or child support payments.[5]

Federal law also comes into the picture under two Supreme Court decisions. In 1979 the Supreme Court refused to recognize the supremacy of state laws which make wives co-owners of certain federally controlled pensions earned by their husbands; and in 1981, the Court reached the same conclusion in the slightly different context of federal military retirement benefits.[6] The 1979 decision ruled that federal pension law which does not provide for payments to divorced spouses of railroad workers takes precedence over state community property law under which the wife is a co-owner of the pension. The case, *Hisquierdo v. Hisquierdo*, involved a woman who was declared co-owner of her husband's railroad pension by a California divorce court. The Federal Railroad Retirement Act which governed his pension prevents creditors from seizing such pension benefits to satisfy the husband's debts. The Supreme Court ruled that this provision, which was designed to protect retired workers from their creditors, also protected the husband from his wife's co-ownership of the pension under California community property law!

In the 1981 case (*McCarty v. McCarty*), the Supreme Court decided that a man receiving federal military retirement pay is similarly protected against his wife's co-ownership of that benefit. Down the road is an even more important issue implicating most private pensions—whether the federal Employee Retirement Income Security Act of 1974 (ERISA), which was designed to ensure that workers actually receive these private pensions, likewise gives the man total ownership of the pension where state law would give him only half ownership. If the Supreme Court decides this issue too in favor of total ownership by the earning spouse (usually the man), the relevant federal law will have to be amended to specify the priority of state laws giving spouses co-ownership of the pension.

In response to the *Hisquierdo* case, several bills were

introduced in Congress to give pension rights to divorced wives (or husbands, where appropriate) of federal employees. Under some of these bills, the former wife of a civil service, Foreign Service, or military employee would be automatically entitled to a share of his retirement benefits if the couple had been married at least 20 years before they were divorced. Another bill would give a wife (or husband) a share of the spouse's civil service pension if they had been married 5 years—but only if the state court refused to consider the pension as marital property.

While these bills have not passed, Congress has passed other laws giving women significant rights. In 1977, Congress amended the Social Security Act to provide some Social Security benefits to divorced spouses whose marriages had lasted at least 10 years.[7] Before 1977 the marriage requirement was 20 years. In late October 1980, the Foreign Service Act was amended by P.L. 96–465 to provide that former wives (or husbands) of Foreign Service officers, married for at least 10 years, should be presumed entitled to a pro rata share of their husband's retirement annuity and survivor's benefits. The divorce court can review and change the presumption which would give the woman one-half of the benefits earned during the marriage, but this is still a valuable starting point for property division. The law also requires that Foreign Service husbands may not opt out of a survivor's benefit plan unless the wife agrees in writing. However, the more equitable solution in all these cases would be to give spouses 50–50 co-ownership of all pension benefits earned during the marriage; this eliminates the unfairness to wives who work in the home but are divorced before specific time periods, whether 5, 10, or 20 years.

Finally, in 1982 Congress passed a law (P.L. 97-252) to overturn the McCarty decision. The new law returns to the states the right to treat military retirement pay as co-owned marital property, subject to division as part of divorce proceedings. Of course, if a state does not treat any other pensions this way, women in that state will not be helped by the new law. This law is also different from the Foreign Service Act provision, in that it does not set up a presumption of entitlement to a pro rata share. Other provisions in the new law, however, give some divorced military wives the right to receive survivor's benefits, medical benefits, and commissary benefits.

For more information about pension rights, women should contact the Pension Rights Center, 1346 Connecticut Ave., N.W., Washington, D.C. 20036, (202) 296–3778; and the NOW Legal Defense and Education Fund (see chart D in the Appendix). For specific information about the most recent bills introduced in or passed by Congress to respond to this issue, contact Congresswoman Pat Schroeder's office (U.S. House of Representatives, Washington, D.C.), since she is the congressional leader on the issue.

Women should also think about asking for their fair share of their husbands' disability pay, workmen's compensation, stock options, and profit-sharing distributions.

How much alimony, child support, and property should a good lawyer be able to get for a woman?

There is no one correct answer. At present, one-third to one-half of the property, plus one-third to one-half of the husband's *net* income as *gross* alimony and child support is considered the upper limit. Women ought to debate whether this is in fact a good standard.

Other views are certainly possible. Those who strongly view marriage as a partnership, in which each partner does work that is equally valuable, might like to see women get one-half of all property and enough alimony to leave each party with equal cash on hand after both deduct certain fixed expenses such as money used solely for the children (child support) and taxes. That is, wife and husband will have equal *net* incomes after the divorce.

Other women might prefer to examine the economic situation of the parties more closely. This view would use property settlement and alimony to compensate women only for financial damages incurred through marriage. Women who have stayed home for years rearing the family and doing housework would charge damages for each year of loss of wages, loss of associated fringe benefits (paid vacations, sick leave, medical insurance coverage, pension plans), and decrease in wage-earning capacity, plus any continued loss of these items after the divorce. Conversely, the woman who has been married for only a few years, has had no children, has continued the career she had prior to the marriage, and whose husband has shared the housework equally, has suffered no financial loss through the marriage. She would not receive alimony, although she would still be entitled to one-half of the property acquired through joint effort during the marriage.

What is the practical difference between the use of gross and net income figures in computing alimony and child support?

Lawyers often compare the gross income a woman receives—including any salary she earns, plus alimony and child support—to the net income the man is left with after deducting taxes, alimony, child support, and other expenses. This makes their relative economic positions look much more equitable than they really are, and thus leads the woman to ask for less. For instance, in *Making the Best of It* Newton Frolich advises the husband to deduct from his gross income the following expenses: taxes, computed at the higher post-divorce rate; life, medical, and hospital insurance premiums; contribution to children's college education fund; and retirement and pension fund contributions. He then deducts one-half of the remaining net figure as alimony and child support.

Frolich's figures, in one example, are as follows:

Husband's income		$15,000
Deductions		
Post-divorce taxes	$2650	
Retirement fund payment	1200	
Life, disability, hospital, and medical insurance premiums	850	
College fund payment	500	
Total:	$5200	
		−5200
		$9800
Alimony and child support		−4900
Total:		$4900

This computation appears reasonable, since each is left with $4900. After all, the man does not have the personal use of all the deductions, so it is only fair that the woman get one half of his usable income. The flaw in this reasoning is that she will not have the personal use of much of her income, either. Frolich has actually compared the husband's net income of $4900 to the wife's *gross* income of $4900. When she deducts income not available for her personal use, such as taxes and money spent on the children, i.e., child support, her net income will be considerably smaller than $4900.

If the husband deducts taxes, medical insurance, child support, and other expenses from his gross income, the wife should deduct comparable expenses and then compare their net incomes. For instance, she will have to pay taxes on alimony, she will have to use the child support money for actual child-rearing expenses, and she may have to pay medical care expenses, too. The husband's claim is that he will not have the personal use of the money that must be spent to meet all these expenses. The wife's claim is the same. It is important to remember this point, especially in connection with the child support payment. The child support money is intended to cover the *actual cost* of rearing the children. It does not matter whether it is the husband or wife who actually walks into the store and lays out this money; it will still not be available for other purposes. Thus, a principal point to keep in mind while negotiating divorce settlements is to compare, and strive to achieve equality in, the *net* incomes of husband and wife.

This same approach can be used where the wife works. It would compensate the woman whose wage-earning capacity has suffered because she stayed home for a time to rear the children. Why should the man continue to be able to enjoy a larger net income just because he had the privilege of working for pay during the entire marriage while the woman worked for free during many years? In such a case, each would deduct taxes, retirement payments, insurance premiums, college fund payments, and child support expense money. The wife would then be entitled to one-half of the difference between their two net incomes as alimony—in order to equalize their net incomes. This compensates her fairly for her earlier contribution to the family, any sacrifice of career, and continued work in caring for the children. The formula also rewards the husband who is willing to take on his share of the care of the children after the divorce and who did not demand that his wife stay home at the cost of her career. In this situation, if their net incomes are roughly comparable, there may be no alimony.

Are there any qualifications to this discussion of the need to equalize the post-divorce incomes of the husband and wife?

Two provisos are needed. First, courts do not accept the views set forth and would not use this standard in awarding alimony and child support to the woman. However, this fact need not prevent a woman from convincing her husband that equal net incomes would be the egalitarian solution and from obtaining a divorce settlement along the suggested lines.

Second, the answer has assumed a strong partnership view of marriage and is intended to stimulate discussion on the issue of how to compensate women fairly in the divorce situation.[8] To date, most discussions of the issue have looked at the woman's income as determined by her needs, and the man's as determined by his right to keep as much of his "own" income as possible. The authors believe that marriage should be legally viewed as a partnership, which implies that the husband and wife have equal economic rights, no matter which one chooses to stay home or to work outside the home or in what combination they do these things. The assumption is that working outside the home for pay is, in a moral sense, a privilege, not a right, and that the person who has the privilege is not automatically entitled to all the benefits of that status—including the pay. Most people assume that the man has the right to support the family by working outside the home for pay and that whatever is left after expenses are met is his. If the husband's work is a privilege and if the wife's work in the home is seen as a necessary half of an important partnership, obviously both partners should get one-half of the proceeds. Where the partnership continues after a divorce because the woman still takes care of the children, or where the wife works outside the home for pay, but the partnership has previously crippled her ability to earn money, she should still be entitled to one-half of the proceeds, although her own earnings will be added into the communal pot for division purposes.

Is it important to get good alimony and property arrangements in the interim before the final divorce is secured?

Definitely. The amount of temporary alimony you receive usually sets the standard for the amount of permanent alimony you'll receive. This holds true for child support payments also. Thus, the effort to secure temporary payments is just as important as the final divorce proceeding itself.

If the husband has a small income at the time of the divorce, is there any way to get an increase in alimony in the future?

Yes. You can request an escalation clause in the separation agreement, which will provide for a stated increase in alimony for every stated increase in your husband's income.

What are the tax differences between alimony and child support?

The husband can deduct alimony from his income for income tax purposes; he cannot deduct child support. Similarly, the wife must pay taxes on alimony; she does not have to pay taxes on child support.

What are the practical consequences of the tax difference?

The tax difference induces husbands to try to disguise child support payments as alimony. For instance, Newton Frolich makes a big pitch in his book that it saves men money to pay alimony. He does not mean that a man should pay adequate child support and then some extra money as alimony. Instead, he literally means that the husband should take the same amount of money he will have to pay anyway as child support, and call some of it alimony in order to get the income tax deduction. Women should be extremely wary of this tactic, since child support money, whether called child support or alimony, is still money that must be used for the children. It cannot be used for personal needs. Since the woman does need alimony for her own support, she should bargain for it as a separate item.

Accepting a large alimony payment in lieu of adequate child support can lead to real financial hardship for the wife and children. First, as already noted, the wife must pay taxes on alimony. This means that while an alimony settlement is a tax advantage for the man, it is a decided disadvantage for the woman. Second, alimony ceases upon remarriage, but child support ceases only when the children come of age. If you have agreed to call some child support alimony, you will lose it when you remarry, even though your children may still need the money. Your new husband may not be able to support your children, since he may already have children of his own. Lack of adequate child support might even discourage him from marrying you.

On the other hand, it is important to bargain for enough

alimony to meet your own personal needs. If you fail to do this and rely instead on child support, you may find yourself really destitute when the children grow up and the child support ceases. A study by the Rand Corporation in California showed that some former wives of wealthy doctors and lawyers were living on welfare[9]—a sad commentary on how well their lawyers had bargained for them. The rule of thumb, then, in bargaining for alimony and child support, is to *keep the two as separate items*. If you get the right amount of money for each category, you ensure that your children will have the money they need as long as they need it, and that you will have the personal income you need as long as you need it. Of course, if you can get more money by departing from this rule, you should do it—provided you are clear about your financial needs once either alimony or child support ceases.

Should you negotiate with your husband about alimony, child support, property, or other matters before seeing your own lawyer?

Definitely not. You should know your rights before making any agreement—financial or otherwise. You might be entitled to much more than you realize, or you might not have seriously analyzed your future situation—and it is always best to have the facts before making a decision.

Should you leave your money or securities in a joint account if you are thinking about a divorce or you suspect your husband wants a divorce?

No. Take out the money you think is your own. Men are often advised to take all the money out of a joint account as a way of preventing their wives from getting any of it. If you have even the slightest suspicion that your husband would do such a thing, out of bitterness or anger, and if you need the money, it is best to take precautionary measures.

If your husband has cleaned out the joint savings or checking account, or sold joint property, is there anything you can do?

Yes. Your lawyer can get a court order forcing your husband to reimburse you in a property settlement. If he has not taken property or funds, but you suspect he plans to do so, your lawyer can also get an order forbidding any such action. This would prevent your husband from removing or selling any assets before the divorce.

Do you need a full-scale trial to get the best property settlement, alimony, and child support payments?

No. In fact, the full-scale trial is a bad idea. It sends attorneys' fees skyrocketing because preparation for trial and a trial itself are very time-consuming. In addition, a trial brings a private controversy out into the open. It makes both parties anxious to show the world that the other side was at fault, and it usually ends with bitterness and hostility on all sides. If at all possible, it is much better to negotiate the details of your divorce, and then go through a pro forma court hearing.

This said, it must still be emphasized that there will undoubtedly be some divorces that women will want to litigate. If a husband will not negotiate, a trial may be the only way the wife can secure the financial arrangements that are her due. In this situation, she should not hesitate to go forward to a full-scale court hearing.

What can a woman do if both she and her husband are so poor that they cannot afford to live apart?

Many families have such a small income that they cannot afford to set up two separate households. In this situation, the woman should think about obtaining welfare; another book in this series, *The Rights of the Poor*, explains in detail what one's rights to welfare are and how to go about asserting them. An alternative for families that cannot afford to live apart on the present income is for the wife to work for pay if she is not yet doing so. This might increase the family income enough so the parties can afford to separate.

What can women's paralegal groups do to help women who are in the process of getting a divorce?

Women in several cities—including Los Angeles, New Haven, Philadelphia, Seattle, and Washington, D.C.—have already undertaken paralegal divorce projects. For further information, contact one of the groups listed in Chart D(3) in the Appendix.

Paralegal workers in these projects have provided women

with general counseling on coping with new life situations and have given them a chance to talk with other women who have been though a divorce. Counseling might also include information on divorce laws, welfare, housing, day care, job opportunities, and managing finances on one's own. Another valuable service is educating women on their legal rights in the divorce situation so that they will know what they can seek in negotiations. Still another service is providing the names of lawyers who have a good reputation and who do not shortchange a woman's needs. In the case of poor women who cannot locate free legal help and who need a default divorce (one the husband is not contesting, either because he has left town or because he doesn't care), a counseling service might show the woman the ropes so she can go into court and get her own divorce.

Another extremely valuable service a paralegal group can provide is to give bar associations and feminist lawyers feedback on complaints women have about the way their lawyers treat them. This action might lead to some meetings with the local bar association, to press for change and re-education of the bar, but such meetings should not take place without the help of a feminist lawyer. As for the complaints, the group's lawyer should give careful thought to the problem of libel; if an individual lawyer is charged with failure to fulfill his duty to female divorce clients, he will almost surely respond with a lawsuit against the accusers. This is not to say that the real problems of poor representation cannot be confronted, but rather that such an effort must be carefully planned with the help of feminist lawyers.

B. Custody

Is a woman automatically entitled to custody of her children if she is a fit mother?

No. For many years, courts followed a legal rule called the tender years doctrine under which the mother was presumed to be the better custodian for children of "tender years" (usually under age seven). The corollary principle was that a husband could obtain custody only if he could show that his wife was "unfit." This led to nasty courtroom battles in which the husband would try to drag in as many negative factors as possible against the wife. It also led to a double standard; any deviation from the "good wife" role—such as an affair—might result in the wife being found "unfit" although similar conduct would not prevent the husband from getting custody. This doctrine is probably unconstitutional under the Equal Protection Clause; it allows an important legal right to be determined solely on the basis of the sex of the parent because of stereotyped notions about the relationships of male and female parents with their children.

But in most states, custody decisions are now based on "the best interests of the child" without regard to a presumption about which parent is best suited. The majority of women are still able to make a strong case for obtaining custody of their children because they have been the primary caretaker. In fact, a few state supreme courts (Oregon and West Virginia, for example), have begun to recognize a legal presumption that custody should be awarded to the parent who has been the child's primary caretaker. In families in which the husband has played a larger role in child rearing, he will have a correspondingly greater chance of convincing a judge in a contested case that he should have custody. Unfortunately, some feminist attorneys believe, the elimination of the "tender years" presumption has led some judges to award custody to the father largely because of his more favorable economic situation while neglecting to consider who the child's primary caretaker has been.

Is there a way to avoid either parent having sole custody?

There is a growing recognition of "joint custody"—in which the parents continue to be jointly responsible for the child, making decisions and arrangements for the child on a day-to-day basis—and "split custody"—in which the parents alternate having sole custody of the child (with the other parent allowed visitation rights). In most states this can be done only by agreement of the parties; in some states it cannot be done at all, although there is a move, prompted by fathers' rights groups, to create a legal presumption in favor of joint custody. Judges and lawyers have tended to believe that it is better for children to have a single, continuous primary caretaker and that it is much better to have one parent able to make a final decision on important questions such as medical treatment and schools in order to avoid repeated fights. For that reason, you may have to be very insistent and shop around for a lawyer if you want a joint or split custody arrangement.

If you are considering split custody, issues to consider include the desirability of a child moving repeatedly versus the importance of equal access to both parents. An important issue in joint custody is whether you will want to continue to deal with your husband on a day-to-day basis to make decisions about the children after divorce. For example, has he been easy to deal with in the past? Do not simply give in and accept joint custody to avoid a fight if you really believe it is preferable for you to have sole custody. In fact, if you agree to joint custody knowing something about your husband that would make him a bad caretaker, you may be in a poor position to bring it up later if the agreement breaks down and you have to go to court to argue over custody. Finally, the amount of child support payments must be very carefully negotiated in joint or split custody arrangements. Fathers sometimes argue they should pay no support if they have the children half of the time—but usually they have far more than half of the income, and often, after initial interest wears off, keep the children little more than they might in traditional sole custody with visitation arrangements.

If the woman wants custody of the children, are there any special steps she should take?

Yes. She should be discreet about any relationship with another man or a sexual relationship with a woman. The legal system still imposes a double standard, and a mother will be judged much more harshly for extramarital affairs than will a father. If your husband is trying to get custody of the children and you want to retain custody, it would be wise to avoid any affairs for the interim period. Some women may choose to fight the issue openly in order to establish precedents to help other women in the same predicament; however, the risk they take is losing custody of their children. Before deciding to fight the issue, you should consider the risks carefully.

Some states require that persons seeking divorce see a social worker, a friend of the court, or a marriage counselor before the divorce is granted. Be as discreet as possible with any of them. This includes being careful about what is on display in your home as well as what you say. Talk to your lawyer about these matters before any interviews or visits. As a practical matter, these people are very powerful. Judges rarely overturn their recommendations on child custody; so if you offend them on matters related to sexual behavior, it is likely to have serious consequences.

Is it important to maintain custody of your children in the period preceding the actual divorce?

Definitely. Women often want to leave their children with their husbands for a much-needed break or to return to school when they first separate. However, this choice has its risks. Just as the amount of temporary alimony you receive sets a precedent for the award of permanent alimony, the party who has temporary custody of the children is usually granted permanent custody.

Does a woman need a court order for temporary custody before the actual divorce if her husband agrees to leave the children with her?

Until there is a court order, husband and wife are equally entitled to custody of their children. Therefore, until there is an order it is perfectly legal for your husband to take the children even if he has signed a written agreement to leave them with you. The police will not intervene and you will have to start the court process from the beginning to regain custody. If you have the slightest suspicion that your husband may take the children, it is best to obtain a temporary custody order prior to the actual divorce. This may be critical if your husband has threatened to take the children out of the state.

If your husband's visits upset the children, can you prevent them after the divorce is final?

Yes. The question of visitation rights can be reopened and new arrangements made if the old arrangements prove unsatisfactory.

C. Enforcement of Support

Do many men default on alimony and child support payments?

So far, no one has conducted an in-depth study in this area. The surveys available to date, however, indicate that most men do default, starting even in the first year after the divorce.[10]

Once a husband has defaulted on payments, can anything be done to get the money?

Definitely, although many lawyers do not like to institute collection proceedings because they can't make very much money on these kinds of cases. In many states, a lawyer can have the man's salary garnished if he defaults on payments. Other judicial proceedings are also available to collect overdue alimony and child support. One way to make collection easier would be for your lawyer to negotiate for a provision in the settlement whereby the husband agrees to pay your attorney's fees for any default proceedings, as well as court costs. The maximum interest allowable on the default payments under state usury laws should also be included. It would be difficult for the husband's lawyer to object to these provisions since that would be tantamount to admitting that the husband intended to default. If the agreement sets the lawyer's fee high enough, your lawyer or another one should find it worthwhile to take the case in the event your husband defaults.

If a woman does not have an agreement which requires her husband to pay attorneys' fees on default, is there anywhere she can go for help?

Yes. In 1974 Congress passed a law, known as Title IV-D of the Social Security Act,[11] which requires states to aid women (or men) in collecting child support payments. Under this program, the state must represent a woman who is seeking child support in court or administrative proceedings. If she receives public assistance, the legal help is provided free of charge (although she is forced to cooperate—which many poor women do not want to do). If she is not receiving public assistance, she will be charged a small initial fee—perhaps $20—for the service, with any extra charge taken out of the amount collected. Collection action is often very slow, especially for women not receiving AFDC, but it is better to get help from this program than to do nothing at all for lack of money for attorneys' fees.

How can a woman find this program in her city?

The program is usually called the "IV-D program" or the "Office of Paternity and Child Support Enforcement." You can locate the program by calling your local public assistance office (which must refer most of its clients there) or the local district, city, or county attorney's office and asking for the program by name.

Can this program help if the father has left the area?

It can locate the absent father and arrange to start an appropriate court action in the city or state where he lives. The fee is the same for these services. In theory, the state will examine its own records—such as motor vehicles, drivers' licenses, and voter and arrest records—to locate him. The state can also ask the federal government to help locate him through IRS or Social Security records. Success is certainly not guaranteed, but if you are unable to locate the father and unable to pay for the help of an attorney or investigator, this program may help.

Can any laws be passed to prevent default on alimony and child support?

Yes. Women's groups can begin lobbying for laws requiring courts to order automatic payroll deductions for all alimony and child support payments. New York has passed a law[12] which requires those deductions if the husband has been delinquent in making payments. Under the law the husband's employer must forward the payments directly to the wife. Since the husband has no choice in the process, it is difficult for him to default—except by changing jobs and moving to another state where it would be hard to locate him.

In addition, women's groups might press to have local courts begin notice and collection procedures automatically when there is a default. There may be money for this purpose available through the IV-D program.

D. Unmarried Partners/Unmarried Parents

Do unmarried couples, whether heterosexual or homosexual, need to make any legal arrangements to protect themselves?

Yes. Ideally, an unmarried couple would do several things. They would explore the various types of co-ownership of property in order to choose the one that best suits their needs and they would keep good records of the financial contributions each made for the property in question. They would enter into a written "relationship agreement" to settle questions of property ownership, support, and division of property if they break up. They would prepare wills if they want property to go to each other at the time of death, because under state inheritance laws no property will be given to an unmarried partner without a will. Finally, they would anticipate crises by executing a power of attorney, a medical consent form, and a form nominating their partner as guardian of any children. These forms will give their partner the rights that usually go to the next of kin in a crisis (except that a guardianship form won't defeat the rights of a living parent).

For further discussion of the rights of unmarried couples, see Barbara Hirsch, *Living Together: A Guide to the Law for Unmarried Couples* (Boston: Houghton Mifflin, 1976).

If an unmarried couple separates, what rights does the woman have to a property settlement or monetary award?

Traditionally, none. In the past, courts have almost always refused to intervene to protect the property interests of either party to a "meretricious relationship." Their agreements were unenforceable because they were based on "immoral consideration"—i.e., illicit sex. In many states, this is still the law.

However, courts in a few states have recognized that changing social mores require a new approach to the property disputes of unmarried couples. In a landmark California case,[13] Michelle Triola Marvin sued actor Lee Marvin for one-half of his earnings during the seven years they had lived together. She claimed that they had orally agreed to pool their earnings and property. The California Supreme Court agreed that express and implied contracts between unmarried partners were enforceable by the courts, but the trial judge later ruled that Ms. Marvin had failed to prove that they actually agreed to pool their resources so she lost her claim to half of his earnings. Instead, she won a much smaller amount ($104,000) for rehabilitation.[14]

It is too soon to tell how many other states will follow California's lead. Meanwhile, women in similar situations should take precautions to protect their property interests. If you and your partner have an agreement to share earnings and property, put it into writing, perhaps as part of a contract dealing with other domestic issues, and be sure the title to any property is in both your names.

If a woman has a common law marriage, does she have to get a divorce to end it?

Yes, and it is important to do so. There is no such thing as common law divorce and if she does not get a regular court divorce, any later marriage, including a ceremonial one, will be invalid. Several states still recognize common law marriage and women should find out if their state does, particularly if they have agreed with their partner to be married or if they have have been holding themselves out to others as married—e.g., taking a lease as husband and wife or introducing the woman as "Mrs. Robert Brown."

Is an unwed mother automatically entitled to custody of her child?

In most cases, yes. However, it is no longer safe to rely on this assumption. Unwed fathers have won increasing rights concerning their children in recent years—for example, the right to notice and a hearing before the child can be placed for adoption.[15] And while the Supreme Court has never ruled that unwed fathers have custody rights equal to unwed mothers, the law may be moving in that direction. In some states, unwed fathers have been granted custody or visitation rights, especially when they have previously lived with the child. The father's rights may also be honored informally by the refusal of police to intervene if the father takes the child, just as they will not intervene if a married father takes the child when there is no custody order.

Is there something an unwed mother should do to be assured of custody?

The only thing she can do to protect herself is to go to court for a custody order. However, going to court requires naming the father in the court papers and notifying him of the case; this in turn may cause him to ask for visitation or custody when he would not previously have thought of it.

What rights do illegitimate children have with respect to support, inheritance, and Social Security benefits?

In every state, it is now possible to get a court order establishing the paternity of the child and requiring the father to pay support. If you are unable to afford a private lawyer, the IV-D program described in Section C can provide legal help. It is important to get this court order even if you are happily living with the father, because some states require a court order showing paternity before an illegitimate child can inherit from its father when the father dies without leaving a will, and because the support order may be necessary to prove that the child was dependent on the father in order to get certain Social Security benefits.[16] Finally, many states impose strict time limits for going to court to establish paternity, so it is important to act quickly.

E. Domestic Violence

If your husband (or ex-husband or lover) beats, harasses, or threatens to harm you, can you take any legal steps to protect yourself?

Yes. In most states, you will have a choice of three legal strategies in dealing with abuse or threats: (1) divorce or legal separation from your abusive husband, plus any needed "stay-away" orders; (2) criminal prosecution of the abuser; and (3) a protection order that requires him to stop abusing, threatening, or harassing you, either while you continue to live together or while you live apart. You generally do not have to file for divorce, even if you are separated, in order to get a protection order. For each state's laws, see Chart E in the Appendix. However, there are impediments to the use of these remedies in some places. For example, some states do not issue protection orders, and others may require a married woman to file for divorce in order to get a protection order (even when she is not yet sure she wants a divorce). Moreover, police, prosecutors, and judges may be slow to enforce the law and give women the protection and assistance they need. Nonetheless, abused women should definitely pursue the legal remedies available to them.

How does divorce or separation work as a remedy for wife abuse?

To use this remedy, a woman has her attorney file for a divorce or legal separation (which can usually be based on the physical abuse). The attorney then asks the judge to issue temporary orders giving the woman the protection she needs and providing for custody, visitation, and child support. The temporary orders stay in effect until the divorce or legal separation is granted, when they should be made part of the final court order.

What is a protection order and how does it work?

A protection order is an order issued by a civil court judge commanding the husband (or ex-husband or lover) to stop abusing, harassing, or threatening the victim. In states with progressive laws, the order may also provide for custody, visitation, and child support; the man's eviction from the family home (even if it is in his name); payment for the wife's moving and medical expenses; and counseling or participation in a drug or alcohol abuse program.

In some states, a woman may ask the court for such an order herself, without the aid of a lawyer (this is called appearing *pro se*). In others, an attorney must be present, whether her own private attorney, a free legal services lawyer, or the local prosecutor. Sometimes the woman may be able to get an immediate short-term *ex parte* protection order, without the abuser being present, on the basis of her own testimony or sworn statements. (However, this temporary order must then be served on the husband and followed by a full court hearing at which he has an opportunity to appear, before it can be extended for a longer period.) In other cases, it may take up to two months to find and serve the husband, hold a court hearing, and issue a longer-term protection order, which can be in effect for six months to two years.

As many women have learned, it takes further action to enforce the order if the man refuses to comply. In theory, the abuser will be in contempt of court if he violates the order and could be fined or jailed. But the police generally will not arrest him unless the state makes it a special crime to violate the order, and one which subjects the violator to arrest on the basis of the victim's report. In addition, the woman usually has to initiate contempt of court proceedings herself (or through her attorney or the prosecutor), and most courts will not order the man to jail. Still, enforcement can be effective if the court orders a jail sentence, but suspends it on condition that the man complies with the order in the future.

When women do obtain these orders, they should carry them in their pocketbooks and leave a certified copy at the local police precinct. While the police often do not respond well to any domestic violence situation, their performance improves—i.e., they may at least investigate the situation—if they know the woman has a protection order.

Is it possible to have the abuser ordered out of the house?

In some states, yes, even if the title or lease is in his name. You should definitely ask for this in the court order, or ask for moving expenses if you must leave.

Are there special considerations when children are involved?

If at all possible, do not leave the children at home with the abuser, even if they are not in danger, as this may weaken your custody case later. Ask your lawyer to arrange to have the court order provide that you will not have to be alone with the children's father when he picks them up to visit—e.g., arrange pickups at a relative's home, a church, or a public place.

Is wife abuse a crime? Will my husband be put into jail?

Yes, it is a crime. No, he will probably not be put into jail. Although the police are often reluctant to respond to "domestic" calls, wife (or lover) abuse is a crime and you are entitled to a police response whether or not you intend to follow through with full criminal prosecution. If you want the abuser arrested, say so. The police may refuse to arrest him on the spot because of their interpretation of the arrest rules. Still, their presence can give you a chance to get yourself and the children out of the house. If they do arrest him, be sure to ask how long it is likely to be before he is released. (Often it is only hours.) If you decide to file criminal charges with the prosecutor and the case goes forward, your husband may be fined, jailed, or put on probation, assuming he is found guilty or pleads guilty. Probation is the most common result. Be sure to tell the prosecutor if you need special conditions for your protection made part of the probation order.

What steps can a woman take to build her case?

Whichever legal route you choose, you will need to collect evidence to prove in court that you were subjected to abuse. You will also need personal support, both for the court action and in putting your life back together. Police logs, medical records, photographs, and the testimony of those who heard a fight or saw your physical condition afterward can provide good courtroom evidence. Call the police and ask your neighbors to call, too; go for medical treatment and tell the doctor the full story; ask that photographs of your physical condition be taken immediately or take them yourself. Contact a shelter or advocacy group for battered women for personal support, legal information and referral, and practical advice. An increasing number of communities now have shelters where abused women and their children can live temporarily until they can begin to put their lives back in order. These shelters can provide help in getting welfare assistance, job training, jobs, and new homes, in addition to the other help listed above.

Where can women get further information on battered women or referral to local battered women's groups?

Two national groups can refer you to shelters in your area:

Center for Women Policy Studies
2000 P St., N.W., Suite 508
Washington, D.C. 20036
  (202) 872–1770

National Coalition Against Domestic Violence
1728 N St., N.W.
Washington, D.C. 20036
  (202) 347–7015

The Center for Women Policy Studies also has excellent free bibliographies on many aspects of wife abuse. An extensive manual for non-lawyers working with legal problems facing abused women should soon be available for $75 through the National Public Law Training Center, 2000 P St., N.W., Suite 600, Washington, D.C. 20036.

What can women's paralegal groups do about battered women?

They can do a variety of things, including starting a shelter; providing individual information, referral, and advocacy services to battered women; pushing for better laws to protect battered women; pressuring police, prosecutors, and judges to carry out their law enforcement responsibilities; and pressing public social service and assistance agencies to provide better services for battered women. The two groups listed above can provide excellent resource material for most of these projects.

NOTES

1. *Orr v. Orr,* 440 U.S. 268 (1979).
2. Eckhardt, "Deviance, Visibility, and Legal Action: The Duty to Support," *Social Programs* (1968); see also Note 9.
3. Arizona, California, Idaho, Louisiana, Nevada, New Mexico, Texas, and Washington.
4. Colorado, Missouri, New Jersey, New York and Wisconsin are among these states, for example.
5. For further discussion, see Foster and Freed, "Spousal Rights in Retirement and Pension Benefits," 16 *Journal of Family Law* 187 (1978).
6. *Hisquierdo v. Hisquierdo,* 439 U.S. 572 (1979); *McCarty v. McCarty,* 453 U.S. 210 (1981). See also *Ridgway v. Ridgway,* 102 S.Ct. 49 (1981). There is also concern that the Supreme Court will interpret similar provisions of ERISA, which governs private pensions, in the same way. See *Stone v. Stone,* 450 F.Supp. 919 (N.D. Cal. 1978), *aff'd,* 632 F. 2d 740 (9th Cir. 1980), *cert. denied, sub nom. Seafarers International Union, Pacific District—Pacific Maritime Assoc. Pension Plan v. Stone,* 453 U.S. 922 (1981).
7. 42 U.S.C. §§402 (b), 416(d) (1970), *as amended* by Social Security Amendments of 1977; Pub. L. No. 95–216, §§402 (b), 415(d).
8. For questions discussing fair compensation during the marriage, see Chapter IX.
9. Winston and Forsher, "Non-Support of Legitimate Children by Affluent Fathers as a Cause of Poverty and Welfare Dependence." The report is available for $2 from Rand Corporation, 1700 Main St., Santa Monica, Calif. 90406.
10. See generally Nagel and Weitzman, "Women as Litigants," 23 *Hastings Law Journal* 171, 187–192 (1971); and Citizens' Advisory Council on the Status of Women, *Women in 1971* (1972), pp. 42–48. Both sources cite a particularly interesting study: Eckhardt, "Deviance, Visibility, and Legal Action: The Duty to Support," *Social Problems*

(1968). Eckhardt compiled statistics from a 1955 sample of fathers ordered to pay child support in a metropolitan Wisconsin county. He found that after one year 38 percent of the fathers had complied fully, 20 percent were in partial compliance, and 42 percent were in total non-compliance. By the sixth year, 17 percent were in full compliance, 12 percent in partial compliance, and 71 percent in total non-compliance. Nagel and Weitzman suggest that non-compliance is probably even higher on alimony awards; and they point out that, in any case and contrary to popular mythology, alimony is awarded very infrequently. They cite a study of Chicago divorces, where the wives waived post-divorce alimony in 93 percent of the cases. The study cited is M. Virtue, *Family Cases In Court*(1956).

11. 42 U.S.C. §650 *et seq.*

12. N.Y. Personal Property Law, §49–b (McKinney (1979 Supp.)).

13. *Marvin v. Marvin*, 18 Cal.3d 660, 134 Cal. Rptr. 815, 557 P.2d 106 (1976).

14. For further discussion of this problem, see Carol Bruch, "Property Rights of De Facto Spouses Including Thoughts on the Value of Homemakers' Services," 10 *Family Law Quarterly* 101 (1976); "Comment, Property Rights upon Termination of Unmarried Cohabitation: *Marvin v. Marvin*," 90 *Harvard Law Review* 1708 (1977); and "Note, Beyond *Marvin*: A Proposal for Quasi-Spousal Support," 30 *Stanford Law Review* 359 (1978).

15. *Stanley v. Illinois*, 405 U.S. 645 (1972); *Caban v. Mohammed*, 441 U.S. 380 (1979); but see *Quillon v. Walcott*, 434 U.S. 246 (1978), and *Parham v. Hughes*, 441 U.S. 347 (1979).

16. *Lalli v. Lalli*, 439 U.S. 259 (1978); *Matthew v. Lucas*, 427 U.S. 495 (1976).

VIII

Names and Name Change—
Symbols of a New Identity

Names symbolize a person's identity, so it is not surprising that the subject of names has become increasingly important to feminists. The system of naming people reflects women's status today. Almost every woman in this country uses the name of a man, whether father or husband, as her last name. Symbolically, then, every woman's identity is still tied to a man.

Many women have begun searching for ways around this male-oriented system. A few refuse to use either their father's or their husband's name.[1] These women choose surnames that are not related to any man: a beautiful word that seizes their fancy; the name of a city; their mother's first name, combined with "child," as in Sara-child. Other women choose to use their father's name, both before and after marriage. Still others prefer a husband's name to the father's, or combine and hyphenate the two. Some decide with or convince their husbands that both should take a new name—whether a combination of their fathers' names or an unrelated third name.

Each solution has advantages and disadvantages. Choosing a name different from either the father's or husband's allows one to express the greatest disagreement with the male orientation of the present system, but it takes time and effort to re-educate friends, parents, and officials to call you by a name social custom has not sanctioned. Using the father's name allows a woman to retain the identity she grew up with and symbolizes equality upon marriage, since the man also retains his father's name. However, every woman who chooses to do this still carries a symbolic tie to her father only—but none to

243

her mother—and if she has children, they will have the same problem. Some women prefer to use their husband's name because they like it better or feel they have some choice in taking it, even though the choice is between identification with one male and identification with another male. Married couples who hyphenate their father's names or take a third name also opt for a symbol of equality, and each partner contributes to the children's surname, but it sets off the family unit in a way some do not wish to perpetuate.

Ideally, we need a new system for naming people. Children should be given surnames that either reflect the names of both parents or the names of neither. When these children marry in turn, both men and women could keep their surnames, combine them,[2] or choose a third name. None of these choices would carry a sexist connotation since none would favor a male's name over a female's name.

Instituting a new system means passing new laws, though, and this may require prolonged effort. Meanwhile many women—and some men—want to deviate from tradition by taking names that reflect a more egalitarian view of the relationship between men and women. These people are sometimes told that the difficulties are insurmountable, or that they will lose important legal rights if they do so. This is not really so. Although there will be no perfect solutions until laws are changed, there are ways of coping with the present system.

Do women and men have the right to use any name they choose?

Yes. Under the common law, our legal system has long recognized the right of any person to use any name she or he likes, as long as he or she is not doing so in order to defraud someone else. To exercise this right in most states, one simply begins using a new name. In addition, most states have passed laws to establish formal name-change procedures, but it is usually not necessary to use these procedures. They are merely a convenient formality. However, in a few states, the only legal way to change your name is by complying with the statutory procedures. (See Appendix, Chart C, "Explanation of Chart," to learn in which states one must use the statutory procedure.)

Must a woman take her husband's surname as her last name when she marries?

Not necessarily. Many legal cases and treatises state categorically that women must take the husband's name. When one examines these statutes and decisions more closely, it appears closer to the truth to state that women generally use their husbands' name as a matter of social custom and not because the law requires it. In fact, in 1973 only one state—Hawaii—and Puerto Rico had a law stating clearly and unequivocally that the wife (and children) must use the husband's name. A group of law students who researched the law on this question could not find a single case where a judge ordered a woman to use her husband's name for all purposes. However, a few married women who have refused to use their husbands' name have been penalized by the loss of some other right (see next question).

What penalties have been or can be imposed on women for refusing to use their husbands' surnames?

Penalties have generally been imposed under state laws requiring people to reregister or notify authorities when their name changes "by marriage or otherwise." Such persons must generally reregister in order to vote and must notify officials to retain a valid driver's license, motor vehicle registration, or certificate of title to a car, or even to remain a notary public. In theory if one does not do so, one can no longer vote, legally drive a car, etc., although laws often do not explicitly prescribe a penalty for failure to register. (For a detailed list showing which laws your state has passed, see Chart C in the Appendix.) Despite the large number of states with these laws, however, only five or six reported cases could be found where a woman was actually penalized for refusing to reregister under her husband's name. In a few cases these women were denied the right to vote; in one case a woman who sued to get a driver's license issued in her maiden name was unsuccessful; and in a case in the 1930's a woman artist was unable to obtain naturalization papers issued in her maiden name.[3]

The number of reported penalties is so low, in part, because most of the laws are ambiguous. They require a woman to reregister when her name changes by marriage, but they do not tell her if her name changes automatically upon marriage or whether the change is voluntary. If it is the latter, any married woman who does not actually change her name cannot be penalized for a refusal to reregister. In order to avoid penalties, then, women need to convince officials and judges to interpret reregistration laws in the second way. Some women have already done so. The best example is a 1961 Ohio case involving a woman named Krupansky, who had not changed her name for any purpose when she married and had voted in the name of Krupansky in three elections. When she decided to run for a local office, a taxpayer sued to have her name taken off the ballot because it was not the name of her husband. The judge refused to do so, stating that: "It is only by custom, in English speaking countries, that a woman, upon marriage, adopts the surname of her husband in place of the surname of her father. The state of Ohio follows this custom but there exists no law compelling it. . . . A wife may continue to use her maiden, married, or any other name she wishes to be known by. . . ."[4] Thus, even though Ohio has a reregistration law, the woman was not penalized in any way because Ohio judges interpret the law to mean that a woman has the option to use whatever name she likes. Other states which have adopted this view of the law include Wisconsin, Tennessee, and Florida.[5]

On the other hand, some states have taken the opposite approach. Illinois has refused to allow a married woman to vote in her maiden name.[6]

Until October 1981 Kentucky required a married woman to apply for a driver's license in her husband's surname despite the fact that she used her maiden name for all other purposes.[7] And the Maryland attorney general once ruled that a married woman must use her husband's surname as a matter of law. Relying on this interpretation, a Maryland voting registrar deregistered a married woman who refused to reregister, claiming she never used her husband's name. Fortunately, the case was reversed on appeal.[8] Most states have not reached such clear interpretations of the reregistration laws, although their position can sometimes be implied or predicted from other laws or cases.

Other kinds of penalties are more widespread but are not compelled by any law. Many married women report difficulties in obtaining a passport in their fathers' names, although passport officials do not act uniformly on this matter. Sometimes they will issue women passports under the names of both the father and husband; other officials will issue them in the father's name alone if the woman presents affidavits that she has always been known by that name. Other people, such as employers and bank or department store officers, may also penalize the married woman who refuses to use her husband's surname. They may refuse to issue mortgages, credit cards, or paychecks in the name a woman chooses or harass her at length before doing so.

If a married woman exercises her common law right to use a name other than her husband's, will she be penalized in all these ways?

No. In fact, the chances are slim that she will lose any of the legal rights mentioned. This is so whether the woman decides to retain her father's name when she marries, chooses a third name, or decides after first using her husband's name to resume her father's name or adopt a new name. In all of these situations, however, the chances of encountering resistance by banks, department stores, and employers run high.

Will going through a state's formal name change procedure help a married woman avoid the imposition of penalties, whether formal or informal?

Yes. Once a woman obtains a legal document setting forth her legal surname, state officials cannot penalize her for refusing to use her husband's name. (Of course, the woman who *does* change her name—whether to her husband's name when she marries, back to her father's name after using her husband's name, or to a third name—should comply with reregistration and notification laws.) Women report that a legal document also works like magic in eliminating the objections of bank, department store, and employer personnel.

What are the disadvantages of using the name change procedure?

First, it symbolizes inequality since no man need use the procedure in order to retain his father's name after marriage.

Second, the procedure costs money and takes some effort. The amount varies from state to state and includes a court filing fee (perhaps $10 or so), the cost of publishing a notice in the newspaper in some states (which can run as high as $100 in some states), and perhaps the services of an attorney (anywhere from $40 to $150, unless one qualifies for free legal help from a legal services program).

Is use of the name change procedure mandatory for a married woman who does not want to use her husband's name?

No, except in those states where this is the only legal method to change one's name (see Chart C in the Appendix). Any woman who is willing to risk the penalties can simply continue or commence using any name she likes. Even if she is then faced with a penalty, she can almost always avoid it by reregistering in her husband's name. Where officials remain adamant, though, the only choices are turning to the name change procedure, using the husband's name in the contested circumstance, or losing the right involved. Of course, if the state has no reregistration or notification laws, the chances of being penalized for using a name other than the husband's are slim.

Is there any way to know whether use of the formal procedures is really necessary?

There is no definitive guide, but the chart on "Name Change" gives some assistance. The last column indicates states whose laws or decisions provide a clue to whether the state will take the position that a woman's name changes automatically upon marriage as a matter of law (L), or whether women have an option to use any name because it is only customary (C) for them to change their names. In states with an L, or where the formal procedures are the exclusive method for changing anyone's name, it would probably be wise to use these procedures. Where there is a C, women may not have to use the procedures. (Blanks indicate states where research has not turned up any clues.) In all states, though, use of the name change procedure is valuable to protect against harassment and the imposition of penalties.

What do the formal name change procedures entail?

The procedures vary slightly from state to state but are generally not complicated. Most women could follow them on their own if they want to save money by avoiding a lawyer's fee.

Some states will not allow anyone to use the procedures unless she or he has been a county resident for six months or a year, but most do not impose this limitation. Usually one must first go to a courthouse and fill out a paper—often called a Petition for Change of Name—listing such standard items as current name, name desired, age, residence, and reason for change. Then the court clerk files this paper, usually for a nominal fee of perhaps $10 or so. Sometimes one must publish a notice of the proceedings in a local newspaper and present copies to the court to prove that this was done. Unfortunately the cost of newspaper publication can be expensive—up to $100. The final step in some states is a short hearing before a judge, who will ask a few questions. If all goes smoothly, one then receives a legal document setting forth one's legal surname.

Chart C in the Appendix tells the kind of court that will grant this name change for each state. For more details on the procedure, call the clerk of the court, who is listed in the phone book for the named court. If there is no such court in the phone book, call any court and ask how to locate the correct one for name changing.

Two cautionary notes should be added. First, the court will probably be most concerned with your reasons for changing your name; it may probe to find out whether you have any intent to defraud someone by the change of name. To avoid this problem, it may be wise, in addition to your setting forth the reasons for change, to state that you have no intention to defraud anyone. The reasons for seeking a change should be phrased somewhat conservatively in order not to alienate the judge, for some judges have strong feelings about a woman's "proper name." A good tactic might be to emphasize a desire to maintain a separate identity from one's husband or father for work purposes, rather than blatantly stating that one does not wish to be identified with a man. Nor does a woman have to state that she changed her name when she married if she did not. She can state that she wishes to establish her legal right to *continue* using her father's name rather than change back to it.

The second note of caution is that if the judge turns down your petition, you should definitely get a lawyer before proceeding further. An appeal can be taken to a higher court to reverse the judge's decision, but appeals are more complicated and require a lawyer's assistance.

What projects could women's groups undertake to help other women change or keep their names?

An ideal project would be to study the state procedures, publicize them, and help women file their own petitions. This would save women the cost of hiring an attorney, which is the major cost in formalizing a name change. Publicity should include a description of the procedures, information on where to go for the proper forms and for filing them, and an offer of assistance in filling them out. Members of the group could also accompany anyone to court if she so desires and help get a notice published in a newspaper, where this is necessary.

The Women's Legal Defense Fund in Washington, D.C., undertook a project like this. Interested readers should write (for the address, see Chart D(1) in the Appendix) for a copy of the fund's pamphlet *Name Change Information for the Washington Area*; the cost is $3. They should also read the applicable state statute, citations for which are given in Chart C.

As a second project, the group could find a lawyer to research state law in more depth than was possible for this book. If the lawyer discovers cases or laws that make it clear that married women can use any name they like in that state, the group should widely publicize the results of her research. Armed with this information, women can take advantage of their legal right to establish their name by usage, without the cost of formal procedures or the fear of penalty. If the law remains ambiguous, the group should consider suing state officials for what is called a "class action declaratory judgment." In such a lawsuit, the women request the judge to declare what their rights are. Here they want a declaration that the class of all married women in the state have the option of using any name they like, as the Ohio judge declared in Ms. Krupansky's case. Lawsuits like this could also be brought in states where married women are barred from using the name change procedures. If the women win the suit, they can use the decision to force state or business officials to deal with women under their chosen name.

Another option—especially where the state forces married women to use their husbands' names—is to lobby for legislative change. The new law would eliminate forced use of the husband's name and the bar to change of name by married women. It may also be possible to get the state attorney general to issue an opinion stating that for all state purposes a married woman may use whatever name she likes.

Are there any federal laws that protect a woman's right to choose her name?

Yes, in some important situations but not across the board. The Equal Credit Opportunity Act gives a woman the right to open or to maintain a credit account using her father's surname, her spouse's surname, or a combined surname. (See Chapter IX, "A Miscellany of Sex Discrimination Problems.") A court decision also suggests that Title VII of the 1964 Civil Rights Act protects women from harassment by their employers because of their choice of name. The plaintiff in this case worked for a county health department in Tennessee. Her personnel forms were filled out in her maiden name. After her marriage she refused to change her name or to authorize a change on her personnel forms to reflect her husband's surname. When the department suspended her without pay, she sued. The federal appeals court ruled it was a violation of Title VII for an employer to require married women, but not married men, to use their spouses' surnames on personnel forms.[9]

Does a married woman with a surname different from that of her husband have any right to give her surname to her child?

Sometimes. Generally a child's surname is that of his or

her father. Until recently, when the father changed his name, the child's name changed at the same time, at least while he or she was a young child. Thus, if the father contested the mother's right to name the child, he was almost always the victor in legal proceedings. However, some recent court decisions have rejected a rule giving fathers first choice and have instead opted for a standard based on the best interests of the child.[10] Of course, if the father agrees, the couple can give the child the mother's surname although there is always the risk that government officials or businessmen will insist that the child use the father's name, just as they insist that the mother use her husband's name.

Is there any practical way for a woman to ensure that her children will use a surname that she has helped choose?

Yes. The woman and her husband can choose as their common name a joint surname to which both contribute. This might be a hyphenated combination of their fathers' names or a third, mutually satisfactory, name or even her father's name instead of his. Whatever choice they make, both should change their names through the name change procedure. Their children would then automatically acquire the new name, obviating any later problems about who gets to name the children. This procedure will even work for couples who already have children.

Some women prefer not to set off the family unit with a family surname. The only way they can ensure their right to give the child their surname is to secure their husbands' agreement. The problem with this solution is that there is no way to enforce it if the man changes his mind.

Does a divorced woman have a right to resume using her father's name or to take on another name?

Usually. Many states have passed laws that provide that a divorced woman may use any name she likes. Some states, however, allow a divorced woman to do so only if she is considered the blameless party in the divorce, or if she has no children or does not have custody of the children. (See Chart C.) But even if a judge tells her that she must continue to use her husband's name, as a practical matter, his decision is probably not enforceable. Certainly once the woman moves to another state, no one will force her to resume her husband's name, and even within the state, enforcement is highly unlikely. To avoid any problems, a woman seeking a divorce who wants to change her name should ask her lawyer to get this approved in the final court decree.

May a divorced woman have her children's name changed?
Sometimes. Some women have done so under the name change statutes, even where the father objected. Most women who have done so, though, have simply changed the children's name from that of husband one to that of husband two. [11]

Do boys and girls have an equal right to change from their fathers' names to other names?
Yes. Both boys and girls may use the name change procedure without parental consent when they reach the age of majority (usually age 18). The age of majority, which is set by the state legislature, must be the same for both sexes because of a 1975 United States Supreme Court decision. In this case the Court held that a Utah statute which set the age of majority at 18 for girls and at 21 for boys violated the Equal Protection Clause of the 14th Amendment. [12] If your state has not changed its law, you can sue under the Equal Protection Clause to change it.

What new laws are needed to achieve equality of names for men and women—both in naming children and upon marriage?
Two kinds of laws are needed. The first would establish the right of any woman, whether single or married, to use any name she likes. The second would create a new, non-male-oriented system for naming children. Although many feminists have begun lobbying for the first kind of law, there has been little thought devoted to the second. Until this is done, the law will continue to symbolize a woman's tie to a man, for most women will continue to use their fathers' names and to have no say in the naming of their children.

What other sources are there on names and name change?
Some interesting law review articles are Carlsson, "Surnames of Married Women and Legitimate Children," 17 *New York Law Forum* 552 (1971); Hughes, "And Then There Were Two," 23 *Hastings Law Journal* 233 (1971); and "Married Women and the Name Game," 11 *University of Richmond Law Review* 121 (1976). *A Booklet for Women Who Wish to Determine Their Own Names After Marriage* (1974) and its 1975 supplement, *A Woman's Own Name*, are available from the Center for a Woman's Own Name, 261 Kimberley, Barrington, Ill. 60010, for $2 plus $.50 postage each. The Women's Rights Project of the American Civil Liberties Union has published a memorandum on the "Right of Married Women to Retain or Regain Their Birth Names." The Project also wrote the brief in the Maryland case in which a woman established her right to vote using her birth name.[13] For copies of both the memorandum and the brief, write to the Project (see Chart D, Section A, for the address). Priscilla MacDougall has also written several articles on name change: "Married Women's Common Law Right to Their Own Surnames," 1 *Women's Rights Law Reporter* 2 (1972–73); "The Right of Women to Determine Their Own Names Irrespective of Marital Status," 1 *Family Law Reporter* 4005 (1974); and "Women's, Men's, Children's Names: An Outline and Bibliography," 7 *Family Law Reporter* 4013 (1981).

NOTES

1. One of the greatest sources of controversy among friends who read over this chapter was what to call a woman's surname: maiden name, birth name, or father's name? All have disadvantages. Each is inaccurate in some circumstances. Thus, some women using a "maiden name" are married; some women using a "birth name" have changed the surname they acquired at birth (referring to any woman—married or single—who changes her name because she wants another name); and some women using a "father's name" in fact acquired their surname from their mother. Moreover, each term has ideological connotations that other women dislike.

   "Father's name" was finally selected to emphasize that most people in our society still give their children the surname of the father. Many feminists have been combating the custom of a woman's changing her name to that of the husband at marriage, but they have ignored the male-oriented system for naming children. By using the term "father's name," the authors hope to encourage more women to see and combat the second problem.

2. If a combined name is elected, modification will be required in the next generation. It would take mean parents to burden a child with four names! Perhaps one name could be dropped from each parent's side, the name to be determined by alphabetical order.

3. A special note for lawyers: this 1930's case, *In re Kayaloff*, 9 F.Supp. 176 (S.D. N.Y. 1936), illustrates the harm that can be caused by the sloppy use of precedents. The federal court cited two New York cases for the proposition that married women must take their husbands' surname; however, the cases cited had not imposed penalties on married women who refused to take their husbands' name. The first cited decision refused to uphold the validity of a lawsuit against a married woman *who in fact used her husband's name*, where notice of the suit was sent to her in her maiden name and she never received the notice. In the second suit, the court refused a wife's request for an injunction forbidding another woman from using the wife's name. Clearly the judge's passing reference that, in his opinion, the common law required married women to use their husbands' surnames was not justified by the cases he cited. In representing women seeking to raise these issues, then, the lawyer must carefully read past precedent; most of it can be distinguished or dismissed as *dictum*.

4. *Krupa v. Green*, 114 Ohio App. 497, 177 N.E.2d 616 (1961).

5. See *Kruzel v. Podell*, 67 Wis.2d 138, 226 N.W.2d 458 (1975); *Dunn v. Palermo*, 522 S.W.2d 679 (Tenn. 1975); and *Davis v. Roos*, 326 So.2d 226 (Fla. App. 1976).

6. *People ex rel. Rago v. Lipsky*, 327 Ill. App. 63, 63 N.E.2d 642 (1945).

7. *Whitlow v. Hodges*, 539 F.2d 582 (6th Cir. 1976), *cert. denied*, 429 U.S. 1029 (1976). However, on October 30, 1981, the Kentucky Department of Transportation began issuing drivers' licenses to married women in their own names, and issued a memorandum to that effect.

8. *Stuart v. Board of Supervisors of Elections*, 295 A.2d 223 (1972).

9. *Allen v. Lovejoy*, 553 F.2d 522 (6th Cir. 1977).

10. For cases dealing with the issue of naming children at birth where the parents have different last names or disagree on the name to be given the child, and the mother has custody of the child, see *Jacobs v. Jacobs*, 309 N.W.2d 303 (Minn. 1981); *In re Schiffman*, 28 Cal.3d 640, 169 Cal. Rptr. 918, 620 P.2d 579 (1980); *In re M.L.P.*, 621 S.W.2d 430 (Tex. Civ.App. 1981) (dispute over first and middle names only); and *Hurta v. Hurta*, 25 Wash. App. 95, 605 P.2d 1278 (1979).

11. For cases on the issue, see *Saxton v. Dennis*, 309 N.W.2d 298

(Minn. 1981), *cert. denied*, 50 U.S.L.W. 3766 (March 23, 1982); Annotation, "Rights and Remedies of Parents Inter Se with Respect to the Names of Their Children," 92 A.L.R. 3d 1091 (1979) (citing cases generally deferring to the father's choice unless he has acted badly).

12. *Stanton v. Stanton*, 421 U.S. 7(1975).
13. *Stuart v. Board of Supervisors of Elections*, *supra*.

IX

A Miscellany of Sex Discrimination Problems

Women have faced sex discrimination in many aspects of public and private life. This chapter discusses a sampling of issues not covered in earlier chapters, including sex discrimination in public accommodations, credit, housing, day care, jury duty, military service, and benefits for housewives. The questions point to some encouraging developments. A number of new laws have already been passed, and a number of cases won. But they also indicate where new laws or further court decisions are needed. Here, as elsewhere, the battle for a fully egalitarian society has not yet been won.

A. Public Accommodations

May a public bar refuse to serve women?
The answer is uncertain, except in those states and cities with laws specifically prohibiting sex discrimination in public accommodations. On the federal level, there is still no statute forbidding sex discrimination in public accommodations (although there is such a law for race discrimination). Women have tried to use the Constitution's Equal Protection Clause to end the exclusion of women from such public accommodations as bars and restaurants. As you will recall from Chapter I, however, a showing that there is some "state action" involved in the public accommodations is required before the Equal Protection Clause applies. Convincing courts that there is enough governmental involvement to amount to state action has been the sticking point in this area.

In the 1970's women won some victories in the federal

court system, using this equal protection theory. The courts decided that when a state chose to regulate the sale of liquor, it became so involved in this business that the business reflected state action. Once the state was involved, the refusal to sell liquor to women had to survive the test of the Equal Protection Clause. Since it was difficult for a bar to come up with any reasonable basis for refusing to sell liquor to women, the bars generally flunked the test.[1]

For example, in one case Faith Seidenberg, a feminist attorney from Syracuse, New York, won the right to buy a drink at McSorley's Ole Ale House in New York City. McSorley's had long been famous among New Yorkers for liederkranz cheese and onions served with ale, and for a refusal to serve women. When Ms. Seidenberg decided to have a sip of ale there, too, she narrowly escaped physical attack for her temerity. The policeman who arrived on the scene threatened to arrest her rather than the men who initiated the violence, and she fled the scene. But eventually she sued McSorley's and won the right to have her drink when the court found that the state regulatory authority over McSorley's business created sufficient state action. Despite this good beginning, more recent Supreme Court decisions have given strong indication that the Supreme Court would not find state action in such a case, and therefore would not apply the Equal Protection Clause to end the practice. (See the next question and answer.)

But while bars may be able to discriminate, at least one lower federal court has held that *police enforcement* of the discriminatory policy is sufficient state action to bring the Equal Protection Clause into play. A Milwaukee restaurateur refused to serve women in the "Men's Grill" section of his restaurant. To enforce his policy, he obtained the cooperation of the city attorney and the police. When Nely Johnson and her friends sought service in the "Men's Grill," the police were called to take their names and ask them to leave. The women sued and a federal district court ruled that the agreement of city officials to enforce the restaurant's discriminatory policy constituted state action. Under the Equal Protection Clause, the presumed preference of male customers for a "males-only" section could not justify a policy of discrimination against women and the restaurant was forced to stop.[2] To fully resolve the problem nationally, however, women's groups must pressure Congress to make sex discrimination in public accommodations illegal.

May a private club refuse to admit women?

Yes, so far as the Equal Protection Clause is concerned, but women nevertheless may be able to get the state to withdraw a club's liquor license unless it will admit women. This they found to their surprise down at Mory's, when some Yale law students decided they had had enough of the club's grand old all-male traditions. The women petitioned the Connecticut Liquor Control Commission to withdraw Mory's liquor license under two Connecticut laws: one defining private clubs, the other bidding state agencies to use their licensing power to combat discrimination. The commission accepted the women's contention that Mory's was not private and that the commission should not give a liquor license to a club that discriminates, and it withdrew the license under the authority of both laws. Mory's finally capitulated and now serves women.

Women elsewhere should look for similar state laws that can be used to harass and build up pressure on many so-called private clubs. Even if state authorities won't condition a liquor license on admitting women, as Connecticut was willing to do, examining the club's bona fides as a private club could open up alternative attack routes. For instance, if the club doesn't fit the state definition of being private, it may have to get a public liquor license and admit the general male public. Then state public accommodation laws can be used to attack the exclusion of women.

If a club is really private, this tactic will not work, but many so-called private clubs may have some embarrassing questions to answer. How closely, for instance, are new members screened? Are all males automatically qualified for membership, simply by virtue of their sex? Are elections ever held to select a board of directors? Do the members really own the club?

Genuinely private clubs will be immune to attack (unless the state has a law like Connecticut's, telling the state liquor control agency to use its licensing power to combat discrimination). This unfortunate state of the law is the result of a Supreme Court decision that state regulation of liquor did not create enough "state action" (government involvement) in a private Moose Lodge to bring the club under the Equal Protection Clause and thus make it unconstitutional for the lodge to exclude black guests.[3] The same interpretation of the Equal Protection Clause will apply to private clubs excluding women. More recently, the Supreme Court established an even tougher standard for finding state action. A woman customer of the Metropolitan Edison Company sued the utility after it cut off her electricity for nonpayment of her bills. Although the utility was subject to extensive state regulation and provided an essential public service, the Court ruled that there was no state action because the "nexus," or relationship, between the state and the challenged cutoff was not close enough.[4]

When other courts have tried to apply this new legal test to other situations they have generally found that there was not enough government involvement in the activity in question to find state action; thus they have refused to bring the Equal Protection Clause into play. Several local chapters of the Jaycees which admitted women members in violation of the national Jaycees' membership policy sued the national organization for expelling them or for revoking their charters. The local chapters argued that state action by the federal government was involved because the national organization had tax-exempt status and received federal grants. Three federal appeals courts rejected this argument. The judge found that there was no relationship between the receipt of federal grants and tax exemptions and the policy of excluding women.[5] In another case, a woman veteran lost her battle to compel the Veterans of Foreign Wars to admit her to membership. Although the VFW was chartered by Congress, makes an annual financial report to Congress, and is granted tax-exempt status, the court again found that there was not a close enough relationship between the government and the VFW's male-only membership policy to justify applying the Equal Protection Clause.[6]

Thus, because of the state action requirement, it is now very difficult to challenge private clubs' discriminatory policies under the Equal Protection Clause even when they receive some governmental benefits. Attacking these clubs by showing that they are not really private, but rather are open to the general (male) public, may be a more successful strategy for desegregation.[7] At that point, state laws prohibiting sex discrimination in public accommodations can be used to force a change in policy.

What other methods can be used to combat discrimination practiced by private clubs and fraternal orders?

Both state and federal governments can prohibit certain economic benefits to these groups. Some receive tax-exempt status (which keeps them from having to pay taxes); others are allowed gifts which are tax-deductible (thus encouraging gifts), and still others receive direct government grants or subsidies.[8] It is obviously unfair to provide such benefits at public expense to groups that discriminate against women, and women should seek legislation to end the practice on both the state and federal levels. Lawsuits can be tried too. While one woman lost a case in which she sought to challenge the tax-exempt status of the "men-only" Portland City Club in Portland, Oregon,[9] blacks have succeeded with this approach in a number of suits against the Elks.[10] The cases do not force the clubs to stop discriminating, but by removing their tax-exempt status, they increase the cost to the club of discriminating. Thus lawsuits or legislation denying these economic benefits to discriminatory clubs provide powerful leverage for change through economic incentive.

Are there any state or city laws forbidding public bars, restaurants, and hotels to discriminate against women?

Yes. More than 20 states and some cities have already passed laws, generally referred to as public accommodation laws. More are needed. Chart B in the Appendix shows the states with these laws, as well as the much larger category of states with public accommodations laws that do not outlaw sex discrimination. The federal government is in the latter category, for Title II of the 1964 Civil Rights Act forbids only discrimination based on race, religion, color, and national origin.

The issues raised under these laws are sometimes complex. For instance, New York City has decided that residential hotels for women should open their doors to men, and that barber and beauty shops should serve all clients. Some women may not desire this result because of an instinct for privacy, and others may not think the issue important. But for women who want to mingle with men and who believe it is insulting to be excluded from any public area, the passage of new public accommodations laws and the inclusion of sex discrimination in existing laws should be a pressing concern.

B. Housing and Credit

Women need credit to make installment purchases, to buy consumer goods, to obtain housing, to finance an education, and for all the other reasons men need credit. Historically, women have faced much tougher obstacles than men in obtaining credit because of creditors' prejudices about women. Some creditors have denied women credit altogether; others have discounted a woman's income or asked if she practiced birth control when deciding whether she was a "good credit risk." To end this discrimination, Congress enacted two laws: the Equal Credit Opportunity Act[11] and the Fair Housing Act.[12] Creditors may still consider such sex-neutral factors as income, indebtedness, length of employment, and history of reliability in repaying debts when deciding whether to extend credit to any individual applicant, man or woman. However, the new laws should help ensure that women are not arbitrarily denied credit because they are women or are divorced, or held to higher standards than are men in determining whether they are good credit risks.

1. The Equal Credit Opportunity Act

What does the Equal Credit Opportunity Act (ECOA) provide?

The Act, passed by Congress in 1974 and amended in 1976, applies to all creditors who regularly extend credit, such as banks, finance companies, department stores, credit unions, and credit card companies.[13] It provides that these creditors may not discriminate in credit transactions on the basis of sex, marital status, race, religion, national origin, age, or receipt of public assistance. The Federal Reserve Board is charged with interpreting the law, and its Regulation B defines the specific practices which are now forbidden.[14] The law may be enforced by individual lawsuits when one woman is discriminated against, by a class action suit on behalf of a group of women, or by orders of the Federal Trade Commission requiring offending creditors to stop the discriminatory practice.

May a creditor require a married woman to apply (or to reapply) for credit under her husband's surname?

No. An applicant has the right to open or to maintain an account under the name she uses, whether it is her birth-given surname or a name she adopted at marriage such as her spouse's surname, or a combined surname (i.e., Jane Smith, Jane Jones, or Jane Smith-Jones). The application form may request the applicant to designate a courtesy title (i.e., Ms., Miss, Mrs., or Mr.), but the form must state that the use of this title is optional.

If a woman changes her name upon marriage, she need only notify the creditor of the name change. The creditor may not require her to submit a new application in order to maintain the account, nor require her to make the account a joint account with her husband, none insist that the account should now be in her husband's name and not her own.

May a creditor change the terms of an account or terminate an existing account because a woman changes her name or marital status?

No. Regulation B prohibits a creditor from lowering the credit limit, or requiring higher monthly payments on an account, or terminating an account because a woman changes her name or marital status. Of course, getting married or changing her name will not protect her from the creditor's actions when there is evidence that she is unable or unwilling to repay her debts.

However, if a woman is divorced or widowed, a creditor may require her to reapply for an "open end account" (an account on which credit is granted repeatedly, such as a department store or credit card account), if (1) the account was originally opened primarily on the basis of her husband's income and (2) her own income at the time they originally applied for the account was not enough to "justify" the amount of credit granted. For example, if a creditor had a minimum income requirement of $12,500 per year when Ann and Bill Jones applied for joint credit in 1978 and Bill was earning

$12,500 annually and Ann $4000, Ann could be required to reapply for an account after her divorce. If she had been earning $12,500 and he $7500, she could not be required to reapply.

May a creditor ask about a woman's birth control method or her capacity or intention to have children?

No. Such offensive questions are now illegal. (Formerly, in order to obtain credit, some women were required to provide letters from their doctors verifying their use of birth control or were required to agree to an abortion if they became pregnant!) Creditors may not infer from a woman's age that she is likely to drop out of the work force because of pregnancy and refuse her credit for that reason, nor may they give her credit on less favorable terms than a similarly qualified man for the same reason. Creditors may ask women how many children and other dependents they have and whether they contribute to their support or are required to do so, as long as these questions are asked of men as well and are asked regardless of whether the applicant is married, single, divorced, or widowed.

May a creditor discount a working wife's income?

No. A creditor may not refuse to count all or part of a wife's income in determining whether a couple qualifies for credit. For example, a creditor may not count 100 percent of a husband's income but only 50 percent of a wife's in determining whether the couple qualifies for a mortgage.

May a creditor refuse to consider alimony, separate maintenance, or child support as income?

No. If a woman chooses to list alimony, separate maintenance, or child support as part of her income in applying for credit, the creditor must count these payments as part of her income "to the extent they are likely to be consistently made."[15] This means that, in each individual case, the creditor must investigate to determine whether the payments are made to her reliably and predictably and must count them as income if they are. The woman may be asked to show proof of payments she has received in the past—such as deposit slips or records of payment through a court—to show that her ex-husband is reliable. Of course the majority of ex-husbands are not reliable in their payments and their ex-wives will not benefit from this provision. Still, it is helpful to those women whose ex-husbands do make support payments regularly and on time.

In deciding whether the ex-husband's payments are reliable, the creditor may consider such factors as whether the payments are paid under a separation agreement or court order, the length of time during which the payments have been made, the regularity of the payments, and whether the ex-husband is a good credit risk. A woman who finds this investigation offensive need not reveal that she receives alimony or child support—provided, of course, that she has enough income from other sources to qualify for credit.

May a creditor refuse to consider income from regular part-time employment, public assistance, annuities, pensions, or other retirement benefits?

No. A creditor may not refuse to count income from these sources when determining whether a person qualifies for credit, but he or she may consider the amount of the income and whether it is likely to continue. The creditor may ask for further information to make this determination.

May a creditor require a woman's husband to sign her credit application?

Yes, under certain circumstances, but no, under others. If a woman applies for an *individual* account in her own name and has enough income or property of her own to qualify for the amount of credit requested, the creditor may not require her husband's signature. However, his signature is required if they apply together for a *joint* account for which both will be responsible. If the woman requests credit in her own name, gives no collateral, and relies upon jointly owned or community property to establish that she is a good credit risk, her husband's signature may be required on the credit application. In an application for a mortgage or other credit for which some collateral is pledged as security, the creditor may require the signature of the husband or any other person who has an interest in the property which will serve as collateral.

May a creditor use a credit scoring system to determine whether a woman (or man) is a good credit risk?

So far, yes. Many of the larger credit companies use credit scoring systems which assign points for certain indicators of financial stability—e.g., type and length of employment, home ownership, and other credit cards. To qualify for credit, the applicant must have a certain minimum number of points based on these factors. If the scoring system does not explicitly differentiate on the basis of sex or marital status, it is legal under the ECOA.

Undoubtedly some scoring systems discriminate against women, but such discrimination is difficult to document and to eradicate because it is not overt. These credit systems do not assign points explicitly on the basis of sex or marital status—a practice which would blatantly violate the ECOA. Instead, they use indicators of financial stability which are drawn from the profiles of people who were good credit risks in the past—i.e., mainly men. For a variety of economic and social reasons, many women do not possess these characteristics although they may be just as able to repay their debts.

To force credit companies to adopt more equitable scoring systems, women must demonstrate that the current systems result in a pattern of discrimination because they disqualify more women than men from receiving credit. This requires detailed knowledge of the mechanics of the scoring systems and access to the credit companies' application files. Credit companies generally refuse to divulge this information on the grounds of confidentiality, and courts are reluctant to order them to do so. A federal district court in North Carolina ruled that Montgomery Ward need not reveal details of its credit system to a woman plaintiff because of the possible fraudulent use of this information.[16] However, it may eventually be possible to win lawsuits against the practice, based on a pattern of undue disqualification of women applicants.

Does a woman have the right to a credit history separate from her husband's?

Yes. A history of how well a person pays his or her bills, generally kept by local credit bureaus, is an important element in obtaining credit. Creditors use these reports in deciding whether a credit applicant is a good credit risk. Creditors used to report credit information only under the husband's name even where both husband and wife were responsible for paying the account. As a result, many women who were divorced or widowed—or who just wanted to get credit in their individual names—could not obtain credit, even though they had enough income for credit purposes. The ECOA made this practice illegal. A creditor must now determine whether a new account is an individual or a joint account. If both husband and wife agree to pay all bills on the account (a joint account) or if both are allowed to use it (an individual account with an additional "authorized user"), the creditor must report credit information in the names of both husband and wife. (For a joint account established before June 1, 1977, creditors must either report credit information separately for both husband and wife or give the account holder the option of separate reporting if he or she wants it. Write to the creditor asking to have credit information on these older accounts reported in both names.)

There is a different rule in community property states. Although credit histories must be reported separately there, creditors in these states are allowed to consider the husband's credit history in deciding whether to grant a wife's application for an individual account because both husband and wife have control over the community property—which includes most of the assets the creditor could look to for payment.

May a creditor deny credit to an unmarried couple—or to two women friends—when a married couple with the same combined incomes and credit history would be given credit?

Probably not. One federal appeals court in Washington, D.C., has ruled that a creditor must treat an unmarried couple applying for joint credit the same way it would treat a married couple. Jerry and Marcia Markham (then Marcia Harris) were engaged to be married and tried to buy a house together before their wedding. A savings and loan association rejected their mortgage application because they were not married, telling them if they married before closing time they would be given the mortgage. Neither had a high enough individual income to justify a mortgage, and the savings and loan refused to combine their incomes to determine if they were a good credit risk—a routine process for a married couple. The appeals court ruled that this was discrimination on the basis of marital status and illegal under the Equal

Credit Opportunity Act.[17] Arguably, it would be illegal to deny credit to any two people applying for joint credit who would qualify if married. (The court specifically stated it was not ruling on how a group of three or more should be treated.)

May a woman examine her file with the credit reporting agency?

Yes. The Fair Credit Reporting Act of 1970[18] gives a woman the right to examine her credit file with her local credit bureau or other credit reporting agency for a small fee or, if she is challenging a denial of credit, for free. To obtain a copy of her file, the woman should ask her bank which credit agency it uses and then contact the credit agency directly. If the credit files contain information which is inaccurate or misleading, the woman should write a letter explaining her version of the facts and ask the agency either to investigate and make a correction or to add her letter to the file. She should check her file again in a month or two to see if the correction has been made or her letter added. Women who have been recently married or divorced may wish to check their credit files to make sure that information on them is being reported correctly.

Does a woman have the right to know the reasons why she has been denied credit?

Yes, if it is not business credit. Within 30 days after receiving a completed credit application, the creditor must notify the woman of the action taken on her application. If credit is denied, the creditor must send the woman a written notice which includes a statement of the action taken, a notice of the anti-discrimination provisions of the ECOA, and the name and address of the appropriate federal enforcement agency. The written notice must also give either specific reasons for denying credit or inform the applicant of her right to a statement of the reasons, as well as the name, address, and telephone number of the person from whom this statement can be obtained. Under this second option, the woman has 60 days after receiving the notice to request the reasons for the denial, and the creditor then has 30 days in which to respond. If the creditor gives his reasons for denying credit orally, the applicant has the right to a written confirmation within 30 days of requesting it; moreover, the original written notice must inform her of this right.

The statement of reasons must be "specific" and indicate the principal reasons for the denial of credit. For example, the creditor might state that the minimum income required for a credit card is $20,000 per year and the applicant's annual income is only $13,000. It is not enough for the creditor to state that the applicant did not meet his minimum standards or failed to achieve a qualifying score on a credit scoring system. However, the creditor may use a standard checklist or a form letter to notify the applicant.

An applicant for business credit is not entitled to the automatic notice of reasons for the denial of credit. However, she can get it upon request if she acts within 30 days of learning of the denial. The creditor then has 30 days to respond.

Women should not let these cumbersome notice procedures stop them from insisting upon a written, specific statement of reasons whenever they are denied credit. A record of the creditor's reasons for refusing credit is important if the woman later decides to file a complaint with a federal agency or to bring a lawsuit against the creditor.

What steps should a woman take before filing a formal complaint if she believes a creditor has discriminated against her?

She should keep a detailed record of the entire credit transaction, including the names of credit officials with whom she talked, notes on her conversations with them and the date of the conversation, and copies of any correspondence or documents. She should be sure to obtain the written statement of the specific reasons for the denial of her credit application. If the reasons are not satisfactory, she should complain to the creditor and ask him to reconsider her application.

How can a woman enforce her rights under the ECOA?

The ECOA provides for two methods of enforcement: administrative actions by federal agencies and private lawsuits. Responsibility for enforcement of the ECOA has been delegated to 12 federal agencies, with overall enforcement power given to the Federal Trade Commission (FTC). Which federal agency is responsible for a particular creditor depends upon the type of creditor involved—e.g., retail store, national bank, or credit union. The FTC issues advisory opinions and guidelines to the credit industry in general (these are in addition to the binding interpretations of the law issued by the Federal Reserve Board, and called Regulation B) and investigates creditors for violations of the law. The FTC can issue "cease and desist" orders to force creditors to stop discriminatory practices. However, such orders do not guarantee that credit will be granted to any individual applicant who may have been denied credit in the past—including the person who filed a complaint. Neither the FTC nor any other federal agency handles cases for individuals, but they do need individual complaints to determine which creditors to investigate.[19]

Any woman who believes a creditor has discriminated against her should send a letter with details of the credit transaction to the appropriate federal enforcement agency. This will help to build a case against creditors with a pattern of illegal credit practices. The creditor must provide the name and address of the appropriate agency when he denies credit. If he does not, the applicant may write to:

> Federal Trade Commission
> Office of the Secretary
> Equal Credit Opportunity
> Washington, D.C. 20580

or to one of the FTC regional offices, or call (202) 523–3598.

A woman who believes she has been denied credit illegally may also bring suit against the creditor under the Equal Credit Opportunity Act in a federal district court. If successful, she may recover her actual damages plus up to $10,000 in punitive damages. Because the creditor also may be forced to pay her attorney's fees and court costs, she may be able to find an attorney willing to take the case on the basis of court-ordered fees at the end of the case. If a number of women have suffered from the same kind of discrimination, one or more of them may file a class action against the creditor. In a class action, the amount of punitive damages may be as much as $500,000 or 1 percent of the creditor's net worth, whichever is less. The possibility of punitive damages may make it worthwhile for a creditor to settle a threatened lawsuit speedily.

2. The Fair Housing Act

Do women have any federal rights against discrimination in housing?

Yes. In 1974 Congress amended Title VIII of the Civil Rights Act of 1968 (the Fair Housing Act)[20] to forbid sex discrimination in the sale or rental of most housing, in the provision of real estate brokerage services, and in the financing of housing. Owners and real estate agents can no longer refuse to show a woman a house which is for sale or refuse to rent to her. Banks, building and loan associations, and other commercial real estate lenders may not discriminate against women by denying them loans, charging them higher interest rates than men, setting different terms and conditions for loans to women, or requiring women to be better credit risks than men before granting credit. These prohibitions apply to any loan to purchase, construct, repair, or maintain housing. The 1974 amendment also requires mortgage lenders to consider the combined income of husband and wife in deciding whether to grant credit to a married couple.[21] The Act does not prohibit discrimination on the basis of marital status, but such discrimination in financing is prohibited by the Equal Credit Opportunity Act.

How are the anti-discrimination provisions of the Fair Housing Act enforced?

Title VIII provides three methods of enforcement: informal conciliation efforts by the U.S. Department of Housing and Urban Development (HUD), private lawsuits against violators for damages, and suits by the U.S. Attorney General to correct a pattern or practice of discrimination.

When a woman believes or suspects she has been discriminated against in the rental, sale, or financing of housing and wants to file a complaint with HUD rather than going to court first, she should begin by sending a letter of complaint to:

Fair Housing
U.S. Department of Housing and Urban Development
Washington, D.C. 20410

or to the nearest HUD Regional Office. (Addresses of these offices may be located by looking in the telephone book under United States Department of Housing and Urban Development.)

The complaint letter should describe in detail what happened—with dates, times and places, your own name and the names of those you believe discriminated against you. It should be notarized and must be filed with HUD within 180 days after the discriminatory event happened. If the discrimination continues, say so in your complaint. HUD must investigate the complaint within 30 days. If HUD decides to take action, it will attempt to eliminate the discriminatory practice through informal conciliation and persuasion.

If a state or local fair-housing law provides protection and remedies equal to or better than those available under the federal law, HUD will send the complaint to the appropriate state or local agency for you. HUD will take no further action on the complaint unless the state or local agency does not begin proceedings within 30 days or fails to carry them forward with reasonable promptness. Women in states with fair-housing laws (check Chart B in the Appendix) should file complaints at the same time with both the appropriate state agency and with HUD to avoid any delay caused by the referral procedure.

You may also get your own attorney and file suit under the Fair Housing Act in federal district court or your state court within 180 days after the discriminatory event, whether or not you have filed a complaint with HUD. If you win, you will be entitled to any actual damages you have suffered— such as increased interest costs—and you may be awarded up to $1000 in punitive damages as well. When immediate action is required to stop the discrimination—such as stopping the transfer of title to another buyer—the court may issue temporary orders to hold off the discriminatory action and may later issue permanent orders to stop discriminatory practices, as well as awarding damages.

If you have filed a complaint with HUD, you may not go to court for 30 days; this provision is designed to give HUD a chance to try to get voluntary compliance with the law from the violator. Therefore, if more than 150 days have passed since the discriminatory event or if you need immediate court action—such as a temporary court order—to protect you, you should obtain a lawyer and go directly to court. If you are very poor, the court may appoint a lawyer to represent you and may decide not to require you to pay court costs and fees. (When your state or local law provides legal protections equal to or better than those of the federal law, your lawsuit must be brought in state or local court.) By 1980 little private litigation had been brought under the sex discrimination provisions of the Fair Housing Act.

Complaints of housing discrimination may also be made to the Attorney General of the United States. If he concludes after an investigation that there is a pattern or practice of discrimination or that a group of people have been denied rights under Title VIII, he may bring suit in federal district court.

Women's groups might survey the practices in the local housing market on selling or renting housing to women. They may set up comparable applications to see whether a landlord will rent more readily to John Smith than to Mary Jones when both have the same income and obligations. Such a study should be planned with a feminist attorney and careful records kept for litigation purposes if necessary.

In general, the Equal Credit Opportunity Act is probably more useful in attacking financing problems than is the Fair Housing Act. It offers higher possible monetary damages and includes discrimination on the basis of marital status. For these reasons, it should be considered before using the Fair Housing Act provisions to deal with financing problems which arise in connection with housing.

3. Local Laws

How should women protest discrimination in public accommodations, housing, and financing under the various state and city laws?

Many of these laws provide for comprehensive enforcement schemes under the same state agency that regulates employment discrimination. It is not possible to explain in this handbook the various procedures under all these laws, but some general advice would be to call the state employment discrimination agency (see Chart A in the Appendix), and ask for information about where to go and what to do next. If the agency cannot help, women could try reading the law itself (see Chart B for the legal citations for all such state laws). If this is not informative, the help of a lawyer will be needed.

An obvious project for paralegal counseling groups would be to research the local laws and write and distribute pamphlets explaining how to use these laws. Lawyers or law students should help—both to locate laws that may not be included in the chart (city laws, or ones passed after publication of this book) and to check the accuracy of the legal advice proposed by the counseling group.

C. Day Care

Can parents legally establish day-care centers for their children?

It depends. They can if the center meets all the requirements set by local, state, and federal governments to regulate day care.

This question is presented to highlight the fact that states and cities throughout the country have enacted a variety of extremely restrictive day-care regulations. By requiring a higher standard of care than most parents achieve in their own home, they raise costs so high that most parents cannot afford to start any day-care center at all.

Typically restrictive features include these: only women can take care of very young children; centers may not accept children below the age of two or three; the center must have plenty of park space, and a defined amount of space per child (even in big cities where land is costly and the children serviced would never have such space at home, anyway). In addition to state licensing laws and local zoning, health and fire codes, day-care centers which receive federal money must satisfy federal regulations.[22] These regulations set standards for the location and safety of facilities, group size, health and nutritional services, educational programs, the training of staff, and parental involvement. There are many other restrictions, too varied to detail at length here, but these few indicate the general problem. Authorities who would prefer that mothers stay home to tend their children have imposed such unrealistic and costly conditions on day-care centers that parents are forced to resort to totally unregulated centers or homes since they must find some place to leave their children while they work. These regulations should be challenged, and new, more realistic ones enacted.

Where can parents get help in establishing day-care centers?

One source of information is the Day Care and Child Development Council of America, the only national organization devoted exclusively to day-care problems. The council publishes a pamphlet, *Basic Facts About Licensing of Day Care*, available for $.50, and a newsletter, *Voice for Children*, which is available to members. (A membership costs $12 for individuals, $20 for libraries, and $25 or $50 for agencies, depending upon their size.) Both publications can be obtained by writing to:

Day Care and Child Development Council of America
1602 17th St., N.W.
Washington, D.C. 20005
  (202) 745–0200

The council also helps interested local groups start day-care centers and can provide information about state licensing regulations.

Other sources include *Day Care: How to Plan, Develop and Operate a Day Care Center*, by E. Belle Evans, Beth Schub, and Marlene Weinstein (Beacon Press); and *How to Have a Child and Keep Your Job* by Jane Price. Also, every state has a day-care licensing division in its welfare or health department which can provide information about regulations and the availability of funding.

Can most parents afford to establish the quality day-care centers that are needed?

No. Parents need federal aid to establish a sufficient number of quality day-care centers. Although there is no comprehensive federal law providing for day care, some federal funding has been available under Title XX of the Social Security Act,[23] and several other programs. But there are problems even with these limited programs. First, state participation is only voluntary. In addition, Title XX provides for one set dollar amount for all services for the handicapped, the elderly, the abused, and other needy groups, as well as for day care. Thus when the state applies for federal aid for day care, that program is in competition with the state's other needs. Although every state receives some day-care money, insufficient federal funding and competition among worthy programs are perennial problems. Women must insist that Congress substantially increase its allocation for day care through some new program.

Another serious problem is that all federally funded day-care facilities determine eligibility on the basis of parental income. For instance, only 10 percent of the children in day-care centers funded under the Headstart Program may come from families whose income exceeds the federal poverty level. Facilities which receive Title XX funds usually accept no children whose family incomes are 115 percent or more of the state median income.

Feminists should resist the idea that only low-income families need public funding for day care. Parents of all income levels need this program, and an absence of low-cost, quality day-care keeps the middle-income woman tied to her home just as much as the lower-income woman. The solution may be to make publicly supported day care available to all, but on a sliding fee scale. Women will have to fight for this provision, though, since it faces resistance from both conservative and liberal Congressmen who are currently preoccupied with cutting or "containing" the federal budget. In the meantime, one possible strategy for feminists is to negotiate for day care as a work benefit from employers under collective bargaining agreements.

Is there any income tax relief for parents who use day care?

Yes. In 1976, Congress enacted a child-care tax credit.[24] This provision allows taxpayers to reduce their taxes for child-care expenses for children under 15 years old. The expenses must be "employment-related," i.e., incurred for household services or child care in order to allow the taxpayer to be gainfully employed. Until 1982 the amount of credit was limited to 20 percent of the actual child-care expense up to $2000 for one dependent (i.e., $400), or 20 percent of expenses up to $4000 (i.e., $800) for two or more dependents. In 1981 Congress slightly liberalized the maximum tax credit amounts for low-income people, to be effective in the 1982 tax year. As of 1982, people earning less than $10,000 will be able to take a maximum credit of $720 for one child, and $1440 for two children. For people with an income between $10,000 and $30,000, there is a sliding-scale decrease in the amount of the maximum tax credit, from the maximum of $720 and $1440 at $10,000 income down to the $400 and $800 maximum credits at the $30,000 income level, and above.

For an unmarried taxpayer, the credit may not exceed her earned income. In the case of a married taxpayer, the credit may not exceed her earned income or that of her spouse, whichever is less. To qualify for the credit, married taxpayers must file a joint return. If the parents of a child are divorced and one parent has custody for over one-half of the year, only that parent is eligible for the credit. Unlike the old child-care deduction, the tax credit may be claimed by all qualified taxpayers, not just those who itemize deductions.

D. Women in the Military

In the 1970's women scored some major gains in the military and won several important legal cases.[25] First the armed forces decided to increase significantly the percentages of women in the different services. Then the military academies accepted their first women cadets. However, though the military now offers women some excellent opportunities, many inequities remain, and women in the military are still second-class citizens in that world. The number of women in the armed services is still strictly limited to a smaller number than would like to join the military. Women are not required to register for the draft although men are. Women are still precluded from combat roles even when they want to serve in that capacity; indeed, even when it is vital to their career advancement to do so. Finally, preferential treatment for veterans, few of whom are women because of the prior quotas, magnifies and extends the original inequities well beyond the time of military service; the virtually all-male veterans get first crack at the best government jobs. Though deep-rooted, these inequities must be attacked.

May United States military academies exclude women?

No. In 1976, Congress ordered the military academies to admit women.[26] Women now attend West Point, Annapolis, and the other military academies, but their numbers are strictly limited "consistent with the needs of the services." However, except for this quota, the same admissions criteria apply to both sexes and once admitted, women must meet the same academic standards as men. Because military schools offer valuable training not available elsewhere and enhance career opportunities, women should use the Equal Protection Clause to attack quotas.

Do women have the same opportunities as men to enlist in the armed services?

No. Quotas for each branch of the military strictly limit the number of women who may enlist to a level far below the number of women who would enlist if they could. However, men and women are now required to meet the same educational and trainability requirements (as measured by minimum aptitude tests). Previously women, but not men, were required to have high-school diplomas. This discriminatory requirement was dropped after women began a lawsuit attacking its legality.

Must the armed services offer men and women the same salaries, fringe benefits, and opportunities for promotion?

Yes on salaries and fringe benefits; perhaps no on promotions. Men and women at any given rank receive the same salaries, but women's opportunities for promotions are severely limited by quotas at all rank levels. One attempt to compensate for this discrimination is the Navy "up or out" statute, which requires that male line officers be discharged from the Navy when they are passed over twice for promotion, but allows women 13 years before they are discharged for non-promotion. A male lieutenant who wanted to stay in the Navy long enough to be eligible for retirement pay challenged the statute on equal protection grounds, but the Supreme Court upheld the law, on the theory that its purpose was to compensate women for other disadvantages the Navy had imposed on them. Statutory restrictions on women's participation in combat and sea duty made it difficult for female officers to compile service records comparable to those of male officers. A longer period of service before discharge for women officers was therefore necessary to provide them with fair opportunities for advancement, the Court stated.[27] A more logical starting point would have been to rule the whole scheme unconstitutional, beginning with the ban on sea or combat duty for women in the Navy. But the male plaintiff did not challenge that discrimination, and it is possible the Court would not act on it without an Equal Rights Amendment.

As for fringe benefits, Sharron Frontiero, an Air Force lieutenant, won the right to claim her husband as a dependent for purposes of obtaining increased quarters allowances and medical benefits in a 1973 Supreme Court decision. She challenged a federal statute that permitted a serviceman automatically to claim his wife as a dependent, but required a servicewoman to prove that her husband depended on her for more than one-half of his support before she could claim him as a dependent and get the additional fringe benefits. The Court ruled that this scheme was clearly unconstitutional.[28]

May the armed services refuse to allow single parents of minor children to enlist?

This question has not been finally resolved. Shirley Mae West, an unwed mother, challenged an Army regulation that prohibits the enlistment of unwed parents. (Divorced parents are eligible for enlistment only if they do not have custody of their children.) Ms. West, who met all the other criteria for enlistment, argued that this regulation illegally interfered with her constitutional right to marry or not to marry as she chose and with her constitutional right to rear her child. One federal court dismissed her claim on the ground that it lacked authority to review the military's criteria for enlistment,[29] but another court challenge to this policy is currently pending.[30]

May a woman be discharged from the armed services because she is pregnant?

No. In 1971 Stephanie Crawford, an unmarried woman who had been discharged from the Marine Corps because she became pregnant, sued to be reinstated as a Marine. Five years later, a federal appeals court awarded her back pay for the 20 months that had remained in her tour of duty and declared that the no-pregnancy rule violated the Constitution's equal protection guaranty.[31] Under the Marine Corps rule, the only temporary physical disability which was cause for automatic discharge was a pregnancy-related disability; all other temporary physical disabilities were considered on an individual basis. The court found this distinction irrational.

After Ms. Crawford began her suit, the Marine Corps and the other branches of the armed services changed their no-pregnancy rules. The present Air Force and Marine Corps regulations provide that a pregnant servicewoman may request a discharge, but that otherwise her status is unaffected. The Army and Navy may waive the discharge of pregnant women.

Can women be drafted?

Yes, although it is highly unlikely. Nothing in the Constitution prevents Congress from drafting women although it has never yet taken that option. Indeed, no one has been subject to the draft since 1973, when the draft law expired. The armed forces are now all-volunteer, but pressure is mounting for a return to compulsory military service. In 1979 bills were introduced in Congress to reinstate Selective Service registration of 18-year-old males as a first step toward reviving the draft. The bills were defeated. In February 1980 President Carter asked Congress for legislation and funds to begin draft registration of men and women between the ages of 18 and 20. The registration of women was strongly opposed by many Congressmen, and only the all-male registration measure passed. It was challenged immediately as a violation of the Equal Protection Clause, but the Supreme Court ruled that this different treatment of men and women was perfectly constitutional.[32]

May women be excluded from combat roles?

So far, yes. All branches of the armed forces prohibit women from serving in combat capacities. This policy is unlikely to change soon because opposition to women in combat roles is strong and visceral, especially among military men and members of Congress. However, the exclusion of women from combat roles severely limits women's opportunities in the military. A group of female officers and enlisted women in the Navy therefore challenged a federal law which absolutely barred the assignment of women to duty at sea, either in combat or non-combat roles. Because Navy women were restricted to shore duty, they were excluded from most job classifications and limited in their opportunities for training and promotion. Citing studies that showed women could perform capably in shipboard positions, a federal district court ruled that the statute was unconstitutional, both as to combat and non-combat positions.[33]

Following this decision, however, Congress passed a new statute which prohibits women from serving on aircraft or vessels that are actually engaged in combat missions; it does allow women to be assigned to other Navy vessels, but only on a temporary basis if the ship is expected to be assigned a combat mission.[34] The new law might be unconstitutional also although the Supreme Court's 1981 decision permitting a male-only registration for the draft suggests the Court might well accept male-only combat rules, too. In any event, women who want combat roles will probably have to file court challenges to get them.

Is it legal for federal, state, and local governments to give job preference to veterans?

Yes. The federal government and most state governments give some preference to veterans for civil service jobs. Usually the preference consists of the addition of five or ten points to a veteran's score on a civil service exam. However, Massachusetts has an absolute veterans' preference system, under which veterans who qualify for state civil service positions must be considered for appointment ahead of all qualifying non-veterans. The effect of this system is to exclude almost all women from most of the best state civil service jobs because veterans get them all and so few women are veterans.

Helen Feeney, a state employee and non-veteran, claimed that the Massachusetts Veterans Preference Statute discriminated against women in violation of the Equal Protection Clause. Although Ms. Feeney had ranked at the top in several civil service exams, the jobs for which she was competing were given to lower-scoring male veterans. A federal court agreed that the statute was unconstitutional, but its decision was reversed by the Supreme Court. Although the Court recognized that the veterans' preference system had an overwhelmingly adverse impact on women, it upheld the law because the *purpose* of the law was not to discriminate against women but to prefer veterans over non-veterans of either sex.[35] The Supreme Court now refuses to look at the disproportionate and harsh impact of a "neutral" law on women in Equal Protection Clause cases unless the explicit purpose of the law is to hurt women—a standard nearly impossible to prove. However, in employment discrimination cases based on Title VII rather than the Equal Protection Clause, the Court applies a standard more favorable to women's rights—the stricter standard of whether an apparently neutral rule actually has a disproportionately bad effect on women.

E. Jury Duty

May women be excluded from jury duty or granted an automatic exemption from jury duty?

No. Some states have excluded all women from their jury pools except those who specifically volunteer for jury duty, or have granted women an automatic exemption from jury service simply because of their sex. The Supreme Court has ruled that both of these practices are unconstitutional.[36] A jury selection process that results in a significant underrepresentation of women on juries violates the Sixth Amendment, which guarantees defendants the right to trial by a jury drawn from a fair cross section of the community. Neither the state's desire to safeguard women's "important role in the home and family life" nor administrative convenience can justify the automatic exclusion of women from juries.

Although men and women are now both obligated to perform jury duty, the Supreme Court decisions do not mean that all women will actually be required to serve on juries regardless of hardship. States may still set relevant qualifications for jurors and provide reasonable exemptions that apply to either sex. A state may legally exempt women (or men) from jury duty because of age, special hardship, responsibility for the care of young children, or other sex-neutral reasons. Usually a state will excuse any prospective juror who requests an exemption based on one of the specified grounds, but it may no longer simply assume that all women are entitled to exemptions without inquiring in each case.

F. Benefits for Housewives

Should housewives be entitled to wages, vacations, sick leave, medical insurance, unemployment compensation, workman's compensation, Social Security benefits, and pension plans?

Why not? Paying housewives a salary and fringe benefits might resolve the contradiction now found in society's attitude. The housewife is praised rhetorically, told that motherhood and care of the home are the backbone of our society, and that this is the finest role she can ever fulfill. But financially, she is told that the job is worthless. Any money she gets is a gift from her husband. It is support—money she has not earned, but which he chooses to give her. She is also informed that she doesn't really work; work is something done only for pay. Thus when her husband gets home from a hard day at the plant or office, she is supposed to wait on him, on the theory that she has not been working all day. The average housewife has been working just as hard as her husband, and they should both share the household duties at night, after both have finished their daytime activities; they should both be compensated; they should both receive fringe benefits.

Compensating the housewife might increase a woman's sense of self-worth. Earnings are a measure of pride and independence in this society. The woman who works in the home does many important things, and she deserves to be rewarded in the same way as are other people in our society.

Is there any practical way for housewives to receive pay?

Yes. The simplest way to pay housewives (or men who take the same job) would be to institute a modified community property system nationwide. Community property is the law in eight states. It declares that all property acquired by either the man or the woman during marriage belongs to both equally, thus recognizing that the woman's contribution to the family unit is just as valuable as the man's.

On a day-by-day basis, the person who has the right to manage and control community assets has the real power over them. In seven of the eight community property states, husband and wife have equal legal rights to manage and control the community property.[37] This means that both husband and wife must sign papers for transactions involving real estate although usually either spouse may manage other assets such as money, personal property, or stocks and bonds for the benefit of both spouses. In practice, men in these states often retain control over the use of their paychecks even though their wives have a theoretical equal right to manage the family income.

Therefore, in addition to co-equal management and control rights in theory, the wife should be given the right to sue the husband (and vice versa when appropriate) to acquire her half of the income, including his paycheck and the property, even if the marriage is ongoing and the parties are living together. The right to sue is vital if her ownership and control of half the family income is to mean anything. This right also represents a radical departure from current legal concepts of the relationship between husband and wife. By and large, courts refuse to interfere in an ongoing relationship between the two—they will leave the couple to work it out in private. (This is why the right to "support" is an illusion; it remains a gift the husband can choose to give. There is no way a woman who wants to live with her stingy husband can sue him for the money. The courts don't want to interfere.) Thus, the concept of intervening—particularly in order to take away what most judges will see as "his" income, to give it to an "undeserving" woman who doesn't even "work"—will be hard to achieve.

Are there any problems with compensating the housewife through a modified community property system?

There may be problems with this scheme, of course. The suggestions above are intended primarily to stimulate discussion of the issue. Some feminists would disagree with the proposed solution for several reasons.

First, they would argue that we should not encourage women to stay home and that this scheme would have the effect of doing so. Other feminists would reply that women who are going to stay home anyway should at least be compensated for the work they do and that paying for this work might encourage more men to stay home for some of the years of child rearing.

Second, giving a woman a salary based on the husband's income de-emphasizes the idea of being paid for the value of one's work. On the other hand, it emphasizes that marriage is a partnership, in a world where many people—both men and women—still believe that young children should be reared by a parent.

Third, some would argue that the housewife married to a rich man can employ household workers to do much of the traditional housewife's job, and therefore gets paid more for doing less than the housewife married to a poor man. On the other hand, the woman with a rich husband may perform other services of a valuable nature, such as entertaining and gardening. This work, too, deserves compensation.

Finally, some people believe that the scheme does not help the woman who works outside the home and still does all the housework; although she does two jobs, she gets paid for only one. However, at least community property would increase the amount of money and property owned by most women holding down two jobs. The average woman is statistically apt to earn less than her husband because of employment discrimination. Since community property gives her one-half of the combined incomes, the system would indeed compensate her in some degree for her "two" jobs; for one-half of the combined incomes would be greater than the outside salary alone for most women working outside the home.

How can women achieve a community property system with co-equal management and control rights and the right to acquire actual possession of their fair share of the assets and income?

They should lobby for new laws instituting this modified community property system throughout the nation. In the interim, women may be able to negotiate contracts with their husbands to accomplish the same result. The courts are not likely to uphold such contracts although the chances are greater if the parties enter into them before marriage rather than after. In either case, many people should still find it worth doing for the psychological effect of formally agreeing to be equal partners.

Women should also explore the possibility of getting a law passed to validate such contracts in states where it is impossible to pass a community property law. Such a contract would provide that both parties equally own and control one-half of all income and property acquired during the marriage, and that if one party retains control over the other party's half, the second person could sue the first for his or her rightful share. A provision that the wrongful party pay for attorneys' fees, court costs, and interest should also be included in order to make it easier to get a lawyer to bring such a lawsuit.

Is there another way in which women might equalize the financial situation in marriage?

Yes. Women could make written agreements with their husbands to lend them money for certain expenses to be repaid at standard interest rates. For example, a young wife who finances her husband's graduate or professional education by working while he goes to school could at least ensure repayment of this money. Such a loan agreement would be legally enforceable.

Is there any way for women to ensure that their husbands share the work of maintaining the house and rearing the children?

No, but women might want to make a second kind of contract, setting forth the duties of each party during the marriage. Lawyers refer to this kind of contract as one dealing with the incidents of marriage, that is, the duties and obligations legally imposed on each partner under marriage law. It is clear that judges will not enforce a contract that seeks to change the common-law incidents of marriage, so this contract is useful only for its psychological effect. Women might also lobby for laws to validate these contracts—although the prospect of suing one's husband for breaking his contract by not doing the dishes has some troublesome overtones. In any case, women should keep these contracts separate from those providing for equal rights in income and property; the latter have a greater chance of being enforced, and if the two are mingled the court might find both invalid.

A "personal incidents" contract would detail the household duties for each party to the marriage, including care of the children. It could also provide for vacations, free evenings and weekends, and so forth, for each party. This would reinforce the point that the wife (or rare husband) who stays home does work all day and deserves some respite from that work.

For a good example of such a contract, read "How To Write Your Own Marriage Contract," by Susan Edmiston in the Spring 1972 issue of *Ms*. The article includes the Shulmans' Marriage Agreement, whose guiding principle is especially interesting:

> We reject the notion that the work which brings in more money is more valuable. The ability to earn more money is a privilege which must not be compounded by enabling the larger earner to buy out his/her duties and put the burden on the partner who earns less or on another person hired from outside.

What ideas might be explored for providing fringe benefits for housewives?

Housewives will find it more difficult to get the other fringe benefits mentioned—sick leave, medical insurance, unemployment compensation, workman's compensation, Social Security, and pension plans. Some women have suggested adding a component to existing social insurance programs for women, or men, who work in the home. For example, if the housewife were injured while working, she would receive compensatory payments under the Workman's Compensation Act. If she were ill, she would be entitled to state payments from the Temporary Disability Insurance Program, in states with such a program. If she were divorced and the husband defaulted on alimony and child support, she would receive unemployment compensation. And she would be entitled to Social Security benefits in her own right, not as someone's wife; she would receive credit for income earned as a housewife during the years in the home, just as she would for income as a paid worker in the outside labor force for those years.

Of course, in-depth economic research is needed before we can know whether these ideas are feasible. Other important problems would also need to be resolved. For instance, under these programs who would be deemed the woman's employer? Should the woman who works both inside and outside the home receive double benefits? But the important thing is for women to begin exploring ways to better the economic position of the housewife. If real solutions can be developed, perhaps even men would become more willing to share the job with their wives.

What can women's paralegal projects do in this area?

They can work with attorneys on drawing up model contracts for women and help individual women write their own contracts. The legal effect of such contracts must be explained, of course, and the group should ask attorneys to research state laws thoroughly on this question. Finally, women's groups can work with attorneys to prepare model legislation for all the problem areas mentioned in this chapter, and then help lobby for passage of such laws.

NOTES

1. *Seidenberg v. McSorley's Old Ale House*, 317 F.Supp. 593 (S.D. N.Y. 1970). Another decision is *Bennett v. Dyers' Chop House*, 350 F.Supp. 153 (N.D. Ohio 1972).

2. *Johnson v. Heinemann Candy Co., Inc.*, 402 F.Supp. 714 (E.D. Wis. 1975).

3. *Moose Lodge No. 107 v. Irvis*, 407 U.S. 163 (1972). Mr. Irvis also filed a complaint against the lodge under a state public accommodations law. The Pennsylvania Supreme Court held that by opening its dining room to any Caucasian who was invited by a member, the fraternal organization came within the ambit of a "public accommodation" and was therefore forbidden by the state Human Relations Act from discriminating on the basis of race or color in these facilities. *Commonwealth Human Relations Commission v. Loyal Order of Moose*, 448 Pa. 451, 294 A.2d 594 (1972).

4. *Jackson v. Metropolitan Edison Company*, 419 U.S. 345 (1974).

5. *Junior Chamber of Commerce of Rochester, Inc. v. United States Jaycees*, 495 F.2d 883 (10th Cir.), *cert. denied*, 419 U.S. 1026 (1974); *Junior Chamber of Commerce of Kansas City v. Missouri State Junior Chamber of Commerce*, 508 F.2d 1031 (8th Cir. 1974); *New York City Jaycees, Inc. v. United States Jaycees, Inc.*, 512 F.2d 856 (2d Cir. 1975).

6. *Stearns v. Veterans of Foreign Wars*, 394 F.Supp. 138 (D. D.C. 1975), *aff'd without opinion*, 527 F.2d 1387 (D.C. Cir. 1976), *cert. denied*, 429 U.S. 822 (1976).

7. See "Sex Discrimination in Private Clubs," 29 *Hastings Law Journal* 417 (Nov. 1977).

8. For a discussion of the difficulties under present law of eliminating the tax-exempt status of discriminatory organizations, see "Taxing Sex Discrimination: Revoking Tax Benefits of Organizations Which Discriminate on the Basis of Sex," *Arizona State Law Journal* 1976:641 (1976).

9. *McCoy v. Schultz*, 73–1 U.S.T.C. 9233 (CCH) (D. D.C. 1973).

10. *Falkenstein v. Department of Revenue for the State of Oregon*, 350 F.Supp. 887 (D. Ore. 1972), *appeal dismissed for want of jurisdiction, sub nom. Oregon State Elks Association v. Falkenstein*, 409 U.S. 1099 (1973); *McGlotten v. Connally*, 338 F.Supp. 448 (D. D.C. 1972); *Pitts v. Department of Revenue for the State of Wisconsin*, 333 F.Supp. 662 (E.D. Wis. 1971). See also *Bob Jones University v. United States*,———U.S.———, 76 L. Ed. 2d 157 (May 24, 1983).

11. 15 U.S.C. §1601 *et seq*.

12. 42 U.S.C. §3601, *as amended by* 42 U.S.C. §5308(b).

13. Regulation B, 12 C.F.R. §202.

14. 2 C.F.R. §202. The regulations in their entirety apply only to retain credit. Business, securities, public utility, and incidental credit are exempted from some provisions of the Act.

15. 12 C.F.R. §202.6(b) (5).

16. *Rice v. Montgomery Ward & Co., Inc.*, 450 F. supp. 668 (M.D. N.C. 1978).

17. *Markham v. Colonial Mortgage Co. Associates, Inc.*, 605 F.2d 566 (D.C. Cir. 1979).

18. 15 U.S.C. §1681g-i.

19. For a fuller discussion of ECOA enforcement problems, see "Equal Credit: Promise or Reality?" 11 *Harvard Civil Rights-Civil Liberties Law Review* 186 (1976).

20. 42 U.S.C. §3601 *et. seq., as amended by* 42 U.S.C. §5308(b), Housing and Community Development Act of 1974.

21. 12 U.S.C. §1738.

22. 45 C.F.R. Part 71 (1978).

23. 42 U.S.C. §1397 *et seq*. (1976).

24. *Internal Revenue Code*, §44A. Further information about this tax credit is available in Internal Revenue Service Publication 503, "Child Care and Disabled Dependent Care."

25. An excellent source on the role of women in the military is Binkin and Bach, *Women and the Military*, (Washington, D.C.: Brookings Institute, 1977).

26. Department of Defense Appropriation Authorization Act, 10 U.S.C.A. §4342 note (1977 Supp.)

27. *Schlesinger v. Ballard*, 419 U.S. 498 (1975).

28. *Frontiero v. Richardson*, 411 U.S. 677 (1973).

29. *West v. Brown*, 558 F.2d 757 (5th Cir. 1977).

30. *Mack v. Rumsfeld* (W.D. N.Y.). For more information on this case, contact Greater Upstate Legal Project, 101 Towers Building, Roch-

ester, N.Y. 14614; (716) 454–6500 or the National Center on Women and Family Law, 799 Broadway, Room 402, New York, N.Y. 10003, (212) 674-8200.

31. *Crawford v. Cushman*, 531 F.2d 1114 (2d Cir. 1976).

32. *Rostker v. Goldberg*, 453 U.S. 57 (1981).

33. *Owens v. Brown*, 455 F.Supp. 291 (D. D.C. 1978).

34. 10 U.S.C.A. §6015 (1979 Supp.)

35. *Personnel Administrator of Massachusetts v. Feeney*, 442 U.S. 256 (1979).

36. *Duren v. Missouri*, 439 U.S. 357 (1979); *Taylor v. Louisiana*, 419 U.S. 522 (1975).

37. Arizona, California, Idaho, Louisiana, Nevada, New Mexico, and Washington. In Texas commingled community property is managed jointly, but either spouse retains control over any property he or she would have owned if single, provided it is kept separate from the community property.

X

The Legal System

For many persons, law appears to be black magic—an obscure domain that can be fathomed only by the professional initiated into its mysteries. Women who might use the law to their advantage sometimes avoid the effort out of excess awe for its intricacies. But the main lines of the legal system, and of the law in a particular area, can be explained in terms clear to the layperson.

Many women are seeking to improve their lot in life generally or are searching for solutions to specific problems. Often they have legal rights to better treatment but don't know about these rights or how to assert them. The purpose of this book has been to describe in direct, concrete fashion the legal rights of women and the ways in which these rights can be implemented so that women can use law to achieve their goals. In this concluding chapter, however, the nature of the legal system and some of its key concepts are described to render more useful the specific information about women's rights.

What does a lawyer mean by saying that a person has a legal right?

Having a right means that society has given a person permission—through the legal system—to secure some action or to act in some way that she or he desires. A woman might have a right to an abortion, a right to employment free from discrimination, or a right to use whatever name she likes.

How does one enforce a legal right?

The concept of *enforcing* a right gives meaning to the concept of the right itself. While the abstract right may be significant to a particular woman because it carries some connotation of morality and justice, enforcing the right yields something concrete—the abortion, the job, the name.

A woman enforces her right by going to some appropriate authority—often, a judge—who has the power to take certain action. The judge can order the people who are refusing to grant the right to start doing so, on pain of going to jail if they disobey. The judge can also order the people to pay the woman money to compensate her for the loss of the right. Sometimes she will turn to other authorities such as federal and state administrative agencies (see below for definition) or a labor arbitrator.

The problem with the enforcement process is that it will often be lengthy, time-consuming, expensive, frustrating, and will arouse hostility in others—in short, it may not be worth the effort. On the other hand, in some cases you may not need to go to an enforcement authority in order to implement your right. The concerned persons or officials may not realize that you have a particular right and may voluntarily change their actions once you explain your rights. Then, too, they may not want to go through the legal process either—it may be as expensive and frustrating for them as it is for you.

If you understand what your rights are, you will be equipped to convince others to recognize them. Should your explanation and effort at persuasion fail to achieve the desired result, knowledge of your rights and their significance will enable you to decide whether to go forward with enforcement. The time and expense may be justified in terms of your own self-dignity or the importance of the right to other women.

What is a moral right?

This question emphasizes the point that although the formal legal system does not always give you important rights, you may still be entitled to them in the sense of a larger justice. Arguably, it may still be legal for a university to admit undergraduate students in the ratio of four men to every one woman. But in a larger, moral sense, we can believe that a woman has a right to an equal chance for admission, and that such a university has acted arbitrarily and unjustly in its preference for men and its maintenance of a restrictive quota for women. The conviction that the woman has a moral right to fair treatment should then lead us to fight for new laws that will secure for her the legal right as well.

An underlying philosophy of this book is that women do have the moral right to equal treatment with men in every facet of life. The preceding chapters have both identified existing legal rights and explored those areas in which women have moral rights with uncertain, if any, legal support—areas in which they should press for corrective legislation.

Where are legal rights defined?

There are several sources. Rights are defined in the statutes or laws passed by the U.S. Congress and by state and city legislatures. They are also set forth in the written decisions of judges—both federal and state. Congress and state and local legislatures have also created institutions called administrative agencies to enforce certain laws, and these agencies interpret the laws in written decisions and rules that further define people's rights.

Are rights always clearly defined and evenly applied to all people?

Not at all, although this is one of the great myths about law. Because so many different sources define people's rights, and because persons of diverse backgrounds and beliefs implement and enforce the law, there is virtually no way to assure uniformity. Nor do statutes that set forth rights always do so with clarity or in great detail. It remains for judges or personnel in administrative agencies to provide interpretation and to flesh out the details; and in the process of doing so, many of the interpreters reach different solutions. For example, the Equal Protection Clause of the 14th Amendment affirms that all citizens are entitled to equal treatment from the state, but it fails to define equal treatment. At different times, two groups of women seeking to be admitted to all-male schools sued state officials on the grounds that they were not getting equal treatment. The first suit witnessed the first time in its then 90-year-old history that women had ever used the 14th Amendment to attack sex-segregated public universities. The judge—a state judge—who interpreted the Equal Protection Clause in this first situation found that the equal treatment requirement did not extend to exclusion of women from a public university; the prospective students lost their lawsuit.[1] Ten years later, a second court—a federal court in a different part of the country—read the same 14th Amendment, decided it does include sex discrimination, and declared that school officials were required to admit women.[2] So do women have an equal right to go to public universities? The answer, based on these two decisions, is sometimes yes, sometimes no.

The situation is not always this ambiguous. The more times a particular issue is decided, the more guidance you have in predicting what other judges or administrative personnel will decide. Similarly, the importance of the court or agency deciding a case or the persuasiveness of its reasoning will help determine the effect of its decisions on other authorities. A decision of the Supreme Court will affect other judges' interpretation of the law much more than a decision of a state court; someone who articulates thoughtful reasons for a decision will have more influence than one who offers no reasons. There are degrees of predictability to rights; some that have been presented in this book will be more certain of attainment than others, but in all cases there will be some solid ground for an effort directed toward recognition of the right in question. But even though one can predict, one can never *know* in advance what the final result of a lawsuit will be—a very important point to keep in mind in reading this book and contemplating legal action.

Law then is not a preordained set of doctrines, applied rigidly and unswervingly in every situation. Rather, law is molded from the arguments and decisions of thousands of persons. It is very much a human process, a game of trying to convince others—a judge, a jury, an administrator, the lawyer for the other side—that your view of what the law requires is correct. The game of convincing others is carried out in a clearly defined forum with clearly defined ground rules, but otherwise it is not really that different from trying to convince people in general that your position is correct and that they ought to act accordingly. Once women understand that law is a process of convincing others, rather than formalized rules dropped from on high, they will be able to use law as an instrument to create change.

What is a decision or case?

Lawyers often use these words interchangeably, although technically they do not mean the same thing. A case means the lawsuit started by one person against another, and it can refer to that lawsuit at any time from the moment it is started until the final result is reached. A decision means the written memorandum in which the judge declares who wins the lawsuit and why.

What is meant by precedent?

Precedent means past decisions. Lawyers use precedent to influence the decision a judge reaches today. If the facts involved in the prior decision are close to the facts in the present case, the judge will be strongly tempted to follow the former decision. He is not, however, bound to do so and, if persuasive reasons are presented to show that the prior decision was wrong or ill-suited to changed conditions in society, he may not follow precedent.

What is the relationship between decisions and statutes?

In our legal system, most legal concepts originally were defined in the decisions of judges. In deciding what legal doctrine to apply to any case, each judge kept building on what other judges had done before him. The body of legal doctrines created in this way is called the common law.

The common law still applies in many situations, but increasingly state legislatures and the Congress pass laws, or statutes, to define the legal concepts that judges or agencies should use in deciding cases. The written decisions of individual judges are still very important even where there is a statute because the statute is generally not specific enough to cover every set of facts. The judges have to interpret the meaning of the statute, apply it to the facts at hand, and write a decision; that decision will then be considered by other judges when they deal with the same statute in another case. Thus it is generally not enough to know what a relevant statute defines as illegal; you also have to know how the judges have interpreted that statute in specific fact situations. For instance, the Civil Rights Act of 1964 says it is illegal to discriminate on the basis of sex in employment. If an employer pays women lower pension benefits than men with the same work history because women as a class live longer than men, has he violated this law? You can't tell just by reading the words of the statute, which do not mention pension benefits explicitly. Instead, you must read the guidelines and decisions of administrators and judges interpreting the statute in that fact situation or in a closely related situation. (So far, the agency and the courts have said the policy is illegal).

What different kinds of courts are there?

The United States is unique for its variety of courts. Broadly speaking, there are two distinct court systems: federal and state. Both are located throughout the country, but each is limited to certain kinds of cases, with substantial areas of overlap. Most crimes are prosecuted in state courts, for instance, although there are a number of federal crimes prosecuted in federal court. People must always use state courts to get a divorce, but they must sue in federal courts to establish their rights under certain federal laws, such as the 1964 Civil Rights Act.

A distinction present in both federal and state court systems is that between trial and appellate courts. In either system, one starts out at the trial court level, where the facts are "tried." This means that a judge or jury listens and watches as the lawyers for each side present evidence of the facts that each side seeks to prove. Evidence can take many forms: written documents, the testimony of a witness on the stand, photographs, charts. Once the judge or jury has listened to or observed all the evidence presented by each side, it will choose the version of the facts it believes, apply the applicable legal doctrine to these facts, and decide which side has won. If either side is unhappy with the results, that side may be able to take the case to the next, higher-level court and argue that the judge or the jury applied the wrong legal concept to the facts, or that no reasonable jury or judge could have found the facts as they were found in the trial court, and that the result was therefore wrong. The process of contesting your initial loss is called an appeal because you are "appealing" to a higher authority to tell the lower court that it was wrong. All courts above the trial court are called appellate courts. Although there is generally only one level of court that conducts a trial, hearing evidence and deciding the facts, there may be two or more tiers of appellate courts.

In the federal system, the trial courts are called district courts. The first tier of federal appellate courts is the court of appeals; above that is the U.S. Supreme Court. Geographically the country is broken into ten circuits, with one court of appeals in each numbered circuit. The court of appeals is generally referred to by the number of the circuit—e.g., the Second Circuit (abbreviated as 2d Cir.). Each circuit is in turn divided into several districts, and the court of appeals for the circuit hears the appeals from all the district courts within its boundaries. The district courts are given geographic names, e.g., the Southern District of New York (abbreviated S.D.N.Y.), the Northern District of California (N.D. Cal.).

In the state system, each state sets up its own series of trial and appellate courts. The number and the names of these courts differ in each state. For example, New York State has a trial court called the Supreme Court (notice that the lowest court here has the same name as the highest federal court), followed by the Appellate Division of the Supreme Court as the first appellate level court. The Court of Appeals is the highest appellate level in New York. Litigants can sometimes appeal a decision of the highest state appellate court to the U.S. Supreme Court.

In addition to these general courts, there are special courts that handle exclusively cases involving a particular subject matter, such as tax. An example is the U.S. Court of Claims, which only handles lawsuits in which people assert a claim against the government.

In general, the higher the court in either the federal or the state system, the more influential the decisions of its judges will be within that system. Thus, a U.S. Supreme Court decision will have enormous impact on both state and federal judges, who will feel bound to try to follow it; the highest state appellate court will have a similar impact on lower-court decisions within that state. High state and federal court decisions may be influential in other states and circuits or in the other system, but in most cases courts of another system will not feel bound in the same way as they do by decisions of a court in a direct line of authority over them. Finally, certain judges acquire a reputation for being better than others and, consequently, their decisions have a greater influence on other courts.

Weighing all these factors can help women interpret the effect of any given decision. By knowing how high a court voiced a decision, how respected a judge issued it, and whether most cases involving the issue will be brought in that system, you can decide whether the results are likely to affect the rights of many women or of just a few. A U.S. Supreme Court decision will always affect the rights of many; a first-level state appellate court decision written by an obscure judge and dealing with an issue normally decided in the federal court system will affect the rights of very few women. You should be aware of these distinctions when trying to convince others of your rights, and you should probe for these factors in evaluating what others tell you about your rights.

What are plaintiffs and defendants?

The plaintiff is the person who sues—that is, who com-*plains* that someone has wronged her and asks the court to remedy this situation. The defendant is the person sued—or the one who *defends* herself against the charges of the plaintiff. The legal writing in which the plaintiff articulates her basic grievance is the com*plaint*, and a lawsuit is generally commenced by filing this document with the clerk at the courthouse. The defendant then responds to these charges in a document appropriately named an *answer*.

One refers to a particular lawsuit by giving the names of the plaintiff and defendant. If Mary Jones sues Smith Corporation for refusing to hire her because she is a woman, her case will be called *Jones v. Smith Corporation* (v. stands for versus, or against).

What is an administrative agency?

Agencies are institutions established by either state or federal legislatures to administer or enforce a particular law or series of laws and are distinct from both courts and legislatures. They often regulate a particular industry. For example, the Federal Communications Commission regulates the broadcasting industry (radio and television stations and networks) and the telephone and telegraph industry, in accordance with the legal standards set forth in the Federal Communications Act; while the Interstate Commerce Commission regulates the ground transportation industry.

The personnel in these agencies establish broad legal principles, referred to as rules, regulations, or guidelines. Rules are interpretations of a statute and are designed to function in the same way as a statute does—to define people's rights and obligations on a general scale, although in somewhat more detailed fashion than the statute itself. Agencies also issue specific decisions in particular cases, applying, as does a judge, a broad law or rule to a factual dispute between particular parties.

In essence, an administrative agency is an institution that works parallel to, and sometimes subordinate to, the courts. People must often take their dispute to an agency first in order to establish some right, but may then appeal the agency's decision to a court. In that instance, the agency functions as an informal trial court.

Women should learn about agencies—they have figured prominently in this book, particularly in the chapters on employment rights and on the mass media—because these institutions administer laws that give women important rights.

How does one find and read court decisions, statutes, and agency rules and decisions?

All these materials are published and can be found in law libraries. In order to find the item desired, one should understand the system lawyers use for referring to, or citing, these materials. Some examples will help clarify the system. A case might be cited as *Watson v. Limbach Company,* 333 F.Supp. 754 (S.D. Ohio 1971); a law, as 42 U.S.C. §1983; a regulation, as 29 C.F.R. §1604.10(b). The unifying factor in all three citations is that the first number denotes the particular volume in a series of books with the same title; the words or letters that follow represent the name of the book; and the second number represents either the page or the section in the identified volume. In the examples above, the case is found in the 333rd volume of the series of books called *Federal Supplement* at page 754; the statute is found in Volume 42 of the series called *United States Code* at Section 1983; the regulation is in Volume 29 of the *Code of Federal Regulations* at Section 1604.10(b). Once you understand the system, all you need do is find out from the librarian where any particular series of books is kept, then look up the proper volume and page or section. It is also important to look for the same page or section in the paper insert at the back of the book, since many legal materials are periodically updated by this insert. The librarian will tell you what any abbreviations stand for if you are unfamiliar with that series.

The other information given in the citation to a decision

includes the last names of the parties to the lawsuit, the name of the court, and the year the decision was written. In the example, Mr. Watson sued the Limbach Company; the court that reached this decision was the U.S. District Court for the Southern District of Ohio, and the year was 1971.

Series of legal volumes are often organized to reflect the institution responsible for the laws or legal doctrines found in those books. The decisions of district court judges are found in the *Federal Supplement* (F.Supp.) series; all laws passed by the U.S. Congress are found in the *United States Code* (U.S.C.); and all regulations issued by federal agencies are found in the *Code of Federal Regulations* (C.F.R.). Another way that legal books are organized is by subject matter. One publisher issues a series of books called *Fair Employment Practice Cases*. These books cover all cases in which discrimination in employment is involved—no matter what kind of court or agency issued the decision.

Given this basic information, anyone can locate and read important cases, statutes, and regulations. Throughout the book, such materials have been cited when deemed particularly important, and women are urged to read them. Although lawyers often use overly technical language, the references cited in this book can be comprehended without serious difficulty, and reading the original legal materials will give women greater self-confidence and a deeper understanding of their rights. Paralegal groups who want to help other women learn and assert their rights would be particularly advised to read these materials in order to get a more fundamental grasp of the law.

Where can one find a law library?

The biggest and best ones will be found at law schools. Another source would be the libraries of bar associations, although access to these by laypersons may be restricted. Ask a lawyer for suggestions if all else fails.

What is the role of the lawyer in the legal system?

A lawyer understands the intricacies and technicalities of the legal system, can maneuver within it efficiently, and helps other people by doing so. Thus, the lawyer knows where to find out about the leading legal doctrines in any given area and how to predict the outcome of your case, based on a knowledge of those doctrines. A lawyer can advise you what to do: forget about the case; take it to an administrative agency; sue in court; make a will; and so on. The lawyer then helps you take the legal actions that you determine are necessary.

For an in-depth exploration of a lawyer's roles, readers might like to consult Johnstone and Hopson, *Lawyers and Their Work* (Bobbs-Merrill, 1967).

How are legal costs determined and how do they affect people's rights?

The cost of using the legal system is predominantly the cost of paying the lawyer for her or his time. Since the cost has become prohibitive for even middle-class individuals, many people are not able to assert their rights, even though they might ultimately win if they had the money to pay a lawyer for doing the job.

This poses a severe problem for women, many of whom have little or no money of their own. One of the aims of this book has been to present ideas for areas where paralegal women's groups can help other women to assert their legal rights on their own. However, there is a fine line between actually acting as another woman's lawyer—which may be illegal—and lending a supporting hand to help other women assert their rights by themselves. One way to draw that line is to question whether the activity of a paralegal group takes money away from a lawyer. If so, some lawyers might consider the activity to be unauthorized, and this could get the group into trouble. Participation of or cooperation with a lawyer sympathetic to the aims of the group can help to avoid problems of this nature.

Is legal action the only way to win one's legal rights?

By no means. Negotiation, education, consciousness raising, publicity, demonstrations, organization, and lobbying are all ways to achieve rights, often more effectively than through the standard but costly and time-consuming resort to the courts. In all these areas, though, it helps to have secure knowledge of the legal underpinning of your rights. One has a great deal more authority if one is protesting illegal action. The refrain "That's illegal" may move some people in and of itself; or it may convince those with whom you are dealing that you're serious enough to do something about the situation—by starting a lawsuit, for instance.

This book, of course, does focus on rights and how to assert them through legal action. This is not because law is the only way, or even the best way, to change women's status; however, it is *one* way to achieve change, and a way women could utilize more than they have in the past. Women have often not acted forcefully enough because of a lack of knowledge. This book has been designed to fill that knowledge gap and, also, to inspire women to assert their legal rights. For if women actually try to enforce the rights now on the books, they could achieve enormous change in our society. It only requires the will to do so.

NOTES

1. *Allred v. Heaton*, 336 S.W.2d 251, *cert. denied*, 364 U.S. 517 (1960).
2. *Kirstein v. Rectors and Visitors of University of Virginia*, 309 F.Supp. 184 (E.D. Va. 1970).

APPENDIX

Chart A:
State Laws Forbidding Employment Discrimination*

Explanation of chart. Most states have passed a wide variety of laws forbidding employment discrimination. This chart is provided as a supplement to Chapter II in order to enable women to apply the maximum amount of pressure by using all remedies available to them at the state as well as the federal level. The end of Chapter II outlined reasons why it is important to know how many different laws there are and what the differences are among them. Although much of that discussion relates to federal laws, the same themes can be applied to the differences among state laws.

For each state, in turn, five columns in the chart list five kinds of laws and information about each: (1) fair employment practice laws, which are generally modeled on Title VII and offer the same kind of broad coverage; (2) equal pay laws, modeled on the Equal Pay Act; (3) state contracts laws, which are modeled on Executive Order 11246, as amended by E.O. 11375, and which generally protect the employees of companies that hold contracts with the state government; (4) state employees laws, which are sometimes modeled on Executive Order 11478 and prohibit the state government from discriminating against its own employees; and (5) age discrimination laws, which are sometimes modeled on the Federal Age Discrimination Act or which may be included within other state anti-discrimination laws.

For each state there are five rows of boxes. Reading down-

---

*The research for this chart, as well as for the charts that follow, may be incomplete. Readers—and especially paralegal groups—are cautioned to do follow-up research on their own state's laws.

ward, the first row of boxes lists citations for the five kinds of laws.

The second row of boxes tells whether the state law prohibits sex discrimination and, in the case of age discrimination laws, what age groups are protected. Women should lobby to have sex added to the coverage of laws that do not already reach sex discrimination. They should also check periodically for changes because states frequently pass new laws or amend existing laws in this field. The Equal Employment Opportunity Commission will help accelerate this trend because it is pressuring states to add sex discrimination provisions to existing laws. In fact, the Commission no longer defers to states that do not prohibit sex discrimination. (For an explanation of deferral, see Chapter II.) This may force a lot of states to change their laws.

The third row of boxes gives the agency (along with its address and telephone number) that enforces each kind of law, if that information was readily available to researchers. The FEP agency is always listed. If other agencies are not listed, women should try contacting the state FEP agency to help in locating them. Although the state contracts and state employees laws often do not indicate the agency that enforces the law the appropriate agency will usually be the one holding the contract with the offending company (referred to as the Contracting Agency, where the law expressly indicates it) or the agency that employs the woman who is charging discrimination (referred to as the State Agency, where the law expressly indicates it). Since the governor often issues both of these laws, his office would be another source of information on how to assert one's rights under these laws.

The fourth row of boxes states the time limit within which employees must assert their rights. Generally this applies to the time they have to file a complaint with the agency. For example, Alaska's FEP law says 90 days; an employee there must file a complaint of discrimination with the State Commission for Human Rights within 90 days after the discrimination occurs. Time limits are extremely important because they can be used to prevent women from asserting their rights. Sometimes the time limit applies to the time women have to file a lawsuit; again, failure to comply can cause loss of the lawsuit. This column also tells the number of employees an employer must have in order to be covered by the law. If a time limit or a number of employees is not listed, the applicable law does not give them. However, there may be a general state law that establishes time limits for bringing lawsuits, so it is important to complain about discrimination as soon as possible in all states.

The fifth row of boxes gives a code for the kind of enforcement process that applicable state law establishes. This information will help women know the steps they need to take to enforce their rights and the options they have among the different processes.

1. This numeral stands for a cease-and-desist enforcement process, under which the agency generally investigates the complaint, holds a hearing, and can order the company or union to cease discriminating and to pay back wages. The orders of the agency may be reviewed by the courts, but a new trial will not be held in court. If the agency enforces the law vigorously, this is one of the best options for women since it requires the least time, effort, and money.

2. This numeral stands for the right of an aggrieved individual to bring a lawsuit against the company or union; the court generally can order cessation of discrimination, and back wages. This option requires more from women complainants, but it can be a better choice in a state where the state agency is pro-business or fails to enforce the law effectively. At the federal level, both Title VII and the Equal Pay Act are enforced in this way.

3. This numeral stands for an agency lawsuit, which means that the agency goes into court on behalf of women complainants. Again, both Title VII and the Equal Pay Act can be enforced in this way. This process is also good for women with scant resources, but it depends on effective action by state agency personnel—which is not always forthcoming.

4. This numeral stands for criminal enforcement, with fines in the range of $500 and jail sentences of up to one year. This method depends on local officials prosecuting offending companies and unions, which they hardly ever do, so as a practical matter the method is virtually useless, even though it sounds more severe than the others.

5. This numeral stands for laws that do not expressly set forth any obvious enforcement scheme, or that are limited to encouraging or recommending compliance, or under which the state agency is supposed to discipline itself or cut off state

contracts. State laws in this category are also virtually useless. In theory, state agency personnel might discipline themselves or cut off contracts of state contractors who discriminate against women employees, but in practice they rarely do.

Summary of enforcement process code

1. The state agency has the power to issue cease-and-desist orders, subject to judicial review.
2. Women have the right to file lawsuits in court against discriminators.
3. The state agency has the power to file lawsuits in court on behalf of complainants.
4. The discriminating company or union may be punished by criminal sanctions—either by fine or imprisonment.
5. There is no enforcement scheme, or the "enforcement" is limited to voluntary compliance, or a state is supposed to monitor its own employment practices or those of its contractors (and enforce the law by cutting off contracts.)

Women can use the information in this last row of boxes by lobbying for more effective enforcement where necessary. It is important to look at more than the paper enforcement scheme, though, since even the best plan can be sabotaged by a lack of state funding, an orientation of agency heads toward business interests, or a lack of education among agency personnel about the full scope and meaning of discrimination. Women's groups should explore all these questions and begin pressuring state agencies to become more effective. Such action will become increasingly important, for the EEOC is likely to leave more and more of the individual discrimination complaints for state agencies to resolve while reserving class-wide complaints dealing with the rights of many employees for itself, as a way of maximizing the commission's slender resources.

A few general caveats about Chart A should be added. First, it is always better to read the laws themselves. The chart gives women the starting point for doing so. Second, the research for the chart was done in the spring of 1980; as the field is rapidly changing, women's groups should check for new laws or amendments to existing laws. Third, some of the legal citations are to little-used sources, particularly for state contracts and state employees laws. If you cannot find a law in the official reporter system for that state's laws, try either the *Fair Employment Practice Manual* (Bureau of National Affairs), or 2 *Employment Practices Guide* (Commerce Clearing House). Both reproduce each state's employment discrimination laws, except that BNA does not include equal pay laws. Fourth, there has been no attempt to list city or local anti-discrimination agencies, even though there are many of these, some of which are more effective than the state agency. For a list of such agencies, write for the *Directory of State and Local Anti-Discrimination Agencies*, published by EEOC and updated on January 1 and July 1 of each year. It is available from Office of State and Community Affairs, EEOC, 1800 G St., N.W., Washington, D.C. 20506. Fifth, the kinds of employees who are protected vary widely from statute to statute. Depending on the law, one or more of the following categories of employees may be excluded: employees of a relative; domestic employees; employees of religious associations; employees of social, fraternal, and other non-profit organizations; and employees of educational institutions. State employees are sometimes protected by the FEP, equal pay, or age discrimination laws, and sometimes not. The protection for employees of state contractors may be narrowed by limiting the kinds of contracts covered or by requiring that the contract reach a certain dollar level for coverage. Obviously, all these exclusions and limitations can dramatically affect the number of people protected by the laws, and lobbying should be undertaken to eliminate such gaps.

Finally, many state laws allow specific discriminatory practices that federal courts have found to violate Title VII. Business interests have often lobbied for the inclusion of provisions such as those permitting different retirement ages for men and women. Women's groups should study state laws and lobby for amendments to eliminate those blatantly pro-business exceptions.

	FEP	Equal Pay	State Contracts	State Employees	Age Discrimination
1. Alaska	Alas. Stat. §§18.80.010 to 18.80.300, 22.10.020, 23.10.192	§§23.10.155 to 23.10.185	Gov. Code of Fair Prac., Art. II, 8/11/67	Gov. Code of Fair Prac., Art. I, 8/11/67	Included in FEP, State Contracts, and State Employees laws
Sex; Age Limits	Yes	Yes	Yes	Yes	
Agency	State Comm'n for Human Rights 520 MacKay Bldg. 338 Denali St. Anchorage 99501 (907) 272-9504	Dept. of Labor E.S.D. Bldg. Box 1149 Juneau 99801	Contracting Agency	State Agency	
Time Limit; Number of Employees	90 days; 1 employee				
Process	1,2,4	2 or 3, 4	5	5	

	FEP	Equal Pay	State Contracts	State Employees	Age Discrimination
2. Arizona	Ariz. Rev. Stat. Ann. §§41-1401 to 41-1403, 41-1461 to 41-1466, 41-1481 to 41-1485	§§23-340, 23-341, 23-311	E.O. 75-5	None	None
Sex; Age Limits	Yes	Yes	No		
Agency	Ariz. Civil Rts. Comm'n 1502 W. Jefferson St. Phoenix 85007 (602) 271-5266	Industrial Comm'n. of Ariz. 2933 N. Central Ave. Phoenix	Office of Affirmative Action (602) 255-3711		
Time Limit; Number of Employees	180 days; 15 employees	6 months; 1 employee			
Process	1, 2, 3, 4	1, 2, 3, 4	1 (by Civil Rights Commission)		

	FEP	Equal Pay	State Contracts	State Employees	Age Discrimination
3. Arkansas	None	Ark. Stat. §§81-623 to 81-629	None	None	None
Sex; Age Limits		Yes			
Agency		Comm'n of Labor Dept. of Labor Little Rock			
Time Limit; Number of Employees		2 years			
Process		2 or 3, 4			

	FEP	Equal Pay	State Contracts		State Employees	Age Discrimination
4. California	Cal. Labor Code §§1410 to 1433	Cal. Labor Code §1197.5	Cal. Labor Code, §1431, §1735	Gov. Code of Fair Prac., 7/24/63	Gov. Code of Fair Prac., 7/24/63	Cal. Labor Code §1420.1 and §1411-1419
Sex, Age Limits	Yes	Yes	Yes	No	No	65
Agency	FEP Comm'n 455 Golden Gate Ave. P.O. Box 603 San Francisco 94101 (415) 557-2000	Dept. of Industrial Relations Div. of Industrial Welfare 455 Golden Gate Ave. San Francisco 94101	Dept. of Industrial Relations Div. of Labor Law Enforcement 455 Golden Gate Ave. San Francisco 94101 and Contracting Agency	Contracting Agency	State Agency	Dept. of Human Resources Development (961) 445-8822
Time Limit; Number of Employees	1 year (plus 90 days extension in some circumstances); 5 employees	2 years				1 year (plus 90-day extension in some circumstances); 5 employees
Process	1, 2, or 3, 4	1, 2, or 3, 4	5	5	5	1, 2, or 3, 4

311

	FEP	Equal Pay	State Contracts	State Employees	Age Discrimination
5. Colorado	Colo. Rev. Stat. §§24-34-301 to 308; Art. II, §29, Colo. Constitution prohibits discrimination on basis of sex	§§8-5-101 8-5-105	§8-16-101	None	§§8-2-116
Sex; Age Limits	Yes	Yes	No		18-60
Agency	Colo. Civ. Rts. Comm'n 312 State Serv. Bldg. 1525 Sherman St. Denver 80203 (303) 892-2621	Industrial Comm'n of Colorado 200 E. 9th Ave. Denver	Industrial Comm'n of Colorado		
Time Limit; Number of Employees	6 months; 1 employee	1 year			
Process	1, 2, 3	1, 2, 3	5		4

	FEP	Equal Pay	State Contracts	State Employees	Age Discrimination
6. Connecticut	Conn. Gen. Stat. Ann. §§31-122 to 31-128	§§31-75 to 31-76	§4-114a	§4-61c Gov. Code of Fair Prac., 2/28/67	included in FEP, State Contracts, and State Employees laws
Sex; Age Limits	Yes	Yes	Yes	No	40-65
Agency	Comm'n on Human Rts. & Opportunities 90 Washington St. Hartford 06115 (203) 566-4895	Labor Comm'r Labor Dept. 200 Folly Brook Blvd. Hartford	Contracting Agency and Comm'n on Human Rts. & Opportunities	Court of Common Pleas	State Agency
Time Limit; Number of Employees	180 days; 3 employees	1 year			
Process	1, 2 ,3	2, or 3, 4	5	2	5

	FEP	Equal Pay	State Contracts	State Employees	Age Discrimination
7. Delaware	Del. Code 19§§710 to 718	None	S.B.266, L. 1972	E.O. 9, 7/15/69	Included in State Employees laws
Sex; Age Limits	Yes		Yes	Yes	40-65
Agency	Div. of Industrial Affairs Dept. of Labor 618 North Union St. Wilmington 19805 (302) 658-9251		Secretary Dept. of Labor	State Human Relations Comm'n Old State House Annex Dover 19901 (302) 658-5738	
Time Limit; Number of Employees	90 days, or 120 days after discovery; 4 employees				
Process	1, 3, 4		5	5	

	FEP	Equal Pay	State Contracts	State Employees	Age Discrimination
8. District of Columbia	D.C. Code Ann. §6-2201 to 2297	D.C. Code Ann. §6-2221	Bd. of Commissioners Order #62-713 (D.C. Regs. §§21-701 to 21-839)	D.C. Code Ann. §1-320(a) (h)	Included in FEP
Sex; Age Limits	Yes	Yes	Yes	Yes	18-65
Agency	D.C. Comm'n on Human Rights 1329 E. St., N.W. Washington, D.C. 20004 (202) 727-3100		Contracting Agency	Individual Agency	
Time Limit; Number of Employees	1 year; 1 employee	1 year; 1 employee	90 days		
Process	1, 2, or 3, 4		1		

	FEP	Equal Pay	State Contracts	State Employees	Age Discrimination
9. Florida	None	Fla. Stat. Ann. §448.07	None	§§112.041, 112.042	§112.043
Sex; Age Limits		Yes		Yes	
Agency				State Agency	
Time Limit; Number of Employees		6 months after termination of employment; 2 employees			
Process		2		1, 2	5

	FEP	Equal Pay	State Contracts	State Employees	Age Discrimination
10. Georgia*	Ga. Code Ann. §§89-1701-1725	Ga. Code Ann. §§54-1001 to 54-1007	FEP and §1722	FEP	Included in FEP and §89-1703 and §54-1102
Sex; Age Limits		Yes			40-65
Agency	Office of Fair Employment Practices Office of the Governor Atlanta	Comm'r of Labor Dept. of Labor State Labor Bldg. 254 Wash. St. Atlanta 30334			
Time Limit; Number of Employees	180 days; 15 employees	1 year; 10 employees			
Process	1, 2, 3, 4 (conspiracy)	2			4

*Act 581 §§1-9 (3/18/66) prohibits discrimination against the wives of servicemen.

	FEP	Equal Pay	State Contracts	State Employees	Age Discrimination
11. Hawaii	Hawaii Rev. Stat. §§378-1 to 378-10	§§387-4, 12	None	§§76-1, 7, 44	Included in FEP law
Sex; Age Limits	Yes	Yes		Yes	
Agency	Dept. of Labor & Industrial Relations 825 Mililani St. Honolulu 96813 (808) 548-3150	Dept. of Labor & Industrial Relations			
Time Limit; Number of Employees	90 days; 1 employee				
Process	1, 3, 4	2 or 3, 4			

318

	FEP		Equal Pay	State Contracts	State Employees	Age Discrimination
12. Idaho	Idaho Code §§18-7301 to 18-7303 §§67-5901 to 67-5912		§§44-1701 to 44-1704	Included in FEP law	Included in FEP law	§§44-1601 to 44-1606
Sex; Age Limits	Yes	Yes	Yes			Under 60
Agency	Comm'n on Human Rts.,* Dept. of Social Services Statehouse Boise 83702 (208) 384-3550		Comm'r of Labor Dept. of Labor Indust. Adm. Bldg. 317 Main St. Boise 83702			Comm'r of Labor
Time Limit; Number of Employees	6 months; 10 employees					
Process	2, 3	4	2 or 3			1, 2 or 3

*The person must first file a complaint with the Board of County Commissioners where either she or the employer resides; if it appears that an "injunction could be entered," she then goes to the Commission on Human Rights.

	FEP	Equal Pay	State Contracts	State Employees	Age Discrimination
13. Illinois	Ill. Stat. Ann. 48 §§851 to 860	48§§4a, 4b	48§§ 1003–4, 1011-12	Included in FEP law	Included in FEP law	48§§881 to 887
Sex; Age Limits	Yes	Yes		No	
Agency	FEP Comm'n 160 N. LaSalle St. Chicago 60601 (312) 793-2240		Director Dept. of Labor Springfield		
Time Limit; Number of Employees	120 days; 25 employees	6 mos.; 6 employees	5 employees		1 employee
Process		2, 4	2, 3, 4	5	4

320

	FEP	Equal Pay	State Contracts	State Employees	Age Discrimination
14. Indiana	Ind. Stat. Ann. §§22-9-1-1 to 22-9-1-6	§§22-2-2-4, 22-2-2-9	§§22-9-1-10; 5-16-6-1	Included in FEP law	§§22-9-2-1 to 22-92-2-11
Sex; Age Limits	Yes	Yes	Yes		40-65
Agency	Ind. Civil Rts. Comm'n 319 State Office Bldg. Indianapolis, 46204 (317) 663-4855	Wage Adjustment Board (317) 633-4473	Contracting Agency		Comm'r Div. of Labor 1013 State Office Bldg. 101 N. Senate Ave. Indianapolis
Time Limit; Number of Employees	90 days; 6 employees	3 years, 4 employees			4 months; 1 employee
Process	1	2	5		

	FEP	Equal Pay	State Contracts	State Employees	Age Discrimination
15. Iowa	Iowa Code Ann. §§601A.1-601 A.15	§§601.4(1),(2), and (5)	§601A.4(3)	§601A.4(1)	§425.36
Sex; Age Limits	Yes				
Agency	Iowa Civil Rts. Comm'n State Capitol Bldg. Des Moines 50319 (515) 281-5129				
Time Limit; Number of Employees	180 days; 4 employees				
Process	1				

	FEP	Equal Pay	State Contracts	State Employees	Age Discrimination
16. Kansas	Kans. Stat. Ann. §§44-1001 to 44-1013	Included in FEP law	§§44-1030-1032	Included in FEP law	None
Sex; Age Limits	Yes		Yes		
Agency	Kans. Comm'n on Civil Rts. Room 1155 W State Office Bldg. Topeka 66612 (913) 296-3206		Contracting Agency		
Time Limit; Number of Employees	6 months; 4 employees				
Process	1, 4		5		

	FEP	Equal Pay	State Contracts	State Employees	Age Discrimination
17. Kentucky	Ky. Rev. Stat. §§344.010 et. seq.	§§337.420 et. seq.	None	Included in FEP law	Included in FEP law
Sex; Age Limits	Yes	Yes			40-65
Agency	Ky. Comm'n on Human Rts. 600 W. Walnut St. Louisville 40203 (502) 583-2775	Comm'r Dept. of Labor State Office Bldg. Annex Frankfort			
Time Limit; Number of Employees	150 days; 8 employees	6 months; 8 employees			
Process	1	2 or 3			

	FEP	Equal Pay	State Contracts	State Employees	Age Discrimination
18. Louisiana	None	None	La. Stat. Ann §38.315 (professional only)	None	La. Stat. Ann. §§23:892 to 23:893
Sex; Age Limits			Yes		Under 50
Agency			Contracting Agency		
Time Limit; Number of Employees					25 employees
Process			5		4

	FEP	Equal Pay	State Contracts	State Employees	Age Discrimination
19. Maine	Maine Rev. Stat. Ann. 5§§4551 to 4573,4611	26§628	5§§784, 789	Included in FEP law; 5§§784(1) and 789	Included in FEP
Sex; Age Limits	Yes	Yes	Yes		
Agency	Maine Human Rts. Comm'n Statehouse, Rm. 120 Augusta 04330 (207) 289-2326		Maine Human Rts. Comm'n		
Time Limit; Number of Employees	1 year				
Process	2 or 3	4	3		

	FEP	Equal Pay	State Contracts	State Employees	Age Discrimination
20. Maryland	Md. Code Ann. 49B§§9-18	100§§55A to 55H	78A§7A	Included in FEP law	Included in FEP law
Sex; Age Limits	Yes	Yes	Yes		
Agency	Comm'n on Human Relations Mt. Vernon Bldg. 701 St. Paul St. Baltimore 21202 (301) 383-3689	Comm'r Div. of Labor & Industry State Office Bldg. 301 W. Preston St. Baltimore 21201	Bd. of Public Works State Office Bldg. Room 101 Annapolis 21404		
Time Limit; Number of Employees	25 employees	1 year			
Process	1	2 or 3	5		

	FEP	Equal Pay	State Contracts	State Employees	Age Discrimination
21. Massachusetts	Mass. Gen. Laws Ann. 151B§§1-10	149§1, 105A-105C	272§98B* and E.O. 74, Art. IV; also included in FEP law	E.O. 74 as amended by E.O. 116, Art. II; also included in FEP law	144§§24A-24J also included in FEP law
Sex; Age Limits	Yes	Yes	Yes	Yes	45-65 (but FEP limits are 40-65)
Agency	Mass. Comm'n Against Discrimination 120 Tremont Ave. Boston 02108 (617) 727-3990	Comm'r Dept. of Labor & Industries 100 Cambridge St. Boston 02202	Mass. Comm'n Against Discrimination	Mass. Comm'n Against Discrimination	Comm'r Dept. of Labor & Industries.
Time Limit; Number of Employees	6 months; 6 employees	1 year			
Process	1,4	2, 3	1, 4	1, 4	4

*Sex is not included in this statute.

328

	FEP	Equal Pay	State Contracts	State Employees	Age Discrimination
22. Michigan	Mich. Comp. Laws Ann. 37.2202§202	M.C.L.A. 37.2202§ 202(1)(2), 408.397§17, 750.556§556	M.C.L.A. 37.2209§209 also included in FEP law	Included in FEP law	Included in FEP law
Sex; Age Limits	Yes	Yes	Yes	Yes	
Agency	Mich. Civil Rts. Comm'n 1000 Cadillac Sq. Bldg. Detroit 48226 (313) 222-1810	Mich. Dept. of Labor Dept. of Labor Bldg. 300 E. Mich. Ave. Lansing 48933			
Time Limit; Number of Employees	90-180 days; 8 employees	3 years; 4 employees			
Process	1, 2 ,3	2, 3 ,4	5	5	

	FEP	Equal Pay	State Contracts	State Employees	Age Discrimination
23. Minnesota	Minn. Stat. Ann. §§363.03	§181.66-§181.67	§181.59	None	M.S.A. §363.03(1)
Sex; Age Limits	Yes	Yes	No		
Agency	Dept. of Human Rts. 60 State Office Bldg. St. Paul 55155				
Time Limit; Number of Employees	6 months; 1 employee	1 employee			
Process	1, 3	2, 4	4, 5		

	FEP	Equal Pay	State Contracts	State Employees	Age Discrimination
24. Mississippi	None	None	None	None	None
Sex; Age Limits					
Agency					
Time Limit; Number of Employees					
Process					

	FEP	Equal Pay	State Contracts	State Employees	Age Discrimination
25. Missouri	Ann. Missouri Statutes §§296.020	§§290.410	Included in FEP law	Included in FEP law	None
Sex; Age Limits	Yes	Yes	Yes	Yes	
Agency	Comm'n on Human Rts. 314 E. High St. Box 1129 Jefferson City 65101 (314) 635-7961	Industrial Comm'n 1904 Missouri Blvd. Jefferson City			
Time Limit; Number of Employees	30 days after agency decision; 6 employees	6 months			
Process	1, 4	2			

	FEP	Equal Pay	State Contracts	State Employees	Age Discrimination
26. Montana	Mont. Rev. Codes Ann. §§64-301 to 64-330	§§41-1307	Included in FEP law	Included in FEP law	Included in FEP law
Sex; Age Limits	Yes	Yes	Yes	Yes	
Agency	Comm'n for Human Rights 1331 Helena Ave. Helena 59601	Dept. of Labor & Industry 1331 Helena Ave. Helena 59601 (406) 449-3472			
Time Limit; Number of Employees	180 days; 1 employee				
Process	1, 2, 4	1, 4			

	FEP	Equal Pay	State Contracts	State Employees	Age Discrimination
27. Nebraska	Neb. Rev. Stat. §§48-1101 to 48-1125	§§48-1219 to 48-1227	Included in FEP law	Included in FEP law	§§48-1001 to 48-1009
Sex; Age Limits	Yes	Yes	Yes	Uncertain	40-65
Agency	Equal Opportunity Comm'n 233 S. 14th St. Lincoln 68509 (402) 471-2024	Equal Opportunity Comm'n			Equal Opportunity Comm'n
Time Limit; Number of Employees	180 days; 15 employees	25 employees			25 employees
Process	1, 4	2, 3, 4			2, 3, 4

	FEP	Equal Pay	State Contracts	State Employees	Age Discrimination
28. Nevada	§§613.330	§608.017	§338.125	None	§613.330(1)\(2)
Sex; Age Limits	Yes	Yes	Yes		
Agency	Nevada Equal Rights Comm'n				
Time Limit; Number of Employees	180 days; 15 employees				
Process	2, 3	3, 4	5		2, 3

334

	FEP	Equal Pay	State Contracts	State Employees	Age Discrimination
29. New Hampshire	N.H. Rev. Stat. Ann. §§354-A:1 to 354-A:14	§§275:37	None	None	Included in FEP law
Sex; Age Limits	Yes	Yes			
Agency	Comm'n for Human Rts. 66 South St. Concord 03301 (603) 271-2767	Labor Dept. 1 Pillsbury St. Concord 03301			
Time Limit; Number of Employees	90 days; 6 employees	12 months			
Process	1, 4	2, 3, 4			1, 4

	FEP	Equal Pay	State Contracts		State Employees		Age Discrimination
30. New Jersey	N.J. Stat. Ann. §§10:5-1 to 10:5-28	§34.11-56.2	§§10:2-1 to 10:2-4, E.O. 21, Art. II	§10:1-10 to 1-12	§§10:1-10 to 10:1-12	E.O. 21, Art. I, 6-24-65	Included in FEP law
Sex; Age Limits	Yes	Yes	Yes	Yes	Yes	Yes	
Agency	Div. of Civil Rts. Dept. of Law & Public Safety 1100 Raymond Blvd. Newark 07102 (201) 648-2700	Div. of Civil Rts. Dept. of Law & Public Safety					
Time Limit; Number of Employees	90 days		180 days	180 days			
Process	1, 4	2	5	4	4	5	

336

	FEP	Equal Pay	State Contracts	State Employees	Age Discrimination
31. New Mexico	N.M. Stat. Ann. §§4-33-1 to 4-33-13; Const. Art. II §18	None	Included in FEP law	None	Included in FEP law
Sex; Age Limits	Yes				
Agency	Human Rts. Comm'n Villagra Bldg., Room 120 Santa Fe 87501 (508) 827-2713				
Time Limit; Number of Employees	90 days; 4 employees				
Process	1,4				

	FEP	Equal Pay	State Contracts	State Employees	Age Discrimination
32. New York	N.Y. Exec. Law §§290-301	N.Y. Labor Law	N.Y. Labor Law §220-e	None	Included in FEP law
Sex; Age Limits	Yes	Yes	No		40-65
Agency	Div. of Human Rts. 270 Broadway New York 10007 (212) 488-5358	Industrial Comm'n Dept. of Labor 12, State Office Bldg. Campus Albany 12226	Contracting Agency		
Time Limit; Number of Employees	1 year; 4 employees				
Process	1,4	3,4	5		

	FEP	Equal Pay	State Contracts	State Employees	Age Discrimination
33. North Carolina	N.Car. Gen. Stat. 143-422.1-3	None	None	N.Car. Gen. Stat. §126-16	N.Car. Gen. Stat. 143-422.2
Sex; Age Limits	Yes			Yes	
Agency					
Time Limit; Number of Employees	15 employees				
Process	5			5	5

	FEP	Equal Pay	State Contracts	State Employees	Age Discrimination
34. North Dakota	None	N.D. Century Code §34-06.1	None	N.D. Century Code 54-44.3-22	§34-01.17
Sex; Age Limits		Yes			40-65
Agency		Comm'r of Agriculture & Labor State Capitol Bismarck 58501			
Time Limit; Number of Employees		2 years; 1 employee			
Process		2, 4, 5		5	4

340

	FEP	Equal Pay	State Contracts	State Employees	Age Discrimination
35. Ohio	Ohio Rev. Code Ann. §§4112.01-4112.99	§§4111.17, 4111.99	§153.58.1, 153.59, 153.60	None	§4101.17
Sex; Age Limits	Yes	Yes	Yes		40-65
Agency	Civil Rts. Comm'n 240 Parsons Ave. Room 234 Columbus 43215 (614) 469-2785	Dept. of Industrial Relations, 220 Parsons Ave. Columbus 43215			Dept. of Industrial Relations
Time Limit; Number of Employees	6 months; 4 employees	12 months			
Process	1,4, 5	2, 3, 4, 5	5		2, 5

	FEP	Equal Pay	State Contracts	State Employees	Age Discrimination
36. Oklahoma	Okla. Stat. Ann. 74§§951 to 954; 25§§1301 to 1311; 25§§1501 to 1508	40§§198.1-198.2	25§1604, 25§1505	74§954	None
Sex; Age Limits	Yes	Yes	No	No	
Agency	Human Rts. Comm'n P.O. 52945 Oklahoma City 73102 (405) 521-2360	Labor Dept. State Capitol Oklahoma City	Contracting Agency		
Time Limit; Number of Employees	180 days; 15 employees				
Process	1	3, 4	5		

342

	FEP	Equal Pay	State Contracts	State Employees	Age Discrimination
37. Oregon	Ore. Rev. Stat. §§659.010 to 659.115	§§652.220, 652.230	None	§243.305	Included in FEP law
Sex; Age Limits	Yes	Yes		Yes	
Agency	Civil Rts. Div. Bur. of Labor Room 466 State Office Bldg. Portland 97201 (503) 229-5741			Div. of Affirmative Action Office of the Governor Portland	
Time Limit; Number of Employees	1 employee	1 employee			
Process	1,2,4	2			

	FEP	Equal Pay	State Contracts	State Employees	Age Discrimination
38. Pennsylvania	Penn. Stat. Ann. 43§§951 to 963	43§§336.1-336.10	43§153	None	Included in FEP law
Sex; Age Limits	Yes	Yes	No		
Agency	Human Relations Comm'n P.O. Box 3145 Harrisburg 17120 (717) 234-8777	Dept. of Labor & Industry 1700 Labor & Industrial Bldg. Harrisburg 17120			
Time Limit; Number of Employees	90 days; 4 employees	2 years			
Process	1,4	4	5		

344

	FEP	Equal Pay	State Contracts	State Employees	Age Discrimination
39. Rhode Island	R.I. Gen. Laws §§28-5-1 to 28-5-39	§§28-6-17 to 28-6-21	None	E.O. 8, 6/9/69	§§28-6-1 to 28-6-16
Sex; Age Limits	Yes	Yes		No	45-65
Agency	Comm'n for Human Rts. 244 Broad St. Providence 02903 (401) 277-2661	Dept. of Labor 225 Promenade St. Providence		Comm'n for Human Rts.	Dept. of Labor
Time Limit; Number of Employees	4 employees				4 months; 1 employee
Process	1	2, 3, 4		5	1

345

	FEP	Equal Pay	State Contracts	State Employees	Age Discrimination
40. South Carolina	None	None	None	Code of Laws of So. Car. 58-11-230	Included in State Employees law
Sex; Age Limits				Yes	
Agency				Comm'n on Human Affairs P.O. Box 11528 Columbia 29211	
Time Limit; Number of Employees					
Process				1	

	FEP	Equal Pay	State Contracts	State Employees	Age Discrimination
41. South Dakota*	S.D. Compiled Laws §§20-13-1 to 20-13-56	§§20-13-10; 60-12-15; 60-12-21	None	None	None
Sex; Age Limits	Yes				
Agency	Comm'n on Human Relations 5th & Highland Sioux Falls 57103 (605) 338-4562	Dept. of Labor			
Time Limit; Number of Employees	6 months; 1 employee	30 months			
Process	1	2			

*S.D. Compiled Laws §20-12-4 authorizes municipalities and counties to investigate discriminatory practices.

347

	FEP	Equal Pay	State Contracts	State Employees	Age Discrimination
42. Tennessee	None	Tenn. Code Ann. §§50-320 to 50-325	E.O. 17, 1/14/72	E.O. 17, 1/14/72	§4-115 (in appointments to state boards or commissions)
Sex; Age Limits		Yes	Yes	Yes	
Agency		Comm'n of Labor	Comm'n of Standards & Purchases, as monitored by Comm'n for Human Development,* C3 305 Cordell Hull Bldg. Nashville 37219 (615) 741-2424	Comm'n of Labor	
Time Limit; Number of Employees		2 years			
Process		2, 3, 4	5	2, 3, 4, 5	

*Agency itself has no power.

348

	FEP	Equal Pay	State Contracts	State Employees	Age Discrimination
43. Texas	None	Tex. Rev. Civ. Stat., art. 6825	None	Art. 6252-16	Art. 6252-14
Sex; Age Limits		Yes (state employees only)		Yes	21-65 (state employees only)
Agency				District Attorney and/or County Attorney	
Time Limit; Number of Employees					
Process		5		2, 4	5

	FEP	Equal Pay	State Contracts	State Employees	Age Discrimination
44. Utah	Utah Code Ann. §§34-35-1 to 34-35-8	Included in FEP law	Gov. Code of Fair Prac., E.O., Art. VII, 10/1/65; also included in FEP regulations	Included in FEP law; Gov. Code of Fair Prac., E.O., Art. VII, 10/1/65	§34-35-1 to 8
Sex; Age Limits	Yes	Yes	Yes	Yes	40-65
Agency	Anti-Discrimination Division Industrial Comm'n State Capitol Bldg. Salt Lake 84114 (801) 328-5552	Anti-Discrimination Division			Anti-Discrimination Division
Time Limit; Number of Employees	30 days; 25 employees			30 days from issuance of written decision of personnel board	
Process	1		5	5	

	FEP	Equal Pay	State Contracts	State Employees	Age Discrimination
45. Vermont	Vt. Stat. Ann 21§§495 to 495c	21§§495	Included in FEP law	Included in FEP law	None
Sex; Age Limits	No	Yes			
Agency	State's Attorney or Attorney General				
Time Limit; Number of Employees					
Process	1				

	FEP	Equal Pay	State Contracts	State Employees	Age Discrimination
46. Virginia	None	$40.1-28.6	§2.1-374	§2.1-374	None
Sex; Age Limits		Yes	Yes	Yes	
Agency					
Time Limit; Number of Employees		2 years after right accrued (for work after July 1, 1974)			
Process		2			

	FEP	Equal Pay	State Contracts	State Employees	Age Discrimination
47. Washington	Wash. Rev. Code Ann. §§49.60.010 to 49.60.320	§49.12.175	E.O. 70-01, 1/30/70; E.O., Art. III, 8/2/66	E.O., Art. I, 8/2/66	§49.44.090; also included in FEP law
Sex; Age Limits	Yes	Yes	Yes	Yes	40-65
Agency	Human Rts. Comm'n 1411 4th Ave. Bldg. Seattle 98101 (206) 464-6500	State or City Prosecuting Attorneys	Human Rts. Comm'n		
Time Limit; Number of Employees	6 months; 8 employees				
Process	1,2	2, 3, 4	5	5	5

352

	FEP	Equal Pay	State Contracts		State Employees	Age Discrimination
48. West Virginia	W.Va. Code Ann. §§5-11-1 to 5-11-19	Included in FEP law	E.O., 10/16/63	E.O., 10/16/65	Included in FEP law	Included in FEP law
Sex; Age Limits	Yes	Yes	No	Yes	Yes	40-65
Agency	Human Rts. Comm'n P & G Bldg. 2019 E. Wash. St. Charleston 25305 (304) 348-2616	Labor Comm'n Dept. of Labor B-451 Capitol Complex Charleston 25305 (304) 348-2195			Human Rts. Comm'n	
Time Limit; Number of Employees	90 days; 12 employees	1 employee				
Process	1, 4	2, 4	5	5	5	

	FEP	Equal Pay	State Contracts	State Employees	Age Discrimination
49. Wisconsin*	Wisc. Stat. Ann. §§111.31 to 111.37	Included in FEP law	$16.765	Included in FEP law; §230.18	Included in FEP law and State Contracts
Sex; Age Limits	Yes		Yes		40-65
Agency	Equal Rts. Div. Dept. of Industry, Labor & Human Relations P.O. 2209 201 E. Washington Madison 53701 (608) 226-7552		Contracting Agency		
Time Limit; Number of Employees	300 days				
Process	1		1		

*Wisc. Stat. Ann. §256.28 forbids discrimination against women attorneys.

	FEP	Equal Pay	State Contracts	State Employees	Age Discrimination
50. Wyoming	Wyo. Stat. Ann. §§27-257 to 27-264; 27-6-101 to 27-6-116	§§27-210.1 to 27-210.4; 27-4-301 to 27-4-304; Included in FEP law	Included in FEP law	Included in FEP law	None
Sex; Age Limits	Yes	Yes			
Agency	Fair Employment Comm'n 304 Capitol Bldg. Cheyenne 82001 (307) 777-7262	Labor Comm'n Dept. of Labor & Statistics 304 Capitol Bldg. Cheyenne 82001			
Time Limit; Number of Employees	2 employees				
Process	1	2, 3, 4			

Chart B:
State Laws Forbidding Discrimination in Public Accommodations, Housing, Financing for Housing, and Education

Explanation of chart. This chart gives the legal citation to the pertinent state law so that readers can look up the law themselves. The symbol **S** appearing below the citation means that the statute outlaws sex discrimination as well as discrimination based on race, religion, and national origin. If there is no **S** below the citation, the statute covers only the last three categories. Where two sections are given, one with an **S** and one without it, the latter does not include a prohibition against sex discrimination.

The statutes vary widely in scope and comprehensiveness, and readers will have to do more work to determine how valuable they are. The research for the chart was done in the spring of 1980. Since this is a rapidly changing field, women should double-check to see whether new laws have been passed in their state.

In most instances, the citation given is either only to the particular section defining the discriminatory practice or to the first section of a chapter. Readers should therefore look at preceding and following sections to find out about the entire enforcement scheme. They should also check the latest supplement to the cited volume, since many of the citations are found in the inserts in the back of the book rather than in the bound volume itself.

To find the agency that enforces the law, try contacting the state employment discrimination agency (Chart A lists these agencies.) In addition, cities often have agencies that enforce laws forbidding discrimination in public accommodations, housing, financing for housing, and education. There has been no attempt to list them here. To locate city or local agencies, try contacting the state employment discrimination agency or write for the *Directory of State and Local Anti-Discrimination Agencies,* published by EEOC, which deals primarily with state and local employment discrimination agencies, many of them enforcing laws covering several kinds of discrimination. To obtain the directory, write to Office of State and Community Affairs, EEOC, 2401 E. St., N.W., Washington, D.C. 20506.

State	Public Accommodations	Housing	Financing	Education
Alaska	Alaska Stat. §18.80.230 S	18.80.240 S	18.80.250 S	14.40.050 S 14.40.769 S 14.40.835 S
Arizona	Arizona Rev. Stat. §41-1442			
Arkansas			Ark. Stat. §70-926 (Equal Consumer Credit)	
California	Cal. Civil Code §51 S	§53 Civil S §35700-35742 Health and Safety S §1419.5 Labor S	§51 Civil S §35811 Health and Safety S §35720(7) Health and Safety §35316 Educ	§40 Educ. S §51004 Educ. S §51500-5150 Educ. S
Colorado	Colo. Rev. Stat. §23-34-501 S §23-34-601 S	§23-34-405 S	§35-1-109 S	Colo. Constitution Art. IX, §8 (race and color)

State	Public Accommodations	Housing	Financing	Education
Connecticut	Conn. Gen. Stat Ann. §53-35 **S**	§53-35 **S** §8-265c **S**	§36-437 **S** (credit)	
Delaware	Del. Code Ann. §6-4504 **S**	§6-4603 **S**	§6-4603(7) **S**	
District of Columbia	D.C. Code Ann. §6-2211	§6-2211 §6-2231(1) **S** §6-2231(4)(5) **S** §6-2231(6)	§6-2231(3) **S** 6-2231(5) **S** 6-2231(6)	§6-2211
Florida			Fla. Stat. Ann. §725.07 **S**	
Georgia		Ga. Code Ann. §99-4901 **S**	§99-4903 **S**	
Hawaii		§515-3,5,6 **S**	§515-5 **S** (real estate); §477E 3 (marital status)	§§290-60, 61 **S**
Idaho	Idaho Code §67-5909(5) **S**; §18-7301 **S**	§67-5909(7) **S**	§67-5909(8) **S** (real estate)	§67-5909(6) **S**
Illinois	Ill. Stat. Ann. 38§13-2		95§303 **S**	122§10-22.5 **S**; 122§34-18(7) **S**
Indiana	§§22-9-1-2 **S**; 35-46-2-1(1) **S**	§§22-9-1-2 **S**; 35-46.2-1920 (public housing) **S**		§22-9-1-2 **S**

State	Public Accommodations	Housing	Financing	Education
Iowa	§601A.7 S	§601A.8 S	§601A.10 S; §537.3311 S	§601A.9 S
Kansas	Kan. Stat. Ann. §44-1009(c) S	§44-1016 S	§44-1017 (real estate)	
Kentucky	Ky. Rev. Stat. Ann. §§344.120; 344.145 S	§§344.360; 207.180 S	§344.370 S; §344.400 S	
Louisiana	La. Const. Art. I §12 S		§9:3583 S	§17:1676 (state scholarships) S
Maine	Maine Rev. Stat. Ann. 17§1301 5§4591-4992 S	17§ 1301 5§§ 4581-4582 S	5§§4595-4596 S	5§§790 (affirmative action in state schools) S
Maryland	49B§5 S	49B§§19-20 S	49B§22 (real estate) S	
Massachusetts	MGLA 272§§92A,98 S	MGLA 151B§4.6, 4.7 S	MGLA 151B§4.3B S	MGLA 151C§2,2A S 76§5 S
Michigan	MCLA 37.2302 §302 S	MCLA 37.2502§502 S	MCLA 37.2504§504 S	MCLA 37.2402§402 S
Minnesota	M.S.A. §363.03 subd.3 S	M.S.A. §363.03 subd.2 S	M.S.A. §363.03 subd.8 §363.03 subd.2(3) S	M.S.A. §363.03 subd.5 S
Mississippi				

State	Public Accommodations	Housing	Financing	Education
Missouri	A.M.S. §314.010 **S**	A.M.S. §213.105 **S**	A.M.S. §314.100 **S**	
Montana	R.C.M. §64-306 (3) **S**	R.C.M. §64-306 (4) **S**	R.C.M. §64-306(5) **S**	R.C.M. §64-306 (7) **S**
Nebraska	N.R.S. §20-132 **S**	N.R.S. §20-107 §20-109	N.R.S. §20-108	
Nevada	N.R.S. §651.070	N.R.S. §118.100 §207.300 **S**	N.R.S. §598B.100	
New Hampshire	N.H.R.S.A. §354-A:8 (IV) **S**	N.H.R.S.A. §354-A:8(V) **S**		
New Jersey	N.J.S.A. §10:5–12(f) §10:1–3 **S**	N.J.S.A. §10:5–12 (g)(h) **S**	N.J.S.A. §10:5–12(i) **S**	N.J.S.A. §10:5–12(f) **S**
New Mexico	N.Mex. Stat. Ann. §4-33-7(f) **S**	§4-33-7(g) **S**	§4-33-7(h) **S**	
New York	N.Y. Exec. Law §296.2 **S**	N.Y. Exec. Law §296.2a,b (public housing); §296.5 **S**; §296.3(b)	N.Y. Exec. Law §296-a **S**	N.Y. Educ. law §3201-a **S**; §313; §3201; §296.4
North Carolina			N.C. Gen.Stat. §53-180(d) **S**; §25B 5-m* **S**	
North Dakota	N.D. Century Code §12.1-14.04 **S**			

State	Public Accommodations	Housing	Financing	Education
Ohio	Ohio Rev. Code Ann. §4112.02 **S**	§4112.02 **S**	§4112.02 **S**	
Oklahoma	Okla. Stat. Ann. 25§1402		14A§1-109 **S**	
Oregon	Oregon Rev. Stat. §30.670 **S**	§659.033 **S**		§345.240 **S**; §659.150 (institutions receiving state money) **S**; §326.051(d) **S**
Pennsylvania	Penn. Stat. Ann. 43§953 **S**; 43§955(i)	43§955(h) **S**	43§955(h (4)) **S**	24§5004 **S**; 24§5154 (scholarships) **S**
Rhode Island	R.I. Gen. Laws §11-24-2	§24-37-4 **S**	§34-37-4.1 **S**	§34-37-4(B) **S**
South Carolina				Code of Laws of So. Car. §59-33-50 (programs for handicapped children) **S**
South Dakota	S.D. Compiled Laws §20-13-23 **S**	§20-13-20 **S**	§20-13-21 **S**	§20-13-22
Tennessee				§49-5013-2 (state student aid) **S**; §49-1770 to 1771 **S**

State	Public Accommodations	Housing	Financing	Education
Texas				
Utah	Utah Code. Ann. §13-7-3			
Vermont	Vt. Stat. Ann. 13§1451	13§1452(2)		
Virginia			§59-21.19 to 59.1–21.28 **S**	
Washington	Wash. Rev. Code Ann. §49.60.215	§§49.60.222, 49.60.224	§§49.60.175–.176 **S**	§§49.60.040, 49.60.215, 9.91.010
West Virginia	W.Va. Code Ann. §5-11-9(f) **S**	§5-11-9(g)	§5-11-9(h)	§5-11-9(d) (on-the-job or occupational training) **S**
Wisconsin	Wisc. Stat. Ann. §942.04	§101.60(2)	§101.60(2)	
Wyoming	Wyo. Stan. Ann. §6-4-610			

Chart C:
Name Change

Explanation of chart. The second column, headed "Name-Change Court and Statute," gives the legal citation to the state law setting forth the court procedures for changing one's name. It also lists the name of the court that handles the procedure in each state. States where the statutory procedure is exclusive or where criminal penalties may be imposed for changing one's name unlawfully are also marked; in these states, women should not change their name by mere usage but should use the statutory procedure, unless they have competent legal advice that the latter is not necessary.

The third column, "Reregistration and Notification Laws and Penalties," lists those states requiring reregistration or notification of state authorities when a person's name changes. The laws generally require reregistration for voting and notification of authorities of one's driver's license, motor vehicle registration, certificate of title for a motor vehicle, and being a notary public (see code below). In a few states, a penalty for failing to comply with these requirements is set forth. In addition, the voting reregistration statutes sometimes specifically require reregistration of a person whose name changes, although this is not noted on the chart. Most state laws do not formally set forth any penalty for failure to comply with the law. (See generally the discussion at pp. 245–254.)

The fourth column, "Divorce Laws and Limits," shows states with laws affirmatively stating that women who have divorced may change their name back to their maiden name, a former husband's name, or another name. States that limit this right to women with no children, or to women with no minor children in their custody are also noted (see code below).

363

The last column is headed "Interpretation: Name Change by Law or Custom." It indicates states where judicial decisions, state statutes, or attorney general opinions strongly suggest that the state will take one of two positions: (1) a woman's name automatically changes when she marries; (2) she has an option and can decide whether or not to change her name (see code below). If the former position is indicated, women should seriously consider using the statutory name-change procedure. (See discussion in Chapter VIII.) An example of how to read the last column can be taken from Alabama, which has "J/L/DL (1972)." This means that a 1972 *judicial* decision, involving a person's *driver's license*, found that under Alabama law a woman's name changes automatically upon marriage as a matter of *law*. Thus, married women in Alabama will have to use the name-change procedure in order to retain their father's name or change to a third name other than their husband's if they want to avoid state penalties (here, loss of one's driver's license). This column does not indicate very old decisions (anything before 1930 is not listed), nor is it the final word; skillful lawyers will often be able to argue successfully against the implications of these precedents. Finally, the research on attorney generals' opinions is incomplete; and in any case, such opinions do not carry a great deal of legal weight.

Code

Name-Change Court and Statute

> Exclusive—a person may not change his or her name by usage but must use the statutory name-change procedure
>
> H—husband
> W—wife

Reregistration and Notification Laws and Penalties

> DL—required as to *driver's license*
> V—required as to *vote*
> MVR—required as to *motor vehicle registration*

CT—required as to *certificate of title* of motor vehicle

NP—required as to being a *notary public*

R—a person whose name changes must *reregister*

N—a person whose name changes must *notify* the proper authorities

Divorce Laws and Limits

X—the state has a law allowing a divorced woman to change her name

NC—a divorced woman must have *no children* in order to change her name

Interpretation: Name Change by Law or Custom

L—the woman's name changes automatically when she marries, as a matter of *law*

C—a woman has an option of changing her name when she marries since a change is only a matter of *custom*

J—a *judge's* decision indicates whether change is by law or custom

S—a *statute* indicates whether change is by law or custom

AG—an *attorney general's* opinion indicates whether change is by law or custom

DL—relates to *driver's license*

MVR—relates to *motor vehicle registration*

NP—relates to *notary public*

V—relates to being able to *vote*

NCS—relates to *name-change statute*

State	Name-Change Court and Statute	Reregistration and Notification Laws and Penalties	Divorce Laws and Limits	Interpretation: Name Change by Law or Custom
Alabama	Probate Court Ala. Code §12-13-1(10) (exclusive)	DL(N) (unwritten regulation)	X (injunction from using husband's name)	J/L/DL (1972)

State	Name-Change Court and Statute	Reregistration and Notification Laws and Penalties	Divorce Laws and Limits	Interpretation: Name Change by Law or Custom
Alaska	Superior Court Alas. Stat. §9.55.010	MVR(N), DL(N), V(R)	X	
Arizona	Superior Court Ariz. Rev. Stat. Ann. §12-601	V(R)	X	
Arkansas	Chancery or Circuit Court Ark. Stat. §34-801, §34-1216 (divorce)	V(R) (constitution)	X-NC	
California	Superior Court Cal. Civ. Pro. Code §1275; Civil Code §4362, §4521	V(R) (optional), DL(N)	X (except for legal separation)	
Colorado	District, Superior, or County Court §13-15-101	V(R) optional, DL(N)		
Connecticut	Superior Court Conn. Gen. Stat. Ann. §52-11, §46b-63(divorce)	V(ambiguous)	X	AG/C (1941) AG/L/MVR (1934)
Delaware	Court of Common Pleas 10§5901, 13§1514(divorce)	V(R)	X	
District of Columbia	U.S. District Court D.C. Code §16-2501, §16-915(divorce)		X	

State	Name-Change Court and Statute	Reregistration and Notification Laws and Penalties	Divorce Laws and Limits	Interpretation: Name Change by Law or Custom
Florida	Chancery Courts Fla. Sta. Ann. §68.07	DL(N), V(N), NP		S/C/NP
Georgia	Superior Court Ga. Code Ann. §79-501, §30-121		X	
Hawaii	Lieutenant Governor Hawaii Rev. Stat. §574-5 (exclusive)	DL(N), MVR(N)	X	S/C
Idaho	District Court Idaho Code Ann. §7-801	V(N&R), DL(N)		
Illinois	Circuit Court Ill. Stat. Ann. 96§1	V(R), DL(N), MVR(N)	X	J/L/V/(1945)
Indiana	Circuit Court Ind. Stat. Ann. §34-4-6-1	V(N) (woman may vote in professional name)	X	
Iowa	District Court Iowa Code Ann. §674.1	MVR(N), V(N)	X	S/L/NCS
Kansas	District Court Kansas Stat. Ann. §60-1401	DL(N), V(R)	X	
Kentucky	District Court Kentucky Rev. Stat. Ann. §401.010	DL(N)		S/L/NCS

State	Name-Change Court and Statute	Reregistration and Notification Laws and Penalties	Divorce Laws and Limits	Interpretation: Name Change by Law or Custom
Louisiana	District Court La. Rev. Stat. Ann. §13:4751 (exclusive)	V(N)		J/C/Marriage License (1931)
Maine	Probate Court Maine Rev. Stat. Ann. 19§781 (exclusive)	V(N), DL(N)	X	AG/L/Marriage License (1951–1954)
Maryland	Court of Equity Md. Ann. Code 16§123; Md. Rules BH70–75	DL(N), MVR(N), CT(N), V(R)		J/C/V (1972)
Massachusetts	Probate Court Mass. Ann. Laws 210§12	MVR(N), DL(N), NP	X	C/J (common law gives woman freedom to change name or not)
Michigan	Circuit Court Mich. Comp. Laws Ann. 552.391; Probate Court Mich. Comp. Laws Ann. 711.1	NP (must use original name until commission expires)	X	C/AG (1974)
Minnesota	District Court Minn. Stat. Ann. §259.10, §518.27	DL(N)	X	
Mississippi	Chancery Court Miss. Code Ann. §93-17-51			
Missouri	Circuit Court Mo. Rev. Statutes §527.270		X	

State	Name-Change Court and Statute	Reregistration and Notification Laws and Penalties	Divorce Laws and Limits	Interpretation: Name Change by Law or Custom
Montana	District Court Mont. Rev. Codes Ann. §93-100-1	DL(N)		
Nebraska	District Court Rev. Stats. of Neb. §61-101,102	NP (must use original name until commission expires), V(R)		
Nevada	District Court Nev. Rev. Stats. §41.270, §125.130	V(R), DL(N)	X	
New Hampshire	Probate Court N.H. Rev. Stats. §547:7; Superior Court §458:24	MVR(N), DL(N)	X	
New Jersey	County or Superior Ct. N.J. Stat. Ann. §2A:52-1	V(R), NP(R) (must use both maiden and married name hyphenated)	X	J/C
New Mexico	District Court N.M. Stat. Ann. §22-5-1	MVR(N), CT(N) (a crime to use a false name to obtain MVR or CT fraudulently), V(N) (optional)		AG (1967–68) (1967–102)
New York	County, Supreme or, in New York City, Civil Court N.Y. Civ. Rts. Law §60	V (married woman may vote in either maiden or married name)	X	S/C/V
North Carolina	Superior Court N. Car. Gen. Stat. §101-2	MVR(N), CT(N), V(N)	X	

State	Name-Change Court and Statute	Reregistration and Notification Laws and Penalties	Divorce Laws and Limits	Interpretation: Name Change by Law or Custom
North Dakota	District Court N.D. Century Code §32-28-01	DL(N)		
Ohio	Probate Court Ohio Rev. Code Ann. §2717.01	V(R)	X	J/C/Election Law (1961)
Oklahoma	District Court Okla. Stat. Ann. 12§1631 (exclusive)	DL(N)	X	
Oregon	Probate Court Ore. Rev. Stat. §33.410	V(R), DL(N)	X	AG/L (1950–1952)
Pennsylvania	Court of Common Pleas Penn. Stat. Ann. 54§1	MVR(N), DL(N), CT(N), NP	X	
Rhode Island	Probate Court R.I. Gen. Laws Ann. §8-9-9	V(N) (optional), DL(N), MRV(N)	X	
South Carolina	Circuit Ct. Code of Laws §15-49-10	MVR(N), DL(N), NP	X (Court may allow)	
South Dakota	Circuit Court S.D. Compiled Laws §21-37-1; §25-4-47		X-NC (minor in mother's custody)*	
Tennessee	Circuit, Probate, or County Court Tenn. Code Ann. §23-801	V(R)		

*But can still petition under §22-37-1 where restriction doesn't apply.

State	Name-Change Court and Statute	Reregistration and Notification Laws and Penalties	Divorce Laws and Limits	Interpretation: Name Change by Law or Custom
Texas	District Court Stat. Family Code §32.21	DL(N)	X	
Utah	District Court Utah Code Ann. §42-1-1	MVR(N), CT(N)		
Vermont	Probate Court Vt. Stat. Ann. 15§811 (married person needs spouse's consent, but when H changes name that of W changes automatically)	DL(N), MVR(N)— $10 penalty for both	X	S/L/NCS
Virginia	Circuit Court Va. Code. Ann. §8-577.1 (person who changes name "unlaw-fully" subject to fine of $10–$100 and up to 60 days in jail)	V(N) (optional)	X	
Washington	Superior Court Wash. Rev. Code Ann. §4.24.130	DL(N), V(R)	X	
West Virginia	Circuit Court W.Va. Code Ann. §48-5-1 (person who changes name "unlaw-fully" subject to fine of up to $100 and up to 60 days in jail)	MVR(N), CT(N), V(R)	X-NC	

State	Name-Change Court and Statute	Reregistration and Notification Laws and Penalties	Divorce Laws and Limits	Interpretation: Name Change by Law or Custom
Wisconsin	Circuit Court Wisc. Stat. Ann. §296.36	V(R), DL(N)—penalty of up to $100 fine and/or up to 6 months in jail for failure to comply	X-NC	
Wyoming	District Court Wyo. Stat. Ann. §1-739			AG/C/DL (1972)

Chart D:
Sources of Legal Help and Women's Organizations

Explanation of chart. Chart D is necessarily incomplete but includes all groups the authors know about. It should help the woman who needs to find a lawyer to take a case or a counseling group to give her advice, who wants to join a woman's organization to work on legal problems, or who wants to do legal research on women's problems. Readers should also check the chapters themselves for additional materials and organizations. Women looking for lawyers should be aware that some women have begun forming feminist or all-woman law firms; this is an additional source that should be checked out in any local community.

1. Feminist Legal Help*

Women's Equal Rights Legal
   Defense and Education Fund
6380 Wilshire Blvd., Suite 1404
Los Angeles, Calif. 90048
   (213) 653–8087

Lesbian Law Project
1370 Mission St., 4th Floor
San Francisco, Calif. 94103

Equal Rights Advocates, Inc.
1370 Mission St., 4th Floor
San Francisco, Calif. 94103
   (415) 621–0505

---

*Groups are listed by alphabetical order of their state.

Comision Feminil Mexicana Nacional
379 S. Loma Dr.
Los Angeles, Calif. 90017
(313) 784–1515

(Concerned with the status of Chicanas. Class action suits against coerced sterilization; employment counseling and job training; newsletter available.)

Chicana Rights Project
Mexican American Legal Defense
and Education Fund (MALDEF)
28 Geary St., 6th Floor
San Francisco, Calif. 94108
(415) 981–5800

Human Rights for Women
1128 National Press Building
Washington, D.C. 20004
(202) 737–1059

WEAL Fund
805 15th St., N.W.
Washington, D.C. 20005
(202) 638–1961

Women's Legal Defense Fund
2000 P St., N.W., Suite 400
Washington, D.C. 20036
(202) 887–0364

Harmon and Weiss
1725 I St., N.W., Suite 506
Washington, D.C. 20006
(202) 833–9070

Women's Rights Project
Center for Law and Social Policy
1751 N. St., N.W.
Washington, D.C. 20036
(202) 872–0670

League of Women Voters Litigation Unit
1730 M St., N.W.
Washington, D.C. 20036
  (202) 296–1770

Women's Rights Clinic
Antioch School of Law
1624 Crescent Place, N.W.
Washington, D.C. 20010
  (202) 265–9500

Employment/Sex Discrimination Clinic
Georgetown University Law Center
605 G St., N.W., 3d Floor
Washington, D.C. 20001
  (202) 624–8071

Center for Women Policy Studies
2000 P St., N.W., Suite 508
Washington, D.C. 20036
  (202) 872–1770

Federally Employed Women (FEW)—LDEF
National Press Building, Room 481
Washington, D.C. 20045
  (202) 638–4404

Legal Assistance Foundation Clinic
343 South Dearborn St., Suite 800
Chicago, Ill. 60604
  (312) 341–1080

Women's Law Center
12 E. 25th St.
Baltimore, Md. 21218
  (301) 366–2232

Women's Law Collective
678 Massachusetts Ave.
Cambridge, Mass. 02139
  (617) 492–5110

Women's Justice Center
651 E. Jefferson Ave.
Detroit, Mich. 48226
  (313) 961–7073

Michigan Feminist Lawyers
Women's Advocate Office
3404 Michigan Union
Ann Arbor, Mich. 48109
  (313) 763–4186

Clinical Course on Women and the Law
Rutgers Law School
180 University Ave.
Newark, N.J. 07102
  (201) 648–5561

Clinical Course on Women and
  the Law
N.Y.U. Law School
Washington Square South
New York, N.Y. 10012
  (212) 598–1212

NOW Legal Defense and Education
  Fund, Inc.
132 W. 43rd St.
New York, N.Y. 10036
  (212) 354–1225

Reproductive Freedom Project
American Civil Liberties Union
132 W. 43rd St.
New York, N.Y. 10036
  (212) 944–9800

(Information and assistance on sterilization, birth control, and
abortion litigation; brochures.)

Women's Rights Project
American Civil Liberties Union
132 W. 43rd St.
New York, N.Y. 10036
  (212) 944–9800

National Center on Women and Family Law
799 Broadway, Room 402
New York, N.Y. 10003
  (212) 674–8200

Women's Law Fund
620 Keith Building
1621 Euclid Ave.
Cleveland, Ohio 44115
  (216) 621–3443

Clinical Program on Sex
  Discrimination in Employment
c/o Professor Jane Picker
Cleveland State Law School
Cleveland, Ohio 44115
  (216) 687–2528

Women's Law Project
112 S. 16th St., Suite 1012
Philadelphia, Pa. 19102
  (215) 564–6280

Mexican-American Legal Defense
  and Education Fund
Chicana Rights Project
201 N. St. Mary's St.
San Antonio, Tex. 78205
  (512) 224–5476

Women's Rights Project
American Civil Liberties Union
1001 E. Main St., Suite 710
Richmond, Va. 23219
  (804) 643–6419

Northwest Women's Law Center
4224 University Way, N.E.
Seattle, Wash. 98105
  (206) 632–8468

Law school "Women and the Law" courses

Many law schools now offer courses on "Women and the Law." Teachers or students in these courses may be able to direct women to lawyers sympathetic to sex discrimination issues. Call the law school for the name and phone number of the teacher. The following is a partial list of law schools offering such courses: American; Boalt Hall (Berkeley); Boston; Case Western Reserve; Catholic; Cleveland State; Columbia; De Paul; Duke; Georgetown; George Washington; Golden Gate; Harvard; Hastings; Howard; Indiana; New York University; Northwestern; Ohio State; Rutgers—Newark; Stanford; State University of New York at Buffalo; Suffolk; Temple; University of Alabama; University of California at Davis; University of California at Los Angeles; University of Chicago; University of Colorado; University of Connecticut; University of Kansas; University of Maryland—Baltimore; University of Michigan; University of New Mexico; University of Pennsylvania; University of San Francisco; University of Santa Clara; University of Washington; University of Wisconsin; Vanderbilt; Villanova; Yale.

Law school women's groups

In many law schools, women law students have formed feminist groups which would probably be willing to work with other women's organizations, and could show women how to do legal research and help develop paralegal projects. The students might also be able to direct women to sympathetic lawyers. Call local law schools for the name of the women's group and a contact person.

2. Other Sources of Legal Help

American Civil Liberties Union
132 W. 43rd St.
New York, N.Y. 10036
  (212) 944–9800

(Consult the local chapter in your state or city; it will be listed in the telephone directory under either ACLU or the state or city name, e.g., New York Civil Liberties Union. ACLU chapters often have staff lawyers and they call on many volunteer lawyers to take civil liberties cases.)

American Indian Law Center
1117 Stanford Dr., N.E.
Albuquerque, N.M. 87131
   (505) 288–5462

Center for Constitutional Rights
853 Broadway
New York, N.Y. 10003
   (212) 674–3303

(A foundation-funded group with a staff of lawyers who provide legal help in a variety of civil liberties and civil rights cases. The center has been very active in the sex discrimination area.)

Center for Law and Social Policy
1751 N St., N.W.
Washington, D.C. 20036
   (202) 872–0670

(A foundation-funded public interest law group with a staff of lawyers who provide legal help in a variety of cases. The center has two women lawyers who work exclusively on sex discrimination studies and litigation.)

Equal Employment Opportunity Commission: Title VII Lawyers' Panels

Local commission offices maintain lists of lawyers willing to take Title VII employment discrimination cases. Women generally work out fee arrangements with the lawyer. For the local EEOC office consult the phone directory under United States Government, or write the national office: Office of Public Information, EEOC, 2401 E St., N.W., Washington, D.C. 20506.

International Union of Electrical, Radio,
    and Machine Workers
1126 16th St., N.W.
Washington, D.C. 20036
    (202) 296–1200

(IUE has a staff of lawyers who provide advice and free
representation for all employees whom the union represents.
IUE lawyers have been very active in fighting sex discrimination and have brought nationwide lawsuits on important issues. They also hold women's conferences for rank-and-file
employees and have established women's representatives in
many locals.)

Lawyers' Committee for Civil Rights Under Law
733 15th St., N.W.
Washington, D.C. 20005
    (202) 628–6700

(This is the national office. The Lawyers' Committee has
offices in other cities: Atlanta, Beverly Hills, Boston, Chicago, Jackson, Kansas City, New York, Philadelphia, and San
Francisco. In these cities, the telephone number will be
listed in the directory under Lawyers' Committee for Civil
Rights Under Law or under Lawyers' Committee for Urban
Affairs. In Beverly Hills, check the Beverly Hills Bar Foundation. Volunteer lawyers and a few paid staff lawyers handle
a variety of civil rights and civil liberties cases for the Lawyers' Committee. A large percentage of their employment
discrimination cases are brought on behalf of women. In
Washington, D.C., Philadelphia, and San Francisco, the Lawyers' Committee has special programs that help women and
minorities find lawyers for employment discrimination cases.)

Legal Aid programs

In many communities there are Legal Aid Societies whose
staff and volunteer lawyers provide free legal help for the
poor. The office number should be located in the phone
book, or officials at a local law school may be able to direct
women to the nearest Legal Aid office.

Legal Services Corporation

The Legal Services Corporation funds neighborhood legal services programs throughout the nation to provide free legal help for the poor. This is an option for any woman who does not have much money. Call the local office to find out what the eligibility levels are. (The programs will not help people who make more than a specified amount of money.) If you cannot locate a program in the telephone directory under "Neighborhood Legal Services," call the main office in Washington for assistance.

The Legal Services Corporation also funds special centers that do concentrated work in particular fields, such as housing, economic development, health, social welfare, youth, and family law. Women with problems in particular areas may find these centers willing to help them.

> Mexican-American Legal Defense and
>   Education Fund (MALDEF)
> 28 Geary St., 6th Floor
> San Francisco, Calif. 94108
>   (415) 981–5800

(The Fund also has branch offices in Denver, Los Angeles, San Antonio, and Washington, D.C., which are listed in the phone directory. It has a paid staff of 20 lawyers, plus 250 volunteer lawyers, who handle a gamut of civil rights cases. The Fund is interested in sex discrimination cases in which the issues affect minority women. It also has a special program to refer women and minorities to lawyers in employment discrimination cases.)

> NAACP Legal Defense and Education Fund
> 10 Columbus Circle
> New York, N.Y. 10019
>   (212) 586–8397

(This group specializes in racial discrimination and civil rights cases but may do some sex discrimination work for minority women.)

National Lawyers' Guild
853 Broadway, Room 1705
New York, N.Y. 10008
     (212) 260–1360

(The national office is located at the above address. The Guild
also has offices in Atlanta, Boston, Chicago, Cleveland, Denver, Detroit, Los Angeles, Milwaukee, Philadelphia, Pittsburgh, Portland, Ore., San Francisco, San Jose, Seattle, and
Washington, D.C., which can be located through the telephone directory. Most Guild help comes through volunteer
lawyers, although a few offices maintain a small paid staff.
Current projects are in areas that include prison law, military
and the draft, police brutality, computer data banks, and
civilian surveillance; a few offices may do some work on sex
discrimination.)

National Education Association—
     DuShane Emergency Fund
1201 16th St., N.W.
Washington, D.C. 20036
     (202) 833–4000

(The DuShane Fund funds litigation to protect teachers, constitutional rights in general. It has spearheaded the litigation
against mandatory maternity leaves, commonly imposed on
teachers in towns across the nation.)

Native American Rights Fund
1712 N St., N.W.
Washington, D.C. 20036
     (202) 785–4166

(This group also has offices in Boulder, Colo.)

Southern Legal Action Movement
P.O. Box 54472
Atlanta, Ga. 30308

(This group puts out a monthly paper, holds conferences, and
has contacts with sympathetic attorneys, law students, and
legal workers throughout the South. It may be a good source

of information on how to find an attorney interested in sex discrimination work in the South.)

3. Women's Paralegal Counseling Groups and Other Specialized Groups

Note: Women should also check with the listed feminist groups—both legal and non-legal—to see whether they offer or know of comparable services.

Abortion

> National Abortion Rights Action League (NARAL)
> 825 15th St., N.W.
> Washington, D.C. 20005
>   (202) 347–7774

(Public education on abortion and sterilization issues. Monitors congressional legislation. Has chapters in various states.)

Business

> National Association of Women Business Owners
> 2000 P St., N.W.
> Washington, D.C. 20036
>   (202) 338–8966

(Clearinghouse on information and referrals to appropriate organizations serving needs of businesswomen.)

Credit

> Women's Law Center, Inc.
> 12 E. 25th St.
> Baltimore, Md. 21202
>   (301) 366–2232

Center for Women Policy Studies
2000 P St., N.W., Suite 508
Washington, D.C. 20036
  (202) 872–1770

(This center has a foundation grant to study credit discrimination and has published *Women and Credit*, which lists all groups around the country that are working on credit problems and what they are doing. The report is available from the Center.)

Women's Legal Defense Fund
Credit Counseling Committee
2000 P St., N.W., Suite 400
Washington, D.C. 20036
  (202) 887–0364

NOW Credit Task Force
1711 Westwind Way
McLean, Va. 22101

National Consumer Law Center, Inc.
1 Court St.
Boston, Mass. 02108
  (617) 523–8010

Consumer Credit Project, Inc.
261 Kimberley
Barrington, Ill. 60010
  (312) 381–2113

(The Project has published a booklet, *New Credit Rights for Women*, which discusses women's rights under five federal credit laws. It is available from the Project for $2 plus $.75 postage.)

Day care

Day Care and Child Development Council of America
1602 17th St., N.W.
Washington, D.C. 20009
  (202) 745–0220

Day Care Council of New York, Inc.
22 W. 38th St.
New York, N.Y. 10018
  (212) 398–0380

Divorce

New Haven Women's Center
140 Orange St.
New Haven, Conn. 06510
  (203) 436–0645

Women's Divorce Co-op
c/o University YWCA
4224 University Way, N.E.
Seattle, Wash. 40165
  (206) 632–4747

(The Co-op, which is open from 10:00 A.M. to 2:00 P.M. Mondays to Thursdays, helps women handle their own uncontested divorces and does some lawyer referrals.)

Women in Transition
Philadelphia Women's Center
4634 Chester Ave.
Philadelphia, Pa. 19143
  (215) 386–4900

(This project provides counseling, crisis housing, and lawyer referrals, and helps women handle their own divorces in certain situations.)

Women's Legal Defense Fund
Domestic Relations Counseling Committee
2000 P St., N.W., Suite 400
Washington, D.C. 20036
  (202) 887–0364

Domestic violence

Center for Women Policy Studies
2000 P St., N.W., Suite 508
Washington, D.C. 20036
  (202) 872–1770

National Coalition Against Domestic Violence
1728 N St., N.W.
Washington, D.C. 20036
(202) 347–7015

Education

National Coalition for Women and Girls in Education
1818 R St., N.W.
Washington, D.C. 20009
  (202) 387–1300

PEER (Project on Equal Education Rights)
1029 Vermont Ave., N.W., Suite 800
Washington, D.C. 20005
  (202) 332–7337

NOW Education Discrimination Task Force
Lucille Toro, Chairperson
156–158 E. 2nd St.
New Castle, Del. 19720

Employment rights

National Commission of Working Women
Center for Women and Work
1211 Connecticut Ave., N.W.
Washington, D.C. 20036
  (202) 466–6770

Women Employed
5 S. Wabash Ave., Suite 415
Chicago, Ill. 60603
    (312) 782–3902

Women Office Workers
680 Lexington Ave.
New York, N.Y. 10022
    (212) 688–4160

Women's Job Rights Project
620 Sutter St., No. 318
San Francisco, Calif. 94102

(There are two clinics, one in Berkeley and one in San Francisco.)

Women's Legal Defense Fund
Employment Rights Counseling Committee
2000 P St., N.W., Suite 400
Washington, D.C. 20036
    (202) 887–0364

Working Women's United Institute
593 Park Ave.
New York, N.Y. 10021
    (212) 838–4420

(Counsels women who have been subjected to sexual harassment at their jobs.)

Working Women—National Association of
    Office Workers
1258 Euclid Ave.
Cleveland, Ohio 44115
    (216) 566–8511

A directory of women's employment projects in the United States, the *National Directory of Women's Employment Programs,* is available for $7.50 from Wider Opportunities for Women, 1511 K St., N.W., Room 345, Washington, D.C. 20005; (202) 638–3143.

Information on traditionally male jobs is available from the following five groups:

Women's Employment Resource Center
216 Crown St.
New Haven, Conn. 06510
    (203) 624–2331

Wider Opportunities for Women
1511 K St., N.W.
Washington, D.C. 20006
    (202) 638–4868

Women's Employment Division
148 International Blvd., Suite 403
Atlanta, Ga. 30303
    (404) 681–0631

Recruitment and Training Program Inc.
162 5th Ave.
New York, N.Y. 10010
    (212) 620–7300

(Has offices nationwide to help women and minorities enter the trades.)

Coal Employment Project
Box 3403
Oak Ridge, Tenn. 37830
    (615) 482–3420

(Assists women who want coal-mining jobs. Works toward eliminating sex discrimination in the coal mining industry.)

Health issues

Federation of Feminist Women's Health Centers
1112 S. Crenshaw Blvd.
Los Angeles, Calif. 90019
    (213) 936–6293

(Self-help clinic with affiliates in Florida, Georgia, and Michigan.)

Women's Occupational Health Resource Center
American Health Foundation
320 E. 43rd St.
New York, N.Y. 10017
   (212) 953–1900

(Clearinghouse and resource center on legal and educational questions related to health. Newsletter $6/year students; $12/year professionals.)

Juvenile delinquency/rights of children and youth

Children's Rights Project
American Civil Liberties Union
132 W. 43rd St.
New York, N.Y. 10016
   (212) 944–9800

Children's Defense Fund
1520 New Hampshire Ave., N.W.
Washington, D.C. 20036
   (202) 483–1470

National Network of Runaway and Youth Services
1705 DeSales St., 8th Floor
Washington, D.C. 20036
   (202) 466–4212

National Youth Work Alliance
1346 Connecticut Ave., N.W.
Washington, D.C. 20036
   (202) 785–0764

National Center for Youth Law
1663 Mission St., 5th Floor
San Francisco, Calif. 94103
   (415) 543–3307
         and

3701 Lindell Blvd., 2nd Floor
St Louis, Mo. 63178
  (314) 533–8868

Names

Center for a Woman's Own Name
261 Kimberley
Barrington, Ill. 60010
  (312) 381–2113

Women's Legal Defense Fund
Name Change Counseling Committee
2000 P St., N.W., Suite 400
Washington, D.C. 20036
  (202) 887–0364

Rape

Rape Response Hotline
8730 Alden Dr.
Los Angeles, Calif. 90048
  (213) 855–3506
        or
Women's Resource Center
5151 University Dr.
Bungalow-C
Los Angeles, Calif. 90032
  (213) 224–3486; rape hotline (213) 262–0944

Rape Crisis Center
Washington, D.C.
  (202) 232–0202

Rape Crisis Line
Chicago, Ill.
  (312) 728-1920

(Hours: Wednesday through Saturday, 6:00 P.M. to midnight.
Women will accompany rape victims to the police, hospitals,

and courts, and will refer people to counselors. They hold groups with rape victims and educate the public on rape.)

Seattle Rape Crisis Line
4224 University Way N.E.
Seattle, Wash. 98105
 (206) 632–7273

Women's Crisis Center
Ann Arbor, Mich.
 (313) 994–9100

N.Y. Women Against Rape
222 E. 19th St.
New York, N.Y. 10003
 (212) 477–0819; rape hotline (212) 777–4000

Boston Area Rape Crisis Center
Cambridge, Mass.
 (617) 492–7273

Bay Area Women Against Rape
Berkeley, Calif.
 (415) 845–RAPE

Women Against Rape
San Francisco, Calif.
 (415) 647–7273

Women in many other cities—among them Baltimore, Cleveland, Denver, Philadelphia, and Tampa, Fla.—have started rape crisis centers. A group's phone number may be available from directory assistance under Rape Crisis Center.

For information on *How to Start a Rape Crisis Center*, write to:

Rape Crisis Center
P.O. Box 21005—Kalorama St. Sta.
Washington, D.C. 20009

The center asks for a donation of $4 to $5. It also publishes a bimonthly newsletter.

Another pamphlet, *Stop Rape*, by Women Against Rape, is available from:

> Women's Liberation of Michigan
> Room 516
> 2230 Witherell St.
> Detroit, Mich. 48201

> Dr. Judith Becker
> Victim Treatment and Research Clinic
> Columbia College of Physicians and Surgeons
> 722 W. 168th St.
> New York, N.Y. 10032
>   (212) 568–4511

(Studies and treats the long-term effects on victims of sexual assaults, including rape, marital rape, and incest.)

4. National Women's Organizations

Note: These groups are generally concerned with women's rights, with a wider focus than legal work, and are not composed primarily of lawyers or law students. There is no attempt to list every women's group. The list names only those groups that have many local chapters and are active on a national level. To contact the local branch, check the local phone directory or write to the national office.

> Federally Employed Women (FEW)
> National Press Building, Room 481
> Washington, D.C. 20045
>   (202) 638–4404

> National Committee on Household Employment (NCHE)
> 7705 Georgia Ave., N.W., Suite 208
> Washington, D.C. 20012
>   (202) 291–2422

(A private non-profit service that helps household workers to organize locally. It publishes a free newsletter.)

National Organization for Women (NOW)
425 13th St., N.W.
Washington, D.C. 20004
  (202) 347–2279

National Women's Political Caucus
1411 K St., N.W., Suite 1110
Washington, D.C. 20005
  (202) 347–4456

Women's Equity Action League (WEAL)
805 15th St., N.W., Suite 822
Washington, D.C. 20005
  (202) 638–1961

Women's Action Alliance
370 Lexington Ave., Room 601
New York, N.Y. 10017
  (212) 532–8330

Women's Legal Defense Fund
2000 P St., N.W.
Washington, D.C. 20036
  (202) 887–0364

Directories

Handbook on Women Workers
  Women's Bureau
  U.S. Department of Labor
  14th and Constitution Ave., N.W.
  Washington, D.C. 20210

(An extremely valuable resource book (1975), which provides detailed statistics and information on women workers. It lists a variety of organizations of interest to women: civil,- religious, and social organizations; professional and business organizations; general service organizations of business and professional women; educational organizations; political and legislative organizations; patriotic organizations; farm and rural organizations; and labor organizations. A revision is in progress. For a free copy, send a self-addressed mailing label.)

> *Women's Organizations and Leaders—1979 Directory*
> Today Publications
> 621 National Press Building
> Washington, D.C. 20045
>   (202) 628–6999

(The most current of the directories, but extremely expensive at $50 per copy.)

5. Women's Lobby Organizations and Newsletters

Note: Many of the national women's organizations have actively lobbied at the federal and state level for important women's rights legislation, including—most notably—the Equal Rights Amendment. Those interested in lobbying should contact those groups and, in addition, the following groups, most of which are devoted solely to lobbying on women's issues.

> National Federation of Business and Professional
>   Women's Clubs, Inc.
> 2012 Massachusetts Ave., N.W.
> Washington, D.C. 20036
>   (202) 293–1100

(The primary purpose of this group is not lobbying, but it was one of the leaders in the nationwide lobbying effort for the Equal Rights Amendment. In addition, it publishes a "Legislative Newsletter," which can be obtained from the above address.)

> WEAL Washington Report
> 805 15th St., N.W., Suite 822
> Washington, D.C. 20005
>   (202) 638–4560

(An excellent newsletter giving concise reports on the status of legislation affecting women. Cost: $10 for a subscription.)

The Woman Activist
2310 Barbour Rd.
Falls Church, Va. 20043

(Another excellent legislative and lobbying newsletter. Cost: $10 for a year's subscription.)

Women United
c/o Margaret Laurence
Box 300
Washington, D.C. 20044

(This group's major activity was lobbying for the Equal Rights Amendment.)

ERAmerica
1525 M St., N.W.
Suite 602
Washington, D.C. 20036
   (202) 833–4354

(This is an umbrella organization consisting of 120 groups which worked for ratification of the Equal Rights Amendment.)

6. Publications and Other Sources of Information on Legal Developments

Employment Practices Guide
Commerce Clearing House, Publications Dept.
4025 W. Peterson Ave.
Chicago, Ill. 60646
   (312) 583–8500

(This law reporter publishes new cases and laws in the field of employment discrimination, in full. A must for any lawyer handling employment discrimination cases, it is generally available in law libraries.)

Fair Employment Practice Cases
Bureau of National Affairs
1231 25th St., N.W.
Washington, D.C. 20037
   (202) 452–4200

(This reporter also publishes new cases and laws in the field of employment discrimination, in full. Again, it is a must for any lawyer handling employment discrimination cases and is generally available in law libraries. Cost: $227 for a one-year subscription, plus $16 per volume for prior bound volumes.)

The National Conference of Law Women is a group of women law students, lawyers, and legal workers which holds a national conference once a year and regional conferences more frequently. Its principal focus is on using members' legal talents to help women in general. The conference is a good place to get information about nationwide legal efforts on behalf of women, as well as to make contact with local groups.

Marjory Fields's *A Handbook for Battered Women* is available from: Brooklyn Legal Services, Family Law Unit, 105 Court St., Brooklyn, N.Y. 11201. (212) 855–8033

> Project on the Status and Education of Women
> Association of American Colleges
> 1818 R St., N.W.
> Washington, D.C. 20009
>   (202) 387–1300

(The project educates administrators, teachers, and students on the status of women in education and on legal requirements for ending sex discrimination. Write for information on these subjects and on affirmative action to eradicate sex discrimination. The Project will provide technical assistance to women who want to promote affirmative action on campus.)

Sex Discrimination and the Law: Causes and Remedies, by Babcock, Freedman, Norton, and Ross (Boston: Little, Brown, 1974), and 1978 Supplement, by Williams, is a legal casebook on sex discrimination and the law, covering constitutional law, family law, criminal law, employment discrimination, media, education, abortion, and public accommodations.

Sex-Based Discrimination and the Law by Davidson, Ginsburg, and Kay (West Publishing, 1974), and 1978 Supplement, is a legal casebook on sex discrimination and the law, covering constitutional law, family law, criminal law, employment discrimination, education, abortion, and public accommodations.

Women's Bureau
U.S. Department of Labor
Washington, D.C. 20210
  (202) 523–6611

(The Women's Bureau publishes a wide variety of very useful
information about women and women's legal status. Write
and ask for their materials, listed in their leaflet *Publications
of the Women's Bureau*.)

Women's Rights Law Reporter
Rutgers Law School
180 University Ave.
Newark, N.J. 07102

(A law reporter that summarizes new cases and laws affecting
women's rights, published quarterly. Annual subscription rate:
$12/individuals; $24/libraries. Single issues: $3.50/individuals;
$7/libraries. A must for anyone who wants to keep abreast of
current developments in all areas affecting women's legal
rights.)

Chart E:
State Laws on Domestic Violence*

Explanation of chart. During the last five years, almost every state has passed extensive legislation on domestic violence. Most of these statutes provide new civil and criminal legal remedies for battered women or others abused by family or household members. Some laws specify the powers and duties of police answering domestic disturbance calls. Some require agencies that offer services to families with violent members to keep records or write reports on family violence. Finally and perhaps most important, many state legislatures have appropriated funds for shelters and other services for families with violent members.

Chart E gives citations to state statutes on domestic violence. Statutes that cannot be found in a law library may be obtained from the legislative counsel's office at your state capitol.

In the right-hand column under "Type of Provision" each statute is categorized as follows:

"Protection order" is listed beside statutes that provide for civil injunctive relief for victims of abuse. Only those statutes that make protection orders available independent of any other proceeding are listed.

"Order pending divorce" is listed beside statutes that provide temporary injunctive relief during a divorce, separation, or custody proceeding.

"Criminal law" is listed beside statutes that create a new substantive criminal offense for physical abuse of a family or

*This chart was prepared by Lisa Lerman, Esq., with the assistance of Mary Bottum, Esq., and Susan Wiviott. It is reprinted in part from *Response to Violence in the Family*, August 1980 (Center for Women Policy Studies). A complete copy of the chart may be obtained by writing CWPS, 2000 P St., N.W., Suite 508, Washington, D.C. 20036.

household member or that provide new procedures for disposition of criminal charges in domestic violence cases, such as conditions on pre-trial release, deferred prosecution, or conditions on probation. General criminal statutes that may be the basis for charges against abusive mates are not listed.

"Police intervention" is listed beside statutes that provide for warrantless arrest based on probable cause in domestic violence cases, or that impose duties on law enforcement officials regarding handling of domestic disturbance calls.

"Data collection and reporting" is listed beside statutes that require agencies that offer services to families with violent members to keep records on cases handled or to write statistical or other reports on family violence.

"Funding and shelter services" is listed beside statutes that appropriate funds for services to families with violent members or that establish standards for operation of shelters for battered women.

Citation	Type of Provision
Alaska Stat. §§09.55.650 to 09.55.770	protection order police intervention
Alaska Stat. §§09.55.200, 09.55.205	order pending divorce
Alaska Stat. §§18.69.010 to 18.60.080	funding and shelter services
Alaska Stat. §§18.55.330	(housing preference for victims of abuse)
1980 Ariz. Legis. Serv. §§13-3601, 13-602 (West) (to be codified as Ariz. Rev. Stat. §§13-3601, 13-3602)	protection order criminal law police intervention
Ariz. Rev. Stat. §25-315	order pending divorce
Ark. Stat. Ann. §§41.1653 to 41.1659	criminal law
Cal. Civ. Code §§4359,5102 (West 1970 Supp. 1980)	protection order
Cal. Civ. Proc. Code §527 (West 1970)	protection order
Cal. Civ. Code §§4458, 4516, 7020 (West 1970 Supp. 1980)	order pending divorce
Cal. Penal Code §§273.5, 1000.6 to 1000.11 (West Supp. 1980)	criminal law

Citation	Type of Provision
Cal. Gov't. Code §§26840.6, 26840.7	funding and shelter services
Cal. Welf. & Inst. Code §§18290 to 18304 (West Supp. 1973-1979)	funding and shelter services
Cal. Welf. & Inst. Code §§18230.5, 18980 to 18995	funding and shelter services
Colo. Rev. Stat. §§13-6-104, 13-6-105 (1973 & Supp. 1979)	protection order
Colo. Rev. Stat. §§14-10-108, 14-10-109 (1973)	order pending divorce
Colo. Rev. Stat. §16-3-401 (1973)	(peace bond)
Conn. Gen. Stat. Ann. §46b-38 (West Supp. 1980)	protection order
Pub. Act. No. 79-321, 1979 Conn. Legis. Serv., p. 346 1979	data collection and reporting
Conn. Gen. Stat. Ann. §§77-87, 78-44, 78-36	funding and shelter services
Del. Code tit. 10, §§902, 921(6), 925(15), 950(5) (1974 & Supp. 1978)	protection order
Del. Code tit. 13, §1509 (Supp. 1978)	order pending divorce
D.C. Code §§16-1001 to 16-1006 (1973)	protection order criminal law
Fla. Stat. Ann. §741.30 (West Supp. 1980)	protection order
Fla. Stat. Ann. §§409.607, 901.15(6) (West Supp. 1980)	police intervention
Fla. Stat. Ann. §409.606 (West Supp. 1980)	data collection
Fla. Stat. Ann. §§409.602 to 409.605, 741.01 (West Supp. 1980)	funding and shelter services
Georgia Senate Resolution No. 261 (1980)	data collection and reporting
Hawaii Rev. Stat. §§585-1 to 585-4 (Supp. 1979)	protection order police intervention
Hawaii Rev. Stat. §§580-9 to 580-12 (1976)	order pending divorce
Hawaii Rev. Stat. §709-906 (1976)	criminal law
Ill. Ann. Stat. ch. 69 §25 (Smith-Hurd 1980)	protection order
Ill. Ann. Stat. ch. 40 §§501, 602, 607 (Smith-Hurd 19)	order pending divorce

Citation	Type of Provision
Ill. Pub. Act No. 81-717, 1979 Ill. Laws (to be codified as Ill. Ann. Stat. ch. 85 §507-a (Smith-Hurd 19))	police intervention
Ill. Ann. Stat. ch. 38 §206-5.1 (Smith-Hurd Supp. 1980)	data collection and reporting
Ind. Code Ann. §31-1-11.5-7 (Burns Supp. 1979)	order pending divorce
Ind. Code Ann. §4-23-17.5 to 4-23-17.5-9 (Burns Supp. 1980)	funding and shelter services
Iowa House File 709, 1979 Iowa Legis. Serv., p. 127 (West) (to be codified as Iowa Code §236 (1981))	protection order police intervention data collection and reporting
Kan. Stat. Ann. §§60-3101 to 60-3111 (Supp. 1979)	protection order
Kan. Stat. Ann. §60-1607 (1976 & Supp. 1979)	order pending divorce
Kan. Stat. Ann. §§23-108, 23-110 (1976 & Supp. 1979)	funding and shelter services
Ky. Rev. Stat. §403.000 (enacted 1980)	protection order
Ky. Rev. Stat. §431.005 (amended 1980)	police intervention
Ky. Rev. Stat. §§209.010 to 209.090 (1977)	data collection and reporting
La. Rev. Stat. Ann. §§46:2121 to 46:2125 (West Supp. 1980)	funding and shelter services
La. Senate Resolution 21 (1977)	data collection and reporting
Me. Rev. Stat. Ann. tit. 19, §§761 to 764 (enacted 1980)	protection order
Me. Rev. Stat. Ann. tit. 19, §§769, 770 (enacted 1980)	police intervention
Me. Rev. Stat. Ann. tit. 15, §301 (enacted 1980)	criminal law
Me. Rev. Stat. Ann. tit. 25, §1544	data collection and reporting
Me. Rev. Stat. Ann. tit. 22, §8501	funding and shelter services
Md. Ann. Code art. 4, §§402(a) 404, 501 to 506 (1974 and Supp.) (enacted 1980)	protection order

Citation	Type of Provision
Md. Ann. Code art. 27, §11F (19)	criminal law police intervention
Md. Ann. Code art. 88A, §§101 to 105 (1979)	funding and shelter services
Md. House Joint Resolution No. 32 (1977)	data collection and reporting
Mass. Gen. Laws. Ann. ch. 209A, §§1 to 4, ch. 208, §34C (West Supp. 1980-1981)	protection order
Mass. Gen. Laws Ann. ch. 208, §§17 to 20 (West 1958 & Supp. 1980–1981)	order pending divorce
Mass. Gen. Laws Ann. ch. 276, §§28, 42A (West 1972 & Supp. 1980–1981)	criminal law police intervention
Mass. Gen. Laws Ann. ch. 18, §2(A)(14) West 19)	funding and shelter services
Mich. Comp. Laws Ann. §552.14 (West 1966 & Supp. 1979–1980)	order pending divorce
Mich. Comp. Laws Ann. §§764.15a, 769.4a (West Supp. 1978–1979)	criminal law police intervention
Mich. Comp. Laws Ann. §§28.251 to 28.257 (West 1967 Supp. 1979)	data collection and reporting
Mich. Comp. Laws Ann. §400.1501 (West Supp. 1979–1980)	funding
Minn. Stat. Ann. §518B.01 (Supp. 1980)	protection order
Minn. Stat. Ann. §§609.135, 609.135(4), 629.72 (Supp. 1980)	criminal law
Minn. Stat. Ann. §629.341 (Supp. 1980)	police intervention
Minn. Stat. Ann. §§241.62(5), 241.66 (Supp. 1980)	data collection and reporting
Minn. Stat. Ann §§241.61 to 241.65, 256D.05(3) (Supp. 1980)	funding and shelter services
Mo. H.C.S. for S.B. 524, 80th Gen. Assembly (1980)	protection order police intervention
Mo. Rev. Stat. §452.315 (1974)	order pending divorce
Mont. Codes Ann. §§27-19-201 to 27-19-204, 27-19-301 to 27-19-306, 27-19-311 to 27-19-313, 27-19-401 to 27-19-406 (1979)	protection order

Citation	Type of Provision
Mont. Codes Ann. §404-106 (1979)	order pending divorce
Mont. Codes Ann. §40-2-402 (1979)	data collection and reporting
Mont. Codes Ann. §40-2-404, 405 (1979)	funding and shelter services
Neb. Rev. Stat. §§42-901 to 42-903, 42-924 to 42-926 (1978)	protection order
Neb. Rev. Stat. §42-357 (1974)	order pending divorce
Neb. Rev. Stat. §§29-2219, 29-2262 (1978)	criminal law
Neb. Rev. Stat. §42-927 (1978)	police intervention
Neb. Rev. Stat. §§42-904 to 42-923 (1978)	funding and shelter services data collection and reporting
Nev. Rev. Stat. §33.020 (1979)	protection order
Nev. Rev. Stat. §171.124 (1979)	police intervention
N.H. Rev. Stat. Ann. §§173-B:1 to 173-B:11 (Supp. 1979)	protection order
N.H. Rev. Stat. Ann. §458:16 (Supp. 1979)	order pending divorce
N.H. Rev. Stat. Ann. §§597:7-a, 651:2, VI, 651:4, I (Supp. 1979)	criminal law
N.H. Rev. Stat. Ann. §594:10, I (Supp. 1979)	police intervention
N.H. Rev. Stat. Ann. §106-B:14 (Supp. 1979)	data collection and reporting
N.J. Stat. Ann. §§30:14-1 to 30:14-14 (West 19)	funding and shelter services
——Ch. 338, 1979 N.J. Laws, p.——(19) (to be codified as N.J. Stat. Ann. §§40:55D-66.1, 40:55D-66.2 (West 19)	(shelter zoning law)
Ch. 178, 1979 N.M. Laws, p. 633 (1979)	police intervention
N.Y. Jud. Law §§155, 168, 811 to 813, 817, 822 to 824, 826(b) to 828, 834, 838, 841 to 847 (McKinney 1975 & Supp. 1976–1979) (amended 1980)	protection order
Chs. 530 to 532, 1980 N.Y. Laws, p.——(1980)	protection order criminal law police intervention

Citation	Type of Provision
N.Y. Crim. Proc. Law §§100.07, 530.11 (McKinney Supp. 1979–1980)	criminal law
N.Y. Jud. Laws §216(1)(d)-(f) (McKinney 1975)	data collection and reporting
N.Y. Soc. Serv. Law §2-31(a)(6) (McKinney Supp. 1979)	funding and shelter services
N.Y. Exec. Order No. 090 (1979)	data collection and reporting
N.C. Gen. Stat. §§50B-1 to 50B-7 (Supp. No. 5, 1979)	protection order police intervention
N.C. Gen. Stat. §§14-134.3, 15A-401, 15A-53A.1 (Supp. No. 5, 1979)	criminal law
N.D. Cent. Code §§14-07.1-01 to 14.07.1-08 29-01-15(4) (1960 & Supp. 1979)	protection order police intervention
Ch. 1979 Ohio Legis. Bull., p. 86 (to be codified as listed below)	
Ohio Rev. Code Ann. §§1901.18, 1901.19, 1909.02, 2919.26, 3113.31	protection order
Ohio Rev. Code Ann. §§2919.25, 2919.26, 2933.16	criminal law
Ohio Rev. Code Ann. §§109.73, 109.77, 737.00, 2935.03	police intervention
Ohio Rev. Code Ann. §3113.32	data collection and reporting
Ohio Rev. Code Ann. §§3113.33 to 3113.39	funding and shelter services
Olka. H.B. 1634 (enacted 1980)	funding and shelter services
Okla. S.B. 617 (enacted 1980)	(mental health facilities to provide services for victims of domestic violence)
Or. Rev. Stat. §§107.7, 133.055, 133.310 (1977)	protection order criminal law police intervention data collection and reporting

Citation	Type of Provision
Or. Rev. Stat. §107.095 (1977)	order pending divorce
Or. Rev. Stat. §§184.885, 184.890 (1977)	funding and shelter services
35 Pa. Cons. Stat. Ann. §§10182 to 10190	protection order police intervention
42 Pa. Cons. Stat. Ann. R.C.P., Rules 1901 to 1905	protection order
R.I. Gen. Laws §15-5-19 (1969)	order pending divorce
R.I. Gen. Laws §11-5-9 (Supp. 1979)	criminal law police intervention
S.C. Code §20-3-110 (1976)	order pending divorce
Tenn. Code Ann. §§36-1201 to 36-1215 (Supp. 1977)	protection order police intervention
Tenn. Code Ann. §39-602 (Cum. Supp. 1976)	criminal law
Tex. Fam. Code Ann. tit. 4, §71.01	protection order
Tex. Crim. Pro. Code Ann. art. 6.01 to 6.07 (Vernon 19)	data collection and reporting criminal law
Tex. Fam. Code Ann. tit. 1, §7.4	funding and family services
Utah Code Ann. §§30-6-1 to 30-6-8 (2d Replacement Vol. 3 & Supp. 1979)	protection order police intervention
Utah Code Ann. §76-5-108 (Supp. 1979)	criminal law
Utah Code Ann. §30-5-9	funding and shelter services
Vt. Stat. Ann. tit. 19, §§1101 to 1108 (enacted 1980)	protection order
Vt. Stat. Ann. tit. 11, §675	order pending divorce
Vt. Stat. Ann. tit. 13, §2451 (enacted 1980)	(custodial interference)
Va. Code §20-103 (1950)	order pending divorce
Va. Code 16.1-279 (L) (Cum. Supp. 1980)	(court may mandate counseling for or payment of shelter fees by abuser)
Va. House Joint Resolution 27	police intervention
Va. Code §§63.1-315 to 63.1-318 (enacted 1980)	funding and shelter services

Citation	Type of Provision
Wash. Rev. Code Ann. §26.09.060 (Supp. 1980–1981)	order pending divorce
Wash. Rev. Code Ann. §§10.99.010 to 10.99.070 (Supp. 1980–1981)	criminal law police intervention data collection and reporting
Wash. Rev. Code Ann. §§70.123.010 to 70.123.900 (Supp. 1980–1981)	funding and shelter services
W.Va. Code §§48-2A-1 to 48-2A-8 (Supp. 1980)	protection order
W.Va. Code §48-2-13 (1976 & Supp. 1980)	order pending divorce
Wis. Stat. Ann. §§767.23(1,m), 940.33 (West 19); §813.025(2)(a) (West 1977)	protection order
Wis. Stat. Ann. §247.23 (West 1957 & Supp. 1979–1980)	order pending divorce
Wis. Stat. Ann. §§940.19(1,m), 971.37 (West 19)	criminal law
Wis. Stat. Ann. §165.85(4)(b) (West 1974)	police intervention
Wis. Stat. Ann. §§15.197(16), 20.435(8)(c), 46.95, 50.01(1), 973.05, 973.055 (West 19)	funding and shelter services
Wyo. Stat. Ann. §§20-2-106(c), 20-2-110 (1977 republished ed.)	order pending divorce

ADDITIONAL TITLES IN ACLU HANDBOOK SERIES

The books are all available from the ACLU, 132 W. 43 St., New York, N.Y. 10036

AMERICAN CIVIL LIBERTIES UNION HANDBOOKS

Facts at Your Fingertips!

SPECIAL
MONEY SAVING
OFFER

Now you can have an up-to-date listing of Bantam's hundreds of titles plus take advantage of our unique and exciting bonus book offer. A special offer which gives you the opportunity to purchase a Bantam book for only 50¢. Here's how!

By ordering any five books at the regular price per order, you can also choose any other single book listed (up to a $4.95 value) for just 50¢. Some restrictions do apply, but for further details why not send for Bantam's listing of titles today!

Just send us your name and address plus 50¢ to defray the postage and handling costs.